A HISTORY OF THE
SIKHS
VOLUME 2: 1839-1964

A HISTORY OF THE

SIKHS

BY KHUSHWANT SINGH

VOLUME 2: 1839-1964

PRINCETON, NEW JERSEY

PRINCETON UNIVERSITY PRESS

LONDON AND BOMBAY: OXFORD UNIVERSITY PRESS

1966

Printed in the United States of America by
Westview Press, Boulder, Colorado

Reissue, 1984
First Princeton Paperback printing, 1984
ISBN 0-691-03022-7
ISBN 0-691-00804-3 (pbk.)

To my Parents
Sardar Bahadur Sir Sobha Singh
and Lady Viran Bai

PREFACE

◆◆◆◆ THE first volume of *The Sikhs* dealt with the birth of Sikhism and the rise of the Sikhs to political dominance in the Punjab under Maharajah Ranjit Singh. This volume takes up the narrative from the death of the maharajah and brings it up to the present times. It is divided into five parts which deal respectively with the conflict with the English and the collapse of the Sikh kingdom, its consolidation as a part of Britain's Indian empire, religious and sociological movements born under the impact of new conditions, the growth of political parties—nationalist, Marxist, and communal— the fate of the Sikhs in the division of the Punjab, and the great exodus from Pakistan. It ends with the resettlement of the Sikhs in independent India and the renewal of the demand for a Sikh state.

The theme of Volume I was the rise of Punjabi consciousness and the establishment of an independent Punjabi state under Sikh auspices. The theme of this volume is the Sikh struggle for survival as a separate community. It started with resistance to British expansionism; it was continued as resistance against Muslim domination; and after independence, it turned to resistance against absorption by renascent Hinduism.

I wish to express my thanks to my friend, Satindra Singh of the *Economic Times* for furnishing me unpublished material on contemporary Sikh affairs; to Major W. Short for guidance on Sikh politics during World War II; to Gopal Das Khosla (one time chief justice of the Punjab High Court) for reading the manuscript; to Dr. M. S. Randhawa for information on Sikh painting; to Mr. J. H. McIlwaine and Mrs. Rimington of the India Office Library for assistance in compiling the bibliography; and to Miss Yvonne Le Rougetel, who collaborated with me in the research and writing of both the volumes. I would also like

· vii ·

to place on record my gratitude to the Rockefeller Foundation and to the Muslim University, Aligarh, for allowing me to continue and complete this work.

KHUSHWANT SINGH

Muslim University
Aligarh

CONTENTS

CONTENTS

ILLUSTRATIONS

follow page 68

MAPS

PART I

FALL OF THE SIKH KINGDOM

"What does the red colour stand for?" asked Maharajah Ranjit Singh when he was shown a map of India. "Your Majesty," replied the cartographer, "red marks the extent of British possessions." The maharajah scanned the map with his single eye and saw nearly the whole of Hindustan except the Punjab painted red. He turned to his courtiers and remarked: *"Ek roz sab lāl ho jāigā—*one day it will all be red."

It took only ten years for the maharajah's prophecy to be fulfilled.

Ranjit Singh's successors were not possessed of the qualities of leadership: their main preoccupation was to secure the throne for themselves by liquidating their rivals. The court split into different factions. The poisoned cup of wine, the concealed dagger, and the carbine took their toll of royal blood; the rabble slaughtered each other in the streets. The Punjabis became dispirited and disunited. Dogra Hindus contended for power with the Sikhs; Muslims became indifferent. Administration broke down. The army grew to a size which the state's revenues could not finance; it became mutinous and ultimately took over the functions of the state.

The English, who had anticipated the chaos that would follow the death of Ranjit Singh, began to move troops up to the frontier and to meddle in the internal affairs of the Durbar. By the autumn of 1845 they were ready to invade the Punjab. They defeated the Sikhs in a series of engagements, annexed Jullundur Doab, and gave Jammu and Kashmir to Gulab Singh Dogra.

Three years later the English allowed a minor revolt in Multan to spread over the province, and utilised it as a pretext to annex the rest of the kingdom. As Ranjit Singh had foreseen, by the spring of 1849, the map of nearly the whole of India had become red.

CHAPTER 1

THE PUNJAB ON THE DEATH OF RANJIT SINGH

RANJIT SINGH, maharajah of the Punjab, died on the afternoon of the 27th of June, 1839. In the forty years that he ruled, he hammered warring Sikh factions into one and welded people of diverse loyalties into a nation; and he made the nation strong and prosperous. Guru Nanak's mission of bringing the Hindus and Muslims together and Guru Gobind Singh's endeavour to raise a warlike fraternity had succeeded. The Punjab was no longer a cockpit for foreign armies contending for the sovereignty of Hindustan; on the contrary, it had become not only the strongest Indian power but also one of the most powerful states in Asia. After many centuries of domination by Pathans and Afghans, the Punjabis had reversed the roles by extending their kingdom across the Pathan country and becoming arbiters of the destiny of the throne of Kabul. They had overcome Chinese satellites in Tibet and stopped British expansion to the west. No longer did the invader dare to set foot in the Punjab, to trample over the young wheat or plunder the peasantry when the harvest was gathered in. Highways had been made safe; once again caravans from central Asia and Hindustan exchanged their wares in the markets of the Punjab. All this had been achieved by the people of the Punjab under the leadership of a man who had risen from their midst.

Ranjit Singh was like a massive banyan tree which cast its shadow over the whole of the Punjab; and like the banyan he had sheltered the land beneath him to such an extent that nothing but weeds could thrive in it. Consequently, when he died there was no one of sufficient stature to step into his shoes and guide the destinies of the state. This applied particularly to the people who were close to Ranjit Singh: members of his family and favourites at court whom

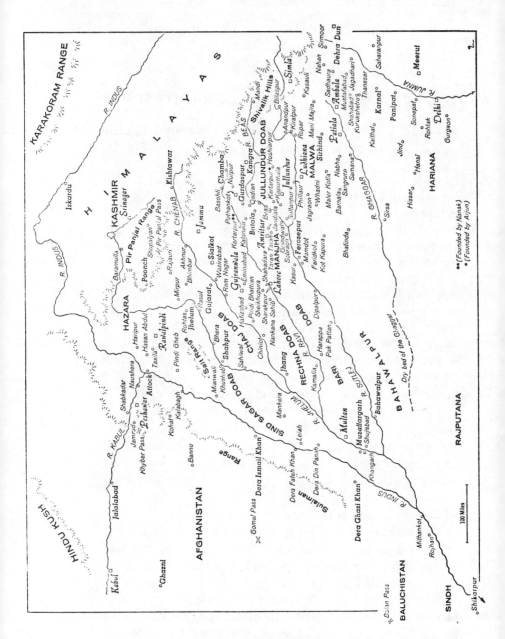

THE PUNJAB IN 1809

he had raised from rustic obscurity to power, from modest circumstances to wealth beyond their imagination.

Ranjit Singh left seven sons. Since they were born of different women, the emotions that determined their attitude towards each other were fratricidal rather than fraternal. The eldest, Kharak Singh, who had been invested as the future maharajah, was the least suited to rule the Punjab.[1] He was an indolent, easy-going debauchee with neither the restless energy that had animated his illustrious father nor the down-to-earth simplicity that had endeared his predecessor to the masses. Kharak Singh was, however, not unwilling to leave the tedium of administration to more willing hands, especially to a favourite, Chet Singh Bajwa, who was related to him through his wife. Kharak Singh's son, Nao Nihal Singh, was cast in a different mould: ambitious, enterprising, and endowed with a pleasant personality.

Ranjit Singh's second son, Sher Singh, was also ambitious and affable. He based his claim on being born of Ranjit Singh's first wedded wife. Kharak Singh refuted the contention and asserted that he (Kharak Singh) was the only legitimate son of his father: the others—Sher Singh, Tara Singh, Kashmira Singh, Peshaura Singh, Multana Singh, and Dalip Singh—were of doubtful paternity.

The council of ministers and the nobility at the court were as divided as the princes. Two major factions emerged soon after the death of Ranjit Singh. The more influential was that of the Dogras, consisting of the three brothers, Gulab Singh, Dhian Singh, and Suchet Singh, and Dhian Singh's son, Hira Singh, who had been a great favourite of the late maharajah. Although the brothers were not always united in their purpose, one or the other member of the family managed to be in power at Lahore, while Gulab Singh converted his fief in Jammu into an almost independent Dogra kingdom.

---

[1] "Besides being a block-head, he was a worse opium eater than his father," wrote the royal physician, J. M. Honigberger. *Thirty-Five Years in the East*, p. 101.

Opposed to the Dogras were the Sikh aristocracy, of which three families—the Sandhawalias, Attariwalas, and the Majithias—were the most prominent. Since the Dogras were Hindus and the Sikh aristocrats were Khalsa, differences between them often assumed a communal aspect of Dogra versus Sikh.

There was among the coterie of self-seekers a small number of men who refused to align themselves with either faction and continued to serve the Durbar as faithfully and honestly as circumstances permitted. Outstanding among them were the Fakir brothers, notably the eldest, Azizuddin, who continued to be the adviser on foreign affairs, and the Kashmiri Brahmin, Dina Nath, who administered the departments of revenue and finance.

In the scramble for power, the decisive factor was the support of the army: rival factions tried to win over the soldiers by offering higher wages and gifts and appealing to their sense of patriotism. Seeds of indiscipline had been sown by Maharajah Ranjit Singh himself when he expanded and modernised the army in 1822. All his conquests had by then been made. Subsequent military campaigns yielded neither profitable territory nor booty to meet the cost of expansion of the army. As a result, payments to the soldiers fell in arrears: some units remained unpaid for over two years. After Ranjit's death, when civil administration deteriorated and provincial governors became tardy in remitting revenues, the army was compelled to reimburse itself. Soldiers acquired the habit of looting civilians and selling their services to the highest bidder. They began to disobey their officers. (Officers had independent incomes and little identity of economic interest with their men.) Officers who tried to assert their authority were manhandled and even murdered. The men resorted to the practice of electing *pances* (elders) to negotiate for terms of service. They left their units without permission to attend family functions or to help their brethren gather in the harvest. The most unfortunate result of the mutinous attitude of the troopers was to make the foreign officers very nervous. Many left the service of the Durbar; most of those who remained sent their money and jewels to banks in India and showed no reluctance in furnishing information to British agents.

With the loosening of central authority, the governors of the outlying provinces began to toy with the idea of becoming independent rulers. Gulab Singh Dogra started expanding his domain at the expense of the Durbar. Muslim tribes, particularly the Yusufzais around Hazara and the Baluchis between the Jhelum and the Indus, became restive. As the Durbar's authority weakened, the British began to mature their plans of stepping in. Their involvement in Afghanistan precluded for some time direct intervention in the Punjab. But as soon as affairs in Afghanistan were settled, they resumed their expansionist policy.

Maharajah Kharak Singh and Prince Nao Nihal Singh

Squabbling among the courtiers began while Ranjit Singh's body lay on the floor of the palace bedroom awaiting cremation.[2] Maharajah Kharak Singh assuaged their fears by assuring them that their *jāgīrs* would not be touched. But his relations with his brother Sher Singh[3]

[2] The chief courtiers foregathered in the palace and agreed unanimously that "no confidence could be placed in Koonwar Kharak Singh Bahadur and Koonwar Nao Nihal Singh Bahadur as regards the continuance of the estates in their possession." The next day after the cremation they came to the palace and again desired the heir-apparent "to console them (the noblemen) by a solemn oath on the *Granth* that the grants respectively conferred on them by the late maharajah should be continued to them." *Panjāb Akhbār*, June 27 and 28, 1839.

[3] Sher Singh approached the British and pressed his "superior" claim to the throne. He was quickly rebuffed by Lord Auckland. Government to Clerk, July 12, 1839.

Sher Singh had kept away from his dying father's bedside because he suspected that Kharak Singh would take the opportunity to seize him. (*Panjāb Akhbār*, June 26, 1839.) When he heard of his father's death he repaired to his estate in Batala and had the message conveyed to the Durbar that he would not attend the obsequies unless he was guaranteed immunity from arrest.

continued to be tense for some time. Sher Singh came to Lahore on the last day of the official mourning and a semblance of harmony came to exist between members of the royal family.[4] Kharak Singh took his father's place as the new maharajah of the Punjab, and Dhian Singh was re-invested chief minister.

The unanimity in the Durbar did not last many days. Nao Nihal Singh quit his post on the frontier and arrived in Lahore resolved to take over effective control.[5] Dhian Singh restrained the impetuous Nao Nihal from wrecking the carefully balanced apple-cart. Instead he accepted the prince's right to make major policy decisions and agreed to play the role of chief counsellor.[6] But Chet Singh Bajwa persuaded Maharajah Kharak Singh not to acquiesce in the usurpation of the royal prerogative. The maharajah made an effort to put his son and the Dogra chief minister in their places. It was, however, obvious to all concerned that the initiative came from Chet Singh Bajwa who, in Punjabi parlance, was resting his gun on the maharajah's shoulder to snipe at the people he did not like. For a short while Bajwa became the power behind the throne. Power turned his head; he became arrogant and then offensive to the Dogras. Dhian Singh and his son were forbidden access to the royal apartments. Gulab Singh was obliged to return to Jammu. Nao Nihal Singh left the capital in disgust, and returned to the northwest to prosecute the campaign against the Afghans.[7]

[4] *Ibid.*, July 13 and 16, 1839. Sher Singh was only biding his time. To George Clerk he expressed his conviction "that many swords will ere long be leaping from their scabbards." SC 24A of 6.11.1839.

[5] "Nao Nihal Singh has made all the Sardars about him sign a document confirming Maharajah Kharak Singh's succession and his own *mukhtārī* or ministership . . . he has issued orders to all Sardars at Lahore to defer the ceremony of *tilak* to his father till his return to Lahore, and to consider themselves responsible for the preservation of all the jewels, treasures, and horses, etc., left by the late maharajah of which he would take an account on his return." *Ibid.*, July 19, 1839.

[6] *Ibid.*, July 21, 1839.

[7] Prince Nao Nihal's presence at the frontier put new zest into his troops. Within a few days of his arrival, the Punjabis under the com-

The discord between the ministers became an open scandal, and disloyal elements began to take advantage of the situation. Prince Nao Nihal Singh decided to intervene. He arrived in Lahore in August 1839 and let it be known to the maharajah that it was the considered opinion of all the advisers that Bajwa should be dismissed. The maharajah not only ignored the advice but made Bajwa's approval a condition precedent for the grant of new jagirs.[8] The prince sounded out Mr. Clerk,[9] who was in Lahore on a business-cum-condolence mission, and, being assured that the British would not create difficulties, quietly assumed the functions of a ruler. In the early hours of October 9, 1839, a band of about twenty men led by Prince Nao Nihal Singh and the three Dogra brothers forced their way into the maharajah's private apartments—the *khwābgāh* or dreamland—dragged the hapless Chet Singh Bajwa from his hiding place, and brought him into the presence of Kharak Singh. With his own hands, Dhian Singh Dogra tore out Bajwa's bowels,[10] shouting at the

mand of Colonel Shaikh Bassawan forced their way through the Khyber Pass, captured Ali Masjid, and marched on to join the British forces at Kabul. Lord Auckland acknowledged that the Durbar had completely fulfilled its obligations under the Tripartite Treaty (SC 18 of 11.9.1839), expressed "high satisfaction" with the conduct of Nao Nihal Singh (SC 116 of 16.10.1839) and other officers of the Durbar, particularly of Colonel Shaikh Bassawan, to whom he sent a sword "in testimony of his gallantry and determination." (PC 117 of 9.10.1839.)

8 *Panjāb Akhbār*, September 25, 1839.

9 George Russell Clerk, political agent at Ludhiana was told of the plot to murder Chet Singh Bajwa. He wrote, "It was lately in contemplation to shoot or sabre the favourites; they consulted me and I advised an impressive remonstrance on all their parts to the maharajah and in the event of his not consenting to cast off the wretches . . . to do everything possible to get rid of Bajwa short of doing injury to his person as that would bring disgrace on the Durbar." SC 24A of 6.11.1839.

10 A graphic account of the murder is given by Col. Gardner, who was an eye-witness. *Memoirs of Alexander Gardner*, edited by Hugh Pearse, pp. 212-22.

Chet Singh's property (estimated at between 50 and 60 lacs of rupees) was attached. Bajwa's chief supporter, Misr Beli Ram, and his brothers

same time: "Take this in the memory of Maharajah Ranjit Singh."

Maharajah Kharak Singh meekly submitted to his audacious son. Nao Nihal Singh occupied the palace in the fort and became the maharajah of the Punjab in all but name.[11] His attitude to his father changed from obstreperousness to filial propriety.[12] He let all the ceremonial functions remain the prerogative of his father while he attended to administrative matters. He had it conveyed to the ministers, governors of provinces, and generals, who had grown accustomed to being left to themselves by the ailing Ranjit Singh and the lackadaisical Kharak Singh, that he meant to govern the Punjab personally and effectively. They soon began to chafe under the prince's iron rule. But the prince gained the support of the British by overruling his counsellors and allowing British troops in Afghanistan to return through the Punjab.[13] Within a couple of months

---

were arrested, and their properties, estimated at over 70 lacs of rupees, were also confiscated. SC 24B of 6.11.1839.

[11] SC 52 of 1.6.1840.

[12] Later, Nao Nihal Singh tried to get absolution from his father for his part in the murder of Bajwa. Kharak Singh continued to chafe at the deprivation of power occasionally remarking, "I am not an idiot." He tried to flee from Lahore but was apprehended by the prince and Dhian Singh Dogra and brought back to Lahore. SC 232 of 18.5.1840.

[13] SC 40 of 20.11.1839. The British government did not honour the terms of the Treaty of Lahore 1809 (appendix 6, Vol. I) and again pressed the Durbar to let reinforcements cross the Punjab on their way to Kabul. Nao Nihal Singh realised the folly of putting all his eggs in the British basket. He is said to have opened negotiations with Amir Dost Mohammed. He also ordered defensive fortifications to be erected at Kasur to prevent British invasion from Ferozepur, which was reported to have been heavily refortified. Despite British objections, the Gurkha general, Matabar Singh, was allowed to continue residing in Lahore.

The Durbar also felt aggrieved with Colonel Wade, who refused to treat Nao Nihal as the *de facto* ruler of Lahore. This was conveyed to Sir John Keane, the commander of the British force returning from Kabul. A few weeks later, when Colonel Wade himself passed through Lahore, he was not allowed to call on Maharajah Kharak Singh. The governor general realised that Colonel Wade had become *persona non grata* with the Durbar and in April 1840 ordered Mr. Clerk to take over.

the Punjab felt as if the spirit of Ranjit Singh had been resurrected in the person of his grandson, Nao Nihal Singh. Nao Nihal Singh's troubles came from the Dogras. Early in May 1840, General Zorawar Singh Dogra reported from Iskardu that in consequence of the disaffection of the people with their ruler, Ahmed Shah, he had intervened and put Ahmed Shah's son, Mohammed Shah, on the throne and was himself firmly established at Iskardu.[14] Nao Nihal Singh, while approving of the acquisition of territory, did not want the Dogras to become king-makers in Little Tibet, and he issued orders for the reinstatement of Ahmed Shah, on condition that he send tribute to Lahore. Zorawar Singh turned to his immediate overlord, Gulab Singh Dogra, and the two devised ways of circumventing the prince's orders without openly flouting them.

The prince realised that the Dogras had become inconveniently powerful. A considerable part of their wealth came from the exploitation of the salt mines, over which they exercised a monopoly. The prince wanted to terminate the monopoly so that the people could acquire salt more cheaply.[15] Before he could take any steps in this direction, however, Gulab Singh Dogra incited his neighbour, the raja of Mandi, to revolt against the Durbar. Nao Nihal Singh ordered two officers known to be hostile to the Dogras, Ajit Singh Sandhawalia and Ventura, to bring Mandi to obedience. This was accomplished, and Durbar troops brought the Mandi raja as prisoner to Amritsar. Ventura established a chain of police posts in the hills. Under instructions from Nao Nihal Singh he abolished arbitrary taxes levied by the petty rajas and prohibited the sale of children and women—a practice common among the poorer sections of the hill people. Ventura's campaign subdued the hillmen for a little while.

During the summer of 1840 the cannons of the fort of Lahore were kept busy firing salvos in honour of victories gained by Punjabi armies over the Dogra-supported hill

14 *Panjāb A<u>kh</u>bār*, May 8, 1840.   15 *Ibid.*, May 20, 1840.

people. Relations with the British were friendly; the Afghans did not matter very much. The countryside was peaceful. The people felt that the old days of glory had returned. But the summer's victories were like a lambent flame flickering to its death.

The rot began at the top and spread to the entire body politic. Maharajah Kharak Singh, who had lapsed into utter idleness, began to drink more excessively and to consume large quantities of opium till he was reduced to a state of imbecility. On the morning of November 5, 1840, he succumbed to an attack of dysentery and high fever. At his cremation two of his wives mounted the pyre to commit *satī*. They made Nao Nihal Singh and Dhian Singh Dogra put their hands on the dead maharajah's chest and swear by all that they held most sacred to serve the state loyally and faithfully.

Fate had ordained otherwise. Nao Nihal Singh consigned the body of Maharajah Kharak Singh and his consorts to the flames, dismissed the mourners, and made his way back to the palace. As he was passing under the gateway which gave access to the fort, the arch gave way, and slabs of stone and masonry crashed down on his head. A son of Gulab Singh Dogra was killed on the spot. Several others, including Dhian Singh Dogra and Dewan Dina Nath, received injuries. Nao Nihal Singh's skull was fractured.[16]

[16] Many English writers, including Cunningham, Gardner (who claimed to be an eye-witness), Steinbach, and Carmichael Smyth, have expressed the opinion that the fall of the archway was contrived by Dhian Singh Dogra. This has been eagerly taken up by Sikh historians Prem Singh and Dr. Ganda Singh, who ascribe the downfall of the Sikh reigning family to Dogra-Hindu machinations. There is little evidence to support this theory, particularly in view of the fact that Dhian Singh himself suffered some injury and lost his nephew. Despite rumours, Gulab Singh never held his brother responsible for the death of Udham Singh. The Hungarian Doctor Honigberger, who was in Lahore at the time and treated the prince and the minister, is quite certain that the fall of the arch was accidental. (See Honigberger, pp. 102-05.) He is supported by Sohan Lal Suri in *Umdāt-ut-Tawārīkh*, IV, 70-71.

Dhian Singh Dogra had the unconscious Nao Nihal Singh removed to the palace, and, though there was little doubt that life was fast ebbing out, he had it bruited about that the prince was well on the way to recovery. When Nao Nihal Singh died[17] a few hours later, the chief minister ordered that the news of the death be withheld till the matter of the succession had been settled. After consulting the senior members of the council, he invited Prince Sher Singh to come to Lahore immediately. There is little doubt · that Sher Singh was the fittest person to succeed to the throne; he was popular with the army, courteous, and amiable; and the English, whose opinions were of consequence in the Durbar's affairs, were known to approve of him.

Dhian Singh Dogra's plans were upset by his rivals in

The *Intelligence Report* from Lahore states:

"This day—[5th November] about 9 o'clock a.m. Maharajah Khurruk Singh expired. His corpse was burnt with Rannee Isur Koonwur, sister of Surdar Mungal Singh and three slave girls. After this, while Koonwur Nownihal Singh was going through the gate of the palace a beam of wood accidentally fell upon his head and upon Meean Oodum Singh. The latter died instantly but Koonwur Nownihal Singh survived in agony a few hours." SC 116 of 7.12.1840.

The British agent, Clerk, in his report written on November 7, 1840, and in a memorandum written two years later, supports General Ventura's opinion that this was an accident.

The facts themselves do not allow for any doubt on the subject. Kharak Singh died early in the morning and was cremated a few hours later on a spot which was alongside a public thoroughfare. It is highly improbable that anyone could, in broad daylight, have been able to set up a contraption by which an arch could come down on a given signal.

The subject has been dealt with by Dr. G. L. Chopra in a paper entitled "The Death of Kanwar Nao Nihal Singh" published by the *Indian Historical Records Commission*, Vol. 18, 1942, 29-33. Dr. Chopra holds the view that the fall of the archway was accidental.

[17] Gardner, an extremely unreliable witness, states that when Nao Nihal Singh was brought into the palace there was only a trickle of blood from his ear, but when the colonel saw him again a little later, the floor of the room was full of blood. He suggests that the prince was battered to death by Dhian Singh's hirelings, two of whom soon paid the penalty of knowing too much by being murdered; two others fled to British India and one was never heard of again. *Memoirs of Alexander Gardner*, p. 225.

· 13 ·

the council, who decided to support Kharak Singh's widow, Chand Kaur,[18] and sent word to her and her Sandhawalia kinsmen to come to Lahore at once.

Dhian Singh Dogra tried frantically to get some sort of agreement from Chand Kaur before the intriguers' brew came to a boil. He temporarily succeeded in persuading her to accept the honorific of a queen, with Sher Singh as the *afsar kalān* (chief adviser). He summoned the British agent, and in the presence of all the courtiers asked him to convey to his government that the arrangement had been "adopted by the whole Khalsa in concord and unanimity."[19] A few hours after the meeting Prince Sher Singh arrived in Lahore. The death of Nao Nihal Singh was made known, and the succession of Sher Singh was proclaimed.

In the afternoon Nao Nihal Singh's body was taken to the spot where his father's ashes still smouldered. Two of the prince's consorts mounted the pyre with him. One pinned the royal aigrette on Sher Singh's turban; the other daubed Dhian Singh Dogra's forehead with saffron to signify that he was chief minister. Before they perished, the *satīs* made the prince and the minister swear loyalty to the state.

Maharani Chand Kaur and Maharajah Sher Singh

It did not take Chand Kaur very long to recover from the shock of the deaths of her husband and son. She exploited the sympathy that the tragedy had generated and staked her claim to the crown.[20] She sent for Gulab Singh Dogra from Jammu to counteract his brother, Dhian Singh's, influence. Dhian Singh suggested many compromises. She could marry Sher Singh or, being childless, adopt Sher Singh's son, Pratap Singh. Chand Kaur spurned the offer of marriage. How could she marry a man whom

[18] Chand Kaur was the daughter of Jaimal Singh of the Kanhaya misl. She was married to Kharak Singh in 1821.
[19] SC 79 of 23.11.1840.   [20] SC 116 of 7.12.1840.

she described as *sheroo cobā*—the bastard son of a dyer? She parried the suggestion of adopting Pratap by offering instead to adopt Dhian Singh Dogra's son, Hira Singh. She also had it noised about that one of Nao Nihal Singh's widows was pregnant. Dhian Singh did his best to bring her to reason. He placed his turban at her feet and implored her to accept the title of "queen dowager" with Sher Singh as the head of a council of regency. Chand Kaur tore up the proposal. In a stormy scene in the Durbar, Dhian Singh warned Chand Kaur of the danger of lending an ear to mischief-mongers. He told her that the government of the Punjab did not depend either on her or on Sher Singh or any of the claimants in the royal family, because it was the government of the entire Khalsa.[21] Gloom spread over the country; soothsayers predicted the doom of the Khalsa government in the year 1840.[22]

A few days later, two Sandhawalia Sardars, Ajit Singh and Attar Singh, arrived in Lahore and took over control. On December 2, 1840, Chand Kaur was proclaimed maharani of the Punjab with the title *malikā mukaddas*—revered empress. The next day Sher Singh left Lahore for his estate in Batala. A month later Dhian Singh Dogra too was compelled to quit the capital. Chand Kaur and the Sandhawalias gained complete control of the administration.

The dice were heavily loaded against Chand Kaur. The Punjabis were unable to reconcile themselves to being ruled by a woman who could not leave the veiled seclusion of the zenana.[23] And Chand Kaur proved to be singularly

[21] SC 116 of 7.12.1840. "Raja Dhian Singh is indefatigable and firm. . . . He at this crisis has upheld the tottering Khalsa."

[22] SC 117 of 7.12.1840. This was based on one of the many spurious versions of the *sau sākhī*—the hundred fables—ascribed to Guru Gobind Singh. It prophesied great misfortune to the K͟hālsā *sarkār* in Sambat 1897 (A.D. 1840) and its restoration the following year by the reincarnated spirit of Hari Singh Nalwa.

[23] Bedi Bikram Singh of Una, who had come to Lahore to carry out the investiture, stated categorically that "he had come to give the *tikkā* (saffron mark) to Kanwar Sher Singh and not to a woman, for no

inept in the art of diplomacy; she was vain, ill-tempered, and given to using language that became a bazaar woman more than a maharani.

The chief problem of the *Māī*—mother, as Chand Kaur came to be known among the people—was the loyalty of the army. Sher Singh was popular with the troops and the European officers. He offered the troops an increase in wages. Desertions to the prince's camp began on a large scale. Most of the crack regiments went over to him, and the Mai's men were refused access to the magazine. Within a fortnight of her assumption of power, the Mai had to have two battalions posted inside the fort to protect her person. The state of uncertainty encouraged lawless elements in the countryside. The English started movements of troops towards the Sutlej.[24]

Sher Singh decided to seize power from the feeble hands of the widow and save the Punjab from disintegration. He sent an envoy to Mr. Clerk at Ludhiana to obtain English reactions to his bid for the throne. The British were bogged down in Afghanistan and were in dire need of help. In the anglophile Sher Singh they saw a potential ally and gave him assurance of support.[25]

---

woman had, or could ever, reign at Lahore." The *Māī* sent word to the Bedi that he had better take care of himself. SC 107 of 21.12.1840.

Panjab Intelligence of December 7, states: "The Mai sits in the Summum Burj to hold her durbar behind a purdah with five or six other women, the chiefs of the council . . . sit outside the purdah and give their opinions." SC 104 of 28.12.1840.

[24] The attitude of the British towards their allies, who had not only helped them to win the war in Afghanistan but were allowing their territory to be used by British armies as if it were a common highway, can be gauged by the correspondence that passed between Sir William Macnaghten and the governor general in Calcutta. Macnaghten proposed that the treaty of 1839 be unilaterally declared by the British to be null and void and Peshawar be added to the Durrani kingdom. (Macnaghten to governor general, November 26, 1840; governor general to Macnaghten, December 28, 1840.)

He also suggested that the Punjab be further divided into two: the hills to be administered by the Dogras and the plains by the Sandhawalias.

[25] SC 66 of 1.2.1841 and SC 93 of 22.2.1841.

Sher Singh arrived at Lahore at the head of an army composed of deserters who had flocked to his colours; most of the Durbar's European officers were with him.

The Mai did not lose heart. She appointed Gulab Singh Dogra as the commander-in-chief and charged him with the task of defending the city. She cleared four months of arrears in the soldiers' wages and lavished presents of gold bangles, necklaces, jewels, and shawls on the officers. She issued orders to the city's bankers forbidding them to lend money to Sher Singh. These measures had the reverse effect. The troops sensed her nervousness and felt that she was again trying to win a lost cause by bribery. Sher Singh had little money, but he was able to infuse confidence that his was the winning side and he would be able to redeem his promise of a permanent increase of Re. 1/- per month in the wages of the troops as well as reward those who joined them. The regiments stationed outside the city walls went over in a body. Sher Singh had 26,000 infantry, 8,000 horses, and 45 guns. The Mai was left with only 5,000 men, a few guns, and a limited quantity of gunpowder.

Sher Singh forced his way into the city. He made a belated proclamation[26] assuring safety of life and property to the citizens and offered pardon to those who would come over to him. The leading courtiers made their submission and forwarded a joint appeal to the Mai and Gulab Singh Dogra to lay down arms.

The Mai, supported by Gulab Singh Dogra, refused to surrender, and the battle was joined. For two days Sher Singh's artillery shelled the fort, and the guns of the fort poured death and destruction on the bazaars lying beneath the ramparts. On the evening of January 17, 1841, Dhian Singh Dogra arrived and arranged a cease-fire. The Mai

[26] "In the kingdom of Guru Ram Das (the 4th Sikh guru who was born at Lahore) by the orders of Maharajah Sher Singh Bahadur, it is proclaimed that anyone touching the property of the people shall be severely punished." SC 60 of 1.2.1841. This proclamation was made after the troops had looted many bazaars and helped themselves to the wine cellars of the officers.

was persuaded to accept a handsome jagir and relinquish her pretensions to the throne.[27] Sher Singh undertook to show her the respect due to a brother's widow and to pardon the men who had sided with her. Her short reign of a month and a half was over. At midnight Gulab Singh and his Dogras evacuated the fort—taking with them all the Durbar's hoard of gold and jewels kept at Lahore.[28] Ajit Singh Sandhawalia fled to seek help from the British agent at Ludhiana. On Mr. Clerk's refusal to receive him, he proceeded to Calcutta to see the governor general. Attar Singh Sandhawalia followed him into British territory.

Sher Singh occupied the fort and was invested with the title of the maharajah of the Punjab.[29] Dhian Singh Dogra was proclaimed chief minister.

Sher Singh's rule began badly. He was unable to redeem his promise to the troops, who continued looting the bazaars. Soldiers went berserk, murdering regimental accountants and officers whom they suspected of having embezzled their wages or having dealings with the English. Sher Singh and Dhian Singh Dogra invited two men each from every company, troop, and gun to the palace and heard their grievances. They agreed to dismiss corrupt accountants but refused to agree to the *pances'* demand to transfer officers they did not like; the meeting became stormy. The weak-willed Sher Singh threw up his hands with the remark, *kacā pakkā sambhālo* (literally, "raw or ripe, it's yours"), which gave the *pances* to understand that they were free to settle things for themselves.[30]

[27] SC 97 of 8.2.1841. Latif's version of the agreement is somewhat different. *History of the Punjab*, p. 506.

[28] SC 88 of 8.2.1841. Gulab Singh Dogra had made immunity from search of himself and his men an absolute condition for the surrender of the fort. The Mai reposing her trust in him appointed him agent of her estate in Kudi Kuddiali, which adjoined Gulab Singh's territories.

[29] The formal *tilak* ceremony was performed on January 27, 1841, by Bikram Singh Bedi of Una. Pratap Singh was proclaimed as the heir-apparent. SC 95 of 8.2.1841.

[30] Carmichael Smyth, *History of the Reigning Family of Lahore*, p. 87. Two Europeans, Colonel Foulkes and Major Ford, were shot dead; Court

Maharajah Sher Singh belied the hopes of his many admirers. With the army in open mutiny, the best he could do was to plead with the men to be reasonable and give them whatever money he had: in the first six months of his rule he parted with nearly 95 lacs of rupees to the soldiers. Even this did not appease the men, who threatened to depose him. Instead of facing them resolutely, Sher Singh sought escape in the cup, the company of courtesans —and the Mai.[31] What the Punjab had prayed for was a dictator. What it got was a handsome and well-meaning dandy who knew more about French wines and perfumes than he did about statecraft.

The attitude of the British Government towards Sher Singh's succession was somewhat ambivalent. The governor general recognised him as ruler of the Punjab but at the same time gave asylum to Ajit Singh Sandhawalia[32] and did nothing to prevent him from raising troops to invade the Punjab.

Sordid tales of the goings on in the palace destroyed whatever respect the people retained for the Durbar. The British added to its discomfiture by refusing to accord it the respect due to a sovereign state. The most flagrant case

---

barely escaped with his life; Ventura's house had to be guarded; Avitabile asked the British agent in Peshawar to help him escape to Europe; Colonel Meehan Singh, the governor of Kashmir, and Sobha Singh, garrison commander of Amritsar, were murdered; Jemadar Khushal Singh, his nephew Tej Singh, and Lehna Singh Majithia had to barricade themselves in their houses.

[31] On January 24, 1841, an old chief made the suggestion in open durbar that Sher Singh should take his brother's widow under his protection (cādar aṅdāzī) by marrying her. SC 97 of 8.2.1841.

Chand Kaur met a tragic end; she was murdered by her maidservants on the night of June 11, 1842. The culprits were apprehended but before they could divulge the motives of their crime, their tongues were cut off and they were executed by the order of Dhian Singh Dogra. This has led historians such as Prem Singh to point the accusing finger towards the Dogra (Maharajah Sher Singh, pp. 163-70). Cunningham accuses Sher Singh of the crime (p. 261). The murder is referred to by Clerk in his letter to his government dated June 15, 1842.

[32] SC 89 of 8.2.1841.

was the abuse of hospitality by Major Broadfoot. Broad-foot was permitted to escort the seraglios of Shah Zaman and Shah Shuja across the Punjab to Afghanistan and was provided with an escort of Mussalman troops. The major's attitude was aggressive from the very start, and on more than one occasion he ordered his men to open fire on the Punjabis who happened to come near his party. The Durbar suffered this kind of behaviour—and worse. When Broadfoot had crossed the Indus, he called on the Pathan tribesmen to revolt against the Durbar.[33]

The Broadfoot episode, following many cases of betrayal of national interest by courtiers, noblemen, and officers, forced the men of the Punjab army to make their own

[33] "It did not appear that his (Broadfoot's) apprehension had even a plausible foundation. . . . The whole proceeding merely served to irritate and excite the distrust of the Sikhs generally, and to give Sher Singh an opportunity of pointing out to his mutineer soldiers that the Punjab was surrounded by English armies both ready and willing to make war upon them." Capt. J. D. Cunningham, *History of the Sikhs* (1st edition, p. 245).

The following lines from a personal letter written by Mrs. Henry Lawrence on May 26, 1841 (when the Punjab armies were helping the British), is indicative of the British frame of mind: "Wars, rumours of war, are on every side and there seems no doubt that *the next cold weather will decide the long suspended question of occupying the Punjab*: Henry, both in his civil and military capacity, will probably be called to take part in whatever goes on." (Emphasis added.)

Lord Ellenborough's letter to the Duke of Wellington dated October 15, 1841, is equally revealing. "I have requested Lord Fitzroy to appoint him [Lieutenant Durand] at once in obtaining all information he can with respect to the Punjab and making a memorandum upon the country for your consideration. I am most anxious to have your opinion as to the general principles upon which a campaign against the country should be conducted." He followed Durand's memo with another letter dated October 26, stating, "At present about 12,000 men are collected at Ferozepur to watch the Sikhs and act if necessary.

"What I desired therefore was your opinion founded as far as it could be upon imperfect geographical information which could be given to you, as to the *best mode of attacking the Punjab*." Ganda Singh, *Private Correspondence relating to the Anglo-Sikh Wars*, p. 47.

English papers published in India made frequent allusions to the designs of the British Government against the Punjab. Maharajah Sher Singh protested about them to Maddock, who led a British mission to the Durbar. SC 5 of 15.1.1843.

voice heard in matters of state. The only institution with which they were familiar was the *pañcāyat*—the council of elders—which regulated the affairs of the villages from which they came. This institution had been introduced in the army, and each regiment had begun to elect its own *pañces*, whose duty was to deliberate on the orders of the commanding officer and then to make their recommendations to the men. In the army, the *pañcāyats* did not develop into a proper administrative system, and much depended on the ability of the elected men. In order to maintain their influence the *pañces* often pressed for concessions and increases in wages which were unreasonable. Some senior *pañces* became powerful enough to be able to auction posts of officers; they appointed deputies (*kar pañces*) to convey their decisions to the troops and ensure their acceptance. The results were disastrous. The army lost its discipline as well as direction by officers who had greater experience in military affairs.

While the Durbar at Lahore was preoccupied with pacifying its mutinous soldiery and helping the British out of their predicament in Afghanistan, the Dogras began the second phase of the conquest of Tibet.

There were economic reasons for extending the frontiers of Jammu and the valley of the Jhelum (which Gulab Singh Dogra had occupied on the murder of its governor) beyond the Himalayas. Since the British had extended their frontiers to the Sutlej, Tibetan caravans which had passed through Kashmir began instead to go through Bushair. The Kashmiri shawl makers, who obtained much of their raw wool from Ladakh and Lhasa, suffered most. There was danger of the Kashmir wool industry dying out. Besides this, Rohtak district of the province of Garo was reputed to be rich in gold, borax, sulphur, and rock salt, and had a thriving market which supplied many parts of Central Asia. There were complementary political reasons for the expansion. By striking out north and then eastwards, the Punjab could establish a common frontier with the only other independent state of India, Nepal, and thus guard itself against the possibility of British encirclement.

Zorawar Singh Dogra had taken Ladakh in 1834 and then driven the wedge a little farther by capturing Iskardu, on the junction of two tributaries of the Indus. Another approach route to these mountainous regions had been opened up by the occupation of Mandi and Kulu. The Dogra general decided to press these points further; one northwards and the other eastwards towards the Nepalese frontier.

It was not difficult to find an excuse for aggression. In April 1841, Zorawar Singh demanded Garo's adhesion to the Punjab on the grounds that Garo was a dependency of Iskardu and Iskardu was now a province of the Punjab. In view of the changed circumstances he also desired that Lhasa should pay tribute to Lahore rather than to Peking. Zorawar Singh marched to Garo while another column proceeded eastwards along the Kumaon hills and cut off British contact with Lhasa. In June 1841 the Dogras captured Garo. Zorawar Singh thought it politic to send information of the fact to the raja of Bushair, who was under British protection. From Garo, the Dogras marched forward towards Tuklakote. A Tibetan force sent to oppose them was annihilated, and a few days later the Durbar's flag was hoisted at Tuklakote. The Dogras had pierced the heart of Tibet to its very core. By the time they were able to consolidate their new conquests, the campaigning season in the mountains was over.

This brilliant feat of arms alarmed the British,[34] and their agent demanded that the Durbar give up its new conquests.[35] While the verbal warfare was going on between

[34] SC 71 of 18.10.1841.

[35] The tension over Punjabi expansion across the Himalayas did not vitiate other relations between the Durbar and the British. On the request of the British Government, the Durbar took steps to regulate duties on merchandise passing to and from British India to the Punjab. The duties on goods entering the Punjab were fixed at reduced rates

Ludhiana and Lahore, the Chinese mustered their armies. With the first fall of snow they encircled the Dogra advanced posts, cut off their supply lines, and waited patiently for the elements to do the rest.

The Dogras were reduced to desperate straits. They were marooned at a height of 12,000 feet in the midst of a vast sea of drifting snow and ice. They ran out of food and fuel, and soldiers began to die of frost-bite. Zorawar Singh offered to withdraw, but the Chinese were unwilling to let a trapped bird slip out of their grasp. "You seized Ladakh and we remained silent. You became bold in consequence and took possession of Gartok and Tuklakote. If you desire peace, give up Ladakh and go back to your own country," was the Chinese reply.[36]

The Dogras were compelled to fight their way out. Hunger and cold had sapped their vitality, and they had to contend with an enemy who not only outnumbered them by ten to one but was also equipped for winter warfare. On December 12, 1841, fell the gallant Zorawar Singh. The rest of the band laid down arms and were butchered in cold blood. Tuklakote was abandoned. Before the spring thaw, the Chinese reoccupied their Tibetan possessions and reinstated their satellites at Iskardu and Ladakh. Only at Leh did the Punjab flag still flutter defiantly in the Tibetan breeze.

Gulab Singh Dogra rushed reinforcements to Ladakh. By the spring of 1842 Dogra troops reached Leh and pushed forward to recapture Ladakh. The advance continued in the form of a pincer movement towards Garo. One column reached the boundary of the district in August 1842 but was dissuaded from proceeding further by a British officer, Lieutenant Cunningham, who happened to be there. The other column decimated a Chinese force sent against it from Lhasa.

---

chargeable at one place. This step had no little effect in promoting commercial traffic between the Punjab and its neighbouring countries.
[36] SC 59 of 6.12.1841.

On October 17, 1842, the Durbar agent and Gulab Singh's personal representative signed a treaty with the representatives of the Chinese emperor at Lhasa. It was agreed that the boundaries of Ladakh and Lhasa would be considered inviolable by both parties and that the trade, particularly of tea and *paśmīnā* wool, would, as in the past, pass through Ladakh.[37]

The British were prevented from taking active steps to check the Dogra incursion into Tibet by a sudden turn of events in Afghanistan. In the autumn of 1841, the Afghans rose and destroyed the British army of occupation. Among those who were murdered was Sir Alexander Burnes—the chief architect of British expansionism in Sindh, the Punjab, and Afghanistan. The attempt to reinstate Shah Shuja on the throne of Kabul had been a joint Punjabi-British venture, and consequently the disaster which overwhelmed British arms at Kabul could not be overlooked by the Durbar. General Avitabile was ordered to go to the relief of the British.[38] The Punjabis recaptured Ali Masjid but were unable to hold it as the winter set in. As soon as the passes were cleared of snow they resumed their offen-

[37] The British took the earliest opportunity to undo the Treaty of Ladakh. When they sold Kashmir to Gulab Singh in 1846, Captain A. Cunningham, who was sent to settle the northern and eastern boundary of Gulab Singh's domains, had it conveyed to the Chinese and Tibetan merchants that their goods could enter British territories without having to pay duty. Lord Hardinge followed this up with a note to Lhasa informing the Chinese of British suzerainty over Kashmir and suggesting that the old treaty be amended to the effect that trade would not be restricted to the Ladakh route. The Treaty of Lhasa of 1842 was consequently redrafted in August 1846 as desired by the British.

[38] The British were surprised at the Punjabis' willing cooperation, as their advisers—Wade, Clerk, and Shahamat Ali—had told them that no faith should be placed in the Punjabis' professions of friendship (see *Calcutta Review*, III, 182). In a letter dated April 11, 1842, Henry Lawrence wrote: "The Sikhs were only bound to employ a contingent of 6,000 men, but they did the work with no less than 15,000, leaving the stipulated number in position, and withdrawing the rest to Jamrood and Peshawar, where they remain ready to support those in the Pass if necessary." Edwardes and Merivale, *The Life of Henry Lawrence*, I, 363.

sive and, with a British contingent, once again occupied
Ali Masjid in the spring of 1842.[39] The Durbar arranged
for the supply of grain, cattle, and other provisions to
British troops and dispatched its own force, which was
larger than the British, to Afghanistan. The Punjabis relieved Jalalabad and helped to re-establish British power
in Afghanistan. Fortunately for the British, Shah Shuja
died (or was killed). They decided to scrap the Tripartite
Treaty and make terms with Dost Mohammed. The Amir
was released from detention to be sent back to Kabul.

The British behaviour in the Afghan campaign soured
Sher Singh. He saw how they had used the Punjab as a
stepping stone to reach Afghanistan, and, having done so,
scrapped the treaty without considering the Durbar's interests.[40] And soon after the debacle in Afghanistan, the
British committed unprovoked aggression against Sindh.
Without even waiting for an excuse, Sir Charles Napier
occupied the province in March 1843.[41] What guarantee
was there that the British would not act in the same way
towards the Punjab?

Relations between the Durbar and the British cooled

[39] The governor general, Lord Ellenborough, in an official notification
of April 19 expressed his entire satisfaction with the conduct of the
troops of Maharajah Sher Singh. He informed the army "that the loss
sustained by the Sikhs in the assault of the Pass which was forced by
them is understood to have been equal to that sustained by the troops of
Her Majesty to the Government of India." Ellenborough instructed his
agent at Lahore to offer his congratulations on this occasion "so honourable to the Sikh Army." Ganda Singh, *Private Correspondence relating
to the Anglo-Sikh Wars*, p. 42.

[40] In the winter of 1842, Lord Ellenborough expressed a desire to meet
Sher Singh and thank him personally for the part played by the Punjabis in
the Afghan campaigns. Sher Singh, who had at first agreed to the meeting, finally excused himself on the flimsy ground of protocol. The governor general had to content himself with shaking hands with Sher
Singh's son, the eleven-year-old Pratap Singh, and Dhian Singh Dogra.

[41] "The real cause of the chastisement of the Amirs," says Kaye, "consisted in the chastisement which the British had received from the
Afghans. It was deemed expedient at the stage of the great political
journey to show that the British could beat someone, and so it was
determined to beat the Amirs of Sindh." *Calcutta Review*, I, 232.

visibly. Sher Singh continued to keep up appearances of friendship but stopped playing second fiddle to the British. He gave Dost Mohammed, who had crossed swords with the Punjabis in innumerable battles, a great reception when he passed through Lahore on his way to Kabul. The Durbar signed a separate treaty recognising him as the Amir of Afghanistan.

The British sensed that they had through their own maladroitness lost the confidence of Sher Singh. They also felt that as long as Dhian Singh Dogra remained the chief minister there was little chance of the Durbar changing its attitude towards them. Persisting in their pretensions of friendship, they asked Sher Singh to allow the Sandhawalia Sardars, known to be inimical towards Dhian Singh Dogra, to return to the Punjab and have their estates restored to them.[42] The maharajah, who had begun to chafe under Dhian Singh's domination, accepted the British suggestion. In November 1842, Ajit Singh Sandhawalia arrived at Lahore and was received with open arms by the simple-minded Sher Singh. Other members of the family were also reinstated in their possessions. As was perhaps anticipated, the Sandhawalias became the pro-British, anti-Dogra party in the Durbar.

Dhian Singh Dogra proved to be too strongly entrenched to be removed at the whims of princes or courtiers. The Sandhawalias were compelled to resort to violence—and, in the process, to make a clean sweep of the set-up at Lahore. Whether they acted on their own initiative or on the assurance of support from the British will never be known for in the holocaust that followed all the evidence was drowned in blood.

[42] In April 1842, when Clerk met Sher Singh, the maharajah told the British agent that, if the Sandhawalias occupied any of the Durbar's possessions across the Sutlej (Kot Kapura, Akalgarh, Naraingarh or Whadni), passage should be given to his troops to seize them and "rip open their bellies." SC 134 of 29.6.1842. Six months later, the same Sher Singh was persuaded by Clerk to welcome back the Sandhawalias.

On September 15, 1843, the first of the month of *Asūj* by the Hindu calendar, it was arranged that Sher Singh would take the salute at a march-past and inspect the troops of Ajit Singh Sandhawalia. Sher Singh took his elder son, Pratap Singh, with him and left the child to amuse himself in a nearby garden. After the march-past, the Sandhawalia came up to the platform where the maharajah was seated to present a double-barrelled gun of English manufacture which he had brought with him from Calcutta. As the maharajah stretched out his hands to receive the weapon, Ajit Singh pressed the trigger. *"Eh kī daghā*—what treachery is this!"* cried the unfortunate maharajah before he collapsed. The Sandhawalia's men fell upon Sher Singh's escort; Ajit Singh hacked off the maharajah's head and mounted it on his spear. At the same time Ajit's uncle seized Pratap Singh and severed the boy's neck. He too impaled his victim's head on his spear and joined his nephew. The regicides rode to the city flaunting their trophies. For reasons still unknown, they were admitted into the fort. They sent invitations to the Dogras—Dhian Singh, Hira Singh, and Suchet Singh— to join them. Dhian Singh fell into the trap and came to the fort with a very small escort. He was killed and his bodyguard of 25 was hacked to pieces. When Suchet Singh and Hira Singh, who were encamped a couple of miles outside the city, received news of Dhian Singh's murder, they immediately sought refuge in the cantonment and appealed to the Khalsa army to avenge the murders.

The Sandhawalias occupied the fort and the palace in the belief that they would now rule the Punjab. They had reckoned without the people.

News of the dastardly crimes sent a wave of horror through Lahore. The army *pances* resolved to take the city under their protection and to punish the malefactors, and they chose as their leader Hira Singh, the son of Dhian Singh Dogra. The fort was surrounded. All through the

· 27 ·

night artillery blasted the ramparts. Next morning Nihangs stormed in through the breaches and captured the citadel. The assassins and 600 of their troops were put to the sword. But Attar Singh Sandhawalia remained. He received the news of the capture of Lahore by the army and fled across the Sutlej, where he was given asylum by the British.[43]

Ranjit Singh's youngest son, Dalip Singh, was proclaimed maharajah with Hira Singh Dogra as his chief minister. Real power, however, had passed from the palace to the cantonment.

The Punjab under the Dogras

The blood bath left the Durbar in a state of exhaustion without lancing it of its malignant factionalism. There was a realignment of courtiers behind the claimants to the throne and the post of chief minister. Maharajah Dalip Singh had two stepbrothers, Peshaura Singh and Kashmira Singh, both older than he and anxious to press their claims to the throne; both had private armies of their own. And although Hira Singh Dogra had been named as the chief vazir, his appointment was not unquestioned. Since the maharajah was only seven years old, his mother, the youthful and comely Jindan,[44] assumed the role of queen mother

[43] The blood bath of September 15 and 16, 1843, must have been foreseen by the British. Lord Ellenborough wrote to the Duke of Wellington on August 2, 1843 (after the Sandhawalias had been in Calcutta for some time), "The affairs of the Punjab will receive their denouement from the death of Sher Singh." At the time Sher Singh was a young man and in the best of health.

A very detailed report on the different factions in the Durbar was submitted by Richmond on September 5, 1843. The following lines dealing with the *rapprochement* between Dhian Singh Dogra and Sher Singh are significant: "The union is but seeming and a few moments under the excitement of passion and of wine may cause an irreparable breach which may end in the death of Sher Singh." SC 455 of 23.3.1844.

The Anglo-Indian press of Calcutta admitted that although there was no proof of the British Government being directly concerned in the murder of Sher Singh, it did "smell a rat." *Friend of India,* December 1843.

[44] Jindan was the daughter of an officer in charge of the royal kennels.

· 28 ·

and introduced her brother, Jawahar Singh, into the council as a sort of guardian-cum-adviser. Besides these two, Suchet Singh Dogra felt that he had a stronger claim to be chief vazir than his nephew, Hira Singh. Gulab Singh Dogra[45] supported Suchet Singh.

The relations between the Dogras were further acerbated by the presence of a Brahmin priest, Jalla, who had been companion-tutor to Hira Singh Dogra since the latter's childhood. Jalla was an extremely arrogant man of peevish disposition and soon came to be disliked by everyone; Gulab Singh Dogra and Suchet Singh loathed him more than anyone else.

Palace intrigues consumed the energies of the court and the council, leaving them little time to attend to the day-to-day business of administration. The British felt that they might be called upon to intervene to restore order and began to move troops up to the Sutlej. These troop movements worsened the situation in the Punjab. Many Sardars opened negotiations with the British to have their jagirs confirmed. The danger of external aggression and internal dissension made the army[46] the most powerful element in the state.[47] The legend of Khalsa invincibility

---

She was married to Ranjit Singh in 1835. Dalip Singh was born in September 1837.

[45] Suchet Singh Dogra had no son of his own. Gulab Singh persuaded him to adopt his youngest son, Ranbir Singh (also known as Mian Pheenoo). This gave Gulab Singh and his sons a vested interest in the fortunes of Suchet Singh.

[46] At the time it numbered 69,500 infantry, 27,575 cavalry, 4,130 artillerymen as on October 1, 1843. SC 521 of 23.3.1844.

[47] Richmond's report of February 13, 1844, states: "With regard to the state of feeling in the army, I may observe that every regiment and every body of men, save a few Gurkhas, Afghans and Hindustanis, have virtually thrown aside their obedience to the state and to their officers. The habit of discipline, a sense of self-interest and a vague feeling of deference to the 'Khalsa' keep them united as an armed body for the present." SC 562 of 23.3.1844.

"We have now to deal with the temporary government of one able man, Raja Gulab Singh, with a large army overbearing and disorganised but never yet beaten; and with the Sikh people without a present

was revived. A man who came to the fore now was one Bhai Bir Singh,[48] a retired soldier turned ascetic who had set up his own gurdwara at village Naurangabad on the Sutlej. In times of national crisis, Sikh soldiers and peasantry began to turn to Bhai Bir Singh for guidance. Attending the bhai was a volunteer army of 1,200 musket men and 3,000 horsemen. Over 1,500 pilgrims were fed in his kitchen every day.

Hira Singh Dogra tackled the problems facing him with great energy. He dismissed European officers known to be intriguing with the British and sent spies to ascertain details of the military preparations which were being made across the Sutlej.[49] In open court he asked the British *vakil*—pleader—to explain why his government was fortifying Ferozepur and why it had given asylum to Attar Singh Sandhawalia, who was known to have been associated with the murders of the previous maharajah and the

---

leader, but victorious on every side, and capable of any exertion, if their spirit is properly called forth in the support of the mystic Khalsa." Richmond, September 26, 1843. SC 487 of 23.3.1844.

[48] Bir Singh (d.1844) came from tehsil Tarn Taran.

[49] *Panjāb Akhbār*, January 1, 1844. Durbar agents succeeded in tampering with the loyalty of British Indian troops on the Sutlej; throughout the winter of 1843-44 there were mutinies of native sepoys in Sindh and on the Sutlej. In Sindh they were occasioned by the reduction in the pay of the troops (after its annexation, Sindh ceased to be a "foreign station" for the British). On the Sutlej, particularly at Ferozepur, they were the result of the disparity between the pay given by the Company—8½ rupees per month—and that received by the Durbar's troops which was 12½ rupees per month.

Lord Ellenborough was very alarmed at the outbreaks and considered success by the Khalsa in inducing mutiny "more dangerous than would be its declared hostility." In another letter written early in 1844, the governor general wrote to the Duke of Wellington "of the great magnitude of the operations on which we should embark, if we ever should cross the Sutlej. I know it would be of a protracted character." Colchester, *History of the Indian Administration of Lord Ellenborough*, p. 425.

The mutinies at Ferozepur were the subject of dispute between the governor general and the commander-in-chief, in consequence of which Sir Robert Dick was removed from the command on the Sutlej frontier and Major General Walter Gilbert posted in his place. Rait, *Life and Campaigns of Viscount Gough*, I, 351-52.

chief minister and who was inimical to the present regime. The *vakīl* protested the goodwill of the British and said he would convey the Durbar's fears to his government.[50] Hira Singh was not satisfied with the explanation and ordered the garrisoning of Kasur (facing Ferozepur) and the strengthening of the defences of Phillaur.

Movements of troops on either side of the frontier spread uneasiness among the people. The rich began to send their money and jewellery to British India, and many families of noblemen fled the Punjab on the pretext of making pilgrimages.

Princes Peshaura Singh and Kashmira Singh took advantage of the state of unrest and proclaimed their right to the throne. Hira Singh asked his uncle, Gulab Singh Dogra, to proceed against the recalcitrant princes at Sialkot. Gulab Singh undertook the expedition with alacrity. (Sialkot adjoined his territory and could be annexed by him.)

The princes put up stout resistance. After they were ejected from Sialkot, they toured through Majha and then joined Bhai Bir Singh at Naurangabad. They whipped up anti-Dogra feeling in the army by pointing out that Hira Singh Dogra had virtually usurped the throne. The *pañces* called on the chief minister and demanded, among other things, that Dalip Singh be formally installed as maharajah; Peshaura Singh and Kashmira Singh have their estates restored to them; and Dogra contingents that had been brought to Lahore be ordered to return to the hills. Hira Singh Dogra accepted the demands. Dalip Singh was seated on the throne and his uncle Jawahar Singh, who was under detention, was released; Kashmira Singh (who had recovered Sialkot) and Peshaura Singh were received at Lahore and their pensions were guaranteed.

The next to challenge Hira Singh's stewardship was his uncle, Suchet Singh Dogra, who stood high in the favour of Rani Jindan. Suchet Singh arrived at Lahore and de-

[50] *Panjāb A<u>kh</u>bār*, February 19, 1844.

manded the dismissal of both Hira Singh and Pandit Jalla. The army *pañcāyat* decided to remain loyal to the chief minister. Suchet Singh fled from Lahore. A column sent in pursuit overtook him and slew him and his escort.

Hira Singh Dogra was not destined to rule in peace. He had hardly finished with his uncle when another danger menaced his position. Attar Singh Sandhawalia, whose hostile activities in British India had been the subject of many protests, crossed the Sutlej into Durbar territory and joined Bhai Bir Singh at Naurangabad.[51] Princes Kashmira Singh and Peshaura Singh also left their estates for Naurangabad; Bhai Bir Singh's camp became the centre of the Sikh revolt against Dogra dominance over the Punjab.

Attar Singh was a formidable foe. He was a kinsman of Ranjit Singh and had served him with distinction. He was considered one of the bravest generals and, in the last few years of Ranjit Singh's life, had become the most powerful of all the Sikh sardars. The British supported him, and even the sons of the late maharajah were willing to acknowledge his claims.

Hira Singh Dogra harangued the soldiers, reminding them that the Sandhawalia had been responsible for the murders of Maharajah Sher Singh, Prince Pratap Singh, and his (Hira Singh's) father Dhian Singh Dogra; that the Sandhawalia had been with the English for the last six months and had promised to give the British six annas out of each rupee collected in revenue if his venture succeeded; that Suchet Singh Dogra's widow had financed the revolt

[51] *Intelligence Report*, May 4, 1844. Ellenborough's letter to Queen Victoria dated June 10, 1844, states: "It is much to be regretted that Uttur Singh should have been permitted to move from Thanesir to the Sutlej with the known object of acting against the Lahore Government. This error of the British agent renders it impossible to protect against the violation of the strict letter of the treaty which was committed by the Sikhs, whose troops were sent to the left bank to intercept Uttur Singh; and, under all the circumstances it has been deemed expedient to make no representation upon the subject but to allow the whole matter to be forgotten." Colchester, *History of the Indian Administration of Lord Ellenborough*, p. 129.

with the money her husband had invested in British India; and that Bhai Bir Singh and the princes had unwittingly become tools in the hands of traitors. The army *pañces* agreed to side with Hira Singh Dogra, and the Durbar troops marched out to Naurangabad.

Bhai Bir Singh tried to bring about a settlement. Whilst the negotiations were going on, the impetuous Sandhawalia lost patience and killed one of the Durbar's emissaries. Durbar artillery blasted the Bhai's camp, killing several hundred men including Attar Singh, Prince Kashmira Singh,[52] and Bhai Bir Singh.

The troops, though victorious, were filled with remorse. They had soiled their hands with the blood of Maharajah Ranjit Singh's family and of a man looked upon as a guru. They turned their wrath against the Dogras. Hira Singh Dogra assuaged their feelings by making offerings in the memory of Bhai Bir Singh and announcing that he might accept conversion to Sikhism.[53] What really saved Hira Singh Dogra was a fresh wave of rumours that the British were ready to invade the Punjab[54] and a small scale rebellion in the state.[55]

[52] Prince Peshaura Singh had meanwhile left the bhai's camp and made his submission to the Durbar. He later crossed the Sutlej and was given asylum by the British.

[53] *Punjab Intelligence* of May 14, 1844, reported that "Raja Hira Singh endeavours to keep the soldiers in good humour and promises them much, giving them at the same time presents and honours. The Sikh soldiers took the gifts but said, 'We killed our guru and we got two rupees, what sort of men are we?'"

[54] The newswriter from Kasauli reported that large quantities of ammunition had been forwarded to Ludhiana and Ferozepur; reports from Ferozepur said that zamindars had been advised not to sow an autumn crop as a very large army was to assemble there; stocking of war matériel in the cantonments and examination of fords on the Sutlej was also reported. H. R. Gupta, *Punjab on the Eve of First Sikh War*, pp. 80, 198, 201, 206, 208, 219.

[55] Fateh Khan Tiwana rebelled in the south; Gulab Singh Dogra refused to send in revenue and incited the frontier tribesmen to plunder Peshawar. Mulraj, governor of Multan, was sent against Fateh Khan. In an action fought at Mitha Tiwana, about 900 men were killed on both sides. Fateh Khan lost his son and was compelled to submit. Gulab

In July 1844, Lord Hardinge, a soldier of great repute replaced Lord Ellenborough as governor general. This appointment caused nervousness in Durbar circles.[56] Consequently, when in October the commander-in-chief of the East India Company's forces in India came up to inspect troops at Ludhiana and Ferozepur, the Punjab army was alerted against a possible invasion; frontier outposts on the river were quickly garrisoned and a twenty-four-hour watch kept on fords and ferries. The tension lasted several weeks.

The final crisis in Hira Singh Dogra's short career was precipitated by Jalla. The Brahmin priest, no puritan himself, cast scandalous aspersions on Rani Jindan's character.[57] The rani and her brother, Jawahar Singh, appealed to the army *pances*, who acclaimed Jindan and her son, and swore to drive Hira Singh Dogra and Jalla out of the Punjab.

Hira Singh Dogra turned to his uncle for help. Gulab Singh hurried down from Jammu with 7,000 Dogras. The news of the descent of the hillmen incensed the Khalsa soldiers, who decided to arrest the chief minister and his priest. Hira Singh and Jalla took an escort of Dogras and fled the capital.

Khalsa troops caught up with the fleeing Dogra and his Brahmin mentor. A running fight ensued in which over

---

Singh's defiance subsided when Durbar troops were ordered to Jammu. He sent his son as hostage to Lahore.

56 When the news was read out in the court, Jalla remarked: "Lord Auckland had invaded Afghanistan and his successor, Lord Ellenborough, had invaded Sindh and Gwalior, and now the new lord was no doubt willing to invade the Punjab." *Punjab Intelligence*, June 23, 1844. The remark was no doubt occasioned by the information sent a few days earlier that the governor general's council at Calcutta had, at its secret sitting, regretted the death of Attar Singh Sandhawalia because, if he had lived, the British would have acquired the Punjab without a fight. Deserters from the Company's forces had augmented fears of invasion by stating that the British had planned to cross the Sutlej in September.

57 Rani Jindan, whose name was linked with many courtiers, was said to have become pregnant through a liaison with Lal Singh. She became very ill after an abortion, and it was said in open court that, if she died, Lal Singh would be executed. She survived the illness and, through her influence, Lal Singh was given the title of raja.

1,000 Dogras were killed. Hira Singh and Jalla were slain and their heads were impaled on spears and paraded through the streets of Lahore.

Hira Singh Dogra had been a man of uncommon talent and courage. If circumstances had been different he might well have become the first Dogra-Sikh maharajah of the Punjab. But the upstart and arrogant Jalla led to his downfall. Jalla's memory is execrated in the doggerel:

Uper Allāh
Talley Jallā
Jalley de sir tey khallā

There is God above
And Jalla below,
And may He smack Jalla on the head with a shoe.

Maharani Jindan and Dalip Singh

For some time after the murders of Hira Singh Dogra and Jalla there was no one to conduct the affairs of the Durbar.[58] Gradually Maharani Jindan took the functions of the court in her hands. She was assisted by her brother Jawahar Singh (who assumed the title of vazir), Raja Lal Singh, and her maidservant, Mangla,[59] who, because the maharani was in purdah, acted as an intermediary for her mistress. Jindan's first task was to win over the army. In this she had to contend with Prince Peshaura Singh.[60]

[58] "The rani with her son and her brother were alone in the fort. The rani sent for the bhai, Ram Singh, but he did not obey the summons. She sent then for the sardars of the council who had but recently left the Durbar but not one would go near her. They declare the kingdom is now in the hands of the troops and they must wait to see what they decree." Broadfoot to Currie, January 4, 1845. SC 58 of 4.4.1845.

[59] Mangla was the daughter of a water-carrier of Kangra who was employed by Jindan in 1835. After the death of Ranjit Singh she became the maharani's confidante and was rumoured to be the go-between her mistress and Lal Singh. She herself became the mistress of Jindan's brother, Jawahar Singh. At the time in question, she was 30 years of age. The relationships of Jindan with Lal Singh and of Mangla with Jawahar Singh were subjects of much scandal.

[60] Broadfoot in a letter to Currie dated January 5, 1845, reports that

Jindan completely outbid Peshaura Singh and for some time was assured of military support for her son, Maharajah Dalip Singh.[61]

Gulab Singh Dogra utilised the dissension at Lahore to set himself up as an independent ruler in Jammu. He opened negotiations with the Barakzai Afghans and the British; he began to strengthen his forts and to inflame the hill people against the Sikhs. "The mountaineers are united against the Seikhs; they regard the war as one of religion," he is reported to have said.[62]

In February 1845 Durbar troops which had been posted along the Sutlej to meet a possible British invasion were directed to Jammu. Gulab Singh Dogra submitted. He handed over 4 lac rupees as tribute, fêted the Khalsa army, and sent it back on the road to Lahore loaded with gifts. The Khalsa had not gone very far from Jammu when they were ambushed by the Dogras and relieved of all the tribute. They returned to Jammu and inflicted several defeats on the Dogras. Gulab Singh again capitulated. He came to the Sikh camp, "placed his sword and shield on the ground . . . and stood with his hands joined as a suppliant,"[63] and protested his loyalty. The credulous *pances*

"the camps of the troops were a scene of commotion, the men declaring that they would have no ruler but Peshora Singh, who would increase their pay and under whom they would conquer Jasrota and Jammu. They declared that the rani and her brother were unfit to govern, and that the sardars of the council and their officers did nothing but get jagirs themselves, while they (the private soldiers) were resolved to have no ruler who did not increase their pay." SC 61 of 4.4.1845.

[61] "Diwan Deena Nath stated that including 25 lacs of rupees remitted in the first days of joy and generosity the extra expenditure amounts in fifteen days to a crore of rupees, of which three quarters have gone to the regular army. This is an exaggeration so far as the troops are concerned, but it is no doubt true as to the treasury, for the *mootusudees* having now to deal only with the inexperienced rani and the ignorant soldiery call the expenditure what they please, and embezzle the difference between that and the real disbursements. The troops know, and speak of this, and one day purpose to recover these sums for themselves." Broadfoot to Currie, January 7, 1845. SC 68 of 4.4.1845.

[62] SC 68 of 4.4.1845.   [63] SC 147 of 4.4.1845.

were again brought round by gold and words of flattery.[64] A treaty of peace was drawn up by which Gulab Singh undertook to pay 35 lac rupees, of which five had to be paid immediately,[65] and to accompany the army to Lahore.

The Dogra displayed great presence of mind and a Machiavellian adroitness in extricating himself from a nasty situation. He showed calculated indifference to the summons to appear before the court, stating that he was the servant of the Khalsa army and not of the Durbar and that he would only answer to the *pances*.[66] (He had announced earlier that the monthly wages of infantry men should be increased from 12 to 15 rupees per mensem.)[67] He joined the faction of Lal Singh and became his brother-in-arms by exchanging swords with him.[68] (A few weeks later he accused Lal Singh of attempting to assassinate him.)[69] He was placed under house arrest; but he bought his way out in a few days. He was fined 68 lac of rupees; but he got away with the payment of only 27 lacs.[70] He let it be known that the Chinese had invaded his northern provinces and gained permission to return to Jammu. As soon as he was back in his mountain fastness, he reopened negotiations with the British and offered them his services in the event of war against the Sikhs.[71]

[64] "In the hills Raja Gulab Singh continues to make in public abject professions of submission to the Durbar and of being broken-hearted, and desirous only of dying in peace, but he is preparing with unwearied energy for war, and is stirring up every enemy to the Sikhs and every ally to himself that his messengers can reach. His intrigues also are incessant at the Durbar with Peshora Singh, with the army, and on this side of Sutlej, and day after day his agents offer and receive fresh terms of submission, which are duly discussed by the council." Broadfoot to Currie, January 16, 1845. SC 102 of 4.4.1845.
[65] SC 22 of 20.6.1845.   [66] SC 58 of 20.6.1845.
[67] SC 49 of 20.6.1845.   [68] SC 53 of 20.6.1845.
[69] SC 34 of 15.8.1845.   [70] SC 58 of 20.6.1845.
[71] Gulab Singh's agent, Sheo Dutt, called on Broadfoot in August 1845 and had it conveyed that "he would at once cause the whole of them (the hillmen) to revolt against the Sikhs and submit to the British or, if desired, he could besides assemble 40,000 troops from the hills, probably 50,000, but certainly 40,000 and more and attack the Sikhs." SC 46 of 25.10.1845.

While the Durbar troops were engaged in Jammu, Prince Peshaura Singh returned to the Punjab and set up a rival court at Sialkot. This was a signal for lawless elements to rise. Gangs of Nihangs roamed about the Majha country and threatened to loot Amritsar and Lahore.[72] Rani Jindan tried to win over the families of powerful chieftains to her son's side against the pretensions of Peshaura Singh and to help restore law and order in the state. She broke off Dalip Singh's engagement with the comparatively poor Nakkais and betrothed him to the daughter of Chattar Singh Attariwala. This did not deter Peshaura Singh. He captured the fort of Attock, proclaimed himself maharajah, and approached the Afghans for help. Chattar Singh Attariwala proceeded to Attock.

Peshaura Singh's attempts to secure help from the Afghans and rouse the populace in his favour were not successful. He accepted the assurance of personal safety from Chattar Singh Attariwala and agreed to accompany him to the capital. Twenty miles from Attock, the prince was seized, brought back to the fort, and murdered. The *pances* discovered that the army had once again been used by one Durbar faction against another. They felt that the murder of Peshaura Singh had been master-minded by Rani Jindan's brother, Jawahar Singh, and ordered him to appear before the army *pancāyat*.

On the evening of September 21, 1845, the terrified Jawahar Singh clutched the infant Dalip to his bosom and rode out on his elephant to answer the summons of the *pancāyat*. Rani Jindan and her maid servant Mangla followed with their escort. At the cantonment, Jawahar Singh refused to alight from his elephant. The guards plucked the maharajah from his lap and speared Jawahar Singh where he sat in the howdah. Next morning the minister's corpse was cremated. His four wives, who committed *satī*, died cursing the Khalsa and prophesying that the

72 SC 147 of 4.4.1845.

wives of Sikh soldiers would soon be widows and the Punjab laid desolate. Jindan returned to the palace screaming vengeance against the army and threatening to immolate herself and her son.

The army *pañcāyat* took over the affairs of state and became the sovereign of the Punjab. It selected Dewan Dina Nath to act as its mouthpiece and issued instructions that no letter was to be issued to the English till the *pañces* had deliberated on its contents. The *pañcāyat* acted in the name of the Khalsa.[73] Its orders were issued under the seal *Akāl Sahāi*—the Lord is our helper.[74]

[73] For a while the army *pañces* were able to introduce strict discipline among the men and to maintain order in the capital. It is curious that in this atmosphere of Sikh resurgence many of the leaders of the army council were Dogra-Hindus: Mian Prithi Singh son of Mian Albel Singh, Mian Pacchattar Singh son of Rai Kesri Singh, and Mian Naurang Singh son of Mian Labh Singh. SC 119 of 20.12.1845. It would appear that the Sikh-Dogra conflict was largely an upper-class phenomenon.

[74] The British were much exercised by what seemed to them to be a change in the form of government. It was noticed that the term *Sarbat Khālsā* had been introduced in the official correspondence of the Durbar since the death of Maharajah Sher Singh and as the army council gained power at the expense of the palace coterie, expressions like *Sarkār Khālsājī* and *Khālsā Pañth* came into vogue. The British agent was instructed to make it clear that his government would recognise no other form of government save a monarchy and regarded "the army with its self-constituted *pañcāyats* in no other light than as the subjects and servants of the government." SC 114 of 4.4.1845.

CHAPTER 2

FIRST ANGLO-SIKH WAR

British Preparations

◆:◆:◆:◆: WHEN did the British decide that the state of
◆:◆:◆:◆: anarchy in the Punjab had come to such a
◆:◆:◆:◆: pass that the security of their possessions required the strengthening of the Sutlej frontier and, if
necessary, crossing the river? And when did the Sikhs come
to the conclusion that the British had resolved to take the
Punjab as they had taken the rest of India and were moving their troops with hostile intent?

It is not possible to answer these questions with any
precision. There were Englishmen who believed that it was
the destiny of their race to rule and civilise the natives;
sections of the British press publicised these views and
wrote of extending the *Pax Britannica* to the furthest geographical borders of the sub-continent—and even beyond.
The Durbar was not ignorant of these views. Reports published in Calcutta newspapers, gists of speeches delivered
by English officials, and talk in regimental messes were
transmitted to Lahore. After the death of Ranjit Singh, the
Punjab campaign had become a common topic of discussion in British circles. By the time Sher Singh became
maharajah, these discussions had crystallised into plans of
conquest. With the arrival in July 1844 of Lord Hardinge,
an experienced soldier, the plans were translated into blue-
prints;[1] men and munitions were moved up to the Punjab

---

[1] Hardinge's policy vis-à-vis the Sikh kingdom underwent a radical
change. At first he believed in maintaining a strong Sikh state as a
buffer between British India and the Muslim countries beyond the Indus.
He pursued this policy till the murders of Hira Singh Dogra and Jalla
in December 1844. Thereafter he was convinced that the Sikhs were
incapable of maintaining a stable government, and he changed his own
policy to one of deliberately weakening the Sikhs by strengthening the
Dogras in the hills and fortifying the Sutlej frontier with a view to annexing the Punjab at an opportune moment. *"The government of the*

FIRST ANGLO-SIKH WAR, 1845-1846

Map labels:
R. JAMUNA
Meerut
Simla
Dagshai
Ambala
Delhi
GOUGH
HARDINGE
HILL GARRISONS
COMBINED BRITISH FORCE
Jullundur
Phillaur
Ludhiana
RANJODH SINGH MAJITHA
R. BEAS
Aliwal
Buddowal
Bassi
Lahore
LAL SINGH
Sabraon
Mudki
TEJ SINGH
Ferozepur
Littler
Ferozeshahr
Chillianwalla
Gujrat
R. JHELUM
R. CHENAB
R. RAVI
R. SUTLEJ
Multan
R. INDUS

frontier to be at their allotted places in time for the campaigning season, which began in the autumn.[2] In September 1844, Broadfoot, who had earned notoriety for his anti-Punjabi behaviour and was known to be "rather too prone to war," was chosen to replace Colonel Richmond as the agent at Ludhiana.

The army mustered along the Sutlej was, however, not strong enough to invade the Punjab, nor was there any semblance of an excuse to do so.[3] The invasion project was postponed, but not abandoned. The movement of troops towards the frontier was maintained.[4] A fleet of sixty flat-bottomed boats, designed to link up into a pontoon bridge and provide passage to 6,000 infantry at one trip,[5] was as-

---

Punjab must be Sikh or British," he wrote to Lord Ripon on January 8, 1845—italicizing the words himself.

[2] "On the northwest frontier, I am in correspondence with Gough to get all our troops of horse artillery and bullocks in complete order; and we propose to send our companies of Europeans, picked men, to fill up vacancies." Hardinge to Ellenborough, September 17, 1844. *Foreign and Political Department Records.*

Lord Hardinge brought two sons with him to handle his secret correspondence.

[3] In a letter dated January 23, 1845, Hardinge apprised Ellenborough of the situation. He wrote: "Even if we had a case for devouring our ally in his adversity, we are not ready. . . . moderation will do us no harm, if in the interval the hills and the plains weaken each other; but on what plea could we attack the Punjab if this were the month of October, and we had our army in readiness?" The letter continues: "Self preservation may require the dispersion of this Sikh army, the baneful influence of such an example is the evil most to be dreaded, but exclusive of this case, how are we to justify the seizure of our friend's territory who in adversity assisted us to retrieve our affairs?" Ganda Singh, *Private Correspondence Relating to the Anglo-Sikh Wars,* p. 72.

[4] "We shall now begin to move up the additional regiments to Ferozepur, Ludhiana and Ambala, the barracks etc. being nearly ready. As the fords deepen and the heat increases, these movements will cause no alarm but quietly we will get the troops in their proper place." Hardinge to Ellenborough, March 8, 1845. *Foreign and Political Department Records.*

[5] Charles Hardinge, who was acting secretary to his father, informed the agent at Ludhiana of their despatch. "They are of equal dimen-

sembled on the eastern banks of the Sutlej; by the summer of 1845 Broadfoot was exercising these boats without "concealment or mystery."[6]

By the autumn of 1845, the invasion force—the largest ever assembled by the British in India—was poised on the Punjab frontier. It had been increased from 17,000 men and 66 guns in the time of Ellenborough to over 40,000 men and 94 guns.[7] In addition to Ludhiana (which had been the only military outpost till 1809), cantonments had been built at Ambala, Ferozepur, and in the Simla hills overlooking the Sutlej. In the first week of December 1845, Lord Gough personally led units from Meerut and Ambala towards Ferozepur, where General Littler awaited him and where the boats had been assembled to bridge the Sutlej. Lord Hardinge decided to join Gough to give the benefit of his experience to his commander-in-chief.

---

sions, each carrying a gun, two grappling irons with strong chains, and 100 men, the 60 boats would therefore for a short distance, such as the passage of a river, carry 6,000 infantry at one trip."

The young subaltern offered advice to the seasoned intriguer. "It is not desirable that the purposes to which these boats can be applied should unnecessarily transpire." If questioned by the *vakil* of the Lahore Durbar, Broadfoot was to state that they were to be used to meet the increase of mercantile traffic on the Indus. Broadfoot, *Career of Major George Broadfoot*, pp. 283-86.

   [6] *Ibid.*, p. 331.

[7] Post	Strength as left by Lord Ellenborough	Strength at first breaking out of war
Ferozepur.	4,596 men	10,472 men
	12 guns	24 guns
Ludhiana.	3,030 men	7,235 men
	12 guns	22 guns
Ambala.	4,133 men	12,972 men
	24 guns	32 guns
Total force exclusive of hill stations, which remained the same.	17,612 men	40,523 men
	66 guns	94 guns

Reference: Charles Hardinge, *Viscount Hardinge*, p. 76.

Sikh Unpreparedness

"At Lahore they are quiet, drinking and intriguing politically and amorously,"[8] wrote Broadfoot in July 1845. A month later he reported in somewhat the same vein. "I sometimes feel as if I were a sort of parish constable at the door of a brothel rather than the representative of one government to another."[9] Even after making allowances for the British agent's gullibility in accepting bazaar gossip as authentic news, one cannot avoid the conclusion that while the British were carefully planning for war—aggressive or defensive—the Durbar lulled itself into a false sense of security and abandoned itself to the delights of the flesh. Rani Jindan, Raja Lal Singh, the chief minister, and Tej Singh, the commander-in-chief of the Sikh forces, and many of the chieftains, both Sikh and Dogra, were in communication with the British and willing to sell the Punjab provided their lives and jagirs were secured.[10] The courtiers were thoroughly scared of the undisciplined soldiery and sought its destruction. British troop movements gave them an opportunity to divert the attention of the army from their own conduct to the British and so whip up the Khalsa's anglophobia.[11]

The Khalsa army was hostile to both the Durbar and the British. The former it blackmailed into granting higher

[8] SC 10 of 5.9.1845.

[9] Broadfoot to Currie, August 6, 1845, SC 10 of 5.9.1845.

[10] "You will be so good as to report whether you have any authentic knowledge of the numbers of these influential chiefs, the identity of their projects and whether the terms they expect have been matured by combinations and agreements amongst themselves, so as to constitute a powerful part representing a large portion of the Punjab property, in land as well as in feudations, and thus to have some approximation as to the importance of these chiefs supposed to represent the natural interests of that country." Hardinge to Broadfoot, September 10, 1845. SC 48 of 25.10.1845.

[11] "The Durbar has also been lately a little excited by the account of our preparations received from their newswriters at our various stations who send in an exaggerated shape every idle rumour of our newspapers or military cantonments." Broadfoot to Currie, July 14, 1845. SC 34 of 15.8.1845.

wages (the Punjabi trooper drew almost twice as much pay as the Company's sepoy); the latter was suspected of buying over the ministers and senior officers in order to facilitate plans of conquest. Although the army was the chief author of the chaos in the state, the *pañces* were able to maintain a certain measure of discipline in the cantonments[12] and to organise the casting of new guns, construction of carriages, laying in stores of gunpowder, muskets and swords, etc.[13] They were also able to infuse a sense of patriotism in the rank and file, resurrect the mystique of the invincibility of the Khalsa, and fire them with the ambition of driving the *feringhee* into the sea.[14]

The British agent asked for an explanation of the military preparations. The Durbar replied that they were defensive measures to counter the aggressive designs of the British. In addition, the Durbar asked for the return of the treasure of Suchet Singh Dogra estimated at over 17 lac of rupees, the restoration of village Moron[15] in Nabha,

[12] "Yet as on former occasions there is a singular species of order in this anarchy; the troops and *pañcāyats*, except at the moment of a tumult use the words of subordinates though they substantially command, and they profess to desire to give the nominal supremacy to anyone of their own body in the same manner. Though their excesses in the hills were great, especially in respect of women, yet they maintain sufficient order in their camps, to have bazars with dealers in grain; whose convoys are respected, and though their officers are looked on rather as servants than commanders and dare not do anything contrary to the inclinations of the *pañcāyats* they are to a considerable extent obeyed in carrying out movements approved by the *pañcāyats* and chaudries." Broadfoot to Currie, March 27, 1845. SC 33 of 20.6.1845.

[13] SC 34 of 15.8.1845.

[14] Col. Gardner describes the atmosphere in Lahore. He says that such was "the real belief that the intentions of the British were aggressive, such the domestic incitements of their families to plunder, and such their devotion to their mystic faith, that one single, dogged determination filled the bosom of each soldier. The word went round, 'we will go to the sacrifice.'" *Memoirs of Alexander Gardner*, edited by Hugh Pearse, pp. 265-66.

[15] In 1819, Moron had been given to Ranjit Singh by the raja of Nabha in exchange for land in the Punjab. Ranjit Singh had given the village to one of his sardars. The raja of Nabha forcibly occupied and looted Moron in 1843. Despite the protest of the Durbar, the British upheld the action of the Nabha raja.

and free passage for the Punjab armed constabulary to the Durbar's possessions across the Sutlej—a right that had been acknowledged by the British on paper but more often than not denied in practice.

The British Government rejected the Durbar's explanation.

Lord Gough continued to advance. Lord Hardinge joined him on November 26 at Karnal, and the two proceeded to march towards Ferozepur. On December 3 the British severed diplomatic relations with the Durbar by handing the Durbar agent his passport. There was little doubt now that the British wanted war. If they were allowed to join their forces at Ferozepur, they would inevitably cross the pontoon bridge and menace Lahore. The Khalsa army decided to forestall this move. One division was ordered to engage General Littler and the other to intercept the army advancing under Gough and Hardinge.

On December 11, 1845, the Punjab army began to cross the Sutlej near Hari ki Pattan[16] to its own territory on the other side of the river. On December 13, Lord Hardinge declared war. He accused the Sikhs of invading British territories "without a shadow of provocation." The Durbar's possessions on the left bank of the Sutlej were confiscated and Cis-Sutlej chiefs were called upon to cooperate in punishing a "common enemy."[17]

[16] There is some confusion regarding the actual date of crossing. The British allege that the Sikhs crossed between the 8th and 12th of December. Some Indian historians (Sita Ram Kohli and Dr. Ganda Singh) put the date later—Dr. Kohli, specifically to December 14 or 15, i.e. after Hardinge's proclamation of war. There is little doubt that Hardinge's proclamation was made after some Sikh units had crossed over. Probably the operation, performed by a handful of small boats and over one ford, took a few days to complete.

[17] Despite the forthright language used in the proclamation of war, Lord Hardinge had his doubts about the morality of his action. Five days later he remarked to Robert Cust, personal assistant to Broadfoot: "Will the people of England consider this as an actual invasion of our frontier and a justification of war?" It is not surprising that Cust referred to the advance of the British force as "the first British invasion of the

· 46 ·

The precise strength of the army sent by the Durbar against the English is not known, but there is no evidence that it was any larger than that of the enemy. There is, however, little doubt that both its commanders, Lal Singh[18]

---

independent kingdom of the Punjab." *Linguistic and Oriental Essays*, v, 46-47.

Opinions of two other British officers closely connected with Anglo-Punjabi politics are worth noting. Major G. Carmichael Smyth of the North Western Agency wrote: "Regarding the Punjab war, I am neither of the opinion that the Seiks made an unprovoked attack, nor that we have acted towards them with great forbearance. If the Seiks were to be considered entirely an independent state in no way answerable to us, we should not have provoked them—for to assert that the bridge of boats brought from Bombay, was not a *causa belli*, but merely a defensive measure, is absurd; besides the Seiks had a translation of Sir Charles Napier's speech (as it appeared in the *Delhi Gazette*) stating that we were going to war with them; and as all European powers would have done under such circumstances, the Seiks thought it as well to be first in the field. Moreover they were not encamped in our territory, but their own.

". . . and I only ask, had we not departed from the rules of friendship first? The year before the war broke out we kept the island between Ferozepur and the Punjab, though it belonged to the Seiks, owing to the deep water being between us and the island.

". . . But if on the other hand the treaty of 1809 is said to have been binding between the two governments, then the simple question is, who first departed from the 'rules of friendship'? I am decidedly of the opinion that we did." *History of the Reigning Family of Lahore*.

Even more emphatic on the subject is Sir George Campbell, who was then posted at Kaithal (a Sikh state escheated by the British). He wrote: "It is recorded in the annals of history, or what is called history, which will go down to posterity, that the Sikh army invaded British territory in pursuance of a determination to attack us. And most people will be very much surprised to hear that they did nothing of the kind. They made no attack on our outlying cantonments nor set foot in our territory. What they did do was to cross the river and to entrench themselves in their own territory." *Memoirs of my Indian Career*, p. 78.

See also W. W. Humbley, *Journal of a Cavalry Officer*, p. 37.

[18] The first thing Lal Singh did on crossing the Sutlej was to write to Captain Nicholson at Ferozepur: "I have crossed with the Sikh army. You know my friendship for the British. Tell me what to do."

Nicholson replied: "Do not attack Ferozepur. Halt as many days as you can, and then march towards the governor general." Ganda Singh, *Private Correspondence relating to the Anglo-Sikh Wars*, p. 907. Also W. W. Humbley, *Journal of a Cavalry Officer*, pp. 40-42.

and Tej Singh, were in treasonable communication with the English, and in all probability Rani Jindan was aware that Lal Singh had written to the British "to consider him and the *bībī sāhibā* (Jindan) as their friends and cut up the *būrchās* (ruffians, i.e. the Khalsa) for them."[19]

Battle of Mudki, December 18, 1845

The Durbar army was divided into two: Tej Singh proceeded towards Ferozepur to reckon with General Littler. Lal Singh entrenched the larger part of his force near village Pheru Shahr (later known as Ferozeshahr) and himself marched on to intercept Gough and Hardinge. He was surprised to find that the British had advanced as far as Mudki. Despite the enemy's superiority in men and arms, Lal Singh ordered his troops to commence hostilities while he himself retired to Ferozeshahr. The leaderless Punjabis fought a grim hand-to-hand battle against the more numerous enemy led by the most experienced commanders of Europe. The battle continued with unabated fury till midnight (and came thereafter to be known as "Midnight Mudki"). After the loss of half of their force and fifteen guns, the Punjabis withdrew from the battlefield.

The field action of Mudki was not of very great military significance except insofar as it gave the British their first experience of the fighting qualities of the Punjabi soldier. British casualties were heavy;[20] reinforcements were sent for from Ambala, Meerut, and Delhi. Lord Hardinge relinquished his superior position of governor general and agreed to become second-in-command to his commander-in-chief. The march to the Sutlej was resumed.

Battle of Ferozeshahr, December 21, 1845

On the morning of December 21 Gough came in sight of the Punjabi entrenchments at Ferozeshahr. By the after-

[19] Nicholson's Diary dated December 12, 1845.
[20] 872 dead and wounded including Quartermaster General Sir Robert Sale, Sir John McGaskill, and Brigadier Boulton.

noon, General Littler, who had eluded Tej Singh, was able to join forces with Gough. The British commanders ordered an immediate attack. The battle commenced late in the afternoon on what happened to be the shortest day of the year. The British tried to overrun the Punjabis in one massive cavalry, infantry, and artillery onslaught. The battle raged with extreme ferocity through the evening till both armies were enveloped in the dark. A shell hit the Punjabi powder magazine and set many tents on fire. The Punjabis turned the misfortune to their advantage by falling on parties of the enemy who had penetrated their entrenchments. At midnight the moon rose over the battlefield giving the Punjabis another opportunity to liquidate enemy pockets and recover the ground they had lost. The British suffered terrible casualties; every single member of the governor general's staff was killed or wounded.[21] That frosty night "the fate of India trembled in the balance."[22]

The sun rose on the plains of Ferozeshahr over a terribly battered British army. It had run out of ammunition, and the men had no stomach left for battle. At this point

[21] Among the dead was the notorious Broadfoot.

[22] Sir Hope Grant, one of the British generals who fought in the Anglo-Sikh wars, wrote: "Truly that night was one of gloom and foreboding and never perhaps in our annals of India warfare has a British army on so large a scale been nearer to a defeat which would have involved annihilation. The Sikhs had practically recovered the whole of their entrenched camp; our exhausted and decimated divisions bivouacked without mutual cohesion over a wide area. . . ." *Life of General Sir Hope Grant*, I, 58-59, edited by H. Knollys.

Lord Hardinge sent his son back to Mudki with a sword he had been given for his services in the Napoleonic campaigns and instructions that in the event of a defeat all his private papers were to be destroyed.

An entry in Robert Cust's diary shows that the British generals had decided to lay down their arms: "December 22nd. News came from the governor general that our attack of yesterday had failed, that affairs were desperate, that all state papers were to be destroyed, and that if the morning attack failed, all would be over; this was kept secret by Mr. Currie and we were concerting measures to make an unconditional surrender to save the wounded, the part of the news that grieved me the most." *Linguistic and Oriental Essays*, VI, 48.

Tej Singh arrived from Ferozepur with troops, fresh and eager for combat.[23]

Tej Singh's guns opened fire. The British artillery had no shot with which to reply. Then, without any reason, Tej Singh's guns also fell silent, and, a few minutes later, Tej Singh ordered his troops to retreat. Lord Gough quickly realised that the Sikh commanders had fulfilled their treacherous promise. He ordered his cavalry to charge the entrenchments at Ferozeshahr. The defenders, who were confidently expecting Tej Singh to give the enemy the *coup de grace*, were taken by surprise. They fled from their encampment, abandoning their guns, 80,000 lbs. of gun-powder, and all their stores.[24]

The disaster at Ferozeshahr broke the morale of the few Durbar notables who had remained loyal to the state. Gulab Singh Dogra sent his agent to Ludhiana to negotiate terms for his assistance to the British;[25] his example was followed by many other chieftains.[26] To induce further desertions Hardinge issued a proclamation[27] inviting all natives of Hindustan to quit the service of the Durbar on pain of forfeiting their property and to claim protection from the British Government.

Buddowal, January 21, 1846; Aliwal, January 28, 1846

Lord Gough decided to wait for reinforcements before crossing the Sutlej and pushing on to Lahore. The Durbar received information that enemy guns and munitions were being moved northwards from Delhi and Ambala. This

[23] See also Vol. II, p. 162, of *The Autobiography of Lt. General Sir Harry Smith*, ed. by G. C. Moor Smith.

[24] Soon after the defeat, Tej Singh visited the British camp and had an interview with Lord Hardinge. What passed between the two is not known; but from the subsequent treatment the British accorded to the traitor, it is not hard to guess.

[25] SC 319 of 26.12.1846.

[26] *Dispatch to Secret Committee No. 2* of 26.12.1846.

[27] SC 246 of 26.12.1846. There were many Hindustani sepoys in the Durbar's forces: Jemadar Khushal Singh and his nephew Tej Singh, the commander-in-chief, were from Meerut.

armament was to be assembled at Ludhiana before being sent downstream to Ferozepur.

Ranjodh Singh Majithia and Ajit Singh of Ladwa crossed the Sutlej at Phillaur with a force of 8,000 men and 70 guns. In rapid marches they liberated the forts of Fatehgarh, Dharamkote, Gangarana, and Buddowal and encamped at Baran Hara, seven miles from Ludhiana. The Punjabis stole into Ludhiana cantonment and set many barracks on fire.

Sir Harry Smith was sent to relieve Ludhiana. He marched northwards from Ferozepur, keeping a few miles away from the Sutlej. Ranjodh Singh Majithia harried Smith's column and, when Smith tried to make a detour at Buddowal, attacked his rear with great vigour and captured his baggage train and stores.[28]

A few days later, Sir Harry Smith received the reinforcements he was expecting and turned on the Punjabis. At Aliwal, Smith inflicted a sharp defeat on Ranjodh Singh Majithia and Ajit Singh of Ladwa (both of whom fled the battlefield). Once more the Punjabi men refused to give in.[29] Large numbers were killed fighting; many were drowned in the river. Fifty-six guns were lost to the enemy.

Sabraon, February 10, 1846

The loss of armour at Aliwal put the Durbar army on the defensive. Its generals were uncertain where the enemy

---

[28] Sir Harry Smith paid tribute to Ranjodh Singh Majithia's tactics at Buddowal. "It is the most scientific move made during the war," he wrote in his autobiography, "and had he known how to profit by the position he had so judiciously occupied he would have obtained wonderful success. He should have attacked me with the vigour his French tutors would have displayed and destroyed me, for his force compared to mine was overwhelming; then turned about upon the troops at Ludhiana, beaten them and sacked and burnt the city. . . ." *The Autobiography of Lt. General Sir Harry Smith* (Vol. II, 186-187.)

[29] "Although their leader Ranjodh Singh was the first to fly and basely quit the field leaving his brave followers to conquer or lose, their courage never quailed," wrote Humbley. "Again they rallied and made one last and vigorous effort. Though defeat had made them desperate they fought like men who jeopardised all." Humbley, *Journal of a Cavalry Officer*, p. 150.

would cross the Sutlej and so they split their forces. To check the enemy advance on Lahore, the larger portion of the army was entrenched in a horse-shoe curve of the Sutlej near village Sabraon; this was under the command of the traitor, Tej Singh. The other traitor, Lal Singh, posted himself a little higher up the river ostensibly to prevent an attack on Amritsar.

Punjabi entrenchments at Sabraon were on the left bank of the Sutlej with a pontoon bridge connecting them with their base camp. Their big guns were placed behind high embankments and consequently immobilised for offensive action. The infantry was also posted behind earthworks and could not, therefore, be deployed to harass the enemy.

Gough and Hardinge decided to make a frontal assault on Sabraon and destroy the Durbar army at one blow. This was undoubtedly planned with confidence that the Sikh commanders were on their side.[30]

On February 7, it began to rain. For the next two days the downpour continued unabated, and the Sutlej rose more than seven inches, making all fords quite unfordable; only one rickety pontoon bridge connected the army encamped on the left bank with its base. Gough was quick to seize the opportunity. As soon as the rain stopped, he marched out of Ferozepur and, under cover of darkness, took his position at Sabraon.

On the morning of February 10, a heavy mist spread from the river over the rain-sodden fields, enveloping both contending armies. When the sun broke through the mist, the Punjabis found themselves encircled between two horse-shoes: facing them were the British and behind them was the Sutlej now in spate. After a preliminary artillery duel, British cavalry made a feint to check on the exact

[30] Through intermediaries, Henry Lawrence was able to glean sufficient information from Lal Singh to enable him to prepare a "rough sketch of the position and strength of the enemy at Sabraon on the night of 7th February" for transmission to the commander-in-chief. Henry Lawrence to the secretary, May 16, 1846. *Henry Lawrence's Private Papers.*

location of Punjabi guns. The cannonade was resumed, and in two hours British guns put the Durbar artillery out of action. Then the British charged Punjabi entrenchments from three sides.

Tej Singh fled across the pontoon bridge and had it destroyed. But most of the other generals stayed to fight. The most famous of them was Sham Singh Attariwala,[31] who rallied the Punjabis in a last desperate stand against the enemy. Those who tried to escape were drowned in the swirling waters of the Sutlej. Nearly 10,000 Punjabis lost their lives in the action. All their guns were either captured or abandoned in the river. It was a complete and crushing defeat.[32]

Lord Gough described Sabraon as the Waterloo of India. He paid tribute to the Punjabis: "Policy precluded me publicly recording my sentiments on the splendid gallantry of our fallen foe, or to record the acts of heroism displayed, not only individually, but almost collectively, by the Sikh sardars and the army; and I declare were it not from a deep conviction that my country's good required the sacrifice, I could have wept to have witnessed the fearful slaughter of so devoted a body of men."[33]

[31] Sham Singh Attariwala was the son of Nihal Singh, one of Ranjit Singh's celebrated generals. Sham Singh Attariwala entered service under the maharajah in 1803 and fought in the Multan, Kashmir, and northwest frontier campaigns. His daughter married Ranjit Singh's grandson, Nao Nihal Singh.

Sham Singh Attariwala won immortal fame for reckless bravery at Sabraon. The Punjabi bard, Shah Mohammad, wrote of him as "squeezing blood out of the whites as one squeezes juice out of a lemon."

[32] "It is due to the Sikhs to say that they fought bravely," wrote General Sir Joseph Thackwell, who was present at the battle; "for though defeated and broken, they never ran, but fought with their talwars to the last and I witnessed several acts of great bravery in some of their sirdars and men." *Military Memoirs of Lieut.-General Sir Joseph Thackwell*, edited by Col. Wylly, p. 209.

Lord Hardinge, who saw the action, wrote: "Few escaped; none, it may be said, surrendered. The Sikhs met their fate with the resignation which distinguishes their race." *Viscount Hardinge*, p. 119.

[33] Rait, *The Life and Campaigns of Viscount Gough*, p. 108.

The attitude of the people of Malwa during the conflict between their trans-Sutlej brethren and the British deserves attention. Of the innumerable Sikh chiefs of this region, only four—Patiala, Jind, Faridkot, and Chachrauli —gave unstinted support to the enemy; others either stayed on the fence or expressed sympathy with the Durbar.[34] Of the two Muslim chiefs, Malerkotla sided with the British; Mamdot, despite the offer of confirmation of his estates, allowed his brother to lead his contingent against the British at Ferozeshahr.[35] The attitude of the common people was uniformly hostile to the feringhee. Peasants refused to sell grain or fodder to the British army.

On the termination of the Sutlej campaign, the British government confiscated Rupar, Ladwa, and Allowala, took a quarter of Nabha territory and distributed it among the collaborating chiefs. The Malwa *jāgīrdārs* were deprived of judicial powers and left only with the right to collect revenue.

The traitors Lal Singh and Tej Singh were "immortalised" in doggerel verse punning on their names:

> *Lālū dī lālī gaī, Tejū dā geā tej*
> *Ran vic piṭh dikhāi ke moḍhā āie pher*

> Laloo lost the blush of shame,
> Tejoo lost his lustre,
> By turning their backs in the field
> They turned the tide and the battle yield.

[34] These included Nabha, Ladwa, Allowala, Malaudh, Thanesar, Rupar, Kheri, Mani Majra, Shahabad, Sikri, Shamgarh, Buria, and the Sodhis of Anandpur.
[35] SC 1300 of 26.12.1846.

CHAPTER 3

THE PUNJAB UNDER BRITISH OCCUPATION

◊⚏◊⚏◊ TWO days after their victory at Sabraon, Brit-
◊⚏◊⚏◊ ish forces crossed the Sutlej and occupied
⌵∧⌵∧⌵∧ Kasur. The Durbar empowered Gulab Singh
Dogra,[1] who had earlier come down to Lahore with regiments of hillmen, to negotiate a treaty of peace. Gulab
Singh Dogra first obtained assurances from the army pañces
that they would agree to the terms he made and then tendered the submission of the Durbar to Lord Hardinge.
Hardinge had already made up his mind about the future
of the Sikh kingdom. He knew that there were still too
many Khalsa soldiers scattered about in the country to permit annexation; so he contented himself with terms which
would facilitate a take-over at a more appropriate time: he
weakened the state by depriving it of valuable territory,
by reducing its army, and by boosting a rival power on its
frontier. These terms were incorporated in the treaty imposed on the Durbar.

[1] Gulab Singh was acceptable to the British because of his earlier
negotiations with them and because he had prevented the Dogras from
joining the Punjabis.

From January 1846 Gulab Singh had been in communication with
the governor general through various agents. One of his emissaries was a
Bengali physician, Bansi Dhar Ghosh, who delivered a letter from his
master to Lieutenant E. Lake (assistant agent to the governor general)
on January 15, 1846. The Dogra wanted to be early in his offer of collaboration. He wrote: "He who wishes to climb the summit of a lofty
mountain, must start at daybreak; should he delay, night may close over
him ere he has gained the desire of his heart; the treasure which is
buried in the depths of the mountain will become the prize of that man,
who is the first to reach its summit." SC 319 of 26.12.1846.

Early in February 1846, Gulab Singh sent a private emissary to Major
Henry Lawrence, who had taken over the governor general's agency from
Broadfoot. It seems clear that an understanding was reached between the
British and Gulab Singh before the battle of Sabraon. As stated in his
letter of February 19, 1846, to the Secret Committee, Hardinge gave
Gulab Singh an assurance that his interests would be given full consideration. According to the editors of the 1955 edition of Cunningham's History of the Sikhs (p. 279), it was chiefly the disclosure of the communication between Hardinge and Gulab Singh which led to Cunningham's
reversion from the political service to the army.

Treaties of Lahore, March 9 and 11, 1846[2]

By the terms imposed by the victorious British, the Durbar was compelled to give up the Jullundur Doab,[3] pay a war indemnity of 1½ crores of rupees, reduce its army to 20,000 infantry and 12,000 cavalry, hand over all the guns used in the Sutlej campaign, and relinquish control of both banks of the Sutlej to the British. A further condition was later added: the posting of a British unit in Lahore till the end of the year on payment of expenses. Although Rani Jindan continued to act as regent and Raja Lal Singh as vazir, effective power was vested in the British resident, Colonel Henry Lawrence.[4]

The Durbar was unable to pay the full war indemnity and instead ceded the hill territories between the Beas and the Indus, including Kashmir and Hazara. Hardinge was reluctant to occupy the whole of this area.[5] In pursuance of the policy to weaken the Punjabis by strengthening the

[2] See Appendices 2 and 3.

[3] Jullundur Doab was annexed because the Beas was considered a better military frontier than the Sutlej, and it was felt desirable to weaken the state which had produced "a more perfect system of military organisation than any which the British army had hitherto faced." The Jullundur Doab was also very fertile, yielding more than 30 lac rupees per annum after defraying all expenses of administration. It could easily pay the expenses of the occupation force.

[4] "In all our measures taken during the minority, we must bear in mind that by the Treaty of Lahore, March 1846, the Punjab never was intended to be an independent state. By the clause I added, the chief of the state can neither make war nor peace nor exchange nor sell an acre of territory, nor admit an European Officer, nor refuse us thoroughfare through his territories, nor in fact, perform any act (except its own internal administration) without our permission. In fact, the native prince is in fetters, and under our protection, and must do our bidding." Hardinge to Henry Lawrence, August 14, 1847; Edwardes and Merivale, *Life of Henry Lawrence*, p. 417.

[5] "It would bring us into collision with many powerful chiefs for whose coercion a large military establishment, at a great distance from our provinces and military resources, would be necessary . . . conflicting interests would be created and races of people with whom we have hitherto had no intercourse would be brought under our rule while the territories, excepting Kashmir, are comparatively unproductive and would scarcely pay the expenses of occupation and management." *Governor General's Dispatch to Secret Committee No. 7 of March 4, 1846.*

Dogras, he drew the line at the Chakkee river and retained only Kulu, Mandi, Nurpur, and Kangra (which were beyond the Beas); the rest was sold to Gulab Singh Dogra for 75 lac rupees.[6] On March 16, 1846, another treaty was signed at Amritsar recognising Gulab Singh Dogra as maharajah of Jammu and Kashmir. The Dogra got considerably more than he had expected as a reward for his services.[7] He accepted the gift, describing himself with more truth than he intended as *zar kharīd*—slave bought by gold. The erstwhile kingdom of the Punjab[8] was divided be-

[6] "On the other hand the tract now ceded includes the whole of the hill possessions of Raja Gulab Singh and the Jammu family; and while the severance of this frontier line from the Lahore possessions materially weakens that state and deprives it, in the eyes of other Asiatic powers, of much of its pride of position, its possession by us enables us at once to mark our sense of Raja Gulab Singh's conduct during the late operations, by regarding him in the mode most in accordance with his ambitious desires, to shew forth as an example to the other chiefs of Asia the benefits which accrue from an adherence to British interests, to create a strong and friendly power in a position to threaten and attack, should it be necessary to do so, the Lahore territories in their most vulnerable point and at the same time to secure to ourselves that indemnification for the expenses of the campaign, which we declared our determination to exact, and which excepting by the cession of territory, the Lahore Government is not in a condition to afford." *Ibid.* of March 4, 1846.

[7] "It was necessary last March to weaken the Sikhs by depriving them of Kashmir. The distance between Kashmir and the Sutlej is 300 miles of very difficult mountainous country, quite impracticable for six months. To keep a British force 300 miles from any possibility of support would have been an undertaking that merited a straitwaistcoat and not a peerage." *Viscount Hardinge*, p. 133.

[8] The revenues of what remained of the state were computed at 1 crore and 60 lacs of rupees (£1,600,000). After deducting expenses there was a net revenue of 108 lacs of rupees (£1,080,000):

Districts	Net Revenue	Gross Revenue
Peshawar	2,64,965	13,39,047
Multan	30,00,000	47,43,755
Punjab [i.e. except the above districts and the Jullundur Doab]	75,54,195	1,00,22,420
	1,08,19,160	1,61,05,222

SC 1325 of 26.12.1846.

tween a triumvirate of Lawrence brothers and Gulab Singh Dogra. Henry as resident administered the Majha from Lahore; John as commissioner ruled the Jullundur Doab; George at Peshawar controlled Hazara[9] and the Derajat. British officers were posted at strategic points on the pretext of redrawing the state boundaries and helping Durbar officials in their duties. The young maharajah and his Durbar were merely the decorative façade of a kingdom that had ceased to exist except in name.[10]

The British experienced some difficulty in enforcing the treaties they had made with the Durbar and Gulab Singh Dogra. Henry Lawrence had to lead a force to Kangra to compel the surrender of the fort. The situation in Kashmir was even more tricky. Shaikh Imamuddin, the governor, received orders from the Durbar to hand over the administration to Gulab Singh Dogra. At the same time he received a secret note from Raja Lal Singh (who had been chagrined by the British Government's generosity to Gulab Singh) advising him to resist Dogra intrusion.[11] The Shaikh, who had hoped to be confirmed in his post, expelled the Dogras sent against him. Once again Henry Lawrence had to com-

[9] Gulab Singh was unwilling (and unable) to take Hazara. He was compensated with territory adjoining Jammu. A public proclamation (No. 6 dated May 25, 1847) was made by the Durbar regarding the exchange of "the country of Hazara situated to the west of the river Jhelum . . . for an equivalent east of the river towards Jammu." SC 134 of 26.6.1847.

[10] In April 1846 an incident took place which has come to be known in history as the "cow row." It indicates the state of mind of the "protectors" and their attitude towards the natives.

An English sentry, irritated by an obstruction caused by a herd of cows, slashed some of them with his sword, and thus outraged the religious susceptibilities of the Hindu and Sikh citizens. The resident and officers who went into the city to explain the misconduct of the sentry were pelted with stones. They demanded the severest punishment for the insult. The next day Maharajah Dalip Singh was taken by Lal Singh to make his apologies to the resident. Many houses in the bazaar where the incident had taken place were razed to the ground and of the three men chiefly concerned in the stoning one was hanged and two deported. The English soldier who had caused the riot was "warned to be more careful in the future."

[11] SC 1224 of 26.12.1846. See also Sethi, *Trial of Raja Lal Singh*

pel obedience. Shaikh Imamuddin did not offer any resistance to the resident, and along with the reins of office he handed over the secret missives he had received from Raja Lal Singh. Raja Lal Singh was tried by a British court, found guilty of duplicity and exiled from the Punjab.[12] Tej Singh replaced him as the chief notable of the Durbar. In December 1846, Lord Hardinge came to the Punjab. In the manner of empire-builders, he made the sardars gifts of watches (few of them could read the time) and arranged for the Durbar to submit a written request[13] that the British force continue to be stationed in the Punjab till 1854, when Dalip Singh would come of age.

Treaty of Bhairowal, December 16, 1846

The Treaties of Lahore of March 1846 were replaced by a new one which was ratified at Bhairowal. By the terms

[12] *Ibid.*, Lal Singh lived in Dehra Dun and Mussoorie till his death in 1867.

[13] The Durbar was somewhat reluctant to submit a written request. In a letter dated December 10, 1846, Hardinge wrote to Currie: "The coyness of the Durbar and the sirdars is natural; but it is very important that the proposal should originate with them; and in any documents proceeding from them this admission must be stated in clear and unqualified terms; our reluctance to undertake a heavy responsibility must be set forth." In another letter, Lord Hardinge instructed Currie to "persevere in your line of making the Sikh Durbar propose the condition or rather their readiness to assent to any conditions imposed as the price of the continuance of our support." In the preamble of the supplementary articles, the governor general added, "this solicitation must clearly be their act." Hardinge to Currie, December 12, 1846. *Private Correspondence relating to the Anglo-Sikh Wars*, p. [107] pp. 12-13. At an earlier meeting between Rani Jindan, Dalip Singh, Lal Singh, Bhai Ram Singh, Faqir Nuruddin, and John Lawrence on the evening of September 10, 1846, Rani Jindan had stated that after consultation with members of the Durbar on the "resolve of the governor general to withdraw the army," the conclusion to which they had unanimously arrived was that the "existence of the government, indeed of her own life and that of the maharajah, solely depended on its presence and that of the British representative in Lahore." She further said that "if the army only stayed the Durbar would agree to any terms which the English government should think proper to impose." Bhai Ram Singh followed up these representations by paying John Lawrence a visit the next morning. SC 1043 of 26.12.1846.

of this treaty the British Government undertook the maintenance of the administration and the protection of the maharajah during his minority. The resident was given full authority over all matters, in every department of the state. The governor general was empowered to occupy with British soldiers such positions as he thought necessary for the security of the capital, for the protection of the maharajah, and for the preservation of the peace of the country.[14] In short the British resident was made independent of the council of regency and elevated to the position of a governor.[15] Rani Jindan was deprived of all power and pensioned off with 1½ lac rupees per annum.

Administrative changes introduced by the conquerors both in the annexed territories and in those they administered in the name of the Durbar are worthy of attention. In the Jullundur Doab, consisting of the districts of Jullundur, Hoshiarpur, and Kangra, John Lawrence introduced land

[14] See Appendix 4.

[15] Article 3 of the treaty gave the resident "full authority to direct and control all matters in every department of state."

Hardinge wrote to the Secret Committee: "Your committee will perceive that, by these arrangements, I take under my direct control the executive administration of these districts and am desirous before I leave this part of the country to introduce into these territories an effective system of administration, founded upon just principles and regulated by salutary rules of practice. Hitherto there has been nothing of the kind, and the character of British administration, for justice and consistency in these tracts which have been hitherto under our control, has not been maintained so fully as might have been desired." *Governor General's Dispatch to Secret Committee No. 1* of 1847.

This was approved by the board of directors. The wording of their statement is significant: "We have already conveyed to you our strong approbation of your project for establishing a British regency in the Punjab, in case you should determine not to evacuate the country. No middle course would be either prudent or safe; and our dominion, so long as it lasts, should be absolute and complete." SC 1250 of 25.1.1847.

Hardinge was more candid to Hobhouse. Referring to the treaty, he wrote: "It is in reality annexation brought about by the suppression of the Sikhs, without entailing upon us the present expense and future inconvenience of a doubtful acquisition." *Broughton Papers* (Add. Mss 36. 475 fascicule 220) British Museum.

reforms which had far-reaching economic and political consequences. He found a baffling variety of land holdings ranging from those of the hill-chiefs with troops of armed retainers which they were under obligation to furnish to the Durbar when required; estates of descendants of the Majha *misldārs* and of the Bedi and Sodhi descendants of the gurus; religious endowments; grants by *sanads,* and grants to officials in rewards for services to the state, etc.

John Lawrence confirmed the hill-chiefs in their estates, but both in their cases and in those of jagirdars he commuted the obligation to furnish troops into cash payment. He also ordered the demolition of most of the forts in the region. As regards the other jagirs, he laid down the rule that all grants made after the death of Maharajah Sher Singh or made by unauthorised persons such as *nazīms* and *kārdārs* were to be resumed. The most important jagirs were those granted by the Durbar to its loyal servants. John Lawrence was strongly of the opinion that this class of jagirdars was now idle, useless, disloyal, and "always drones except when opportunity allows them to be wasps to sting us."[16]

John Lawrence's measures, though largely beneficial to the peasant proprietors, adversely affected the land-owning class. They also caused uneasiness in Lahore circles as Trans-Sutlej chiefs owned large estates in the Jullundur Doab. The chiefs realised that if the British took the rest of the Punjab, they would be deprived of whatever jagirs remained to them.

As important as the disposal of the jagirs was the fixing of land revenue. John Lawrence made a summary settlement for three years which, though lighter than the Durbar's assessment, caused hardship because payment was demanded in cash instead of in agricultural produce. He also made revenue settlements directly with representatives of village communities, thus bypassing chaudharis and lambardars, who were in consequence deprived of the privilege

[16] Note by John Lawrence dated December 16, 1846, para 8.

of rent-free lands. The revenue officials became as disgruntled as the jagirdars.[17]

In the Punjab that remained nominally under the Durbar, the resident proposed similar changes. Henry Lawrence tried to carry the Durbar with him; his brother John,
who acted for him for a while, did not bother to do that.
The Durbar's dominions were divided into four judicial
districts, each under a judge.[18] Each judge was given a
deputy and provided with troops to enforce his orders. The
judges were to hear appeals from the decisions of *kārdārs*
and were empowered to decide civil and criminal cases
(but not revenue matters nor appoint *kārdārs*). British
officers superintended the functioning of these courts. John
Lawrence had the code of criminal law operative in British
India printed at Lahore[19] (a lithograph press had been

[17] "If the introduction of our rule has been popular to the majority of
cultivators, and generally the lower classes of society, it has been decidedly
contrary to the (interests of) higher. The jagirdars have seen their power,
influence and property entirely destroyed; the chaudharis and headmen
of talooquas and villages have in the same way been reduced to the level
of their poor brethren and being restrained on the one hand from en-
riching themselves by appropriating an undue portion of the village
profits, they have also at the same time been shorn by government of
the highly prized possession of cash, *inams*, rent free lands or favourable
assessments." R. N. Cust, deputy commissioner, Hoshiarpur, to commissioner and superintendent, Trans-Sutlej, July 8, 1847. *Board's Collections 117172*, pp. 160-61, India Office Library.

"The jagirdars are unfavourably disposed towards us, for their jagirs
have been resumed. The chaudharis of villages are already losing their
influence. Their *inam* or money allowances are reduced, and their claims
to hold rent free lands are summarily dismissed." H. Vansittart, deputy
commissioner, Jullundur, to commissioner and superintendent, Trans-
Sutlej, September 7, 1847. I.P.C. 31.12.1847, Part 8, No. 2289, India Office
Library.

[18] General Kahan Singh Man was appointed for Lahore; Ram Singh
Jallawala for the Chaj Doab; Chattar Singh Attariwala for the country
between the Jhelum and the Indus; Lehna Singh Majithia for the Majha
including lands southeast of the Ravi up to the hills and down to Kasur.

[19] Punjab Government Records, *Lahore Political Diaries 1847-1848*, III,
444.
Death by hanging was introduced into the kingdom for the first time.
(In Ranjit Singh's days even murder was punishable by fine payable
to relations of the deceased or by mutilation.)

set up in the capital in January 1848) and circulated to judicial officers. The summary land settlement that John had introduced in the Jullundur Doab was later introduced in the Durbar's territories.

It did not take Rani Jindan and the Durbar chiefs long to realise that they had dissipated Ranjit Singh's kingdom: two-thirds of it had been divided between the invader and the upstart Dogra; and, in the third that remained, the writ that ran was that of the feringhee. They had looked to the British to protect their persons and properties from the rapacity of the Khalsa army. The British had saved them from the army but had exacted a heavy price for doing so. In the new dispensation, the Durbar was shorn of all power, and the economic supremacy of landed aristocracy was seriously jeopardised. Rani Jindan was most perturbed with the way things were going and began to meddle in affairs of state.[20] The resident was dismayed to find that such was the magic of the name of Ranjit Singh that the people overlooked the past misdeeds of his widow and acclaimed her as their queen mother. It became necessary for the resident to remove her from the scene.[21] An excuse

---

Many progressive measures were introduced by the Durbar under British influence. The Durbar was persuaded to issue a proclamation against practices such as *satī*, infanticide, slavery, and forced labour (*begār*). The proclamation was not, however, enforced, and the practices continued till after the annexation of the country.

[20] Jindan strongly opposed the Treaty of Bhairowal and tried to persuade the sardars that they could govern the country without British assistance. "Passion and not patriotism was the secret of this opposition," was the opinion of Henry Lawrence. The resident forbade the sardars (notably Sher Singh Attariwala) to visit Jindan's private apartments. SC 166 of 30.1.1847.

[21] In February 1847, a conspiracy to murder the resident and Raja Tej Singh was unearthed. It was also discovered that Prema, the instigator of the plot, was on visiting terms with a servant of Jindan. This was not considered enough to implicate the maharani. The governor general, however, encouraged the resident to try other means of getting rid of her. *Governor General's Dispatch to Secret Committee* of September 5, 1847; Hardinge to Currie, June 10, 1847.

was provided when, at a formal ceremony to honour nobles, Dalip Singh refused to put the saffron mark on the forehead of Raja Tej Singh.[22] The resident saw the hand of Jindan behind the episode and two days later ordered her removal to Sheikhupura. She was, according to her complaint, "dragged out by the hair"[23] to be taken to the fort; her allowance was reduced to less than a third. The outraged queen protested: "Surely, royalty was never treated the way you are treating us! Instead of being secretly king of the country, why don't you declare yourself so? You talk about friendship and then put us in prison. You establish traitors in Lahore, and then at their bidding you are going to kill the whole of the Punjab."[24]

A strict guard was placed on Jindan. But the more restrictions and dishonour the British heaped on Jindan, the more she became a heroine in the eyes of the people. Most chieftains openly expressed their sympathy for her. Bhai Maharaj Singh, who had succeeded Bhai Bir Singh at Naurangabad and was held in as great esteem as his predecessor by the peasantry and nobility, acclaimed her.[25] The bhai was arrested by order of the resident but escaped from custody. He eluded the police and addressed large meet-

---

Prema and 3 others were sentenced to imprisonment for life and 5 others to various terms in gaol. Punjab Government Records, *Lahore Political Diaries 1847-1848*, III, 284.

[22] This was on August 7, 1847. The resident reported to the governor general: "His Highness shrunk back into his velvet chair, with a determination foreign both to his age and gentle disposition."

[23] Jindan to John Lawrence, September 10, 1847. SC 119 of 30.10.1847.

[24] "You say that I shall receive a monthly sum of 4,000 rupees, and from this I suppose that you have reduced my allowance. I am the owner of a country yielding 3 crores of rupees, in revenue. . . . By what reckoning do you make out my allowances, to be 4,000 per month? I will take what was fixed in the treaty, and if any alteration is made, it should be by way of increase and not of decrease. . . . You have not only destroyed my character, but have also imprisoned me, and separated me from my child. Give me bread, why take away my life by starvation. I am the owner of a kingdom; I will have redress from your queen. You have acted towards me unjustly." SC 119 of 30.10.1847.

[25] SC 142 of 31.7.1847. Maharaj Singh belonged to village Rabbon (district Ludhiana) and was present at the death of Bir Singh.

ings in central Punjab, exhorting the people to rise and expel the feringhee.

Resentment against the English began to mount. The abolition of jagirs in the Jullundur Doab, radical changes introduced in the system of land revenue and its collection angered the landed classes and revenue officials. The insolence of the individual Englishmen did not endear them to the people. They outraged the religious sentiments of the non-Muslim populace by allowing the slaughter of kine;[26] they did not understand Sikh resentment against persons entering gurdwaras with shoes on.[27] Vile abuse, maltreatment of natives, and molesting of women by English soldiers became common occurrences. The Punjabis began to listen credulously to the wildest of stories: that for two months European soldiers would be given liberty to accost any woman they chose; that all the Durbar's ministers would be gaoled;[28] that the sahibs were extracting *mumiāī* (human oil) from the corpses of natives.[29] Among the most eager listeners to this kind of gossip were the soldiers disbanded after the Sutlej campaign; over 20,000 had been let loose in the country without any occupation.[30]

[26] Punjab Government Records, *Lahore Political Diaries 1846-1849*, IV, 431, refers to sale of beef in the open market.

[27] After the Treaty of Lahore, 1846, a tablet bearing the following inscription was placed near the entrance of the Harimandir:

"The priests of Amritsar having complained of annoyance, this is to make known to all concerned that by order of the governor general, British subjects are forbidden to enter the temple (called the Darbar) or its precincts, at Amritsar, or indeed any temple, with their shoes on.

"Kine are not to be killed at Amritsar, nor are the Sikhs to be molested or in any way to be interfered with.

"Shoes are to be taken off at the *bhoonga* at the corner of the tank and no person is to walk round the tank with his shoes on.
Lahore, March 24th, 1847.   Sd: Henry Lawrence, Resident"

[28] Punjab Government Records, *Lahore Political Diaries 1847-1848*, III, 232.

[29] *Ibid.*, 413. The legend of the *mumiāīvālā*, operating on behalf of the British continued right up to 1947. The word is probably derived from Mumai Khan, a Mongol chief, who tortured his victims by hanging them by their feet over a slow fire.

[30] "I see around me and hear of so many men who having been generals and colonels in the Seikh army, are now struggling for existence." Henry Lawrence, April 29, 1847, to the governor general. SC 112 of 26.6.1847.

CHAPTER 4

SECOND ANGLO-SIKH WAR

LORD HARDINGE handed over the reins of office in January 1848, assuring his successor that "it should not be necessary to fire a gun in India for some years to come."[1] Hardinge's policy of bolstering a friendly but subservient Sikh (or Sikh-cum-Dogra) state as a breakwater against central Asian Mohammedanism had foundered on the rocks of the Sikhs' refusal to befriend the British and be as hostile to the Pathans and the Afghans as was hoped. Hardinge was succeeded by a haughty young aristocrat, Lord Dalhousie. The mounting unrest in the Punjab gave the young laird the chance to reorientate British policy towards the Durbar. Instead of only weakening the Sikh state, he believed in "grasping all rightful opportunities of acquiring territory or revenue as may from time to time present themselves." The opportunity was not long in coming; and at an opportune moment. Henry Lawrence, who was against encroachment on the Durbar's powers, was away in England on sick-leave. His brother, John, and Edward Currie, who acted as residents in his absence, belonged to Dalhousie's expansionist school.

The trouble began at Multan. Dewan Mulraj, was assessed by the resident to pay 20 lacs of rupees for his province. At the same time the district of Jhang, which formed a third of his estate, was taken from him. Mulraj agreed to these terms but was unable to fulfil them because the resident had abolished excise duty on goods transported by river, which formed a substantial part of the income of Multan. Mulraj also resented his judgments' being reviewed by the resident. He submitted his resignation in December 1847. The resignation was accepted, but the dewan was persuaded to continue in office till March

[1] Bosworth Smith, *Life of Lord Lawrence*, I, 214.

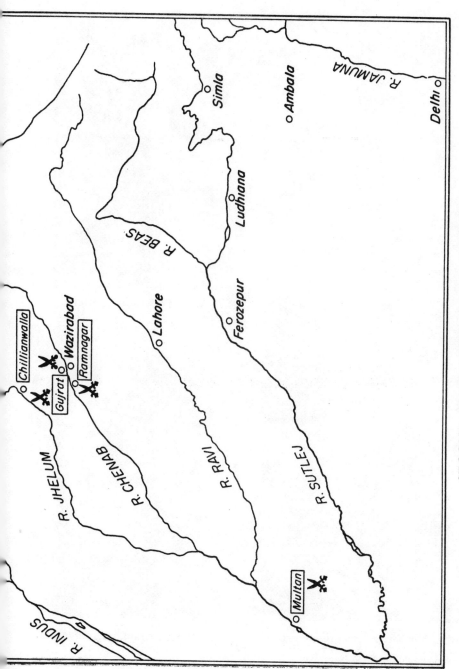

SECOND ANGLO-SIKH WAR, 1848-1849

Amrita Shergill, painter

Bhai Vir Singh, poet-theologian
Photograph by T. S. Nagarajan,
Yojana, New Delhi

Amrita Pritam, poet-novelist

Pratap Singh Kairon

Swaran Singh

Photograph by T. S. Nagarajan, Yojana, New Delhi

Master Tara Singh with Sant Fateh Singh

Photograph by Marilyn Silverstone—Magnum Photos, Inc.

Guru Jagjit Singh (Namdhari)

Photograph by T. S. Nagarajan, Yojana, New Delhi

Guru Hara Singh (Nirankari)   Guru Charan Singh (Radha Soami)

Maharajah Sher Singh

1848, by which time the winter harvest would be gathered.

General Kahan Singh Man was chosen to succeed Mulraj. Two British officers, Vans Agnew of the civil service and Lieutenant Anderson, were sent down by river to superintend the take-over. The Durbar party encamped outside the fort. The next day Mulraj welcomed Kahan Singh Man and the Englishmen, showed them round the fort, and formally presented them with the keys of the citadel. The Multan garrison was discharged, and the Durbar troops took over. As the Englishmen were passing out through the gate of the fort on their way back to camp, they were assaulted. In the melee that ensued, Vans Agnew, Lieutenant Anderson, and a few others were injured. Mulraj rode back to get help and sent a note to the Durbar camp regretting the incident. Vans Agnew acknowledged the dewan's note and exonerated him from all responsibility for the assault. He also sent a report to the resident stating clearly, "I don't think Mulraj has anything to do with it. I was riding with him when we were attacked."[2] He asked for help from Lieutenant Edwardes and General Van Cortlandt, who were at Dera Fateh Khan and Dera Ismail Khan, respectively.

The disbanded soldiery of Multan forced Mulraj to become their leader. They appealed to the Durbar troops to join them in expelling the feringhee. With the exception of Kahan Singh Man and a dozen or so others, the Durbar troops went over to the Multanis. The next evening they mobbed the British camp and killed Vans Agnew and Lieutenant Anderson. Sikh soldiers issued an appeal to their co-religionists in the Punjab.

[2] Edwardes, *A Year on the Punjab Frontier*, II, 78. Lt. Edwardes' note to the resident is pertinent. "I think Mulraj has been involved in rebellion against his will, and being a weak man, is now persuaded by his officers that there is no hope for him but in going all lengths; that the origin of the rebellion was the natural dislike of the Pathans, Baluchis and Multanis (men of high family, courage and false pride) to be turned adrift, after a life spent in military service well rewarded and that these men will fight desperately, and die hard. . . ." II, 100.

"Now we, in accordance with the guru's command, have written to all of you, our Khalsa brethren. Those of you who are true and sincere Sikhs, will come to us here. You will receive pay, and will be received honourably in the durbar of the guru. . . .

"The Maharajah Duleep Singh will, by the guru's grace, be firmly established in his kingdom, the cow and the Brahmin will be protected and our holy religion will prosper. . . .

"The maharajah and his mother are in sorrow and affliction. By engaging in their cause, you will obtain their favour and support. _Khālsājī_, gird up your loins under the protection of the guru and Guru Gobind Singh will preserve your honour. Make much of a few words. Dated 12 Baisakh 1905." (22nd April 1848.)

So strong was the feeling against the British that within a few days the Rechna Doab and the doab between the Chenab and the Indus swarmed with Pathan and Baluch swordsmen willing to make common cause with the Sikhs to reinstate a Hindu governor against the fiat of the feringhee.

The resident's (Edward Currie's) immediate reaction on getting news of the attack on Vans Agnew was to order troops to Multan. But the very next day, when he heard that both Vans Agnew and Lieutenant Anderson were dead and that the Durbar troops had joined the rebels, he countermanded his order. He summoned the council and told it plainly that since the rebellion was against the authority of the Durbar it was up to the Durbar to suppress it. He preferred to ignore the provisions of the Treaty of Bhairowal by which British troops paid by the Durbar were kept specially for preserving the peace of the country.

Members of the council confessed their inability to cope with the situation.[3] Lord Dalhousie and his commander-

---

[3] "The chiefs returned yesterday morning, and having heard what I had to say regarding the necessity of their putting down the rebellion,

in-chief (who pleaded that it was the wrong time of the year for English soldiers to fight in the plains)[4] agreed with the resident to let the situation deteriorate and then exploit it to their advantage.[5]

The resident did his best to fan the flames of rebellion. Rani Jindan, who was under house arrest in Sheikhupura fort and did little besides squander money consulting soothsayers and feeding Brahmins, was ordered to be deported from the Punjab. The resident believed that, although "legal proof of the delinquency would not perhaps be obtainable," she was deeply implicated in a conspiracy to tamper with the loyalty of native soldiers.[6] Despite the

---

and bringing the offenders to justice, by their own means as the only hope of saving their government, they retired to consult and concert measures. After much discussion they declared themselves unable, without British aid, to coerce Dewan Mulraj in Multan and bring the perpetrators of the outrage to justice. After what has happened, I feel that if the question were one merely affecting the maintenance of the Sikh Government and preserving the tranquillity of their provinces we should scarcely be justified in expending more British blood and British treasure in such service." Currie to Dalhousie, April 27, 1848. L. 139/Bk. 178, Punjab Government Records.

[4] Not all English officers were aware of what was passing in the minds of the governor general and the resident. Herbert Edwardes protested that: "Some of the hardest campaigns in Indian history were fought in the hot weather, and men do not sicken when their minds are on the stretch. . . . There is an argument still stronger for our settling this affair ourselves. Our national faith as pledged in the treaty solemnly demands that we should do all in our power to preserve little Dalip's throne. Now if we wished to appropriate the country, and upset that throne, we have only to concentrate a Sikh army on Multan; and disloyalty would follow union, national insurrection would follow disloyalty, and the seizure of the Punjab in self-defence follow insurrection, as inevitably as the links of a chain. The world would acquit us, being ignorant of what we know; but, neither God, nor our conscience could do so." Edwardes to Currie, May 4, 1848. L. 44/Bk.191, P.G.R.

[5] "The Government of India had decided to let the Punjab abscess come to a head, and when ripe to lance it freely in the coming cold weather." Thorburn, *The Punjab in Peace and War*, p. 101.

[6] Three men were hanged in this conspiracy. Evidence of Jindan's guilt rested on the statement made by one of the condemned men prior to his execution. He also implicated General Kahan Singh Man as Jindan's agent to Mulraj. This part of the statement was disbelieved by the governor general.

unanimous disapproval of the hitherto pliable council of regency, the order was carried out with due severity. Jindan was taken to Benares under heavy armed escort; her allowance was further reduced to Rs. 1,000 per month.

A wave of resentment swept over the Punjab. At the time of the Multan rebellion, there was perhaps no one who would shoulder a musket at Rani Jindan's bidding; a week after she had been removed from the state, there were few who would not lay down their lives for her sake. The resident admitted to the governor general: "The Khalsa soldiery on hearing of the removal of the maharani were much disturbed: they said that she was the mother of all the Khalsa, and that as she was gone, and the young Dalip Singh in our hands, they had no longer anyone to fight for and uphold. . . ."[7] Even Amir Dost Mohammed of Afghanistan, expressed sympathy with the people of the Punjab.[8]

The banishment of Jindan shook the confidence that the Durbar notables had placed in the British. Till this time they had been loyal because the British had saved them from the Khalsa army, guaranteed their possessions and privileges, and given them a sense of security.[9] But the

[7] Currie to Elliott, May 25, 1848; No.515/W.E. 27.5.1848 P.G.R. George Lawrence at Peshawar records a conversation he overheard between two Sikh soldiers on the separation of Jindan and her son: they "wondered whether we meant to play him [the young maharajah] fair." One replied, "Rely upon it they do; they always are true to their engagements." "Ah but," said the other, "the bait is great; can they withstand it!" Punjab Government Records, *Lahore Political Diaries 1846-49*, IV, 397.

[8] "There can be no doubt that the Sikhs are daily becoming more and more discontented. Some have been dismissed from service, while others have been banished to Hindustan, in particular the mother of Maharajah Duleep Singh, who has been imprisoned and ill-treated. Such treatment is considered objectionable by all creeds and both high and low prefer death." Dost Mohammed to Captain Abbott; enclosure 13 in No. 44, *Parliamentary Papers (1847-49)*.

[9] "The sirdars are true, I believe; the soldiers are false, I know." Currie to the governor general, June 1848.

Edwardes echoed the same opinion: "With respect to the sirdars, I believe them to be heart and soul on our side, which is the side of jagirs,

removal of Jindan and the confiscation of the jagirs of those suspected of too close an association with her[10] caused them to question their attitude towards their "protectors." The family most concerned were the Attariwalas because Chattar Singh's daughter was engaged to Maharajah Dalip Singh. They overlooked the slights offered to Jindan in the hope that if all went well an Attariwala would become maharani of the Punjab and they would become the most powerful family in the state. Although both the aging Chattar Singh, who was *nāzim* in the northwest frontier districts, and his son, Sher Singh, who was a member of the Council of Regency, tacitly acquiesced in the expulsion of Jindan, they too began to suspect that the British had no intention of restoring the Punjab to Maharajah Dalip Singh when he came of age.

The policy of deliberate inactivity did not percolate down to the junior officers, among whom the most enterprising was Lieutenant Edwardes, who, as we have noted earlier, received Vans Agnew's note at Dera Fateh Khan. He did not wait[11] for orders but asked Van Cortlandt to join him in his march on Multan. He raised levies from the neighbouring Muslim tribes as he went along. He crossed the Indus and occupied Leiah; then he withdrew

---

titles, employments, and whole throats. But their force, with equal confidence, I report to be against us to a man."

10 Punjab Government Records, *Lahore Political Diaries 1846-49*, IV, 562.

11 Edwardes' comment on Lord Gough's reluctance to fight a campaign in the summer was forthright. "As if the rebellion could be put off like a champagne tiffin with a three cornered note to Mulraj, to name a date more agreeable." W. W. Hunter, *The Marquess of Dalhousie*, p. 73.

"This Doab is full of Puthan mercenaries in and out of employ, and entertaining those in the forts will, I have no doubt, secure the posts themselves. Indeed I am inclined to believe that the whole disturbance in Mooltan has originated in the dread of the dewan's Puthan troops of being thrown out of employ." Punjab Government Records, *Lahore Political Diaries 1847-49*. V, 320.

from Leiah and captured Mangrota.[12] In mid-May, he and Van Cortlandt captured Dera Ghazi Khan and approached Multan from the south. Edwardes' spirited moves shamed the resident to action. He ordered General Whish and Sher Singh Attariwala to Multan and induced the nawab of Bahawalpur to join in the assault.

Mulraj fought an engagement with the Bahawalpuris at Kineri (June 18, 1848) and then withdrew. Edwardes and Van Cortlandt joined forces with the Bahawalpuris, pursued Mulraj, and inflicted another defeat on him at Saddosam (July 1, 1848). Mulraj was compelled to withdraw to Multan. With the Durbar troops coming down from the north, and with Lake, Edwardes, and Van Cortlandt in full pursuit from the south, Mulraj's time seemed to be running out.

Bhai Maharaj Singh came to the beleaguered dewan's rescue. At the time of Jindan's deportation, he had been active in Majha. When he heard of the revolt in Multan, he proceeded southwards with his followers. He exhorted the people to join Mulraj's colours and assured them that it was written in the *sau sākhī*[13] that in sambat 1905 (1848) the Khalsa would regain sovereignty in the Punjab.

Durbar troops were sent in pursuit of Bhai Maharaj Singh. They overtook him near the Chenab and inflicted heavy casualties on his followers. The bhai managed to

[12] On May 8, 1848, Edwardes received a note from the resident (dated April 29) ordering him to keep away from Multan and restrict his activities to the Trans-Indus region. *Ibid.*, p. 322.

[13] Many versions of this collection of prophecies ascribed to Guru Gobind Singh have plagued the Sikh community from time to time. Versions of this book (with appropriate changes) were circulated during the Mutiny of 1857 (they prophesied a joint Anglo-Sikh victory over the Mughals); by the Namdharis in the 1860s supporting the claim of Ram Singh to be a reincarnation of Guru Gobind Singh and the future ruler of Hindustan; by the supporters of Dalip Singh in the 1880s (prophesying his return to the Punjab as maharajah with the help of the Russians).

New editions of the *sau sākhī* continue to appear to boost the claims of impostors.

escape and joined Mulraj. His arrival raised the flagging spirits of the dewan, who was elevated from the status of a reluctant rebel to a national hero. What had been a local rebellion became a war of independence. From all over the Punjab came reports of troops declaring for Mulraj.

The Attariwalas turned against the British only when their suspicion that the British did not mean to honour the terms of the Treaty of Bhairowal turned to certainty. At the instance of his father, Sher Singh persuaded Lieutenant Edwardes to write to the resident to fix a date for the marriage of Dalip Singh: the Attariwalas felt that the response would indicate how the minds of British officials were working. The resident promised to consider the matter but ended his note with words that could scarcely have reassured the Attariwalas. He wrote: "I do not see how proceeding with the ceremonies of the maharajah's nuptials can be considered as indicative of any line of policy which the government may consider it right to pursue now or at any future time in respect of the administration of the Punjab."[14]

Soon after this unsatisfactory reply, the relations between Chattar Singh Attariwala and Captain Abbott, who was meant to assist him, became extremely strained. Early in August 1848, without any provocation, Abbott roused the Muslim tribes against the Sikhs.[15] The tribesmen threatened to attack Haripur. For his own safety, Chattar Singh Attariwala ordered Colonel Canora (an American officer of the Durbar) to evacuate the fort for him. Canora refused to comply unless Abbott confirmed the order. The Attariwala ordered his troops to occupy the fort by force. Canora was killed while trying to fire on the Attariwala's troops. Abbott charged Chattar Singh with "cold blooded

[14] Currie to Edwardes, August 3, 1848.
[15] "I called upon them in the memory of their murdered parents, friends and relatives to rise and aid me in destroying the Sikh forces in detail." Abbott to Currie, August 17, 1848.

murder." The resident was constrained to reprimand Captain Abbott;[16] but a few days later he confirmed the order of a subordinate investigating officer sequestrating Chattar Singh's jagirs and suspending him from the post of *nāzim*.[17] Chattar Singh, old and sick as he was,[18] had no option but to fight against the wrong done to him. He opened negotiations with Amir Dost Mohammed and his brother Sultan Mohammed. They agreed to support the Sikhs[19] against the British, provided Peshawar and the Derajat were restored to them. Chattar Singh also approached his friend Gulab Singh Dogra for help. The Dogra marched his troops up and down the Punjab frontier, keeping both the Sikhs and the British guessing about his real intentions.

At Multan, Sher Singh Attariwala heard of the way the resident had treated his aged father but refrained from taking a precipitate step; on September 9, he fought alongside the British in an attempt to capture the fort.[20] But a few days later, when he had reason to believe that the British planned to kidnap him, he left the British camp with his troops. The next day he issued a proclamation:

[16] He wrote: "It is clear that whatever may have been the intention of the brigade (under Chattar Singh) no overt act of rebellion was committed by them till the initiative was taken by you by calling out the armed peasantry, and surrounding the brigade in its cantonment. I have given you no authority to raise levies, and organise paid bands of soldiers to meet an emergency, of the occurrence of which I have always been somewhat sceptical. It is much, I think, to be lamented . . . that you have judged of the purposes, and feelings and fidelity of the *nāzim* and the troops, from the report of spies and informers, very probably interested in misrepresenting the real state of affairs. None of the accounts that have yet been made justifies you in calling the death of Commedan Canora a murder, nor in asserting that it was premeditated by Sardar Chattar Singh." Currie to Abbott, August 19, 1848.

[17] Nicholson to Currie, August 20, 1848.

[18] Punjab Government Records, *Lahore Political Diaries 1846-49*, IV, 149.

[19] *Ibid.*, p. 267.

[20] "The Sikhs fought splendidly—what pricks they are!" Pearse, *Journal Kept during the Siege of Multan*, (mss) p. 48.

"It is well known to all the inhabitants of the Punjab, to all the Sikhs, and those who have cherished the Khalsa and in fact the world at large, with what oppression, tyranny and violence, the feringhees have treated the widow of the great Maharajah Ranjit Singh and what cruelty they have shown towards the people of the country."[21]

Sher Singh offered to join Mulraj. The dewan's suspicions had been aroused by a forged letter which the British contrived to let fall into his hands—in this letter Sher Singh was mentioned as privy to a plot to take Multan by stratagem—and Mulraj refused to admit Sher Singh in the fort. In sheer disgust Sher Singh left Multan to go to the assistance of his father. The defection of the Attariwalas was a signal for other sardars to declare for freedom. Thus did a minor fracas develop into a national revolt. Only at Lahore, Raja Tej Singh and a few of the same ilk held durbar in the name of a hapless minor and did as they were bid by the feringhee.

Lord Dalhousie was pleased with the course of events because it gave him the excuse he was waiting for. "The insurrection in Hazara has made great head. . . . I should wish nothing better. . . . I can see no escape from the necessity of annexing this infernal country. . . . I have drawn the sword and this time thrown away the scabbard."[22] He received the news of Sher Singh's defection with unconcealed pleasure because it had brought matters to that crisis that he had for months been awaiting. He noted, "we are now not on the eve of but in the midst of war with the Sikh nation and kingdom of Punjab." Before leaving Calcutta, Dalhousie made the declaration of war in his usual forthright manner. "Unwarned by precedents, un-influenced by example, the Sikh nation has called for

21 Enclosure in Edwardes to Currie, September 16, 1848. No.1591/W.E. 23.9.1848, P.G.R.
22 Baird, *Private Letters of the Marquess of Dalhousie*, pp. 33-34.

war and on my word, sir, they shall have it with a vengeance."[23] He discreetly refrained from including the Durbar in his pronouncement so that British reinforcements
could enter "Lahore territories not as enemy to the constituted government but to restore order and obedience."[24]

It was an unequal contest. Under the terms of the
treaties of Lahore, 1846, most of the Punjabi guns had
been surrendered and their army reduced to 20,000 infantry and 12,000 cavalry. The peasantry had been disarmed. The British, on the other hand, had massed 50,000
trained soldiers along the Sutlej, cantoned 9,000 in Lahore
and another 9,000 at Ferozepur. Many of the most powerful forts—Lahore, Kangra, Sheikhupura—were in their
hands.

The situation in November 1848 was somewhat as follows. The Chaj and the Sind Sagar Doabs had declared
for freedom; the other doabs were under the British.
There were two centres of resistance—one led by the
Attariwalas in the northwest, the other by Mulraj in the
south.

Sher Singh Attariwala passed close by Lahore; the rising
of citizens that he expected did not take place. He heard
of Lord Gough's advance to Lahore and retreated northwards to hold the British on the Chenab.

Gough marched up to the Chenab and came in sight
of the Attariwala's forces on the opposite bank. The Pun-

---

[23] Dalhousie to Currie, October 8, 1848. Trotter, *Life of Marquess of
Dalhousie*, p. 38.

[24] This confusion in the minds of British officers continued right
through the campaign. Even the commander of the British forces, Lord
Gough, was not sure whether he was fighting for or against the Durbar.
His biographer writes: "It was not till after leaving Lahore that he
knew the definite decision of the governor general and that the war was
to be against, and not in support of, the Durbar. . . . 'I do not know,' he
said on the 15th, 'whether we are at peace or war or who it is we are
fighting for.'" R. S. Rait, *The Life and Campaigns of Viscount Gough*,
II, 178.

jabis crossed the river, captured the fort of Ramnagar, and repulsed a British force under General Campbell which attacked them.[25] Lord Gough came to the relief of Campbell. British forces crossed the Chenab at two points and engaged Sher Singh Attariwala in a sharp artillery duel near village Sadullapur.

British superiority in fire power compelled the Punjabis to abandon their positions on the Chenab and retreat to the Jhelum. They dug themselves in at a place where the river was behind them and an expanse of thick brushwood intersected by deep ravines was in front of them. The British took up their position about three miles southeast of the Punjabi entrenchments. For some time the two armies remained inactive. Then the Punjabis began to run short of provisions and tried to draw out the enemy from their position. News from other fronts induced the combatants to start hostilities on the Jhelum. Chattar Singh Attariwala had liberated Attock and sent whatever troops he could spare and promised to join his son in an attack on the enemy. The British received even a greater fillip with the news from Multan. A British cannonball had fallen on the magazine in the fort, blowing up 400,000 lbs. of gunpowder and killing over five hundred of its defenders.[26] The tide of battle had turned in favour of the British. They awaited the arrival of their siege guns to compel Mulraj to surrender.

[25] Ramnagar was not an engagement of any great consequence, but it gave a much needed boost to Punjabi morale. A British subaltern wrote: "The enemy are in great feather, and ride along within half a mile of our camp and close to our pickets." Sandford, *Leaves from the Journal of a Subaltern*, November 24, 1848, p. 66. The Punjabis captured a British gun and the colours of a regiment.

Sher Singh Attariwala sent a note to the British offering to stop hostilities if they promised to vacate Lahore. No notice was taken of this offer.

[26] This was on December 30, 1848. General Kahan Singh Man and his son, who were confined in a dungeon, were killed in this explosion. Punjab Government Records, *Lahore Political Diaries 1847-49*, v, 329. Mulraj surrendered on January 22, 1849.

Battle of Chillianwala, January 13, 1849

The British[27] and the Punjabis jockeyed for position. Lord Gough tried to avoid the jungle and attack the Punjabis in the flank. Sher Singh Attariwala forestalled the move and took up another formation—with the jungles and ravines still separating him from the enemy.

On the afternoon of January 13, 1849, the British launched their attack. The Punjabis sighted them advancing from the direction of village Chillianwala and promptly opened fire. For an hour Punjabi guns kept the enemy at bay. When their fire slackened, the British, who had the advantage of numbers, charged in an attempt to force the Punjabis into the river. The Punjabis scattered into the brushwood jungle and began their harrying *dhāī phat* (hit and run) tactics.[28] The battle raged till the night enveloped both the armies. The Punjabis captured four British guns and the colours of three regiments. Chillianwala was the worst defeat suffered by the British since their occupation of India.[29] Next morning the Punjabi

[27] The Dogras under Col. Steinbach (one-time servant of the Durbar) and Rohillas, who deserted the Punjabis, joined the British at Chillianwala.

[28] "The Sikhs," wrote an English observer, "fought like devils . . . fierce and untamed even in their dying struggle. . . . Such a mass of men I never set eye on and as plucky as lions: they ran right on the bayonets and struck at their assailants when they were transfixed." Sandford, *Leaves from the Journal of a Subaltern*, pp. 106-08.

[29] The night was one of great terror for the British. General Thackwell wrote: "Confusion pervaded the whole army. Fears were generally entertained that the enemy (the Punjabis) would attempt a night attack. If they had been enterprising and could have perceived the extent of their advantage, they would assuredly have thrown themselves on us. . . . The jungle which had befriended them in the commencement of the action now formed a protection to us." The scene of the next morning is also painted by General Thackwell: "Prince Albert hats and military shoes might be seen in all directions strewn on the ground in great abundance . . . the camp next day was overspread with funeral gloom." And it might well have been, for nearly 3,000 British lay dead or wounded in the ravines and brushwood. Thackwell, *Narrative of the Second Sikh War*, p. 173.

· 79 ·

guns boomed a twenty-one-gun salute to a Punjabi victory.[30]

Once again, as at Ferozeshahr, the Punjabis failed to drive home their advantage. Their own losses had been considerable, and they were not aware of the magnitude of the punishment they had inflicted on the enemy. The elements also came to the rescue of the British. As soon as the fighting stopped, it began to rain; for the next three days it poured incessantly, turning the ravines which separated the Punjabis from their quarry into deep moats. On the fourth day when the sun shone again on the sodden plain, the British pulled out of Chillianwala and retreated across the Chaj to the banks of the Chenab.[31]

The Attariwalas sent George Lawrence, who was their captive, with terms for a truce. They asked for the investment of Dalip Singh as maharajah and the evacuation of British troops from the Punjab. The offer was rejected.

Battle of Gujarat, February 21, 1849

The Attariwalas advanced towards the Chenab and entrenched their forces in horse-shoe formation between the town of Gujarat and the river. They were weaker both in

---

Lord Gough was superseded; Sir Charles Napier was appointed commander-in-chief.

30 The British also claimed Chillianwala as a victory. Lord Dalhousie, however, made candid admission of the true state of affairs in a private letter dated January 22, 1849, to Lord Wellington. He wrote: "In public I make, of course, the best of things. I treat it as a great victory. But writing confidentially to you, I do not hesitate to say that I consider my position grave. . . ." *The Marquess of Dalhousie*, p. 209.

31 British historians have commented adversely on the Sikh treatment of British prisoners and wounded; George Meredith, who published his first poem on Chillianwala, described them as "the savage plundering devils doing their worst among the slain . . . the wounded and the dying." A British subaltern wrote: "Two of the 9,000 lancers who were taken prisoners the other day were sent back this morning with Sher Singh's compliments. They seemed rather sorry to come back as they had been treated like princes, *pilāwed* with champagne and brandy to the mast-head and sent away with Rs.10 each in his pocket." Sandford, *Leaves from the Journal of a Subaltern*, p. 12.

guns (59 to the British 66) and in man power. The British attack began at 7:30 a.m. The Punjabis as usual opened fire too soon; they exhausted their ammunition and betrayed the position of their guns. In a cannonade lasting an hour, British guns silenced the Punjabi artillery.[32] Then their cavalry and infantry charged Punjabi positions. Afghan cavalry, which had joined the Punjabis, tried to deflect the enemy but withdrew without achieving its purpose. The Punjabis engaged the enemy in a hand-to-hand combat. "In this action as well as at Chillianwala," wrote General Thackwell, "Seikhs caught hold of the bayonets of their assailants with their left hands and closing with their adversaries dealt furious sword blows with their right. . . . This circumstance alone will suffice to demonstrate the rare species of courage possessed by these men."[33]

The weight of numbers and armour decided the issue. The Punjabis gave way. The British occupied Gujarat and pursued the Punjabis till they had destroyed all they could find.[34]

The battle of Gujarat ended organised Punjabi resistance to the feringhees. On March 11, 1849, the Attariwalas formally surrendered their swords to Major General Gilbert at Hurmuck near Rawalpindi.[35] They were followed

[32] General Thackwell remarked, "The fidelity displayed by the Seikh gunners is worthy of record: the devotion with which they remained at their posts, when the atmosphere around them was absolutely fired by the British guns, does not admit description." E. J. Thackwell, *Narrative of the Second Sikh War*, p. 213.

[33] *Ibid.*, p. 213.

[34] "Little quarter, I am ashamed to say, was given—and even those we managed to save from the vengeance of our men, I fear, were killed afterwards. But, after all, it is a war of extermination." Sandford, *Leaves from the Journal of a Subaltern*, p. 155.

[35] *Secret Dispatch to the Secret Committee No. 18*, March 21, 1849. When the Attariwalas and their armies laid down their arms, many men resolved to continue the struggle. Narain Singh was captured alive; Colonel Rachpal Singh was killed near Aligarh. On the night of December 28, 1849, Bhai Maharaj Singh on whose head there was a price of Rs.10,000 was taken with a band of twenty-one unarmed followers. "The guru is no ordinary man," wrote Mr. Vansittart, who had arrested

on the 14th by the whole Sikh army. General Thackwell described the scene: "The reluctance of some of the old Khalsa veterans to surrender their arms was evident. Some could not restrain their tears; while on the faces of others, rage and hatred were visibly depicted." The remark of one veteran grey beard as he put down his gun summed up the history of the Punjab: "*Āj Rañjīt Singh mar gayā*"— today Ranjit Singh has died.

On March 29, 1849, a durbar was assembled in the fort. A proclamation was made declaring the kingdom of the Sikhs at an end. Maharajah Dalip Singh handed over the Koh-i-noor diamond and stepped down from his illustrious father's throne—never to sit on it again.

---

him. "He is to the natives what Jesus is to the most zealous of Christians." SC 49 of 25.1.1850. The government could not risk a public trial in India, and decided to deport him to Singapore. For several years, the bhai was kept in a solitary cell. He died on July 5, 1856.

Mulraj was tried for murder and found guilty. The sentence of death was commuted to one of transportation for life. He died near Benares on August 11, 1851.

colonise many of these barren wastes became the most prosperous peasantry in Asia. It was not surprising that they became the staunchest supporters of the British Raj, because—in the words of the governor general, Lord Dufferin—"their future was merged with that of the British Empire in India."

colonise many of these barren wastes became the most prosperous peasantry in Asia. It was not surprising that they became the staunchest supporters of the British Raj, because—in the words of the governor general, Lord Dufferin—"their future was merged with that of the British Empire in India."

CHAPTER 5

ANNEXATION OF THE PUNJAB

◆◇◆◇◆. LORD DALHOUSIE did not believe in half-measures. Even before the Punjabis had laid down arms, he had resolved to decimate Sikh political power.[1] "The right to annex the Punjab is beyond cavil," he wrote.[2] He had, however, to contend with the opinions of some senior colleagues, notably Henry Lawrence, who had hurried back from England and resumed his post as resi-

[1] "There never will be peace in the Punjab so long as its people are allowed to retain the means and the opportunity of making war. There never can be now any guarantee for the tranquillity of India until we shall have effected the entire subjection of the Sikh people and destroyed its power as an independent nation." *Governor General's Dispatch to the Secret Committee No. 20 of 1849.*

[2] Baird, *Private Letters of the Marquess of Dalhousie*, p. 30. In his dispatch to the Secret Committee dated 7.4.1849, Dalhousie gave three reasons for the annexation. Firstly, that while the British had observed the Treaties of Lahore and Bhairowal, the Durbar had not, inasmuch as that it had not paid even a rupee towards the annual subsidy of 22 lacs of rupees nor sent troops against Mulraj. Secondly, that the Durbar army and the people led by the "sirdars of the state, the signers of the treaties, the members of the Council of Regency itself" (one of whom had "commanded the Sikh army in the field") had risen against the British. Thirdly, the Sikhs had invited the Afghans to fight the British.

Mahajan in *Circumstances leading to the Annexation of the Punjab 1846-49* (p. 126) followed by Ganda Singh in *Private Correspondence relating to the Anglo-Sikh Wars* (p. 158) accuses Dalhousie of deliberately misrepresenting the facts given in the first reason, viz. that no portion of the annual subsidy was paid by the Lahore Durbar, and they quote a letter from the resident at Lahore to the governor general dated February 23, 1848 reporting the payment of over Rs. 13 lacs in gold into the British treasury to support their contention. It is clear, however, from the accounts maintained by the resident of Lahore that this gold was credited against debts owed by the Lahore Durbar to the British Government prior to the Treaty of Bhairowal (SC 245 of 30.12.1848) and that a loan made by the British Government to the Lahore Durbar in April 1847 was still due for repayment at the time of annexation (SC 78 of 2.5.1851). Still less was there money available to meet the annual subsidy, the first payment of which was debited in May 1848.

Dalip Singh was much later to compare his case to a betrayal of guardianship when he agitated for the return of his kingdom. "I was

dent. Henry Lawrence was against annexation.[3] John Lawrence was with Dalhousie in holding that the case for annexation was "both undeniable and pressing." Lord Hardinge and later the Court of Directors of the East India Company also backed Dalhousie.[4] Assured of this support, the governor general instructed Henry Lawrence to draft the proclamation of annexation. Henry did not have his heart in the job, and he also desired to accept personally the surrender of Dewan Mulraj. When Dalhousie reacted strongly to Henry's draft and his wish to appear as the arbiter of the Punjab's destiny,[5] Henry put in his resig-

---

a ward of the British nation; and it was unjust on the part of the guardian to deprive me of my kingdom in consequence of a failure in the guardianship." (Letter in *The Times*, September 8, 1882.)

[3] "My opinion, as already more than once expressed in writing to your Lordship, is against annexation. I did think it unjust: I now think it impolitic." Henry Lawrence to Dalhousie, February 2, 1849.

Henry Lawrence's desire, according to his biographer, Herbert Edwardes, was to "erect that great mystical Khalsa corporation of the Sikhs into an aristocratic state, at once leaning on and lending support to our empire on the side of the northwest; to make it after the death of Runjeet, an allied and independent power—to reconcile it when hostile, to spare it when subdued, and to utilise its great military force as a barrier against Afghanistan, and, if need were, against Russia. The rebellion of 1848—which broke out in his absence, but of which he had not foreseen the probability—rudely disturbed, but did not wholly dissipate his dream." Edwardes and Merivale, *Life of Sir Henry Lawrence*, p. 470.

[4] "The energy and turbulent spirit of the Sikhs are stated by one section (of politicians here) as ground for not annexing. In my judgment, this is the argument which would dispose me, if I were on the spot, to annex." Hardinge to Henry Lawrence. W. W. Hunter, *The Marquess of Dalhousie*, p. 83.

[5] "I now remark on the proclamation you have proposed. It is objectionable in matter because, from the terms in which it is worded, it is calculated to convey to those who are engaged in this shameful war an expectation of much more favourable terms, much more extended immunity from punishment, than I consider myself justified in granting them. It is objectionable in manner; because (unintentionally, no doubt) its whole tone substitutes you personally, as the resident at Lahore, for the government which you represent. It is calculated to raise the inference that a new state of things is arising; that the fact of your arrival with a desire to bring peace to the Punjab is likely to affect

nation. He was persuaded by his friends to withdraw it and, despite being overruled and snubbed, agreed to carry out the orders of the governor general. Dalhousie ordered the removal of Maharajah Dalip Singh from the Punjab.[6]

---

the warlike measures of the government; and that you have come as a peacemaker for the Sikhs, as standing between them and the government. This cannot be. . . . There must be entire identity between the government and its agent, whoever he is. . . . I repeat, that I can allow nothing to be said or done, which should raise the notion that the policy of the Government of India, or its intentions, depend on your presence as resident in the Punjab. . . . I do not seek for a moment to conceal from you that I have seen no reason whatever to depart from the opinion that the peace and vital interests of the British Empire now require that the power of the Sikh Government should not only be defeated, but subverted, and their dynasty abolished." Edwardes and Merivale, *Life of Sir Henry Lawrence*, pp. 433-34.

[6] Having convinced himself that the Sikh nation was to be subverted, Dalhousie maintained that he could not permit himself to be turned aside from fulfilling the duty which he owed to the security and prosperity of millions of British subjects "by a feeling of misplaced and mistimed compassion for the fate of a child." W. W. Hunter, *The Marquess of Dalhousie*, p. 82.

The rest of the careers of Dalip Singh and his mother are of more human than historical interest. In 1853 Dalip Singh was converted to Christianity. A year later he and his cousin, Prince Shiv Dev Singh, left for England. Dalip Singh was given an estate at Elvedon in Suffolk. He became a great favourite of Queen Victoria, who treated him as her godson. Rani Jindan, who had escaped to Nepal, later joined him in England where she died in 1863. Dalip Singh brought his mother's ashes to India. On his way back to England he married, in Alexandria, Bamba Muller, the daughter of a German merchant through an Ethiopian woman. They had five children, two sons and three daughters.

Dalip Singh lived beyond his means and ran into debt. He tried to reclaim his kingdom through an appeal first to the British Government and then to the Privy Council. When that failed, he tried to interest European powers in helping him recapture his kingdom. He began to describe himself as the "implacable foe of the British people." He announced his reconversion to the Sikh faith and opened correspondence with several Indian princes and Sikh chieftains. The bout of megalomania lasted till he discovered that no one really took him seriously. Many Sikh organisations passed resolutions condemning him and advising him to seek the forgiveness of the queen. In 1890 Dalip Singh's debts were paid and he was granted the queen's pardon. After the death of Bamba Muller, Dalip Singh re-married in June 1889, Ada Douglas Wetherell. He died on October 22, 1893, of paralysis and was buried a week later at Elvedon.

The Sikh flag was lowered, the Union Jack hoisted on the ramparts of the Lahore fort. Sikh currency, of which there were many varieties (*nānakśāhī, harī singhī, gobind śāhī,* etc.), was withdrawn, and the Company's *sicca* rupee introduced.

Demilitarising the Punjab

The Punjab's cities and villages were placarded with notices demanding the surrender of arms. More than 120,000 stands of arms of matchlocks, swords, and other weapons were voluntarily handed over. A muster of the Durbar's forces was called at Lahore. A small number of troops were retained; the rest of the army was disbanded. Forts and defensive fortifications—practically every Punjabi village had defensive bastions—were levelled. The only part of the erstwhile kingdom which was not demilitarised was the district of Peshawar. (The exception was made on the ground that there was not a large enough British force to defend the people of the area from the incursions of tribal raiders.) All military grants were abolished.[7]

Board of Control

There were diverse views on the sort of government that would best suit the Punjab. Sir Charles Napier, who had taken over as commander-in-chief from Lord Gough, was of the opinion that the Punjab, like Sindh, should have military rule. Others believed that, like the rest of India, it should be ruled by civilians. Lord Dalhousie decided

---

[7] Dalhousie overruled Henry Lawrence, who recommended leniency towards holders of military jagirs. He wrote: "Nothing is granted to them [the military jagirdars] but maintenance. The amount of that is open to discussion, but their property of every kind will be confiscated to the state. . . . In the interim let them be placed somewhere under surveillance; but attach their property till their destination is decided. If they run away, our contract is void. If they are caught, I will imprison them. And if they raise tumult again, I will hang them, as sure as they now live and I live then." W. W. Hunter, *The Marquess of Dalhousie,* p. 99.

to combine the two by giving the Punjab a civil administration manned by both civilian and army officers.[8] He
established a Board of Administration consisting of three
members. Henry Lawrence was appointed president and
entrusted with matters connected with defence and relations with the sardars. John Lawrence was put in charge of
the settlement of land and other fiscal matters. C. G. Mansel
was entrusted with the administration of justice and the
police.[9] These three thus constituted the heart, the back-
bone, and the arm of the Punjab's body-politic. The Board
was made the final court of appeal with powers of life and
death. It was also charged with regulating matters of excise, revenue, and police.

"You shall have the best men in India to help you,"
wrote Dalhousie to Henry Lawrence. He sent to the Punjab the most experienced Englishmen available in India.
Of the 56 covenanted officers, 29 were from the army and
27 from the civil service. The policy Henry Lawrence followed was to "rule by strength rather than precision."[10]
Every civil functionary from a member of the Board down
to the humblest *kārdār* was vested with judicial, fiscal, and
magisterial powers.

Two regions, the Cis-Sutlej and the Trans-Sutlej, were
reunited to the Punjab. The Punjab along with the Trans-
Indus territories which were placed under the same ad-

[8] The disagreement between Sir Charles Napier and Dalhousie became
quite acrimonious and personal. Napier described Dalhousie as "the
young Scots laird . . . as weak as water and as vain as a pretty man or
an ugly woman." Dalhousie in no uncertain terms told Sir Charles to
mind his own business. "I have been warned, Sir Charles," wrote Dalhousie, "not to let you encroach upon my authority and I will take
good care you shall not." Arnold, *The Marquis of Dalhousie's Administration of British India*, I, 225. This however, did not deter Sir Charles
from expressing his contempt for the Board. "Boards rarely have any
talent and that of the Punjab offers no exception to the rule."

[9] Montgomery later replaced Mansel. The president did not however
have the power to overrule his colleagues in matters specifically assigned
to them.

[10] C. L. Tupper, chief secretary, Punjab Government, in Paper read
to the East India Association, July 25, 1891.

ministration comprised of an area of about 73,000 square miles. Its population was roughly estimated at 10 million.

The Punjab was divided into seven divisions or commissionerships, which were further divided into districts (of which there were 25 in the province). A five-tiered administration was set up. Next to the Board were the commissioners of the seven divisions. Below the commissioners were deputy and assistant commissioners; and below them, extra assistant commissioners—a cadre specially constituted to provide jobs for "such natives as might have filled offices of trust under the Durbar."[11] The lowest grade of gazetted officer was the *tehsīldār*, whose civil powers extended to deciding cases up to the value of Rs.300/.

The Board at Work

Defence was given top priority. The Guide Corps, which had been raised by Henry Lawrence in 1846, was increased in strength and included troops of horse as well as infantry. Recruits were drawn from the toughest elements in the country; professional hunters and even brigands were accepted. The Guides were charged with guarding the chain of fortresses which were built to prevent tribal incursions from the northwest and with maintaining peace in the Derajat. For internal security ten regiments, five cavalry and five infantry, were raised. Some of the Durbar's soldiers were absorbed in these regiments. A military police force consisting of 8,000 men, largely Punjabi Mussalmans, was raised. The foot constabulary was meant to guard treasuries and gaols, the mounted police to patrol highways. A secret intelligence service (*khufiā*) police comprised of informers and detectives (*jasūs*) was attached to the police to keep the government in touch with the political temper of the people. Also attached to the police were professional trackers (*pagī, khojī* or *khure pat*), who brought with them their uncanny gifts for following spoors of missing cattle over long, dusty tracks. The old village watch-and-ward was

11 *Punjab Administration Report, 1849-50 & 1850-51*, para 91.

revived. Village watchmen—*caukīdārs*—continued to be employed by the villagers but were expected to keep the police informed of the movements of strangers.

These new units of the police and the army numbered over 50,000 men. Special precautions were taken in policing the Majha, where Bhai Maharaj Singh and his two colleagues, Colonel Rachpal Singh and Narain Singh, were reported to be active.

Once the peace of the province was assured, the Board started on a programme of public works. The Grand Trunk Road from Peshawar to Delhi was re-opened; work was started on connecting the bigger cities and military outposts.[12]

The Punjab had a fairly extensive network of canals. The Public Works Department cleared the Hasli (which supplied water to the many temple-tanks in Amritsar and the Shalamar Gardens in Lahore), made plans to extend it and to dig branch canals. Trees were planted on the banks of canals and alongside roads. Rest houses (*dāk* bungalows) were built to accommodate officials on tour. A programme of afforestation of barren lands was taken in hand. In the districts of Lahore, Gurdaspur, and Gujranwala, a million saplings were planted. These included as many as ninety different varieties of timber. Large tracts were set apart as grasslands—*rakh*. Landholders were encouraged to plant trees, and coppice lands were exempted from taxation.

The Board's greatest contribution, however, was in improving the condition of the agriculturists who formed the vast bulk of the population. New varieties of crops were introduced. New Orleans cotton, sugar cane, flax, tobacco, and a variety of root crops began to be grown in the plains;

---

[12] The 264 miles from Lahore to the frontier crossed 103 large and 459 small bridges and went through six mountain ranges. *The Punjab Administration Report of 1849-50 & 1850-51* claimed that in the first two years after annexation: "1,349 miles of road have been cleared and constructed; 853 miles are under construction; 2,487 miles have been traced and 5,272 miles surveyed, all exclusive of minor cross and branch roads" (para. 346).

tea was planted on the slopes of the Murree hills and in the Kangra Valley. The Punjab had already a large number of mulberry trees; the import of silkworms gave sericulture a boost. Italian merino rams were crossed with local breeds, with beneficial results for both the yield of meat and wool.

The full impact of the changes in the system of revenue introduced by John Lawrence when he was acting resident was now felt. Despite the reduction in the rate of assessment, revenue from land increased from 130 lacs of rupees in 1849 to 160 lacs in 1851. The Board was able to show a balance sheet with surpluses of 102 and 96 lacs, respectively, for the first two years in which it administered the province.[13]

Steps to regularise taxes had also been initiated before annexation. The Durbar had as many as 48 different kinds of levy and maintained innumerable octroi posts. The Board confirmed the abolition of all internal duties and built a chain of octroi posts on the frontiers to collect taxes on imports. Excise was levied on spirits and drugs; tolls were charged on ferries; the salt mines were taken over and, instead of being farmed out to contractors, were exploited by the state itself with a levy of Rs.2 per maund. (Import of salt from Rajasthan was prohibited.) The Board more than made up the loss of revenue from the abolition of internal levies by introducing stamp duty on civil suits. Thus the complicated tax structure of the Dur-

[13] *Punjab Administration Report, 1849-50 & 1850-51*, paras. 264, 402-05. The surpluses were however largely the result of confiscation of jagirs and the sale of Durbar property. And it is also relevant to mention that the expenditure of the province took no account of the cost of maintaining regular troops.

Dalhousie instructed a Dr. Jamieson to make a report on the physical features, geology, flora, and fauna of the annexed territories; Dr. Fleming was instructed to report on the possibility of further exploiting the salt range and the mineral resources of the sub-montane areas. A French mineralogist, M. Marcadien, surveyed Kangra; his report confirmed the existence of rich iron ores in the Kangra region. (SC 115-16 of 23.9.1853.) In Spiti and the Kulu uplands, borax was found. In 1891 the first oil wells were bored near Rawalpindi and Attock. *Civil and Military Gazette*, January 29, 1891.

bar, which yielded only 16 lacs per year, was simplified and yet made to yield a quarter of a lac more. It also had the further advantage of saving the common man from the caprice of officials.

Evil practices such as the destruction of female children on birth, *satī*, etc., were forbidden. Marriage customs, dowry, divorce were modified to ameliorate hardship on women. Rules of inheritance of property were recognised.[14] Since the *tehsīldār* was the only official conversant with these rules and customs, he was entrusted with the necessary judicial powers. Village *pañcāyats* were allowed to function in less important matters affecting the village community. In cities, town councils were constituted to advise and assist English magistrates on civil matters.

The Board discovered to its surprise that the incidence of literacy was higher in the erstwhile Punjab kingdom than in some British provinces[15]—the Punjab had many elementary schools, including 16 for girls in Lahore. The Board allowed the native *madrasās* to function and in addition set up a number of central schools for higher education in the bigger cities. It also decided to continue the use of Persian for official records in the new annexed region and Urdu for eastern Punjab.

The administration by the Board was an unqualified success. It brought peace and prosperity to the country which had passed through ten years of civil strife. In Au-

[14] Four years after annexation, Sir Richard Temple with a revenue official as assistant drew up the *corpus juris* consisting of the laws and customs of the Punjab. This became the Punjab Civil Code of 1854, and, although it did not receive official sanction, it was administered for sixteen years throughout the province. Later Sir James Stephen, law member of the viceroy's council from 1869-72, drafted legislation for the Punjab. Crime was regulated by the Indian Penal Code, revenue by the Punjab Land Revenue Act, and several matters by the Punjab Laws Act (which superseded the Punjab Civil Code). An amendment by Sir George Campbell provided that local custom be given priority to enforce the tribal and family customs of the Punjab as long as they were not opposed to justice, equity, and good conscience.

[15] Arnold, *The Marquis of Dalhousie's Administration of British India,* I, 345.

gust 1852 the Board presented a report on its work in the first two years. It stated with pride that "in no part of India had there been more perfect quiet than in the territories lately annexed." It also complimented the people it had to deal with. "There are less prejudices and elements of hindrance in the Punjab than elsewhere. . . . Sikh fanaticism is dying out, the Hindus are less superstitious and priest ridden and the Mohammedans less bigoted and less bound by traditional practice than their co-religionists in any part of India."[16] The governor general and directors of the East India Company felicitated the Board "for the prosperous and happy result."

How did the change affect the Sikh community? The succession of defeats in the field of battle in addition to the knowledge of betrayal of national interests disillusioned the Sikh rank and file with the royal family and the aristocracy. Consequently, much as Bhai Maharaj Singh was respected, he was unable to arouse enthusiasm among the masses to continue fighting for the Durbar; when he was arrested and deported to Singapore, there was hardly any agitation among the Sikhs.

Dalhousie expelled the royal family and liquidated the Sikh nobility of the Trans-Sutlej region.[17] Sikh peasants and soldiers were suspect and given little chance for employment in the army or the police force, both of which were largely Muslim. Under the circumstances it was not very surprising that the militant spirit of the disbanded Khalsa soldiery (over 40,000 of whom were let loose after the Anglo-Sikh wars) turned to crime. The central districts

[16] "To deal with the best manhood of India, we had the best men of the Indian Government, the warmest interest of the governor general himself, and a lavish employment of time, labour and treasure. It was an imperial experiment, imperially conducted, and crowned with an auspicious result which must be divided between the rulers and the ruled." *Ibid.*, I, 351.

[17] Personal and service jagirs of 25 Sikh chiefs were confiscated. SC 68-71 of 26.5.1849. The Sikhs had no educated middle class; consequently, of the eleven extra assistant commissioners, the Board was able to select only one Sikh.

of the Punjab became infested with dacoits, almost all of whom were Sikhs. Thuggee became rampant—most of the fraternity being either Mazhabi or Sainsi Sikhs. The government was constrained to appoint a superintendent for the suppression of thuggeeism,[18] and the crime was put down with a firm hand.

The most important effect of annexation was the new relationship between Sikhs and Hindus. It has already been noted that, from the time the Khalsa became a political power, large numbers of Hindus, who had looked upon it as the spearhead of Hinduism, had nominally accepted the *pahul* (baptism). During Sikh rule the distinction between Sikh and Hindu became one of mere form; the Khalsa wore their hair and beards unshorn, the Hindus did not. For the rest, Brahmanical Hinduism had come back into its own. The new Sikh Jat nobility aped the practices of Hindu Rajput princes; they worshipped Hindu gods alongside their own *Granth*, venerated the cow, went on pilgrimages to Hindu holy places, fed Brahmins, consulted astrologers and soothsayers, and compelled widows to immolate themselves on the funeral pyres of their husbands. Among certain sections, notably the Bedis, the caste to which Guru Nanak had belonged, the practice of killing female children on birth had been revived.[19]

[18] Mr. Brereton made a detailed report on the thug fraternity in the Punjab. He mentions a Mazhabi Sikh, Wazir Singh, as the founder of the order in the province. He was eventually caught and hanged. Sher Singh introduced vigorous measures to suppress thuggee but the period of anarchy following his murder was favourable to the growth of the crime. FC 259 of 14.1.1853.

[19] John Lawrence had come across this practice when he was commissioner of Jullundur Doab. When renewing the leases of the landholders he made them repeat loudly: "*Bevā mat jalāo*"—Do not burn widows. "*Betī mat māro*"—Do not kill daughters. "*Korhī mat dabāo*"—Do not bury lepers. Bosworth Smith, *Life of Lord Lawrence*, I, 197.

John Lawrence's biographer states that infanticide was not only practised by Rajputs but was universal among the Bedis . . . "they had never allowed a single female child to live." *Ibid.*, I, 206.

This statement appears somewhat exaggerated. Amongst the practices that Guru Gobind Singh forbade was infanticide. He excommunicated

As soon as power passed out of Sikh hands, large numbers of Hindus who had adopted the practices of the Khalsa abandoned them to return to orthodox Hinduism. With them went a considerable number of those who had been Khalsa for several generations. In the two short visits that Lord Dalhousie made to the Punjab he was able to detect this tendency. "Their great Gooroo Govind sought to abolish caste and in a great degree succeeded," noted the governor general. "They are however, gradually relapsing into Hindooism; and even when they continue Sikhs, they are yearly Hindooified more and more; so much so, that Mr. now Sir Geo. Clerk (governor of Bombay, 1847-48) used to say that in 50 years the sect of the Sikhs would have disappeared. There does not seem to be warrant for this view, though it is much more likely now than six months ago."[20]

Break-up of the Board

The differences between Henry Lawrence and his brother, John, had often strained relations to the breaking point (Montgomery confessed that he had to serve as a "regular

---

kurīmārs (those who killed female children) and disallowed them admission to Sikh temples. His injunction still stands imprinted in large letters at the entrance of the *Akāl Takht* alongside the Golden Temple.

Two years after annexation, the deputy commissioner of Gurdaspur reported the continuance of this crime among the Bedis. Thereafter it was discovered that it was prevalent also among Hindu and Muslims Rajputs, i.e. everywhere with the exception of the districts of Leiah, Dera Ismail Khan, Peshawar, and Hazara. FC 185-90 of 9.9.1853. On the Divali of 1853 a large meeting of Sikhs, Muslims, and Hindus, was called in Amritsar, where the matter was discussed and resolutions condemning the practice were passed. Thereafter similar meetings were held in various towns in the province. A code of rules restricting the size of dowries—one of the chief reasons for the destroying of female children—was drawn up. Within a few months infanticide ceased to be practised.

[20] Letter of May 7, 1849. Baird, *Private Letters of the Marquess of Dalhousie*, p. 69.

"With the disappearance of the Khalsa prestige, these votaries have fallen off; they joined in hundreds, and have deserted in thousands. The ranks of Hindooism receive them again, and their children will never drink the *pahul* at Amritsar." Arnold, *The Marquis of Dalhousie's Administration of British India*, I, 386.

buffer between two high powered engines"). In these disputes Lord Dalhousie openly showed preference for John and often went out of the way to belittle Henry.[21] The conflict came to a head when both brothers put in their resignations. Dalhousie promptly abolished the Board, transferred Henry Lawrence to Rajputana, and appointed John Lawrence chief commissioner of the Punjab. This change was more one of form than of substance as John continued to be assisted by two "principal commissioners." Montgomery remained in charge of the judiciary as well as education, roads, police, local and municipal administration. George Edmonstone was appointed financial commissioner.

Once John Lawrence was left to himself, he began to see the wisdom in the policies which his brother had advanced and he (John) had opposed. His handling of jagirs and rent-free tenures, of which over 60,000 still remained to be decided, was liberal enough to evoke a sharp rebuke from the governor general. The most important aspect of John Lawrence's administration was his success in winning over the Sikh masses. When he was convinced that the Sikh peasantry had little sentiment for the restoration of a Sikh state, he allowed them to be recruited for the army. The peasants joined the Company's forces with enthusiasm. Their performance in the skirmishes against Pathan tribesmen and in the Anglo-Burmese War (1852) encouraged the British commanders to enlist them in larger numbers.

[21] In a letter of June 13, 1851, Henry wrote to his brother John: "I am at a loss to understand the governor general. . . . Bad enough to snub us when we are wrong, intending to do right; but to be insulted by assumptions and tittle tattle is too bad. . . . One works oneself to death, and does everything publicly and privately to aid the views of a man who vents his impertinences on us, in a way which would be unbecoming if we were his servants." Edwardes and Merivale, *Life of Sir Henry Lawrence*, pp. 441-42.

CHAPTER 6

SIKHS AND THE MUTINY OF 1857

Causes of the Mutiny

◆❖◆❖◆ CAUSES of the Mutiny of 1857 can be traced
❖◆❖◆❖ back to some well-intentioned but ill-timed
◆❖◆❖◆ measures introduced by successive governors
general: Amherst, Bentinck, Auckland, Ellenborough, and
Dalhousie. These measures adversely affected all classes,
ranging from princes and landowners to peasants and sepoys—most of all the sepoys.

Many states were annexed when their rulers failed to
produce natural heirs. Nana Sahib, the last of the Peshwas,
was deprived of his pension. The rani of Jhansi, was in-
formed that on her death her state would lapse to the
British. These two became leaders of the Maratha rebels.[1]
The crowning act of perfidy was the annexation of Oudh.[2]
The people of Hindustan began to say: "If the British
Government dethrones a king who has ever been so faith-
ful to them, what independent nawab or raja is safe?"[3]
Even the Mughal royal family was not spared. Lord Dal-

---

[1] Other important states taken over were Sambalpur, Satara, Tanjore,
Nagpur, Murshidabad, and Carnatic. Of the last named the following
note is recorded in the *Private Letters of the Marquess of Dalhousie*. "The
young nawab of the Carnatic died suddenly a week ago. He has left no
son, and it is probable that the title will now be made to cease; if so,
it will be another windfall for the Company, and another text for abuse
of my insatiable rapacity and inordinate ambition" (p. 359).

[2] "The King has refused to sign the treaty offered to him. Accordingly
the Government of India has assumed the government of Oudh. The
King has issued a proclamation calling on all his subjects to render
obedience to the British Government. So our gracious Queen has
5,000,000 more subjects and £1,300,000 more revenue than she had yesterday." *Ibid.*, p. 369.

[3] Norgate and Phillott, *From Sepoy to Subedar*, p. 112.
"The unjust appropriation of Oudh," states a contemporary English
writer, was "a finishing stroke to a long course of selfish seeking of our
own benefit and aggrandisement." Mrs. Harris, *A Lady's Diary of the
Siege of Lucknow*, p. 60.

housie extracted an understanding from the emperor's favourite son that the Red Fort of Delhi would be handed over to the British after his father's demise. Although the royal family had ceased to be of political consequence, people had sentimental attachment to the dynasty of Babar and looked upon the Red Fort and its palace with nostalgic affection.

Landowning classes were affected by measures designed to eliminate large estates and by demands for documentary evidence of titles—a practice till then not prevalent in the country.[4]

English officials were not close enough to the people to realise how innocuous measures could be misconstrued by the illiterate masses. Thus the abolition of *sati*, validation of widow remarriage, legislation enabling converts to inherit ancestral property were passed at a time[5] when Christian missionaries were claiming large numbers of proselytes, thus strengthening the Indians' conviction that the English rulers meant to destroy their ancient faiths and traditions.

The sepoys were particularly affected by the anti-British feeling that prevailed in the country. Orders forbidding the wearing of caste-marks, beards, or turbans were looked upon by them as infringements of religious rights.[6] Superstitious Hindus lent a willing ear to the gossip that their ration of flour had bones of animals ground and mixed in it. When, in the autumn of 1856, the old musket, the Brown Bess, was replaced by the more efficient Enfield rifle, the story that the grease on the cap of the new cartridge was extracted from the fat of cows and pigs was readily accepted. The sepoys, both Hindu and Muslim, felt that the time had come for them to make a choice:

[4] The Inam Commission operating in Bombay and the land settlement of Bengal caused great uneasiness among the zamindars of the two provinces.

[5] The act was passed in 1850.

[6] Such orders had been passed in 1806 and led to a serious mutiny in Vellore.

they could either throw up their jobs and serve their gods or stick to them and serve the English.

The sepoys had many other grievances. Their pay was low. The highest rank they could attain was that of a subedar at Rs.60-70 per month; for the equivalent rank, an Englishman drew ten times more.[7] At the time of enlistment, sepoys were given assurances that they would not be called upon to go overseas. Nevertheless attempts were made to send them to Java and Burma. An example that defiance could pay dividends was set by English officers themselves who, when Lord Bentinck ordered reductions in their pay, threatened mutiny. If the *sāhib log* could defy their own *sircār*, why not the natives?

All classes of Indians—princes, merchants, the intelligentsia, peasants, and workers—who had come into contact with the white man had at one time or other been slighted by him. Terms such as nigger and *suar* (pig) had become common in the vocabulary of the Englishman, the country-born Anglo-Indian, and the half-caste Eurasian.

The proclamation of Prince Birjis Qadr of Oudh summed up the grievances: "All Hindus and Mohammedans are aware that four things are dear to every man. First, religion; second, honour; third, life; fourth, property. All these four things are safe under a native government. . . . The English have become enemies of the four things above named."[8]

Sporadic acts of violence had taken place in different parts of the country since the autumn of 1856 and continued throughout the following winter and spring. But when the sepoys at Meerut murdered their white officers on the 10th of May 1857 and proceeded to Delhi to proclaim Bahadur Shah emperor of Hindustan, news of the

---

[7] A retired English army officer wrote: "The entire army of India amounts to 315,520 men costing £9,802,235. Out of this sum no less than £5,668,110 are expended on 51,316 European officers and soldiers." *The Mutiny of the Bengal Army*, p. 25.

[8] S. N. Sen, *Eighteen Fifty-seven*, p. 31.

rising spread like wild-fire and soon most of central and northern India stretching from Delhi to Bengal was in flames. Sepoys were joined by civilians in assaulting Europeans, their cantonments, homes, churches, and public institutions like post and telegraph offices. For some time the rising appeared to be a national revolt against a usurping foreigner. But very soon after it became plain that there was little identity of purpose between the Muslim mutineers and the Hindu. The Muslims sought the restoration of Muslim rule; the Hindu hoped to put the Marathas back into power. The two communities were only united to the extent that they were fighting a common enemy, the English.

The Punjab on the Eve of the Mutiny

The situation in the Punjab was different from that which obtained in the rest of India. The Sikhs, who might well have gambled with the chance of recovering power, were leaderless: Maharajah Dalip Singh had renounced Sikhism and was assiduously trying to convert himself from a Punjabi prince into an English country gentleman; Sher Singh Attariwala was living under surveillance at Calcutta on a pension granted by the British;[9] Bhai Maharaj Singh and Raja Dina Nath (the only notable who spoke nostalgically of the old days) were dead;[10] Bedi Bikram Singh to whom the Sikhs looked for guidance as a descendant of Guru Nanak was interned in his village, Una.[11]

Sikh soldiers did not share the grievances of the Hindustani sepoys. They were allowed to wear turbans and beards and observe the practices of the Khalsa. If they

[9] Nevertheless, in August 1857, a police informer reported that some of the headmen of village Raja Jang were in treasonable correspondence with Sher Singh Attariwala. Punjab Government Records, *Mutiny Reports*, Vol. VIII, Part 1, 247.

[10] On April 27, 1857, "death had removed in Raja Deena Nath a palpable thorn in our side." F. Cooper, *Crisis in the Punjab*, p. 20.

[11] Punjab Government Records, *Mutiny Reports*, Vol. VIII, Part I, 273. There was some excitement among the Bedis of Dera Baba Nanak, but it did not lead to any disturbance. *Ibid.*, p. 294.

had any ill-will, it was towards the Hindustani sepoy (known to Punjabis contemptuously as *purabiah*—easterner—or by the one name *Mātā Dīn*), who disdained to mix with the Sikhs as men of low caste.[12]

The Punjab peasantry, including the Sikhs, was content because the harvest had been good[13] and the share demanded by the government as revenue was modest.

The Board of Administration and thereafter the chief commissioner, John Lawrence, had done a good job: they had brought peace to a land which had lived through ten years of chaos and bloodshed; they had regularised the legal system and both civil[14] and criminal courts were functioning smoothly; they had ruled with an iron hand but without offending the racial or religious susceptibilities of

[12] "The animosity between the Sikhs and the Poorbeeahs is notorious, and the former gave out that they would not allow the latter to pass through their country. It was therefore determined to take advantage of this ill-feeling and to stimulate it by the offer of rewards for every Hindoostanee sepoy who should be captured." *Ibid.*, Vol. VIII, Part I, 234. "The Khalsa held the Hindustanee in 'supreme contempt and there was at least policy in reviving the term at this juncture, for it revived the contempt and hatred with which the class had ever been regarded; it widened the breach between the Punjabee and the Hindustanee, and rendered any coalition the more difficult.'" Cave-Browne, *The Punjab and Delhi in 1857*, I, xvi.

"Hindustani" preponderance in the civil services was as overwhelming as in the army, e.g. of the six Indian extra assistants in Lahore division, five were Poorabias. Punjab Government Records, *Mutiny Reports*, Vol. VIII, Part I, 227.

[13] *Ibid.*, Part II, 201.

"Providence had blessed the Punjab with a golden harvest, such as had not been known for many long years." F. Cooper, *Crisis in the Punjab*, p. 27.

[14] The institution of the Small Cause Court, with its cheap and expeditious disposal of civil suits, and the passing of a new Statute of Limitation in December 1856 reducing the period within which suits for bonded debts could be initiated from twelve to six years, brought a record number of suits for recovery of money. In the first four months of 1857, 45,953 suits were instituted; "From one end of the Punjab to the other, the amount of litigation was great beyond example. The courts were thronged, thousands and thousands were intent on outwitting each other in forensic controversy." *Punjab Administration Report, 1856-58*, para 3.

the people;[15] they had introduced social reforms; they had laid roads, built schools, hospitals and rest-houses in a land whose only experience of foreigners—Turks, Mongols, Pathans, Afghans, and Marathas—had been of systematic plundering.

When the mutiny broke out in Meerut on May 10, 1857, the army cantoned in the Punjab numbered about 60,000, of which considerably more than half were Hindustanis. The British soldiers numbered a mere 10,000.[16]

Hindustani sepoys in the Punjab were as thoroughly disaffected as other sepoys of the Company's army. In March and April, mysterious fires were reported in several cantonments, notably in those where sepoys were being trained in the use of the new Enfield rifle. In short, in the summer of 1857, the only people who could save the English in the Punjab from the wrath of the Hindustani sepoys, who outnumbered them by three to one, were the Punjabis.[17] And of the Punjabis, the one people who could be expected to turn a deaf ear to appeals to restore Mughal or Maratha rule were the Sikhs. The English fully exploited Sikh animosity towards Hindustani Hindus and Mussalmans.[18]

Disarming of the Sepoys and Suppression of the Mutiny in the Punjab

Since the uprising had not been planned, sepoy regiments in the Punjab knew nothing of what had transpired at Meerut and Delhi on the 10th and 11th of May 1857. On the other hand, Montgomery (acting in the

[15] In June 1851, a Colonel Jiwan Singh was murdered by a drunken British soldier in Amritsar. Dalhousie refused to commute the sentence of death on the English soldier. This impressed the Punjabis, who had not expected the government to be impartial in a case in which a white man had done injury to an Indian.

[16] Punjab Government Records, *Mutiny Reports*, Vol. VIII, Part II, 328.

[17] Cave-Browne, *The Punjab and Delhi in 1857*, I, 41.

[18] Punjab Government Records, *Mutiny Reports*, Vol. VIII, Part I, 234.

absence of John Lawrence) received full details by telegraph of the uprising, the proclamation of Bahadur Shah,
and the massacre of the English population of these cities.
Montgomery called a meeting of the senior civil and military officers to consider the situation, and it was decided to
deprive the sepoys at Mian Mir of their ammunition. On
the morning of May 13th native regiments were compelled
to pile arms.[19] On the same day, a council of war was held
at Peshawar. General Reed assumed command in the Punjab and a movable column[20] was formed at Jhelum "ready
to move on every point in the Punjab where open mutiny
required to be put down."

John Lawrence, who was at Rawalpindi for the first two
months of the mutiny, kept in constant touch with his
subordinates. He considered it most important to recapture Delhi. For this purpose he suggested that the troops
in the hills should march to Ambala, and he urged the
commander-in-chief to free the Ambala force for action.
To this end was his planning directed[21]—to disarm those

[19] SC 40 of 29.5.1857.

[20] This proposal originated with Lt. Col. John Nicholson. Not only
did the movable column put down mutiny (after the flight of the
Jullundur mutineers) wherever it occurred but its services were also
utilised in the disarming of native regiments.

[21] "Trust the irregulars and the natives of the Punjab generally, but
utterly distrust the regular army. Utilise the irregulars in every way
you can. Bring them in from the frontier, where their work has been
well done, to the points of danger in the interior of the country where
they may have plenty of work of a novel kind. Add largely to the numbers of each existing regiment. Raise fresh regiments, as occasion may
require, but do so under proper precautions, remembering that the
weapon with which you are arming yourselves may, unless it is well
wielded, be turned against yourselves. As for the regulars, watch them,
isolate them, send them to detached frontier forts, where it will be
difficult for them to act in concert. If any symptoms of mutiny show
themselves, disarm them at once. If mutiny breaks forth into act, destroy them, if possible, on the spot; and if they take to flight, raise
the native populations against them and hunt them down. A few stern
examples at first will save much bloodshed in the end. Find out the Sikh
chiefs living in your respective districts and enlist their martial instincts
and their natural hatred of the Hindustanis on your side at once."
Substance of address by John Lawrence. Bosworth Smith, *Life of Lord
Lawrence*, II, 42-43.

troops whose loyalty was suspect, to raise new regiments and levies, and to release every available soldier from the Punjab to swell the ranks of the army marching to Delhi.

As these plans were shaping in Lawrence's mind, news came of the first outbreak in the Punjab at Ferozepur. Forewarned, the English officer-in-charge took steps to secure the magazine and successfully repulsed the mutineers' attack. At the same time the forts at Phillaur, Govindgarh, Kangra, Attock, and Multan were taken over; the sepoys' plan to make Phillaur a rallying point was thus frustrated.[22] The situation in Simla hill cantonments at Jutogh, Sabathu, Dagshai, and Kasauli caused anxiety. Gurkha regiments refused to obey their English officers, and those at Kasauli looted the treasury. Their demands were conceded, and they were prevailed upon to return to barracks.

As soon as news of the rising in Meerut and Delhi spread, "a season of open violent crime"[23] set in in the Cis-Sutlej states and in some towns of the Punjab, notably Ambala, Panipat, and Thanesar. Ranghar and Gujar tribes began to plunder in broad daylight.[24] Some zamindar princes of Hariana—the nawabs of Jhajjar and Dadree and the raja of Ballabhgarh—threw in their lot with the mutineers; the nawab of Loharu remained neutral. In eastern Punjab, although the Muslim chieftains—the nawabs of Karnal and Malerkotla—sided with the British, Muslim peasantry was sympathetic towards the mutineers. The Hindus remained indifferent. The people of the Trans-Sutlej were loyal to the British. With a few exceptions,[25] the Sikhs of both the Cis-Sutlej and the Trans-

[22] Cave-Browne, *The Punjab and Delhi in 1857*, I, 120.
[23] *Punjab Administration Report 1856-58*, para. 14.
[24] "Every Gujar plundered as if he had been used to it all his life. Then began robberies in broad daylight in every thoroughfare, almost in every village. One village would turn out en masse to fight another." *Ibid.*
[25] There was an abortive rising at Nalagarh and Rupar which was promptly suppressed. One Mohar Singh, a factor of the chief of Rupar, whose attempt to forbid the slaughter of kine had led to some dis-

Sutlej, princes and peasants, expressed unreserved support for the British. The rajas of Jind, Patiala, Nabha, Kalsia, and Kapurthala, the chiefs of Malaudh, Kheri, Bhadaur, and Lodhran, the Singhpurias and the Sodhis of Kartarpur volunteered for service.

At the other end of the Punjab, the outbreaks at Naushera and Mardan[26] had put the authorities on their guard. The men at Peshawar were suspected of conspiring to strike during the Id festival; three native regiments were consequently disarmed. The sepoys at Mardan got wind of these moves, and some 500 fled to Swat,[27] where they offered their services to the wali.

John Lawrence ordered the Punjab to be sealed at either end. Troop concentrations were maintained on the northwest frontier to prevent Pathan tribes[28] and the volatile Dost Mohammed, amir of Afghanistan, from taking the opportunity to descend on the plains. Forces were posted at the southeastern end in Hariana to prevent the mutineers from entering the Punjab and to apprehend those fleeing the province towards Delhi. In the Punjab itself, mobile columns of English and trustworthy Punjabis were

turbance was executed. Punjab Government Records, *Mutiny Reports*, Vol. VIII, Part I, 38-39.

26 Upwards of 100 Sikhs in the 55th regiment of native infantry volunteered to fight the rest of the regiment if led by their officers (SC 5 of 31.7.1857). Though this proposal went unheeded, it was later decided that Sikhs should be separated from the Hindustanis and together with Punjabi Mohammedans and hillmen should form the nucleus of new regiments.

27 Civil war had broken out in Swat the same day the mutiny broke out in Meerut. The wali was not well-disposed towards the British.

28 "'Peshawar once gone', said a trusty Sikh chief to the magistrate of Amritsar, 'the whole Punjab would roll up like this', and as he spoke he began slowly with his finger and thumb to roll up his robe from the corner of the hem towards its centre. 'You know on what a nest of devils we stand,' writes Edwardes to the chief commissioner. 'Once let us take our foot up, and we shall be stung to death.' And Edwardes and his companions had no intention of taking their foot up, but rather of putting it down and keeping it there." Bosworth Smith, *Life of Lord Lawrence*, II, 63.

ordered to round up deserters. Guards were placed on ferries, and high embankments were raised at points where rivers were fordable.

The flame of mutiny spread to Jullundur, where officers had been tardy in carrying out orders to disarm the native regiments. The mutineers made their way to Phillaur, where they were joined by the 3rd regiment of native infantry and then headed for Delhi.

John Lawrence concluded that the disarming of suspected regiments and the escape of so many mutineers had adversely affected the loyalty of others. He decided to deprive the Hindustani sepoys of their arms irrespective of their past record wherever practicable. In pursuance of this policy, disarming took place in the Punjab cantonments including Multan and Phillaur. This was not effected smoothly in all cases. At Jhelum there was considerable bloodshed,[29] and some mutineers eluded their pursuers by escaping into Jammu. Two days after the Jhelum episode, the sepoys at Sialkot shot some of their officers and proceeded towards Delhi. Nicholson intercepted them near Trimmu Ghat on the Ravi. In the two encounters that followed nearly every one of the sepoys was either killed or drowned.

The disarmed regiments at Lahore became restive. Men of the 26th native infantry regiment suddenly attacked their officers and then headed northwards along the Ravi. They were ambushed by a posse of constabulary and armed villagers. One hundred and fifty were slain in this encounter. The main body, which took shelter on an island, was later attacked by a force led by F. Cooper, deputy commissioner of Amritsar. Fifty were drowned or shot while trying to swim away. The remaining (about 280) were captured and taken to the police station at Ajnala village. Cooper had 237 men shot in batches of tens; others refused to come out of the dungeon into which they had been

---

[29] 180 were killed in two days of fighting; 116 were captured and executed. Cooper, *The Crisis in the Punjab*, p. 128.

thrown. Cooper left them there for the night. The next morning 45 were found to have died of suffocation.[30] Another 42 captured subsequently were blown away from cannons.[31]

A similar tragedy was enacted on the northwest frontier. In the last week of August, sepoys of a disarmed regiment at Peshawar assaulted soldiers searching barracks for illicit arms. Fifty mutineers were shot; others who fled were chased and killed.[32] The barracks of the regiment were levelled by commissariat elephants.

The speed with which disaffected regiments were disarmed and the summary "justice" meted out to those whose

[30] "The doors were opened and behold! They were nearly all dead! Unconsciously, the tragedy of Holwell's Black Hole had been re-enacted. No cries had been heard during the night, in consequence of the hubbub, tumult and shouting of the crowds of horsemen, police, tehseel guards, and excited villagers. 45 bodies, dead from fright, exhaustion, fatigue, heat and partial suffocation, were dragged into light, and consigned, in common with all the other bodies, into one common pit, by the hands of the village sweepers." F. Cooper, *The Crisis in the Punjab*, pp. 162-63.

[31] Cooper explained the crime of the mutineers to the public who, according to him, "marvelled at the clemency and the justice of the British" for not killing the rabble of men, women, and children who had joined the mutineers. Cooper, *The Crisis in the Punjab*, p. 163.

Cooper's acts were commended by Lawrence and Montgomery. "I congratulate you on your success against the 26th N.I. You and your police acted with much energy and spirit, and deserve well of the state. I trust, the fate of these sepoys will operate as a warning to others. Every effort should be exerted to glean up all who are at large.

"Roberts will no doubt leave the distribution of the rewards mainly to you. Pray see that they are allotted with due regard to merit, and that every one gets what is intended for him." (Demi-official letter from Sir John Lawrence dated Lahore, August 2, 1857.)

[32] Edwardes wrote: "Almost all the 51st Native Infantry have been picked up and shot. More than seven hundred have been already killed. Four or five got to Khuddum in the Khyber, where the Hurikheyl said they would let them go to Kabul as Mussulmans, but not as Hindus; so they were converted on the spot." Bosworth Smith, *Life of Lord Lawrence*, II, 179.

Cooper's account of the hunt of the 51st (which numbered 871 men) is graphic. "Standing crops were beaten up, ravines probed, as if for pheasants and hares, and with great success . . . total [killed] within about 30 hours after the mutiny, no less than 659." F. Cooper, *The Crisis in the Punjab*, p. 177.

loyalty was suspect spread terror and obviated all chances of rebellion spreading in the Punjab. The stock of the *sircār* rose: in bazaar parlance, the price of "pearls," "white sugar" and "red chillies" (symbolic of the English) went up, while that of "red wheat," "brown *gur*" (molasses), and "black pepper" fell.

Except for the incidents narrated above (and an uprising of the Muslim Kharal tribes around Gugiara district in September 1857) the Punjab was not affected by the rebellion which convulsed the rest of northern India. Punjabi Mussalmans turned a deaf ear to their Hindustani co-religionists' exhortation to *jihād* against the pig-eating despoilers of Islam. Punjabi Hindus and, with greater reason, the Sikhs refused to listen to the belated appeal to save Hindu *dharma* from beef-eating foreigners who used cow fat to grease their cartridges. This was not surprising because those, who in the summer of 1857 claimed to be crusaders for freedom, were the very people who eight years earlier had been the feringhees' instruments in reducing the Punjabis to servitude.

The loyalty of the Punjabi princes and rich zamindars was decisive in saving the Punjab and the rest of India for the British. They helped to maintain order in the Punjab, kept the roads leading to Delhi open for movement of troops, armour, and treasuries, and supplied money, men, and munitions.

Of the Punjabis, the role of the Sikhs in suppressing the uprising was the most significant. Sikh soldiers defended English establishments and families in Allahabad, Benares,[33] Lucknow, Kanpur, Arrah, and other centres of revolt. Since the Meerut and Delhi mutineers had proclaimed the restoration of Mughal rule, Sikhs who had

[33] There were stray cases of Sikhs joining the mutineers. In Benares, a battalion of "Ludhiana Sikhs" of the 37th native infantry mutinied on June 3, 1857. Many were killed or hanged. This triggered off a mutiny at Jewanpur, 70 miles from Benares. The Sikhs guarding the courthouse and treasury at Benares remained loyal. Hilton, *The Indian Mutiny*, pp. 73-75.

been brought up on tales of Mughal atrocities against their forefathers reacted sharply to Bahadur Shah's proclamation. The British exploited the anti-Mughal sentiment of the Sikhs. A new version of the *sau sākhī* prophesying a joint Anglo-Sikh conquest of Delhi was circulated. Thus the prospect of loot was given the sanction of prophecy; the Sikhs eagerly joined the Company's forces marching towards Delhi.[34]

Sikh soldiers were in the van of the assault on Delhi, and, when the city capitulated on September 20, 1857, they were allowed to help themselves to whatever they could lay their hands on. Hodson with his Sikh horsemen first captured Bahadur Shah, Begum Zeenat Mahal, and their son Jawan Bakht. A day later they arrested two other sons and a grandson of the emperor. In the security provided by his Sikhs, Hodson ignored the presence of an armed mob of several thousand, stripped the three princes naked and shot them with his carbine. Sikhs took the corpses of the princes to Chandni Chowk and laid them out for display in front of Gurdwara Sis Ganj, where 182

[34] At first John Lawrence mistrusted the Khalsa. In a note dated May 18, 1857, he wrote: "I do not like to raise large bodies of old Sikhs. I recollect their strong nationality, how completely they were demoralised for some twelve years before annexation, and how much they have to gain by our ruin. I will not therefore consent to raise levies of the old Sikhs. There is a strong feeling of sympathy between Sikhs and Hindus, and though I am willing to raise Sikhs gradually and carefully, I wish to see them mixed with Mohammedans and hillmen." Bosworth Smith, *Life of Lord Lawrence*, II, 53.

Gradually John Lawrence came round to the view that either the Sikhs would have to be fully trusted or treated as rebels; the Sikhs' readiness to enlist helped him to resolve his doubts.

Sikh soldiers who were disarmed along with their Hindustani compatriots at Mian Mir had, on protestations of loyalty, been separated and reformed into purely Sikh regiments. Sikhs belonging to regiments quartered south of Ambala, who were on leave in their homes in Majha, were asked to report at Lahore and were made the nuclei of new units. Cave-Browne, *The Punjab and Delhi in 1857*, I, 228. John Lawrence invited retired gunners of the Durbar army to rejoin colours—which they did with alacrity (*ibid.*, p. 296). Sappers and miners were raised from Mazhabi labourers working on roads and canals.

years earlier their guru, Tegh Bahadur, had been executed by the orders of Emperor Aurangzeb. The "prophecy" of the English version of *sau sākhī* was thus fulfilled in ample measure.

The Sikhs were handsomely rewarded for their services: the princes with grants of territory and palatial residences;[35] commoners with loot and employment opportunities.

Sikh Recruitment in the British Army

An important outcome of the mutiny, as far as the Sikhs were concerned, was that service in the armed forces was thrown open to them, and they became the most sought-after recruits for the British army. It is worthwhile recapitulating the steps by which this came about.

At the end of the first Sikh war in 1846, an irregular[36]

[35] The princes were given additional territory, titles, and property. Patiala was rewarded with Narnaul division of Jhajjar, jurisdiction over Bhadaur, and a house belonging to Begum Zeenat Mahal in Delhi; FC 188 of 2.7.1858. Jind was given Dadree, 13 villages in Kooleran Pargana, and a house of Prince Abu Bakr in Delhi; FC 189 of 2.7.1858. Nabha was rewarded with the divisions of Bawal and Kanti in Jhajjar; FC 190 of 2.7.1858.

The transfer of Jhajjar's territories was calculated. A semi-official document explains the motives: "The territories granted at the suggestion of the chief commissioner of the Punjab have been most judiciously selected from the Jhujjur district. By giving the Maharajah of Puttiala a *locus standi* in that portion of the country, a friendly Hindoo power is placed in the midst of a turbulent Mohammedan population, and a barrier is interposed towards the independent states of Ulwur and Jeypoor with its feudatories of Shekawattee and Ketru, the population of which proved themselves unfriendly during the late crisis. To protect the Jhujjur border would require a strong frontier police, backed by a large military force, and this task will now be undertaken by Puttiala. The divisions of Bhawul and Kantee, granted to the Nabha Rajah, are adjacent to that of Narnoul granted to the Maharajah of Puttiala; and thus we have two staunch adherents on the border of our territories on whom we can place strict reliance." Cave-Browne, *The Punjab and Delhi in 1857*, II, 243.

The chieftains and jagirdars of districts Ambala and Thanesar were rewarded with remission of dues and with titles.

[36] The term "irregular" as opposed to "regular" was applied to units raised for rough and ready local work with Indians holding fairly senior posts and a few selected British officers in command. They were specially trained for guerilla warfare.

force was raised out of the disbanded troops of the Durbar army. At the end of the second Anglo-Sikh war, this force was increased in strength and transferred to the northwest frontier; it came to be known as the Punjab Irregular Force and later the Punjab Frontier Force—the famous Piffers. In 1849, Dalhousie decided to take a few real Khalsas[37] into the British army. Although the number was very small, he was criticised for this action.[38]

The question of Sikh recruitment was considered by the governor general, the commander-in-chief, and the Board of Administration. Brigadier Hodgson, who had commanded the Sikh corps, drew up a memo on the subject which, after its approval, became a sort of *magna carta* for Sikh recruitment. It provided that the number of the Punjabis to be enlisted in the regular army should be limited for the time being to 200 per regiment of whom only half were to be Sikh, making the total number of Sikhs in the 74 regiments 7,400. Recruits were to be under 20 years of age—thus the old Khalsa of the Durbar army were debarred. To make soldiering an honourable profession, only Jat Sikhs were enlisted; Sikhs of lower castes such as Mazhabis, Ramdasias, etc., were rigorously excluded. The most important decision taken, and one which had a far-reaching effect in preserving the separate identity of the Sikhs, was to assure the Sikhs who joined the army that the traditions of the Khalsa would not be interfered with. The regulation provided that:

"The paol, or religious pledges of Sikh fraternity, should on no account be interfered with. The Sikh should be permitted to wear his beard, and the hair of his head gathered up, as enjoined by his religion. Any invasion, however slight, of these obligations would be construed

[37] It should be borne in mind that although the term "Sikh" was used for the re-employed Durbar units, few were in fact Sikhs; they were largely Punjabi Mussalmans, Gurkhas, and Hindustanis of the Durbar army.

[38] Baird, *Private Letters of the Marquess of Dalhousie*. pp. 84-85.

into a desire to subvert his faith, lead to evil consequences, and naturally inspire general distrust and alarm. Even those, who have assumed the outward conventional characteristics of Sikhs should not be permitted after entering the British army, to drop them."[39]

Discrimination against the Mazhabi was felt to be invidious[40] as he was as good a fighter as the Jat. A beginning was made when they were recruited as labourers to build roads in mountains infested with hostile Pathan tribesmen; they also dug the Bari Doab Canal. The Mazhabis were treated as *mati*-men (earth workers) and given neither uniform nor arms. Their promotion to regular soldiering came with the mutiny.

Sikh soldiers proved their fighting quality and loyalty in the Anglo-Burmese war of 1852[41] and two years later against the Mohmand tribe on the northwest frontier.[42] Consequently when the mutiny broke out the English officers were assured that Sikhs would not make common cause with the mutineers, and they selected them to replace the disbanded Poorabiah. At the same time, the Mazhabis were elevated from gangs of labourers to a corps of Pioneers.[43]

Early in May 1857, Hodson raised a unit of horse and foot to work with the military intelligence department and

[39] SC 38 of 28.2.1851. Lord Dalhousie gave his assent to these regulations and remarked, "Soon after I entered the Punjab during the present march, I heard that Sikhs had been enlisted, but that, in compliance I presume with existing regulations, they had been required to cut off their beards—an act to which no real Sikh can submit; or if he for a time submits to it of necessity, it is impossible that he can do so without the deepest discontent. . . . No true Sikh will submit to it—and the intelligence that such a regulation is enforced, rapidly spreading among the other Sikh corps in the service, may produce alarm or at best restlessness which is much to be deprecated. This point, therefore, should at once be set at rest." SC 39 of 28.2.1851.

[40] SC 44 of 28.2.1851.

[41] Baird, *Private Letters of the Marquess of Dalhousie*, pp. 200-201.

[42] *Ibid.*, p. 321.

[43] The credit for the recruitment of Mazhabis goes to Robert Montgomery, the judicial commissioner. MacMunn, *The History of the Sikh Pioneers*, pp. 20-22.

keep the road between Karnal and Meerut open. Hodson borrowed his first 100 Sikhs from the raja of Jind. He then raised three *risālāhs* (cavalry) from the disbanded *ghorca-rāhs* of the old Durbar army. This was the origin of what later became famous as Hodson's Horse.[44] Other English officers raised irregular forces of their own. The names of Brasyer, Rothney, and Rattray came to be attached to Sikh units.

Reviewing the course of events, British army officers after consulting the maharajahs of Patiala, Jind,[45] and Nabha decided "to trust to no race in particular . . . and to mix races in our native army as far as practicable."[46] The Sikhs were, however, handsomely complimented for their role in suppressing the mutiny.[47]

In 1858 a commission under General Peel was appointed to explore the subject of reorganisation of the Indian army. It recommended that the proportion of native to English troops should be fixed at two to one and that no natives should be taken into the artillery. The recommendations were accepted and put into effect straightaway. In two years, the native army was reduced to 140,500 (75,300 Europeans) and by 1869 further reduced to 122,000 (62,000 Europeans). The ethnic change in the constitution of the native army was given permanence by Lord Roberts (commander-in-chief, 1885-93). Some races including the Sikhs, Gurkhas, Dogras, Rajputs, and Punjabi Mussalmans

[44] Because of their red turbans and kummerbunds on their khaki uniforms, Hodson's Horse came to be known as "The Flamingoes."

[45] Patiala advised against raising the proportion of Punjabis to more than one-third of the whole of the native soldiery; Jind went further stating that—"the race [Sikhs] is not entirely trustworthy." SC 1 and 2 of 29.10.1858.

[46] SC 1 of 29.10.1858.

[47] "The Sikhs were raised at a most critical season when other re-cruiting grounds were in the hands of the mutineers or in a state of rebellion. They were called out to save the Empire and have fulfilled their mission, and we all owe our warmest thanks to that bold and sagacious policy which called them into the field and which, I am sure, will also devise means for keeping them under command for the future." SC 2 of 29.10.1858.

were recognised as "martial"; others including the Poora-biah, who had won most of the Englishman's battles in India, were declared "non-martial" and unfit for military service. Of the martial races the favourites of English officers were the Sikhs and Gurkhas.

Administrative Changes—India and the Punjab

After the mutiny, the Court of Directors of the East India Company was abolished and its powers transferred to Parliament. The Parliament appointed a secretary of state and entrusted him and the governor general with the administration of India.

The most important administrative change as far as the Punjab was concerned was the adhesion of Hariana and Delhi to the province. The new districts were inhabited by a people who did not speak Punjabi nor have the Punjabi's spirit of enterprise. Their way of life and their values were as different from those of the Punjabis as their economy. Most of Hariana was a desert woefully deficient in food. And Delhi was a commercial city with little in common with pastoral Punjab. This misalliance created difficulties for subsequent governments.

The status of the administrative head of the Punjab was raised from chief commissioner to lieutenant governor. John Lawrence occupied the post for a month. He was succeeded by Robert Montgomery.

By the Indian Councils Act of 1861, the number of Indians on the governor general's council was increased. The services rendered by the Sikhs in the mutiny were recognised by the nomination of the maharajah of Patiala to this council.

CHAPTER 7

CRESCAT E FLUVIIS[1]

AFTER the mutiny, the government resumed the work of reclaiming the desert and opening up the country by a network of roads and rail lines. The Hasli Canal was extended. The Ravi was tapped from the place it entered the plains, and a canal was dug which, after traversing the districts of Amritsar and Lahore, fell back into the parent stream above Multan. This was accomplished in 1861 and came to be known as the Upper Bari Doab Canal.

Ten years later the waters of the Jumna were similarly canalised. The Western Jumna Canal watered the southern districts of Ambala, Karnal, Hissar, and Rohtak.

In the years 1886-1888 an attempt was made to reclaim the desert surrounding Multan. Water was taken from the Sutlej, and 177,000 acres of barren land were brought under the plough. The experiment was not a success as the canals could not guarantee a perennial flow of water. The mistakes made in Multan were turned to profit by both engineers and colonisers when four years later (1892) over a million acres were irrigated with the waters of the Chenab.[2]

The success of the Chenab Colony was followed by the equally successful irrigation of the Shahpur Thal desert (in 1892 and 1897) by the waters of the Jhelum.

The most daring of all irrigation schemes was the Triple Project, begun in 1905 and completed twelve years later. This project was chiefly designed to bring water to Montgomery (the district named after Sir Robert). Since the Ravi, which ran through the district, had already been tapped by the Upper Bari Doab Canal and had no more

[1] "Strength from the waters"—the motto of the Punjab.
[2] In 1922 the Lower Chenab Canal irrigated 2½ million acres of land. M. Darling, *The Punjab Peasant in Prosperity and Debt,* p. 130.

water to spare, the plan was to feed the Ravi with the waters of the Jhelum and the Chenab and then "milk" it for Montgomery. The Upper Jhelum Canal took the waters of the Jhelum and, after irrigating 350,000 acres of the Chaj Doab, fell into the Chenab. The Upper Chenab Canal then took off from the Chenab and, after irrigating 650,000 acres of the Rechna Doab in the districts of Gujranwala and Sheikhupura, joined the Ravi, where a "level crossing" of a 550-yard barrage helped the water to cross to the other side. The third of the Triple Project canals, the Lower Bari Doab, then took off, ran 134 miles through Montgomery into Multan and back into the Ravi.[3]

The digging of these canals was accompanied by a massive rehabilitation of the desert lands. Till then the doabs had been scenes of "unparalleled desolation . . . miles of dry and barren waste, dotted with sparse scrub jungle and stunted trees, but devoid of any whisper of life."[4] The indigenous inhabitants of these intrafluvial mesopotamias —the cattle-stealing nomads—were compelled to settle in villages and direct their energies to lawful occupations.

The area specifically chosen for the Sikhs was a tract known as *nīlī bār*, irrigated by the Chenab Canal.[5] Colonisation officers scoured Sikh villages in the districts of Amritsar, Ludhiana, and Ferozepur to pick up the best farmers. The colonists were divided into three categories. At the bottom were common peasants, who were granted be-

[3] The Triple Project was designed by Sir John Benton.
[4] Paper by Sir J. Douie, May 7, 1914, Royal Society of Arts, London. An anecdote current at the time was that the lieutenant governor and his senior officers were visiting one of the *bārs* and were doubtful whether farmers could be persuaded to settle on the inhospitable land even if canals were laid out. They consulted an old Punjabi farmer who replied: "Sirs, I see no flies here. But if you put some sugar here, you will soon have flies and if you put water on the land you will not lack colonists."
[5] From the Chenab were taken 427 miles of canal, 2,280 miles of distributory channels, and 12,000 miles of water course. These cultivated 2¼ million acres of land. The total outlay was 26 million rupees. The revenue yield was 34% of the capital. The yearly value of the irrigated crop was more than 78 million rupees, i.e. three times the cost of the canal.

tween 14 to 16 acres free of cost. The next grade were yeomen, who were given 111 to 139 acres on payment of a *nazrana* of Rs.6 to 9 per acre. On top came the "capitalists" with 167 to 556 acres who had to pay Rs.10 to 20 per acre. The settlers were given "heritable and inalienable rights of occupancy." The vast majority of the Sikh colonists were Malwa Jats with a sprinkling of non-Jat agriculturist tribes—Kambohs, Labanas, and Mazhabis.

The colonists got to work with great zeal. What had been a great expanse of yellow sand became within a couple of years a flourishing country of cornfields and villages.[6] Special grants were made to set up "remount depots" (stud farms for horses and mules for the army) and later for select breeds of cattle.

The production from the new lands was far in excess of the requirements of the province, and the first harvest rotted in storehouses. The building of railways and feeder roads was speeded up. In 1861 a beginning had been made by linking Lahore and Amritsar by rail. In the next thirty years a criss-cross of rail lines was laid across the province connecting the canal colonies with the cities of India. Wheat, cotton,[7] and oil-seeds from the Punjab were taken by rail to Bombay and Karachi to be exported: the export of wheat alone reached over a million tons a year. The price of land, which at the time of annexation had been

[6] The financial commissioner's review claimed: "Cultivation has now become more careful; comfortable and commodious houses have been built; all villages have now a good well, many of them have a mosque or a dharamsala and a rest house; the growth of good shade-giving trees is remarkable, both in villages and fields. Many villages are a pattern of cleanliness and comfort, and the people evidently take pride in them and their imposing houses of brick and mortar. There are of course, some exceptions among 100,000 colonists, but the general impression is one of great prosperity, comfort and content, from which a feeling of gratitude to government for the extraordinary benefits its colonisation scheme has conferred on these fortunate individuals in the short space of fifteen years is not absent." *Civil and Military Gazette*, May 26, 1909.

[7] The first attempt to erect a cotton mill in the Punjab was made in March 1883, when citizens of Lahore met under the chairmanship of Raja Harbans Singh to consider the matter. *Tribune*, March 18, 1883.

only Rs.10/-an acre, rose to over Rs.400/-per acre in the new colonies.[8] The Punjabis became the most prosperous peasantry of India; and, of the Punjabis, the Sikhs became the most prosperous of all.

The prosperity ushered in by the development of the canal colonies and the preference shown towards the Sikhs in recruitment to the Imperial army had an important bearing on the future and the caste complex of the community. The economic advantages of being Sikh checked the disintegration of Sikhism and its lapse into Hinduism. On the contrary, the last decade of the 19th century and the first decade of the 20th, saw a phenomenal rise in the numbers of Sikhs.[9] This was due largely to the patronage of the government, which required posts reserved for Sikhs in the army (and later in the civilian services) to be filled exclusively by the *kesādhārī* Khalsa. This patronage paved the way for the success of the proselytisation movement, the Singh Sabha (discussed in Chapter 9). Thus the gloomy foreboding of Lord Dalhousie[10] of the possibility of the disappearance of the Sikhs was staved off by policies initiated by Dalhousie himself and supplemented by army commanders and administrators of the Punjab.

The proportion of Sikhs in the Imperial army was considerably more than that warranted by their numbers. Of the total strength from the Punjab of 42,560 at the turn of the century, 20,060 were Muslims, 11,612 Hindus, and 10,867 Sikhs.[11] (There were another 4,122 Sikhs in the armies of the Punjab states.) In other words, the Sikhs, who formed only a little more than 12 percent of the population of the Punjab, constituted about 25 percent of its army. Of the Sikh soldiery, the largest number were

[8] H. Calvert, *The Wealth and Welfare of the Punjab*, p. 219.
[9] See footnote on p. 146.
[10] See p. 96.
[11] P. H. Kaul, *Census of India, 1911*, Vol. xiv, Punjab, Part ii, Tables, pp. 438-39.

Jats (6,666 in the Imperial army; 1,845 in the armies of native states). The Mazhabis came next with 1,626. Preference for Jats stabilised their position at the top of the caste hierarchy among the Sikhs. This upward mobility of Sikh Jats (considered as *sudras*, the lowest of the four castes of Hindus) had begun in the time of Guru Gobind Singh, when a large majority of those baptised were Jats. It was the baptised *kesādhārī* Jats who had been the chief instruments of the Sikh rise to power and consequently became the land-owning aristocracy during the rule of Maharajah Ranjit Singh. Under British rule, Jats maintained their position as the premier caste among the Sikhs —superior to the Brahmins, the Kshatriyas (from whom the gurus had sprung), and the Vaishyas. This position was not achieved by Muslim or Hindu Jats in their respective communities.

A similar upward mobility was evident with respect to the Mazhabi and Ranghreta Sikhs—and for the same reason, viz. recruitment in the army and the acquisition of land.[12] Apart from tradition, the real cause of the denigration of these castes was their occupation as scavengers (*cūhras*) or skinners of carrion (*camārs*). With new avenues of employment, many belonging to these castes abandoned their hereditary callings to become soldiers or farmers—and began to lay claim to equal status with other soldiers and farmers. Although they did not wholly succeed in erasing the stigma of low caste, they did succeed in winning a better place in Sikh society than untouchables who remained Hindus or Muslims.

[12] For a detailed analysis of the caste structure among the Sikhs with special reference to the upward mobility of the Jats and the untouchable castes see Marenco, *Caste and Class among the Sikhs of North West India.*

PART III

SOCIAL
AND RELIGIOUS REFORM

The climate of the Orient has always been productive of messiahs and prophets. Every age has had its quota of men claiming kinship or communion with God; some even professing to be His human reincarnations.

The Sikhs have had their share of messiahs; the messianic pattern was, however, Sikh-oriented. The gurus had assured their disciples that no one could attain salvation without the mediation of a teacher. Consequently Gobind Singh's declaration that the line of human gurus was at an end and thereafter the Sikhs should look for guidance to the *Ādi Granth* was ignored by many of the succeeding generations; and the *sau sākhī* was forged to sanctify pretensions of prophethood.

The first two sects dealt with in the following pages were born out of the changing fortunes of the Sikhs: out of their rise from rustic poverty to sovereign opulence; and then out of their reduction to a subject people under an alien race. In the first phase, power produced wealth and wealth irreligiousness; in the second phase, the loss of power roused passion to re-create the golden age that had passed. The Nirankaris and the Namdharis exemplify these themes.

The Radha Soamis stand apart as a non-denominational group born of the impact of Sikhism (minus the Khalsa tradition) on Hinduism. It illustrates the sort of mélange of Hinduism and Sikhism which is gaining currency in educated circles of both communities.

More important than the three sects mentioned above was the religious-cum-social movement which went under the name Singh Sabha. On the religious plane, it remained true to the orthodox tradition of "no guru save the *granth*"; on the social, it met the challenge of modern times with modern weapons.

The first task was to adapt the Sikhs to the post-annexation situation. The annexation had reduced the Sikhs from a position of dominance to one of subservience not only to the British but also to the Muslims and the Hindus, who considerably out-numbered them. This sense of numerical inferiority was accentuated by the fact that, while the annexation brought the Punjab Muslims and Hindus into direct contact with their more enlightened Indian co-religionists, the Sikhs of the annexed territories were only reunited to their Malwai brethren, who were even less educated than themselves. The Sikhs had no option but to turn to their rulers for guidance. Under the auspices of the Singh Sabha, the Sikhs sought and won the collaboration of English officials in their drive for literacy.

The second task was to preserve their identity. The annexation exposed the dispirited and leaderless Sikh masses to the preaching of Christian missionaries and the proselytising activities of the Hindu Arya Samajists. The Singh Sabha met this challenge by reviving interest in Sikh religion and tradition.

CHAPTER 8

RELIGIOUS MOVEMENTS

The Nirankaris

DURING the reign of Maharajah Ranjit Singh, the Hindus of western Punjab and Derajat came under the influence of Sikhism. A few accepted the *pahul* and joined the Khalsa fraternity; most others continued to describe themselves as Hindus but gave up the worship of Hindu gods and the recitation of the Vedas, instead reading the *Granth* and joining Sikh congregations at the gurdwaras. Among these Hindus there grew a custom of bringing up at least one son as a *kesādhārī* Sikh. This half-Hindu, half-Sikh community belonged to the Khatri, Arora, or Bania castes. They continued to marry within their castes regardless of the change in their religious beliefs.

Dyal Das (d.1855), a bullion merchant of Peshawar, belonged to this Hindu-Sikh community. He condemned idol worship and making obeisance to "holy" men; he disapproved of going on pilgrimages and performing Brahmanical ritual. The positive aspect of his teaching was that God was formless—*nirankār* (hence the futility of worshipping idols or "saints"); consequently he described himself as a *nirankārī*. He coined the phrase:

> *dhan nirankār*
> *deh dhārī sab khwār*

> Praise be to the Formless Creator;
> Worship of mortals is of no avail.

Dyal Das soon acquired the status of a guru and gathered around him disciples who, like him, described themselves as Nirankaris. They ran into opposition first from Hindu Brahmins and, after Dyal Das moved from Peshawar to Rawalpindi, from the Bedi descendants of Guru

Nanak, who had a large following in the district. The Nirankaris were ostracised by both the Hindus and the Sikhs and had to build their own places of worship. The biggest was raised on the banks of the stream Layee four miles outside Rawalpindi. When Dyal Das died, his sandals became an object of veneration. They were placed on an altar alongside the Granth, and the temple on the Layee was named after him as Dayalsar. It became the headquarters of the Nirankari sect.

Dyal Das was succeeded by the eldest of his three sons, Darbara Singh. Darbara Singh built new centres (bīṛās) for the Nirankaris and began the practice of issuing encyclicals (hukumnāmās) for the instruction of his followers. His chief contribution was to standardise ritual connected with births, marriages,[1] and deaths. These rituals were a departure from the Hindu tradition inasmuch as they were based on the Granth and not on the Hindu sacred texts. Darbara Singh (d.1870) was succeeded by his youngest brother, Rattan Chand (d.1909), and Rattan Chand by his son Gurdit Singh (d.1947). The present head of the Nirankaris is Gurdit Singh's son, Hara Singh.

Various estimates of the numbers of the sect have been made.[2] The Nirankaris themselves claim a following of nearly 100,000 comprised mainly of non-Jat Sikhs and Hindus of the Arora Zargar (goldsmith) and Kshatriya castes.[3] Until 1947, their influence was restricted to Sikh and Hindu communities of the North West Frontier Province and Kashmir. After the partition of India, Dayalsar was abandoned, and the centre was shifted first to Amritsar and then to Chandigarh, the new capital of East Punjab.

The differences between orthodox Sikhism and the

---

[1] The Nirankaris claim that they were the first to introduce the Anand marriage which is performed by circumambulating the Granth. The Anand Marriage Act legalising such marriages was passed in 1909.

[2] The census of 1891 records the number of Nirankaris as 50,724, of which 11,817 were Sikhs and 38,907 Hindus. Captain A. H. Bingley in his Handbook for the Indian Army estimates the total figure of Nirankaris at 38,000.

[3] Information supplied by Dr. Man Singh, son of the Nirankari guru.

Nirankaris are limited to the latter's worship of gurus other than the ten recognised by the Sikhs. Nirankaris style Dyal Das and his successors with honorifics such as *srī satgurū* (the true guru) and *srī hazūr sāhib* (his holy eminence). They also disapprove of the militant Khalsa.[4]

The Nirankaris are fast losing their separate identity and may, within a few decades, merge back into the Hindu or Sikh parent body. The importance of the movement lies largely in the fact that it initiated ceremonial rites which inculcated among the Sikhs a sense of separateness and thus checked the process of their absorption into Hinduism.

Radha Soamis of Beas

The founder of the Radha Soami sect was a Hindu banker, Shiv Dayal (1818-1878), of Agra. Shiv Dayal was greatly influenced by the teachings of the *Ādi Granth*, and he propounded a doctrine which contained elements of both Hinduism and Sikhism. He described God as the union between *rādhā* (symbolising the soul) and *Soāmī*, the Master; hence himself as a worshipper of *Rādhā Soāmī*.[5] Shiv Dayal attracted a following of Hindus and

---

[4] Two of the four Nirankari gurus were not baptised as Khalsa, and Nirankaris substitute the word *"nirankār"* for *"srī bhagwatī"* (the sword) in the invocation recited at the end of prayer because, say the Nirankaris, *bhagwatī* is also the name of a Hindu goddess. The only other point of difference from orthodox Sikhs is in their form of greeting, which is *dhan nirankār* instead of the orthodox *sat srī akāl*.

[5] Shiv Dayal's beliefs are set out in his book *Sār Bacan* (Essential Utterances) and can be briefly summarised as follows:

Human beings, who are the highest of God's creation, are afflicted with sorrow because they have been unable to achieve the perfection of which they are capable; such perfection can only be attained under the guidance of a guru who can give *diksā*—the secret formula—consisting of instructions in physical and mental discipline to achieve *samādhi* (meditation). The human body is divided into two separate compartments: the higher which is above the eyes is the seat of the soul; and the baser which is below the eyes is controlled by the mind. Realisation of God comes by reproducing the image of the guru at a spot between the eyes (*śiv netrā*) and repetition of *śabd* (the word) or *nām* (name of the Lord). This practice is known as the *surat śabd yoga*, or the union (*yoga*) of the soul (*surat*) with the sound current (*śabd*). The company of

Sikhs and became the first guru of the sect. On his death, the Radha Soamis split into two: the main centre was at Agra;[6] a branch started by a Sikh disciple, Jaimal Singh[7] (1839-1913), was on the bank of river Beas, not very far from Amritsar.

The Beas Radha Soamis soon became independent of the Agra centre and had a succession of gurus—all Sikhs—of their own. On Jaimal Singh's death, one of his disciples, Sawan Singh Grewal, an engineer, became the head of the Punjab Radha Soamis. Sawan Singh enlarged the Beas centre and named it Dera Baba Jaimal Singh. During Sawan Singh's tenure, the number of Beas Radha Soamis increased rapidly. Besides Sikhs, who formed the nucleus, they included Hindus, Muslims, Parsis, and Christians. Sawan Singh (d.1948) was succeeded by Jagat Singh, a retired professor of agriculture. After a short term of three years, Jagat Singh (d.1951) nominated Charan Singh Grewal (a grandson of Sawan Singh) as his successor. Under Charan Singh's leadership—he is an educated man with great charismatic charm—the Beas Radha Soamis have grown into a community of substantial proportions: over 100,000 followers assemble to celebrate the birthdays of their gurus. They claim the adherence of a million

---

truthful people (*satsaṅg*) is essential. (The organisation is known as the Radha Soami Satsang.)

6 Shiv Dayal died in 1878 and was succeeded at Agra by Rai Saligram Saheb Bahadur (1828-98). Rai Saligram composed religious verse of which two anthologies, *Prem Bānī* and *Prem Patr*, are the better known. He also wrote *An Exposition of the Radha Soami Doctrine* in English.

The third guru of the Agra Radha Soamis was a Bengali Brahmin, Brahma Sankar Misra (1861-1907). After Misra the Agra Radha Soamis broke up into different factions. Today they have a flourishing industrial estate in a suburb called Dayalbagh. The Agra centre is more of economic than religious importance.

7 Jaimal Singh was a Sikh Jat from village Ghuman (district Gurdaspur). He was a soldier in the forces of the East India Company and met Shiv Dayal while he was posted in Agra. On retirement from active service, he returned to the Punjab and set up a Radha Soami centre on the left bank of the Beas.

men and women of different nationalities and denominations.[8]

The Beas Radha Soamis have some basic differences with orthodox Sikhism. They believe in a living guru, who initiates[9] the disciples, who thereupon become *guru bhāīs* or *guru bahins* (brothers-in-faith or sisters-in-faith) and greet each other with the words *"rādhā soāmī."* Radha Soami temples do not have the *Granth Sāhib* but only a raised platform where the guru sits to deliver a discourse. They have no *kīrtan* because they believe that music diverts people's minds from the meaning of the hymns to the simple enjoyment of sound. And, although the Radha Soami gurus of Beas as well as their Sikh adherents remain *kesādhārī*, they do not believe in *pahul* (baptism) nor in the militant vows of the Khalsa.

Although the Radha Soamis owe much to Sikhism—their gurus' discourses are largely drawn from the *Ādi Granth* —it would be wrong to describe them as a sub-sect of Sikhism. The only justification for treating them along with other Sikh religious movements is their close resemblance to the *sahajdhārīs*. The *sahajdhārīs* nominally accept the teachings of all the ten gurus and keep up the fiction that in due course they will be baptised as the Khalsa. The Radha Soamis only accept the teachings of the first five gurus contained in the *Ādi Granth* and reject the rest. The Radha Soamis present a new version of *sahajdhārī* Sikhism. Their faith has considerable attraction for the religiously inclined educated classes, for the Hindu-oriented Sikh, and the Sikh-oriented Hindu.

Namdhari or Kuka Movement

The Namdhari sect was founded by Balak Singh,[10] of village Hazro in the northwest frontier region. Balak Singh

---

[8] It is impossible to verify the number as the Radha Soamis do not form a distinct and separate sect and are not therefore listed in the census.

[9] Radha Soami initiation involves certain vows, e.g. strict vegetarianism, abstinence from alcohol, and two and a half hours of meditation every day.

[10] Balak Singh (1797-1862) was the son of a goldsmith of village Sarvala

had been inspired by the sermons of one Jawahar Mal,[11] who preached the virtues of poverty and denounced the rich as godless. Balak Singh followed suit by exhorting his followers to live simply and practise no religious ritual other than repeating God's name or *nām* (hence *nāmdhā-rī*).[12] It was Balak Singh's personality more than the substance of his sermons that induced his followers to look upon him as a reincarnation of Guru Gobind Singh. Before Balak Singh died he chose one of his most ardent disciples, the carpenter Ram Singh,[13] as his successor. The headquarters of the Namdharis shifted from Hazro to Ram Singh's village Bhaini in Ludhiana district.

Ram Singh introduced some changes in the forms of worship, appearance, and form of address which distinguished his followers from the rest of the Sikhs. Following his example, his disciples chanted hymns and, like dancing dervishes, worked themselves into a state of frenzy and emitted loud shrieks (*kūks*): they came therefore to be

---

(district Attock) who later shifted his business to Hazro. They were Aroras of the Batra sub-caste.

[11] Jawahar Mal, known for his piety as *sāiṇ sāhib*, was the son of Dayal Chand, of village Sarai Saleh near Haripur. Dayal Chand, though a Vaishnavite Hindu, was strongly drawn to the simple tenets of the Sikh faith. He started to expound the *Granth* and drew large crowds to his centre. Dayal Chand came to be known as "Bhagat," and thereafter his descendants, who are of the Kalal caste, styled themselves as "Bhagats." In 1847 Jawahar Mal opened a centre for divine worship entitled the *Jagiāsi Abhiāsi Āśram*.

[12] Namdharis were to rise at 3 a.m., brush their teeth, and bathe. They were ordered to live simply and thriftily. The destruction of female children was rigorously forbidden—so also was the giving or accepting of dowries. Namdharis were enjoined to live on their earnings and forbidden to beg for alms. Tobacco, snuff, and alcohol were tabu. Meat was also excluded from the diet of the Namdharis.

[13] Ram Singh (1816-1885) was a Ramgarhia of village Bhaini (Ludhiana district). He was in the Durbar's artillery and met Balak Singh when his unit was posted on the frontier. When Sikh artillery was disbanded after the first Anglo-Sikh war, Ram Singh came to live at Hazro. On the annexation of the Punjab, he returned to Bhaini and resumed his ancestral profession and the preaching of Balak Singh's message.

named *Kūkās*. The Kukas wore only white handspun cloth; they bound their turbans in a style of their own (flat across the forehead instead of forming an angle); they wore necklaces of woollen rosaries; they carried staves in their hands; and they greeted each other with *sat akāl purakh* instead of the customary *sat srī akāl*. Although most of the Kukas came from the poorer classes of Ramgarhias, Jats, cobblers, and Mazhabis, Ram Singh made them feel as if they were the elect—the saintly *sant Khālsā* —while the others were *mlecha* (unclean). Ram Singh issued *hukumnāmās* to his followers which embraced ethical, social, hygienic, as well as political matters.[14]

Ram Singh's religious discourses began to have a political flavour. When he administered *pahul*, besides the usual sermon delivered on such occasions, Ram Singh spoke of the wickedness of the Sikh princes and landowners; of the assumption of guruship by the Bedi and Sodhi descendants of the gurus; of the wickedness of idolatry and casteism.[15] Despite his criticism of many Hindu prac-

[14] *Ethical*: Do not lie, steal or commit adultery. *Personal*: Do not imbibe tobacco, alcohol or meat of any kind. Wear turbans flat across the forehead. *Social*: Do not destroy or trade in female children; do not give girls under eight in marriage; do not give or take large dowries (Ram Singh performed mass marriages of his followers in village Khote in 1863. He forbade his followers to spend more than Rs.13/- at a wedding). Do not lend or borrow money on interest; do not castrate bulls; protect cows and other animals from slaughter. *Hygienic*: Rise before dawn and bathe every day; (pray and tell beads of rosaries made of wool). *Political*: Do not accept service with government; do not send children to government schools; do not go to courts of law but settle disputes by reference to *pancāyats*; do not use foreign goods; do not use government postal services.

[15] "Gobind Singh's *Granth* is the only true one, written by imagination, and is the only sacred writing extant. Gobind Singh is the only true guru. Any person, irrespective of caste or religion, can be admitted a convert. He said Sodhis, Bedis, *mahants*, Brahmins and such like are impostors, as none are gurus except Gobind Singh. Temples of Devi, Shiva, are a means of extortion, to be held in contempt and never visited. Idols and idolworship are insulting to God, and will not be forgiven. Converts are allowed to read Gobind Singh's *Granth*, and no other book." Mr. Kinchant's description of the Kuka Articles of Belief, 1863. *Papers Relating to the Kuka Sect*.

tices, Ram Singh became an ardent protector of the cow.

Ram Singh had separate gurdwaras built for his follow-ers. He appointed *sūbās* (governors) who collected funds which were remitted to Bhaini. He arranged for the train-ing of young men in the use of weapons and built up a paramilitary organisation. The Kukas had their own postal runners to carry secret messages.

By 1863 Ram Singh had a well-knit following of several thousands. A new version of the *sau sākhī* was circulated. It prophesied the rebirth of Guru Gobind Singh in the person of one Ram Singh, carpenter of village Bhaini, who would resurrect the Khalsa, drive the English out of Hin-dustan, and establish a new Sikh dynasty. Ram Singh ordered his followers to assemble at Amritsar for the Bai-sakhi festival to listen to a special proclamation. The fact that this was exactly what Guru Gobind Singh had done at Anandpur when he baptised the Khalsa could not have been lost on the Kukas.

Ram Singh arrived in Amritsar and found the city bris-tling with police. He was unable to make his proclamation. On his return to Bhaini, he was served with a notice for-bidding him to leave the village. He complained that he had been victimised by "government bodies, Brahmins and many other people. . . ."[16] Ram Singh remained under surveillance till the government had assured itself that the Kukas would cause no disturbance.

On the Dussehra festival in the autumn of 1867, Ram Singh visited Amritsar with nearly 3,500 of his followers. He was received with honour at the Harimandir and other shrines and baptised over 2,000 Sikhs, including members of some well-to-do families of zamindars. By this time Ram Singh had acquired, perhaps without any volition on his part, the status of secular chief. He travelled with a body-guard of soldiers and, like a prince, held court every day.

[16] Letter to Bhagat Jawahar Mal, October 1865, quoted by Ganda Singh, *Kūkian dī Vithiā*, p. 59.

He exchanged presents with several ruling chiefs and sent a mission to Nepal.

Kukas who had been fed on prophecies of a Sikh resurgence could not remain quiescent for too long. But when it came to making an issue, they fastened on a matter which barely touched the sentiments of the Sikh masses, viz. protection of cows. And on this issue too they chose to vent their spleen on Muslim butchers rather than on the English. Their collision with the authorities came as a result of their attempt to stop the slaughter of kine.

Kuka fanatics murdered some Muslim butchers and their families in Amritsar and later at Raikot (Ludhiana district).[17] For these crimes, eight Kukas were hanged and others sentenced to long terms of imprisonment.[18] The government reimposed orders restricting Ram Singh to his village and forbade the assemblage of Kukas at religious festivals. But Kuka passions had been inflamed, and, on the Maghi festival in January 1872, they flocked in the hundreds to Bhaini. Speeches were made extolling the heroism of the men who had been hanged. It was also bruited about that the time prophesied by the *sau sākhī* for the restoration of Sikh power was at hand. Ram Singh had some difficulty in persuading his followers to return peacefully to their homes. However, one band decided to ignore their guru's advice and to attack Malerkotla, a Muslim state where slaughter of cows was permitted.

On the way to Malerkotla the gang raided the house of

[17] In November 1871, J. W. MacNab, commissioner of Ambala, was asked to make a report on the Kukas. MacNab was convinced that Ram Singh had instigated the murders of the butchers and recommended criminal proceedings against him. No action was taken on MacNab's report.

[18] *Crown Vs. Fateh Singh and others.* Judgment of the Punjab Chief Court, dated 9.9.1871 (reference 53) and *Crown Vs. Mastan Singh and others.* Judgment of the Punjab Chief Court dated 1.8.1871. See also Dr. Ganda Singh's letter on the subject in *The Spokesman* of June 29, 1964. Among those who were executed was one Gyani Rattan Singh, a zamindar of Patiala, who was held in great esteem by the Kukas and believed by them to have been innocent.

the Sikh zamindar of Malaudh to acquire arms. They were engaged by the zamindar's retainers and, when they entered Malerkotla, by the state constabulary. L. Cowan, the deputy commissioner of Ludhiana, joined the pursuit and captured 68 of the band. Cowan sent a note to his commissioner, T. D. Forsythe, and without any formality blew up 66 of the prisoners by tying them to the mouths of cannons.[19]

Kuka headquarters at Bhaini were searched: only a few kirpans, hatchets, and a pair of ornamental khukries were found. Ram Singh and eleven of his followers were arrested and deported to Burma.[20]

Forsythe then joined Cowan at Malerkotla, where another 16 Kukas were blasted off by cannons. Subsequently, the party went to Malaudh, where four Kukas were in

[19] "The gang of rebels, for no other name will adequately characterise them, never numbered more than 125: of these there were at Malodh 2 killed, 4 captured; at Kotla 8 killed, 31 wounded. Of those wounded, 25 or 26 escaped at the time; but 68, including 27 wounded, have been captured in the Patiala state. . . . The entire gang has thus been nearly destroyed. I propose blowing away from guns, or hanging, the prisoners tomorrow morning at daybreak. Their offence is not an ordinary one. They have not committed mere murder and dacoity; they are open rebels, offering contumacious resistance to constituted authority, and, to prevent the spreading of the disease, it is absolutely necessary that repressive measures should be prompt and stern. I am sensible of the great responsibility I incur; but I am satisfied that I act for the best, and that this incipient insurrection must be stamped out at once." *Parliamentary Papers on the Kuka Outbreak*, p. 11.

The commissioner, T. D. Forsythe, who had earlier advised Cowan not to be too hasty, supported the action of his deputy. He wrote: "My dear Cowan, I fully approve and confirm all you have done. You have acted admirably. I am coming out." Letter dated January 18, 1872. *Ibid.*, p. 53.

[20] Forsythe wrote: "The complicity of Ram Singh in the outrages committed by his followers at Malodh and in the state of Malerkotla has not yet been thoroughly inquired into; and it is a fact that he reported to the police the intention of Lehna Singh and Hera Singh, the chief actors in the present case, to commit outrages. But by his own admission his followers make use of his name and take advantage of his presence among them to call on their fellows to commit murders and create disturbances." Letter dated January 18, 1872. *Ibid.*, p. 12.

custody. Forsythe relented and sentenced them to life imprisonment.[21]

Whatever little sympathy the Sikhs may have had with the revivalist aspect of the Namdhari movement was forfeited by the resort to violence against poor Muslims and the defiance of the administration. The community was strongly pro-British, and Sikh leaders took the earliest opportunity to reaffirm their loyalty. The maharajah of Patiala ordered the arrest of all Kukas in his state.[22] A meeting of Sikh sardars in Amritsar presented an address to the lieutenant governor describing the Kukas as a "wicked and misguided sect" who "by their misconduct and evil designs" had injured the honour of the Sikh community in the estimation of the government, "and well-nigh levelled with the dust the services we [i.e. the Sikhs] had rendered to the government, such as those for instance performed in 1857. . . ."[23]

After some years in gaol, Ram Singh was allowed to receive visitors as well as to communicate with his followers. Once again he toyed with the idea of fomenting revolution in the Punjab. His followers discovered more copies of the *sau sākhī*[24] predicting a Russian invasion of India and the founding of the dynasty of Ram Singh. Ram

[21] There was strong criticism in the Anglo-Indian press of the barbarous action taken by Cowan. The Government of India ordered an enquiry, as a result of which Cowan was dismissed and Forsythe was transferred to a post outside the Punjab.

The viceroy's opinion was conveyed in the following words: "The course followed by Mr. Cowan was illegal, that it was not palliated by any public necessity, and that it was characterised by incidents which gave it a complexion of barbarity." Letter dated April 30, 1872 from E. C. Bayley to the Punjab Government. *Ibid.,* pp. 54-58.

[22] The maharajah's *firmān* (proclamation) dated January 19, 1872.

[23] *The Englishman,* March 23, 1872.

[24] These *sau sākhīs* were claimed to have been found in a tank near Sirsa. Under instructions of the lieutenant governor, Sir Robert Egerton, they were translated into English. (See note by D. E. McCracken, assistant to the inspector-general of police, Punjab Home Department, Judicial Proceedings, August 1882, Nos. 217-218B.)

Singh sent an emissary to Russia to elicit help;[25] but the mission produced no results. He also realised that the Sikhs were unwilling to revolt against their rulers. Ram Singh gave up hope and in his later days lost faith in the prophecies fabricated by his enthusiastic followers. His later letters from gaol show clearly that he did not consider himself a guru but a *rapatī* (mouthpiece) of the guru. Occasionally, when the way he had been treated made him angry, he invoked the aid of his guru (and, strangely enough, of the Hindu goddesses of destruction Sakti, Bhagwati, Jagdamba)[26] to rid the land of the filthy cow-eating whites.

Ram Singh died in Rangoon in 1885 and was succeeded by his younger brother Hari Singh. Hari Singh was not allowed to move out of Bhaini for the 21 years he was guru. On his death in 1906, he was succeeded by his son Pratap Singh (d. 1961), who was, in his turn, succeeded by the present head, Jagjit Singh.[27]

No reliable figures of the numbers of Kukas have been compiled.[28] They have two centres, one at Bhaini and the other at Jiwan Nagar near Sirsa in Hissar district. They publish four journals, of which the *Satyug*, a weekly paper in Gurmukhi, is the oldest and the most widely circulated.[29]

The Kukas are a distinct sub-sect who maintain little intercourse with the parent community. They have their

[25] See P. C. Roy, *Gurcharan Singh's Mission in Central Asia*, pamphlet published by author.

[26] See Ram Singh's letters from gaol published in Ganda Singh, *Kūkiāṇ dī Vithiā*, pp. 213-14.

[27] Jagjit Singh has no son and is likely to be succeeded by his younger brother, Bir Singh, or Bir Singh's son, Dalip Singh.

[28] In 1871, the Kukas claimed a membership of nearly one million. The census of 1891 however listed only 10,541, and the figure had only gone up to 13,788 in the census of 1901.

Today the Kukas claim to have a following of between 5-10 lacs, consisting largely of Jats, Ramgarhias, Aroras, and Mazhabi Sikhs. They are concentrated in the districts of Hissar, Amritsar, and Ludhiana. (Author's interview with Guru Jagjit Singh.)

[29] Other Kuka journals are *Nawāṇ Hindustān*, a Gurmukhi daily published in New Delhi; *Nāmdhārī Samācār*, a Hindi quarterly published in Delhi; *Sacā Mārg*, a Gurmukhi weekly published in Samana.

own gurdwaras and only on rare occasions deign to join Sikh religious processions. They do not intermarry with Sikhs unless the party concerned accepts their persuasion.

The Kukas, nevertheless, more strictly adhere to the puritanical faith of Guru Nanak and Guru Gobind than other Sikhs. Their gurdwaras are not ostentatious, and their worship is devoid of the elements of idolatry (rich canopies and coverings over the Granth, waving of censers, etc.) which have become common practice in orthodox circles. And the Kukas themselves lead austere lives; they wear the simplest of clothes and observe a rigid code of conduct; they are punctilious in attending service in their gurdwaras and in observing the tabus of food, drink, and personal deportment. They also have a place in the history of the freedom movement of India. Ram Singh was the first man to evolve non-cooperation and the use of *swadeshi* (indigenous goods) as political weapons. The boycott of British goods, government schools, law courts, and the postal service and the exhortation to wear only hand-spun cloth (*khaddar*) which Ram Singh propagated in the 1860's were taken up again sixty years later by Mahatma Gandhi.

CHAPTER 9

SINGH SABHA AND SOCIAL REFORM

The Background: Christian and Hindu
Missionary Activity

 THE Nirankari, Radha Soami, and Namdhari movements made small impact on the Sikh masses. The first was confined to the urban community in the northwest; the second was largely concerned with theistic problems; while the third was temporarily blasted out of existence on the parade ground of Malerkotla. All three developed into schismatic coteries owing allegiance to its particular guru and practising its own esoteric ritual. The evils they had set out to abolish continued unabated. Sikhs of lower castes continued to be discriminated against; the rich continued to indulge in drink and debauchery; Brahmanical Hinduism, with its pantheon of gods and goddesses, mumbling of Sanskrit *maṅtras*, belief in soothsayers, astrologers and casters of horoscopes, continued as before. Even Sikhs who criticised these sects for worshipping gurus other than the recognised ten, were not averse to prostrating themselves before the Bedi and Sodhi descendants of Nanak and Gobind or paying homage to some saint or the other exactly as if he were a guru.

As serious as the decline in moral standards was the decline in the number of Sikhs. When the Khalsa was in the ascendant, large numbers of Hindus had begun to grow their hair and beards and pay lip-worship to the Sikh gurus. After annexation, these time-servers returned to the Hindu fold. Genuine Sikh families who had cultivated close social relations with such Hindus either followed suit or became clean-shaven *sahajdhārīs*. Sikhs, most of whom had been Hindus a few generations earlier and had never given up social intercourse with the Hindus, were now faced with the prospect of being reabsorbed into Hinduism and ceasing to exist as a separate community.[1]

The inherent weakness of the Sikh body politic was only one factor of disintegration; there were three others: the activities of Christian missions, the proselytisation by a new Hindu organisation known as the Arya Samaj, and the rationalism that came with the introduction of scientific concepts.

In 1835, an American Presbyterian Mission had been established at Ludhiana. Immediately after annexation, it spread its activities from Malwa to Majha;[2] the Church Missionary Society opened centres around Amritsar and Lahore and in the hill districts. The Society for the Propagation of the Gospel, the Salvation Army, the Methodists, Episcopalians, Moravians, and several Roman Catholic orders vied with each other in gaining converts.[3] Christian missionaries were actively supported by English officials.[4]

The conversion of Maharajah Dalip Singh in 1853 was the first feather in the cap of the Christian missionaries and a grievous shock to the Sikhs. The same year a Christian mission school was opened in Amritsar. With the

[1] This was the opinion of as shrewd and scholarly observers as Sir Richard Temple and Denzil Ibbetson, who noted in the *Census Report of 1881*: ". . . The Sikhs are the most uneducated class in the Punjab. . . . On the whole there seems reason to believe that notwithstanding the stimulus of the Kabul campaign (tales of the heroism of Sikh soldiers in the northwest frontier campaign were given wide publicity), Sikhism is on the decline."

[2] Rev. John Newton and Rev. C. W. Forman visited Lahore in 1849. Maconachie, *Rowland Bateman.*

[3] *Imperial Gazetteer of India 1908*, xx, 291-92.

[4] Bateman's biographer records a meeting at Lahore on February 19, 1852, with Archdeacon Pratt of Calcutta in the chair, where it was stated that: "Henry and John Lawrence, Robert Montgomery, Donald McLeod, Herbert Edwardes, Reynell Taylor, Robert Cust, Arthur Roberts, William Martin, C. R. Saunders and others, were all interested in starting the Punjab Church Missionary Association." Maconachie, *Rowland Bateman*, pp. 12-13.

The growth of Christianity in the Punjab is borne out by census figures: 1881—3,796; 1891—19,547; 1901—37,980; 1911—163,994; 1921—315,931; 1931—414,788.

ardour usual to new converts, the exiled maharajah offered to support it.

Apart from Maharajah Dalip Singh, most of the early Sikh converts to Christianity were from the untouchable castes. Within a short time *isāī*, the word meaning Christian, acquired a pejorative sense and became synonymous with *cūhṛā*, the Punjabi word for the untouchable sweeper. It was then that the neophytes realised that neither the patronage of the padre nor the seeming dignity of the sola topee could eradicate the stigma of untouchability. Thereafter the rate of conversion from the lower castes declined. Christian missionaries turned their attention to the well-to-do Jat and Kshatriya castes. Several Sikh families of note accepted Christianity.[5] The conversions of educated and aristocratic families disturbed the Sikh leaders more than the loss of their untouchable brethren.[6]

More serious than the activities of Christian missionaries, however, was the challenge of renascent Hinduism, chiefly from the Arya Samaj.

The Arya Samaj was founded by Swami Dayanand[7] Saraswati, whose motto was "Back to the Vedas." According

[5] The best known of these families was that of Raja Harnam Singh, brother of the maharajah of Kapurthala. Raja Harnam Singh's sons and daughter rose to eminent positions. Amrit Kaur, a friend of Mahatma Gandhi, was minister of health in the central government; Maharaj Singh became governor of Bombay; Dalip Singh, a judge of the Punjab High Court.

Sadhu Sundar Singh (b.1889), Jat Sikh of Rampur (Patiala state), was the most celebrated Indian convert to Christianity. He was a mystic. He spent most of his years walking up and down the Hindustan-Tibet Road. He disappeared some time after 1935.

[6] In 1873, when four Sikh boys of the mission school of Amritsar announced their decision to turn Christian, there were protest meetings all over the Punjab; Sikh preachers talked to the boys and prevented them from abandoning their ancestral faith.

[7] Dayanand (1824-1883) was the son of a Saivite Brahmin of Kathiawar. Dayanand left home at the age of 21 and spent the next eighteen years studying the Sanskrit religious texts under the guidance of a blind scholar, Swami Virajanand. He spent the remaining twenty years of his life preaching in northern India.

to him, the Vedas inculcated belief in one omnipresent but invisible God and in the equality of human beings: he was therefore against the worship of idols and the caste system. Dayanand was a forceful orator. Within a few years his voice was heard all over India. His iconoclastic monotheism and egalitarianism had special appeal for the Sikhs.

In the summer of 1877, Dayanand came to the Punjab, where he received a great welcome from the Hindus and Sikhs. He opened a branch of the Arya Samaj at Lahore. Proselytisation (*śudhī*-purification) was an important part of its activities, and it gained many Hindu and Sikh adherents.

It did not take the orthodox Sikhs long to appreciate that Dayanand's belief in the infallibility of the Vedas was as uncompromising as that of the Muslims in the Koran.[8] The *Granth* was to him a book of secondary importance, and the Sikh gurus men of little learning; Nanak, he denounced as a *dambhī* (hypocrite). Dayanand was contemptuous of Sikh theologians because of their ignorance of Sanskrit: his favourite phrase for any one who did not measure up to him was *mahā mūrkh* (great fool). Dayanand set the tone; his zealous admirers followed suit.[9]

[8] "I regard the Vedas as self-evident truth, admitting of no doubt and depending on the authority of no other book; being represented in nature, the Kingdom of God." Dayanand, *Handbook of the Arya Samaj*, p. 35.
Max Muller's opinion on Dayanand's attitude to the Vedas is illuminating: "By the most incredible interpretations Swami Dayanand succeeded in persuading himself and others that everything worth knowing, even the most recent inventions of modern science, were alluded to in the Vedas. Steam-engines, railways and steam boats, were all known to have been known, at least in their germ, to the poets of the Vedas; for *veda*, he argued, means knowledge, and how could anything be hid from that?" *Biographical Essays*, ii, 170.

[9] The *Āryā Samācār*, an organ of the Samaj, published the following lines:

  Nānak śāh fakīr ne nayā calāyā panth.
  Idhar udhar se jor ke likh mārā ik granth
  Pahle cele kar liye, piche badlā bhes
  Sir par sāfā bāndh ke, rakh līne sab kes.

The Sikhs turned their backs on Dayanand; instead they joined the Muslims and Christians in demanding the suppression of Dayanand's book, *Satyārth Prakāś*,[10] which maligned the prophets of their three faiths.

Besides the activities of the Christian missions and the Arya Samajists, other winds of change began to blow across the province. There was an influx of Bengali intellectuals, who brought with them the message of liberal Hinduism of Raja Ram Mohan Roy (1771-1833) and the Brahmo Samaj. They opened a branch in Lahore in 1864 and won a notable convert in Dayal Singh Majithia.[11] Equally influential were the Theosophists, many of whom (including Dr. Annie Besant) lectured in the Punjab. The interest in India and Hindu religion generated by the publication of the works of Max Muller, Sir Edwin Arnold, and Dr. Monier Williams was followed by the publication of many works on the Punjab.[12] The Sikhs were

---

Nanak, the king of fakirs, founded a new community.
He collected an assortment of writings and put them in a volume.
He gathered a few disciples and then changed his garb;
He wound a turban round his head and grew his hair long.
Ganda Singh, *A History of the Khalsa College*, p. 7.

[10] *Satyārth Prakāś* was published in 1874. It was banned by the Punjab Government because of offensive references to Prophet Mohammed. An amended version is now in circulation.

[11] Dayal Singh Majithia (d.1898) was the son of the famous Lehna Singh, minister of Maharajah Ranjit Singh. He became president of the Indian Association, which was affiliated to the Indian National Congress. He financed the *Tribune* and set up a trust which founded the Dayal Singh College and a public library. The *Tribune* started publishing in 1881. It continues to this day to have almost a monopoly of circulation in English-educated Punjabi circles.

[12] The more important of these were Sir Richard Temple's *Legends of the Punjab, Names and Name Places*, and the monthly magazine, *Punjab Notes and Queries*; Bosworth Smith's *Life of Lord Lawrence*; Ross's *Land of Five Rivers*; and above all Rudyard Kipling's stories, many of which had Punjab's cantonments as their background.

Western interest in the Punjab was an important factor in reviving the interest of the Punjabis in their own history and cultural traditions. What Monier Williams did for India, Dr. Leitner sought to do for the Punjab. He was the spirit behind the *Anjuman-i-Punjab* and the *Panjāb Akhbār*, published at Lahore. He set up a Punjab Institute at Woking near London.

once again unlucky in their European interpreter. A German philologist, Dr. Ernest Trumpp, was engaged by the India office to translate the *Granth* into English. Trumpp tried his hand at the first few pages and abandoned further translation because the language did not conform to the rules of Sanskrit grammar, and Sikh theologians refused to collaborate with him. Trumpp's opuscule when published caused no small disappointment. His preface had ill-natured comments on the text of the *Granth*; and his translation was inaccurate, dull, and prosy. Yet who could the Sikhs blame except themselves?

The literary and educational movement gathered momentum. In the 1870's and 1880's an Oriental College, a University library, museum, school of arts, science institute, and a medical college were opened in the Punjab. Hindus and Muslims started schools and colleges of their own; only the Sikhs lagged behind.[13]

Singh Sabhas of Amritsar and Lahore

Four years before the setting up of the Arya Samaj, the Sikh gentry of Amritsar had convened meetings to protest against the speeches of a Hindu orator who had made scurrilous remarks against the Sikh gurus. These protest meetings had been organised by a society which described itself as the Singh Sabha. It had the support of the rich, landed gentry and the orthodox.[14] The society's objects included the revival of the teachings of the gurus, production of religious literature in Punjabi, and a campaign against illiteracy. The founders also sought to "interest high placed

[13] "The Catholic principles which it [*Granth*] inculcates are known but to a few and clouds of prejudice and superstition have spread over the horizon of the Sikh religion. Now many Singh Sabhas have sprung up in different parts of the Punjab and the leaders of the community have awakened to their present condition; and there are ample grounds now to hope that there would be a Sikh revival." *Tribune*, February 7, 1885.

[14] Leaders of the Amritsar Singh Sabha were Khem Singh Bedi, Bikram Singh Ahluwalia of Kapurthala, and Thakar Singh Sandhawalia. Several Sikh theologians including the celebrated Gyani Gyan Singh took active interest.

Englishmen in, and assure their association with, the educational programme of the Singh Sabha." To ensure the patronage of the government the Sabha resolved "to cultivate loyalty to the crown."[15] Thakar Singh Sandhawalia was president and Gyani Gyan Singh secretary of the Amritsar Shri Guru Singh Sabha. The government extended its patronage to the educational programme of the organisation.[16]

In 1879 another Singh Sabha was formed at Lahore. Leaders of this Sabha were a group of educated and energetic men of the middle class.[17] The governor of the Punjab, Sir Robert Egerton, agreed to become its patron and induced the viceroy, Lord Lansdowne, to lend his support.[18]

[15] The mood of sycophantic loyalty to the British can be gauged from the message of farewell that was sent to Lord Ripon by the Sri Guru Singh Sabha by Man Singh, president of the Golden Temple Committee: "Our bodies are the exclusive possession of the British. Moreover, that we are solemnly and religiously bound to serve Her Majesty; that in discharging this duty we act according to the wishes of our Great Guru, the ever living God and that whenever and wherever need be felt for us, we wish to be the foremost of all Her Majesty's subjects, to move and uphold the honour of the crown; that we reckon ourselves as the favourite sons of our empress-mother, although living far distant from Her Majesty's feet and that we regard the people of England as our kindred brethren." *Tribune*, November 15, 1889.

[16] The policy of educating the landed aristocracy and training it for leadership was started by the lieutenant governor, Sir Charles Aitchison (1882-87). The Aitchison Chiefs College at Lahore admitted only sons of princes and rich zamindars listed in Griffin's *Rajas of the Punjab*. Extension of the same policy produced, in the earlier stages, close collaboration between leaders of the Singh Sabha (drawn almost exclusively from the rich and loyal classes of Sikhs) and the English rulers.

[17] They were Gurmukh Singh Chandhur, Dit Singh, and Jawahar Singh Kapur. Gurmukh Singh Chandhur (1849-98) was employed as a cook in the palace kitchen of the raja of Kapurthala. He was given a stipend by the raja and after completing his studies became the first professor of Punjabi at the Oriental College (1885). He was the author of many books in Punjabi including a History of India. Dit Singh (1853-1901) was a Mazhabi of Patiala. He was amongst those most eager to welcome Dayanand and later his most vigorous critic. Jawahar Singh Kapur (1859-1901), a Khatri Sikh, was employed as a clerk in the north-western railway.

[18] At a function at Patiala the viceroy said: "With this movement the

The Lahore Singh Sabha opened branches in many towns, sent missionaries to the villages, established liaison with Sikh regiments, and began publishing journals in Punjabi. In 1883 the Lahore and Amritsar Sabhas were merged, but the association proved a failure. The Amritsar Sabha had been constituted by an easy-going group of conservatives dominated by men like Khem Singh Bedi, who, by virtue of his descent from Nanak, was wont to accept homage due to a guru. The Lahore group was radical and strongly opposed to the institution of "gurudom." The two groups clashed on the right of untouchable Sikhs to worship in the gurdwaras; the conservatives sided with the priests who allowed untouchables to enter only at specified hours without the right to make offerings. The debate became acrimonious. The conservatives dissociated themselves from the movement and then became openly hostile.[19]

The rapid expansion of the Arya Samaj[20] and the anti-Sikh bias of many of its leaders[21] constituted a challenge to

---

Government of India is in hearty sympathy. We appreciate the many admirable qualities of the Sikh nation, and it is a pleasure to us to know that, while in days gone by we recognised in them a gallant and formidable foe, we are today able to give them a foremost place amongst the true and loyal subjects of Her Majesty the Queen Empress." *Tribune*, October 23, 1890.

[19] In 1887, Udai Singh Bedi, a nephew of Khem Singh Bedi, filed a libel suit against *The Khālsā Akhbār* run by the Lahore Sabha. The paper had described the Bedi as the "guru of Satan." The editor was fined and the Lahore Sabha's publishing enterprise had to close down for some time. *Tribune*, March 7, 1888.

[20] The Arya Samaj opened many schools in the province. In 1886, the D.A.V. (Dayanand Anglo-Vedic) College was opened at Lahore.

[21] At the eleventh anniversary meeting of the Punjab branch of the Arya Samaj in November 1888, the speakers again chose to make derogatory references to Sikhism. Prof. Guru Dutt said, "If the Swami had wished to become a general, he would have shown himself several thousand times better than Bonaparte. . . . Yes, Keshab Chander (Sen) and Guru Gobind Singh were not even one hundredth part of our Swami Dayananda Saraswati ji. The Sikhs might have some religion in them, but their guru had no learning whatever. . . . If Swami Dayananda Saraswati ji Maharaj had called Guru Nanak a *dambhī* (a hypocrite, an

· 143 ·

the Singh Sabha movement. It also brought about the final rupture between the Samaj and some of its Sikh supporters.

The two Singh Sabhas again rejoined hands and doubled their efforts to start a college of their own.[22] At a largely attended meeting held in Lahore, a plan was drawn up; a *hukumnāmā* was issued from the Golden Temple asking Sikhs to give a tenth of their income (*dasvandh*) towards the building of the college.[23] English well-wishers organised a committee in London to raise funds in England. Sikh princes, encouraged by the viceroy and the commander-in-chief, made handsome donations; the Anglo-Indian *Civil and Military Gazette* supported the cause with enthusiasm. Money began to pour in from all over the province. On March 5, 1892, the lieutenant governor, Sir James Lyall, who had taken personal interest in the venture, laid the foundation stone of the Khalsa College at Amritsar.[24]

---

impostor), then what is wrong therein? He (the Swami) had the sun of the Vedas in his hands. . . . He was not the person to be suppressed by anyone." Ganda Singh, *History of the Khalsa College*, p. 8.

[22] Jawahar Singh Kapur addressed meetings in Amritsar telling his Sikh audiences that the Arya Samaj had its institutions to teach Sanskrit and the Vedas, the Muslims had made provision for the teaching of the Koran at Aligarh, but the Sikhs had no institution for the study of Gurmukhi and the *Granth. Tribune*, August 15, 1890.

[23] The trustees of the College Committee included both Sikhs and Englishmen. They were Maharajah Pertap Singh of Nabha, Sir Attar Singh of Bhadaur, Gurdayal Singh, Dharam Singh, Dewan Gurmukh Singh of Patiala, Mr. Bell, Colonel Holroyde, and General Black. *Civil and Military Gazette*, May 9, 1890.

[24] An Englishman, Dr. S. C. Oman, was appointed principal. The chief justice of the Punjab High Court, W. H. Rattigan, became president of the college establishment committee, which was controlled by the vice-president, Sir Attar Singh of Bhadaur, and the secretary, Jawahar Singh Kapur.

Gratitude to the English patrons can be judged from the proposals submitted for the name of the college. The maharajah of Nabha wanted to name it the "Loyal Lyall Khalsa College" (letter to Gurmukh Singh dated December 22, 1899); the establishment committee was content to name it just Lyall Khalsa College. It was only the reluctance of Sir James himself that saved the College from being prefixed either Loyal or Lyall.

It was inevitable an organisation such as the Singh Sabha which had such multifarious activities should evolve its own politics as well. These crystallised in the formation in 1902 of the Chief Khalsa Diwan pledged "to cultivate loyalty to the crown," to safeguard Sikh rights vis-à-vis the other communities, and to fight for adequate representation of Sikhs in services, particularly the army. Almost from its inception its most effective leader was Sunder Singh Majithia.[25]

The most important aspects of the Singh Sabha movement were educational and literary. From 1908 onwards, an education conference was convened every year to take stock of the progress of literacy in the community and collect money to build more schools. The teaching of Gurmukhi and the Sikh scriptures was compulsory in these Khalsa schools.[26]

The impetus given to education in its turn stimulated the publication of books,[27] magazines, tracts, and newspa-

[25] Sir Sunder Singh (1872-1941), a descendant of the Majithias in the service of Maharajah Ranjit Singh, was a Shergil Jat of village Majitha near Amritsar. He was an ardent supporter of the British Raj. He was secretary of the Chief Khalsa Diwan from its inception in 1902 to 1921 and president of the Khalsa College Committee from 1920 till his death. He was a member of the provincial council and central assembly and held innumerable ministerial appointments. Majithia was a wealthy landowner and a sugar magnate. There will be many references to him in the following pages.

Senior colleagues of Sunder Singh Majithia were Harbans Singh of Attari (grandson of the hero of Sabraon) and Arjan Singh Bagarian, whose family had been religious mentors to the Sikh aristocracy.

[26] In 1856 the Education Department of the Punjab Government was constituted and a beginning made to set up schools independent of mosques, temple, or gurdwaras, to which they had till then been attached. In northwest Punjab Sir Khem Singh Bedi took a prominent part in building Khalsa schools. Sikh schools were also built in Amritsar, Lahore, Ferozepur, and in some villages such as Kairon, Gharjakh, Chuhar Chak, and Bhasaur. One of the best known institutions was the Sikh Kanya Mahavidyalaya of Ferozepur founded by Takht Singh.

[27] The *Anjuman-i-Panjāb* (founded in 1865) was responsible for translating many important English books into Punjabi. In 1877 Punjabi was introduced as a subject in the Oriental College at Lahore; in 1882 the Singh Sabha organised a *Panjābī Pracārini Sabhā* to popularise the use of Punjabi.

pers.[28] The earliest venture in Punjabi journalism was the weekly _Khālsā Akhbār_. In 1899 the _Khālsā Samācar_ was founded and soon became the leading theological journal of the community. Its circulation increased under the editorship of Vir Singh, who rose to prominence as a novelist, poet, and a commentator of scriptural writings.[29] Vir Singh also started the _Khalsa Tract Society_ and published literature on different aspects of Sikh history and religion.

A spate of books on Sikhism, both in Gurmukhi and English, were published. Of the Gurmukhi, Gyani Gyan Singh's _Panth Prakāś_ and _Tawārīkh Guru Khālsā_ and Kahan Singh's voluminous encyclopaedia of Sikh literature (_Guru Śabdaratnākar Mahānkoś_) were of lasting significance. M. A. Macauliffe's monumental work on the life and teachings of the Sikh gurus[30] was also published at this time.

The Singh Sabha movement not only checked the relapse of the Sikhs into Hinduism but retaliated by carrying proselytising activities into the Hindu camp. Large numbers of Hindus of northern and western Punjab and Sindh became _sahajdhārī_ Sikhs and the _sahajdhārīs_ were baptised to become the Khalsa.[31]

The rise and expansion of the Arya Samaj in the Punjab

[28] Over a dozen papers owed their existence to the Singh Sabha movement. _Sukabi Subodhinī_, Amritsar (1875); _Akāl Prakāś_, Amritsar (1876); _Gurmukhī Akhbār_, Lahore (1850); _Khālsā Prakāś_, Lahore (1884); _Srī Gurmat Prakāś_, Rawalpindi (1885); _Panjāb Darpan_, Amritsar (1885); _Khālsā Akhbār_ restarted in Lahore in 1886; and the _Vidyārak_, Lahore (1886); _The Khālsā Gazette_ and _Loyal Gazette_ (which later became the _Sher-i-Panjāb_) were published in Urdu.

[29] See Appendix 1.

[30] _The Sikh Religion_ was published in 1909 in six volumes by the Oxford University Press.

[31] The following figures show the increase in the Sikh population:

Year	Actual Number of Sikhs	Variation Percent in: Sikhs	Total Population
1881	1,706.165		
1891	1,849,371	+ 8.4	+ 10.1
1901	2,102,896	+ 13.7	+ 6.3
1911	2,883,729	+ 37.1	− 2.2
1921	3,110,060	+ 7.8	+ 5.7

Punjab Census Report, 1921.

had a decisive bearing on the course of Hindu-Sikh relations and on the pattern of anti-British political movements in the province. The *sudhī* crusade launched by the Samaj was fiercely resisted by the Sikhs. The more the Samajists claimed Sikhism to be a branch of Hinduism, the more the Sikhs insisted that they were a distinct and separate community. This action and reaction broke up the close social relationship which had existed between the two sister communities. It found expression in the publication of a booklet *Ham Hindū Nahiṅ Haiṇ*—we are not Hindus—by the scholarly Kahan Singh, who was then chief minister of Nabha. Although the Singh Sabha movement petered out in the 1920's it left a legacy of a chronically defensive attitude towards Hinduism.

Dayanand's teachings also had a strong political flavour. In proclaiming his intention to purify Hinduism of its post-Vedic accretions, he desired to liberate Hindu society from non-Hindu domination. His criticism of Islam and Christianity in effect was the criticism of Indian Muslims and the English. Consequently the renaissance of Hinduism brought about by the Arya Samaj had a strong anti-Muslim and anti-British bias which was often discernible in the utterances of Punjabi Hindu nationalists, large numbers of whom were Arya Samajists, e.g. Lajpat Rai,[32] Ajit Singh, Hans Raj, and the majority of Punjabi Hindu terrorists. The domination of the Indian National Congress by Arya Samajists gave the freedom movement an aspect of Hindu resurgence and was chiefly responsible for the aloofness of the Muslims and the Sikhs.[33]

[32] Lala Lajpat Rai (1865-1928), the most eminent of Punjab's nationalists, was born into a Hindu-Sikh family. He was also an active Samajist and for a while president of the Hindu Mahasabha.

[33] The remarks of Dr. Griswold are illuminating. "The watchword of Pandit Dayanand was back to the Vedas. With this religious watchword, another watchword was implicitly, if not explicitly, combined, namely India for Indians. Combining these two we have the principle, both religious and political, the religion of India as well as the sovereignty of India ought to belong to the Indian people, in other words, Hindu religion for the Indians and Indian sovereignty for the Indians." *Indian Evangelical Review*, January 1892, quoted by Farquhar, *Modern Religious Movements in India*, pp. 111-12.

PART IV

POLITICAL MOVEMENTS: MARXIST, NATIONAL, AND SECTARIAN

The reclamation of desert lands by the extension of canals, patronage in the services, and the introduction of the western system of education produced economic, social, and political changes in the Sikh community. The canal colonies eased the pressure on land and brought unprecedented prosperity to the peasantry. Their prosperity was, however, short-lived; within a few years, holdings were fragmented and became uneconomical. Rural indebtedness increased. Families which could raise money sent their younger sons to explore other avenues of employment or to seek their fortune in foreign lands. Sikh communities sprang up in Burma, Malaya, Singapore, Thailand, Cambodia, the Philippines, and China; and from the Asian coast the more enterprising ventured across the Pacific to Canada and the United States. At the same time small entrepreneurs set up business in countries on the eastern coast of Africa. On the American continent Sikh emigrants came up against racial discrimination and in turn developed a xenophobia which provided fertile ground for the dissemination of Marxism.

Enthusiasm for the British Raj, which had reached its climax during the first world war (1914-1918), rapidly declined. The government's refusal to protest against Canadian and American maltreatment of Sikh immigrants, disappointment over constitutional reforms, the shooting at Amritsar (April

1919) followed by the repression of the movement to gain control of shrines from hereditary priests, created resentment against British rule. From these movements three political parties emerged: the Communists, the Nationalists, and the Akalis. In the years following the first world war, when steps were taken to increase people's participation in the administration, these three political parties contended for power; much the most influential of them being the Akalis.

CHAPTER 10

RURAL INDEBTEDNESS AND
PEASANT AGITATION

The Punjab Peasant in Prosperity and Debt

◊:◊:◊: THE reclamation of desert lands by the exten-
◊:◊:◊: sion of canal irrigation, combined with facili-
▽·▽·▽ ties for marketing agricultural produce, ushered in an era of prosperity that the Punjab had never
seen. But this prosperity brought in its wake other economic changes which radically altered the social fabric of
life in the Punjab. A direct consequence of the increase in
the earning from agriculture was the increase in the price
of land; it rose from a mere Rs. 10 per acre in 1870 to more
than Rs. 100 per acre by the turn of the century.[1] Land became a valuable commodity, and small farmers were unable
to resist the temptation to sell their holdings.[2] The number
of landless farmers assumed alarming proportions. The
famine of 1869[3] attended by heavy mortality of livestock
accentuated the problem. Agriculturists were unable to pay
revenue due from them and were compelled to borrow.

The 1870's ushered in an era of peasant indebtedness
which had never been known in the country before. From
1877—which was another year of serious shortages—it as-

[1] H. Calvert, *The Wealth and Welfare of the Punjab*, p. 219. The price
of land continued to rise. In 1925 it was Rs.438/- per acre; in 1933-34,
it touched Rs.477/- per acre.

[2] "That dull animal [the peasant] by degrees realised that he was the
possessor of, in his eyes, unlimited credit and used it." Thorburn, *Report
on Peasant Indebtedness and Land Alienations*, p. 10.
And once the agriculturist started borrowing, he lost his self-reliance
and made it a habit—*carhiā sau te lathā bhau*—when the debt mounts
to a hundred, one loses all fear, or, in for a penny in for a pound.

[3] In the famine of 1869, 600,000 head of cattle were lost in four
districts of southeastern Punjab alone. A cattle epidemic in 1877 killed
two-thirds of the livestock in Ambala. In 1919-21 the failure of five out of
six harvests reduced the cattle at Sirsa by 40%. M. Darling, *The Punjab
Peasant in Prosperity and Debt*, p. 97.

sumed alarming proportions. The elaborate legal system introduced by the British contributed towards the impoverishment of the peasantry and the enrichment of moneylenders and lawyers.[4] "To permit the profits of husbandry to pass to moneylenders is an intolerable revolution of an odious kind never yet known in India," wrote Thorburn, "and yet it is exactly what our system is bringing about."[5]

Moneylending became a popular occupation.[6] In the past moneylenders had disdained to advance money on anything as worthless as land; now they were eager to lend against the fruits of the land without being encumbered with its ownership. Their business methods were far from ethical; they falsified accounts and charged rates of interest which kept their clients in a state of perpetual indebtedness.[7] The agriculturist did little, however, to ameliorate

[4] The process began in 1859, when three years was fixed as the limitation of all debts unprotected by registered bond—thus forcing creditors to hurry to courts. The introduction of the Civil Procedure Code, the setting up of the Chief Court at Lahore (in 1866), the passing of the Evidence Act and Contract Act in 1872 gave ingenious lawyers and their clients (moneylenders could afford them more than agriculturists) opportunities to prolong litigation. The straw that broke the back of the peasantry was the creation in 1874-75 of munsiffs' courts to try debt disputes. Till then district officers with close knowledge of the peasants' problems and revenue matters had dealt with these disputes simply, cheaply, and equitably. The munsiffs, largely urbanites ignorant of rural affairs, proved to be harsh and often corrupt. Thorburn, *Report on Peasant Indebtedness and Land Alienations*, p. 47.

[5] *Ibid.*, p. 11.

[6] Between 1902 and 1917 the number of moneylenders almost doubled. In 1902 there were 8,400 registered moneylenders in the Punjab. By 1917, their number had increased to over 15,000. H. Calvert, *The Wealth and Welfare of the Punjab*, p. 255.

The Punjab had three communities of moneylenders: Aroras in the western districts, Khatris in the central, and Banias in the southern districts. The first two communities were equally Hindu and Sikh; the Banias were invariably Hindus. Moneylending was seldom practised by Punjabi Mussalmans and very rarely by Jats of any community.

[7] Moneylenders did not necessarily have to be dishonest. Even "with honest lenders," wrote Thorburn, "a good solvent customer's money debt is doubled inside three years and his grain debt inside two years." *Report on Peasant Indebtedness and Land Alienations*, p. 7.

his condition. The Sikh Jat in particular reverted to his traditional habit of drowning his sorrows in drink; in some districts of Malwa, the preference was for opium.[8] These addictions led to an increase in crime. In addition to family feuds and altercations concerning the use of canal water which were common to all agricultural communities, the Sikh Jat indulged in violence without motive or provocation and had to borrow money to defend himself in court.

There were other causes of indebtedness: inordinate expenses at weddings, providing dowries for daughters or— in some districts where there was acute shortage of women —the cost of buying wives. Punjabi peasants also proved to be more quarrelsome and litigious than any other people of India.[9] A little less than half the adult population of the province attended law courts and spent between 3-4 crores of rupees in litigation every year. In addition, there were natural causes of indebtedness such as the increase of population; in the Punjab, between 1855 and 1881 the population was estimated to have increased by nearly 20 percent.[10] The pressure on land became heavy and holdings became uneconomical.[11] The halcyon days ushered in by the opening up of the canal colonies were soon over.

The accepted rate of interest was *dām deorhe, jins dūnī* (for cash 50%, for grain double).

[8] The Sikhs of Ferozepur district earned notoriety for indulgence in drink, opium, and crimes of violence.

[9] The Civil Justice Committee in its report published in 1925 found that, in proportion to their numbers, the Punjabis filed twice as many suits as the people of the United Provinces. About 2½ million, i.e. 40% of the adult population, attended the courts every year as parties or witnesses. H. Calvert, *The Wealth and Welfare of the Punjab*, p. 372.

[10] To make a fair comparison between the first (1855) and third census (1881), to the figures of the 1855 census must be added two sets of figures—"the corresponding census of the Delhi territory, namely Delhi, Gurgaon, part of Karnal, Hissar and Rohtak was taken under the N. W. Provinces Govt. on 1st January, 1853 while the census of Bhattiana or Sirsa was a settlement census taken village by village between 1852 and 1863." See Ibbetson's report on the *Punjab Census 1881*, I, 8.

[11] Thorburn reporting in 1896 on conditions in villages in Sialkot district wrote: "Congestion can hardly go further, and the sub-division of

Land Alienation Act, 1900

Murders of Hindu and Sikh moneylenders by exasperated peasant debtors became a common phenomenon in the western districts.[12] The government realised the dangers of having disgruntled peasantry—particularly a peasantry from which it drew the largest number of recruits for the army and on whose loyalty depended the internal security of the country.[13] The Land Alienation Act was

---

holdings is consequently so great that quite half of the proprietary families have less than five cultivated acres to live on, enough in average and good years, but insufficient in seasons of drought, even though land be well-irrigated." *Peasant Indebtedness and Land Alienations*, p. 2.

According to Calvert, the average holding of land was 7-8 acres per head constituted as follows:

> 17.9% of the people owned less than one acre; their holdings amounted to 1% of the land.
>
> 40.4% of the people owned between 1-5 acres; their holdings amounted to 11% of the land.
>
> 26.2% of the people owned between 5-15 acres; their holdings amounted to 26.6% of the land.
>
> 11.8% of the people owned between 15-50 acres; their holdings amounted to 35.6% of the land.
>
> 3.7% of the people owned more than 50 acres; their holdings amounted to 25.7% of the land.

H. Calvert, *The Wealth and Welfare of the Punjab*, pp. 172-73.

[12] Muslims formed 56% of the population and owed at least 50-60 crores of Punjab's rural debt calculated at 100 crores of rupees. M. Darling, *The Punjab Peasant in Prosperity and Debt*, pp. 19-20.

The census of 1921 is not sufficiently detailed to give all the information required, but, roughly, the proportion of agriculturists to others in the three communities was as follows:

	Agriculturists	Non-Agriculturists	Total
Muslims	6,728,000	4,716,000	11,444,000
Hindus	2,211,000	4,368,000	6,579,000
Sikhs	1,508,000	784,000	2,292,000
	10,447,000	9,868,000	20,315,000

Calvert, *Wealth and Welfare of the Punjab*, p. 269.

[13] In a note in 1895, on the proposal to check alienation of land, the lieutenant governor, Sir D. Fitzpatrick, warned that if landowners were reduced to the condition of tenants or labourers they would constitute "a political danger of formidable dimensions." Government of India Records, *Agricultural Indebtedness and Land Transfers*, II, *Punjab Correspondence*, p. 2.

designed to protect the agriculturists from the clutches of the moneylenders. It forbade the attachment of land in execution of decrees and outlawed mortgages which had a conditional sale clause attached to them. It also forbade (except by special sanction) the sale of land by members of agricultural tribes to non-agriculturists and declared illegal mortgages of land by agriculturists to non-agriculturists unless provision was made for automatic redemption. To ensure implementation of these provisions, the act limited leases of land to periods of not more than five years.

The act succeeded in safeguarding the interests of cultivators; but it also sowed the seeds of racial separatism. The question as to who was or was not an agriculturist was not decided by actual occupation but by caste. Thus all Jats, Rajputs, and members of scheduled castes were declared agriculturists, while all Khatris, Aroras, and Banias were classed as non-agriculturists. The act did not provide for an exception in the case of Jat moneylenders or Arora agriculturists. In certain districts Brahmins were declared agriculturists, in others, non-agriculturists. Cases of individual hardship were not as serious as the breaking up of the population on a new racial basis. Muslims, amongst whom caste considerations mattered little, were not particularly affected, nor, for precisely the opposite reason, were the Hindus. Hindi-speaking Hindu Jats were concentrated in Hariana and had little in common with the Punjabi-speaking Khatri or Arora Hindu of the Punjab. The community most adversely affected was the Sikhs. They had gone a long way in breaking the barriers of caste; and there were a sizeable number of Khatri and Arora Sikhs who, because they were in agriculture, had developed an identity of economic interest with their Jat co-religionists. The Land Alienation Act severed the links between the Jat Sikh farmer and the non-Jat Sikh farmer and put them in opposing camps. As a result, while the Jat Sikh was drawn closer to the Jat Mussalman and the Jat Hindu, the Khatri and the Arora Sikh drew closer to the Khatri and Arora Hindu.

Common economic interests were reflected in political life with the Sikh Jats aligned with other Jats against non-Jat Sikhs. Economic and political differences ultimately affected social life as well. Sikh Jats preferred to marry into Hindu Jat families rather than into non-Jat Sikhs. And Sikh Khatris and Aroras preferred to intermarry with corresponding Hindu castes rather than with Jat Sikhs. Finally, there was the third racial group amongst the Sikhs— the untouchables. Sikh untouchables found that they had more in common with Hindu untouchables than with the higher caste Sikhs. They sought the statutory privileges accorded to "scheduled castes." In short, with the Land Alienation Act, race came to matter more than religion. The Sikh community split into three racial divisions—the Jats, the non-Jats (which included Brahmins, Kshatriyas, and Vaishyas), and the untouchables (Mazhabis, Ramdasias, Siklighars, Kabirpanthis, etc.).

Peasant Agitation, 1907

The Land Alienation Act saved agricultural land from passing to moneylenders, but did not solve the problem of rural indebtedness. The Punjab was visited by a series of calamities. Some districts were twice ravaged by famine, and the whole of the province was swept by an epidemic of bubonic plague which took a toll of over four million lives. The administration remained insensitive to these disasters; instead of remitting land revenue, it continued to increase it with each new settlement[14] and inflicted heavy punishment on defaulters.

The immediate cause of unrest was the introduction of a bill affecting the newly colonised lands opened by the Chenab Canals. The bill was passed on the assumption that

14 In 1891, the land revenue from the Punjab amounted to £1,500,000; by 1906 this had gone up 30% to £1,925,000. O'Donnell, *The Causes of Present Discontent in India*, p. 94.

land was the property of the government and the farmer was a mere tenant. This was contrary to prevailing notions of peasant-proprietorship. Provisions which caused the most heart-burning were those which restricted the rights of colonisers to make wills and denied them the right to cut trees on their land.[15] Provisions regulating the pattern of housing and standards of sanitation were not objectionable in themselves except for the clause which gave the administration the right to resume the grant in case of default.[16]

The bill was vigorously criticised in the Indian press and by members of the Punjab Legislative Council. Pratap Singh Ahluwalia, speaking on behalf of the Sikhs, protested that the bill sought to make the government both landlord and administrator; it enhanced the rights of the administration at the expense of the tenants and deprived them of the protection of the civil courts.[17] His objections were overruled.

While the colonisation bill was agitating the minds of the people, a new settlement of Rawalpindi district[18] was made at a higher rate of assessment, and the rate on water taken from the Bari Doab Canals was increased. The districts most affected by these measures were Lyallpur (mainly colonised by Sikhs) and Rawalpindi.

A distressed peasantry made the Punjab fertile soil for revolutionary seed. And the seed blew in profusion from all over India—and indeed from Asia. The Punjabi rustic, who had looked upon the European as his *māī-bāp* (mother-father) divinely ordained to rule over the "lesser breeds" of yellow and brown and black races, heard of the resounding victory of Japanese arms over the Russian. He

[15] The bill required colonisers to plant a minimum of 55 trees per square but denied them the right to cut trees without permission.
[16] J. M. Douie, settlement commissioner, *P.L.C.D.*, February 28, 1907.
[17] *P.L.C.D.*, February 28, 1907, pp. 13-15.
[18] Land revenue from the district increased from £27,500 in 1864 to £36,400 in 1884 to £45,000 in 1904. O'Donnell, *The Causes of Present Discontent in India*, p. 101.

also heard of his own countrymen's triumph in forcing the government to rescind the partition of Bengal (1905). In India the gentle politics of Dadabhai Naoroji and Ranade had given way to the radical and the revolutionary method of Tilak and the terrorists. "Swaraj is our birth-right," proclaimed Tilak. "If you deny us swaraj we will blow you to smithereens," added the terrorists. It was hardly likely that the gale that was blowing across the length and breadth of Hindustan would bypass the Punjab.

Urban politicians took the lead in organising protest meetings. The nationalist press supported their cause and in its eagerness to help enlarged the grievance against the colonisation bill into a racial issue between the brown and the white man. The *Tribune* and the *Punjabi* were sued for libel by English officers; *India* and The *Hindustan* were prosecuted for sedition against the government.[19]

By March 1907 the atmosphere in the cities and the affected colonies had become tense. A new song was on the lips of the people *"pagṛī sambhāl jattā*—peasant, guard your turban." Students of the Khalsa College, Amritsar, staged a hostile demonstration at the farewell visit of the outgoing lieutenant governor, Sir Charles Rivaz.[20] Protest meetings in bigger cities were organised by lawyers and members of the Arya Samaj.[21]

The fiftieth anniversary of the sepoy mutiny was chosen as the occasion for a province-wide protest. In some places, particularly Lyallpur, the demonstrations had to be dispersed by force. Lajpat Rai, Ajit Singh, and some lawyers who were suspected of fomenting the trouble were arrested. The first two were deported to Burma.

Despite the repression, criticism of the bill continued

[19] The *Hindustan* addressed a message "to the native forces in British India: *Bande Mātaram. Sepoy mat bano*—Salutation to the Motherland do not join the army." *Civil and Military Gazette*, July 28, 1907.

[20] Among the organisers of the student demonstrations was young Tara Singh, who was destined to become the dominant figure in Sikh politics.

[21] A leading part was taken by Lajpat Rai, Sufi Amba Prasad, and Ajit Singh of the *Bharat Mata Society*, and Pindi Das, editor of *India*.

unabated. The authorities sensed that the measure had caused uneasiness among Sikh soldiers,[22] many of whom had relatives in the colony areas, and governor general, Lord Minto, vetoed the bill. The land tax and the water rate were reduced.[23]

The king emperor's birthday was made the excuse to proclaim an amnesty, and the Punjab leaders returned home after six months in Burma.[24]

[22] Mr. Morley, secretary of state for India, in a speech in Parliament, said "In this agitation special attention, it is stated, has been paid to the Sikhs, who, as the House is aware, are among the best soldiers in India. . . . Special efforts have been made to secure their attendance at meetings to enlist their sympathies and to inflame their passions. So far active agitation has been virtually confined to the districts in which the Sikh element is predominant." *Indian Debates Session, 1907*, House of Commons, June 6, 1907, p. 177.

It was the opinion of the Punjab Government that of the 28 meetings organised by the agitators only five dealt with peasants' grievances; the rest were of a political nature.

[23] Returns of water tax are significant. The capital of 7 million sterling invested in the Punjab canals yielded in 1906-07 a handsome net profit of 10½%, whereas in the case of the Chenab Canal colonies the returns were nearly 22%. It was in the Chenab colonies that the agitation was the strongest. O'Donnell, *The Causes of Present Discontent in India*, p. 98.

[24] The arrested lawyers were kept in gaol for five months before being released on bail. A few days later they were acquitted by the judge, Mr. Martineau, because the evidence tendered by the prosecution was "untrustworthy and malicious." *Ibid.*, p. 100.

CHAPTER 11

WORLD WAR I AND ITS AFTERMATH

Sikh Contribution to the War (1914-1918)

EVER since the Mutiny of 1857, the Sikhs had formed a very substantial portion of the British army. When war broke out, Sikh recruitment was speeded up. The number of Sikhs in the services rose from 35,000 at the beginning of 1915 to over 100,000 by the end of the war,[1] forming about a fifth of the army in action.

Recruitment from the princely states was more impressive than in British India. Over 60,000 men from Patiala (which had a total higher than the best of any British district and four times as much as that of any other Indian princely state), Jind, Kapurthala, Nabha, Faridkot, and Kalsia went to the front. The maharajahs of Patiala, Jind, and Kapurthala offered their personal services, and all the princes made generous contributions in cash and equipment.

Sikh soldiers fought on all fronts of the war in Europe, Turkey, and Africa, and did credit to their race by their bravery. Of the 22 military crosses awarded for conspicuous gallantry to Indians, the Sikhs won 14. The official chronicler of the Punjab's war effort recorded: "It is true that in practically every part of the province the Sikhs came forward in strength and established an all-round record which leaves little room for criticism.[2]

---

[1] M. S. Leigh, *The Punjab and the War*, p. 44.

[2] *Ibid.*, pp. 107-09.

On the conclusion of hostilities, Sikh legislative councillors lauded the services of their community. Gajjan Singh said: "My community has supplied recruits in almost every Sikh district much larger in number as compared with the sister communities of the Muhammadans and Hindus. . . . I am not in possession of correct figures but I believe that out of the nearly four lakh brave sons of the Punjab who went to fight the battles of the King Emperor about one-third were members of my community.

Aftermath of the War. Massacre of Amritsar, April 13, 1919

Because the Sikh contribution to the war both in men and material was bigger than that of any other community of India, it was not altogether surprising that they exaggerated their role in the allied victory and expected to be specially rewarded for their services. They were, consequently, pained to find that local officials and the police continued to treat them as common rustics instead of heroes. They heard for the first time the full story of the maltreatment of Sikh emigrants by Canadian and American whites and of the Ghadr rising;[3] of the infamous conspiracy trials—the hangings, deportations, and the internment in their villages of nearly 5,000 of their Ghadrite co-religionists. Their fellow villagers also told them of the persecution by the authorities, of the "Indent System" by which every village had been forced to provide a certain number of recruits,[4] and the pressure used to raise war funds.[5] Other factors added fuel to the smouldering fire. The summer monsoon failed; the *rabī* harvest was extremely meagre; the cost of living rose higher than ever before.[6] Urban population was further hit by the imposition of a special income-tax: the increase in some cases ranged from 100 to 200 percent.[7] To cap it all, an epidemic

---

We, the Sikhs are very proud of this record. If we were proud of our loyalty and devotion to government we are prouder today." *P.L.C.D.,* November 20, 1918, pp. 387-88.

[3] Discussed in Chapter 12.

[4] There was extra strain on man-power requirements in the last two years of the war. It was caused by the collapse of Russia and the rising of the Mahsud, Mohmand, and Mari tribes on the northwest frontier.

[5] The expression "pressure and persuasion" was used by Lord Willingdon, governor of Bombay. Bombay police often sealed wells till the villagers paid the sum marked against them. B. G. Horniman, *Amritsar and Our Duty to India,* p. 24.

[6] Wheat was 47% above the normal price of 1914, foreign cloth 175%, Indian cloth 100%, sugar 68% higher than prewar prices. German submarine warfare restricted imports; coal shortage cut down railway transport.

[7] Hunter Committee Report, *Disorders Inquiry Committee Report,* p. 152.

of influenza raged across the entire country taking a heavy toll of life. By the end of the year (1918), over 100,000 Punjabis had succumbed to the 'flu. An atmosphere of disillusionment and depression came to prevail in the province. When the people needed succour and reassurance, a balm to soothe their nerves—the government rubbed salt into their wounds.

Restrictive measures introduced during the war were not withdrawn; on the contrary, legislation of a more drastic nature was planned. Sir Michael O'Dwyer, lieutenant governor of the Punjab, scouted the notion of self-government for India as a preposterous figment of the mind of the urbanite babu and the wog barrister.[8] He prohibited nationalist leaders from entering the province and took stern measures to repress agitation against the Rowlatt[9] bills intended to combat revolutionary crime. In the Punjab, Sir Sidney Rowlatt came to be known by the sobriquet *raulā* (turmoil). The drastic changes he proposed were summed up in the slogan: *nā dalīl, nā vakīl, nā apīl* (no argument, no lawyer, no appeal). Nevertheless, the bills became law in March 1919.[10]

Mahatma Gandhi, who had been leading the agitation against the Rowlatt bills, called for a complete *hartāl* (cessation of work) to mark the people's sense of resentment. There were riots and casualties caused by police firing in many cities. The Mahatma was arrested.

[8] "If it is clear that the demands emanate not from the mass of the people, whose interests are at stake, but from a small and not quite disinterested minority, naturally enough eager for power and place, we must, if we are faithful to our trust, place the interests of the silent masses before the clamour of the politicians however troublesome and insistent." Sir Michael O'Dwyer quoted in the *Congress Punjab Inquiry Report 1919-20*, p. 14.

[9] A Committee under Sir Sidney Rowlatt produced a report on revolutionary crime in India since 1907 and proposed a series of measures empowering the executive to override ordinary legal processes in dealing with violent political agitation.

[10] These were the Indian Criminal Law Amendment Bill and the Criminal Law (Emergency Powers) Bill. They were introduced in February 1919 and passed within a month.

In the Punjab, the protests were conducted in a peaceful and orderly manner till the police precipitated matters. In Amritsar, Doctors Saifuddin Kitchlew and Satyapal, who had successfully organised a "striking demonstration in furtherance of Hindu-Mohammedan unity" were arrested and whisked away to Dharamsala.[11] News of their deportation spread in the city, and a crowd of citizens proceeded to the deputy commissioner's bungalow to register their protest. The police stopped them en route and, in trying to disperse them, killed half a dozen people and wounded over 30.[12] The mob got out of hand and began to assault white people. It set fire to English-owned banks, a church, the offices of the Christian Religious Text Book Society, the telegraph office, and the town hall. In this riot five Englishmen were killed and an English missionary severely assaulted. The deputy commissioner's foolish action yielded a bitter harvest of racial hate.

From Jullundur, Brigadier General R. E. H. Dyer[13] arrived with troops and armoured cars. The next afternoon when he marched his troops through the bazaars he was greeted with shouts of *Hindū-Mussalmān kī jai* and *Mahātmā Gāndhī kī jai*. In the evening he received information of vandalism: cutting of telegraph wires and tampering with fishplates on the railway track. The general proclaimed a state of emergency and declared all meetings illegal. Meanwhile the local Congress had already announced a meeting at Jallianwala Bagh for the Baisakhi fair. From the early hours of the morning, Sikhs, for whom the first of Baisakh was also the birth anniversary of the

[11] Hunter Committee Report, *Disorders Inquiry Committee Report*, p. 29.

"Mussalmans and Hindus have united . . . I have been expecting this . . . there is a big show coming." General Dyer to his son on leaving Jullundur for Amritsar. Colvin, *Life of General Dyer*, p. 162.

[12] The figure of casualties in the *Congress Punjab Inquiry Report* was twenty dead and many wounded (p. 48).

[13] R. E. H. Dyer (1864-1927) belonged to a well-known family of brewers, Dyer Meakin & Co., of northern India. He was schooled in Simla and later in Sandhurst. He got his commission in 1886 and served mostly in India.

Khalsa, started arriving at the Golden Temple. Those who had come from the outlying villages and had not heard of the proclamation went to the nearby Jallianwala garden to while away the hours till it was cool enough to return home. Local Congress leaders utilised the opportunity to tell them about the occurrences of the previous day. For the Sikh villagers it was just another diversion, a *tamāsā*.

As soon as General Dyer received news of the meeting, he marched a platoon of infantry to Jallianwala. He occupied the only entrance and exit to the garden and, without giving any warning to the people to disperse, opened fire. He killed 379 and wounded over 2,000. He imposed a curfew on the city and returned to his camp leaving the dying with the dead without any possibility of help reaching them. When the news was conveyed to Sir Michael O'Dwyer, he fully approved of the action.[14]

Martial law was proclaimed in Amritsar and subsequently extended to other districts: Lahore, Gujranwala, Lyallpur, and Gujarat.

Martial Law in the Punjab

Hartals and black-flag processions to protest against the Rowlatt bills had taken place in most cities of the Punjab, and in some the police had dispersed passive resisters by opening fire on them. After Jallianwala, the demonstrations took an extremely violent form. Bridges, churches, post offices, and other public buildings were burnt; telegraph and telephone lines were cut; railway lines torn up; white men assaulted. The army took over the administration, and whatever vestiges of a civilised government had remained also vanished.

[14] "I approved of General Dyer's action in dispersing by force the rebellious gathering and thus preventing further rebellious acts. . . . Speaking with perhaps a more intimate knowledge of the then situation than anyone else. I have no hesitation in saying that General Dyer's action that day was the decisive factor in crushing the rebellion, the seriousness of which is only now being generally realised." Hunter Committee Report, *Disorders Inquiry Committee Report*, p. 48.

General Dyer's actions at Amritsar set the tone of "Dyer-archy" (the word coined for lawlessness) for the rest of the province. He had the city's water and electric supply cut off. In the street where a missionary lady had been assaulted, he made Indian passers-by crawl on their bellies; people were flogged without trial; bicycles, carts, and cars "other than those owned by Europeans" were commandeered. Lawyers were compulsorily recruited as special constables and made to patrol the streets; specially constituted courts tried nearly 300 men and summarily sentenced 51 to death and hundreds of others to terms of imprisonment.

Lahore suffered a worse fate than Amritsar. The army administrator ordered tradesmen to open their shops on pain of being shot and having their stores distributed free to the public; not more than two persons were allowed to walk abreast on the sidewalks; electric fans and other electric gadgets belonging to Indians were requisitioned for the use of British soldiers; Badshahi mosque, where meetings had taken place, was closed except for the Friday prayers; for several days flogging was carried out in public. Educated classes came in for special attention. Students of several Lahore colleges were ordered to report four times daily—in some cases four miles away from their colleges.

Kasur, where two Englishmen had been murdered, was collectively punished with fines and public flogging of suspects; an Indian who failed to *salām* a white man was made to rub his or her nose on the ground; a local poet was ordered to compose verses in praise of martial law and its administrator; gallows were erected in the market place to strike terror in the populace.

Gujranwala and its neighbouring villages were subjected to bombing and machine-gunning from the air; one of the targets successfully hit was the Khalsa High School at Gujranwala, where many people were killed and wounded.

Other places in the Punjab which suffered at the hands of martial law administrators were Wazirabad, Nizamabad,

Akalgarh, Ram Nagar, Hafizabad, Sheikhupura, Chuhar-
kana, Sangla, Moman, Manianwala, Nawanpind, Jalapur
Jattan (a Sikh village), Malakwal, Lyallpur, Gojra and
Chak No. 149 (colonised by Sikh Jats), and Gujarat. In
the seven weeks that the Punjab was administered by martial law nearly 1,200 were killed and at least 3,600
wounded.[15]

The effect that Jallianwala and martial law administration had on the people of the Punjab can hardly be exaggerated. Racial tension, reminiscent of the most savage days
of the mutiny when every white man looked upon the
coloured as his enemy, was re-created. Even people of tried
loyalty, including those who had served in the forces, were
victimised. Sir Michael O'Dwyer, who claimed that he had
saved the empire, had in fact dealt it the most grievous blow by alienating almost all Indians, including its
staunchest supporters, the Sikhs.[16]

General Dyer tried to win over the Sikhs as best he
could. He summoned the manager of the Golden Temple

[15] The Jallianwala Bagh massacre and the martial law regime was subjected to the most searching enquiry by a committee appointed by the
Indian National Congress headed by Mahatma Gandhi himself. The
committee severely censured the lieutenant governor, Sir Michael O'Dwyer, General Dyer, and the English officers concerned. Subsequently, the
government appointed its own committee for the same purpose. It was
presided over by Lord Hunter and consisted of seven other members,
including three Indians. The Hunter Commission was unanimous in its
verdict on General Dyer's action and recommended his dismissal. On the
other issues, the English and the Indian members were at variance; the
latter submitted a minority report.

The matter was also debated in the British Parliament. Winston
Churchill made the most scathing criticism of General Dyer's action—he
described it as "an episode which appeared to be without parallel in
the modern history of the British Empire . . . an extraordinary event,
a monstrous event, an event which stood in singular and sinister isola-
tion." R. Furneaux, *Massacre at Amritsar*, p. 153.

General Dyer had his supporters. The *Morning Post* raised a fund for
him and he was presented with a golden sword as "Defender of the
Empire." The general received a sum of £26,317 from his English admirers.

[16] Sir Michael O'Dwyer was murdered by a Sikh, Udham Singh, at a
public meeting in London on March 13, 1940. Udham Singh was hanged
on June 13, 1940.

and Sunder Singh Majithia and asked them to use their influence with the Sikhs in favour of the government. He sent out movable columns through the Sikh villages to wean them away from the influence of mischief makers and to prove that the *sircār* was still strong. Priests of the Golden Temple invited the general to the sacred shrine and presented him with a *siropā* (turban and kirpan).

Mahatma Gandhi later visited Jallianwala Bagh and the sites where atrocities had been committed by the army and the police. He addressed mammoth gatherings and told the people that the most important quality for a patriot was to be *nirbhai*—fearless. Under his inspiration a new organisation, the Central Sikh League, consisting of nationalists who were opposed to the Chief Khalsa Diwan's toadying to the British, came into existence.

CHAPTER 12

XENOPHOBIC MARXISM

Sikh Emigration to Canada and the United States

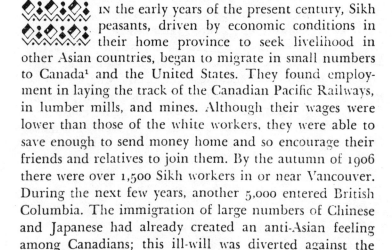 IN the early years of the present century, Sikh peasants, driven by economic conditions in their home province to seek livelihood in other Asian countries, began to migrate in small numbers to Canada[1] and the United States. They found employment in laying the track of the Canadian Pacific Railways, in lumber mills, and mines. Although their wages were lower than those of the white workers, they were able to save enough to send money home and so encourage their friends and relatives to join them. By the autumn of 1906 there were over 1,500 Sikh workers in or near Vancouver. During the next few years, another 5,000 entered British Columbia. The immigration of large numbers of Chinese and Japanese had already created an anti-Asian feeling among Canadians; this ill-will was diverted against the Sikhs, who looked more distinctive with their turbans and long flowing beards and were less docile than their fellow Orientals.[2] In a short time Sikhs became the cynosure of

[1] The presence of Indians attracted official notice in 1904 when 258 "Hindus" (a term applied by Canadians and Americans to all Indians irrespective of their religion) were listed in the census of British Columbia. Over 90% of the Indian emigrants to Canada and the United States were Sikhs—of these over 90% of those who went to Canada settled in British Columbia and over 90% of those who went to the United States settled in California.

[2] To whip up racial prejudice, stories were spread that the Punjabis were polygamous, full of caste prejudices, unclean in their personal habits, riddled with disease (particularly trachoma), and therefore altogether unassimilable. A song which became popular at the time in British Columbia was entitled "White Canada for Ever."

> This the voice of the West and it speaks to the world:
> The rights that our fathers have given
> We'll hold by right and maintain by might,
> Till the foe is backward driven.

Canadian eyes.[3] Assaults on Sikh workers became a feature
of daily life in Vancouver.[4] Unemployment consequent
upon a slump in the lumber trade accentuated the com-
petition between white and coloured workers. White trade

We welcome as brothers all white men still,
But the shifty yellow race,
Whose word is vain, who oppress the weak,
Must find another place.

Chorus:

Then let us stand united all
And show our father's might,
That won the home we call our own,
For white man's land we fight.
To oriental grasp and greed
We'll surrender, no never.
Our watchword be "God save the King"
White Canada for ever.

[3] In October 1906, a ship bringing a party of Indians had to be diverted
to Victoria because the mayor refused to allow it to dock in Vancouver
harbour. A mass meeting was held in Vancouver Town Hall on October
18, 1906, at which resolutions were passed against further immigration
of Indians. Some voices were raised in protest on behalf of the Sikhs;
among them was that of Henry H. Gladstone (nephew of the famous
prime minister), who had served 15 years in India. Answering the charge
that Indians had filthy habits, he wrote: "The Sikhs are scrupulously
clean and I regard them as a very fine race of men." *Pacific Monthly*,
Vol. 17 of 1907.

Dr. S. H. Lawson, who was a ship's surgeon on the Canadian Pacific
Railway steamers *Monteagle* and *Tartar*, wrote: "It was my duty to make
a thorough physical examination of each immigrant at Hong Kong and,
although at first I was strongly prejudiced against them, I lost this
prejudice after thousands of them had passed through my hands and I
had compared them with white steerage passengers I had seen on the
Atlantic. I refer in particular to the Sikhs and I am not exaggerating in
the least when I say that they were one hundred per cent cleaner in
their habits and freer from disease than the European steerage passengers
I had come in contact with. The Sikhs impressed me as a clean, manly,
honest race. My more recent impressions as a surgeon in mining camps
among thousands of white men, where immorality is rife, has increased
my respect for the Sikhs." *The Indians Appeal to Canada*, p. 11; R. K.
Das, *Hindustani Workers on the Pacific Coast*, p. 75.

[4] There were anti-Asian riots in the city of Vancouver in July 1907.
These were largely directed against the Chinese and Japanese and resulted in $36,000 worth of damage to property. The Sikhs escaped by dis-
creetly remaining indoors.

unions pressed the Federal Government to exclude coloured immigrants. As a result of the measures passed, only six Indians were allowed to enter Canada in 1909.

The fact that Sikh immigrants were British subjects created legal complications. British Columbian legislation required the sanction of the Federal Government; the Federal Government had to consult the government of the United Kingdom, which in its turn had to watch the reaction of the Government of India. Canada's immigration policy vis-à-vis the Indians was thus formulated after prolonged negotiations between Vancouver, Ottawa, London, and Calcutta. All the governments were however agreed that British Columbians had every right to exclude Indian immigrants; their only concern was that measures should be so framed that no suspicion of racial discrimination should attach to them.[5]

From 1907 onwards, British Columbia's state legislature passed several enactments to check Indian immigration and prohibit employment of Indians in certain industries. These enactments were invalidated by the courts. The Government of India was then requested to stop immigration at source.[6]

[5] At first an attempt was made to persuade the immigrants to leave Canada voluntarily and settle instead in British Honduras. It was believed that in view of the unemployment in British Columbia in the years 1907 and 1908 this proposal would receive favourable response. A delegation of representative Sikhs visited the Honduras, studied the conditions and recommended that their countrymen reject the proposal as the wages in the Honduras, where most of the labour was indentured, were low and the climatic conditions were unsuitable for Punjabis.

[6] Sir Wilfred Laurier, prime minister of Canada, repeated the allegation that the Indians were "unsuited to live in the climatic conditions of British Columbia and were a serious disturbance to industrial and economic conditions in portions of the Dominions." Order-in-council, March 2, 1908.

In a letter to the viceroy, Lord Minto, Sir Wilfred wrote, "Strange to say the Hindus . . . are looked upon by our people in British Columbia with still more disfavour than the Chinese. They seem to be less adaptable to our ways and manners than all the other Oriental races that come to us." April 1909, quoted by Morse in his unpublished thesis "Immigration and Status of British East Indians in Canada," 27.

In 1908, Mr. McKenzie King[7] (later prime minister of Canada) visited London and Calcutta to press the Canadian point of view. As a result the Government of India ordered shipping companies to stop advertising travel facilities and employment opportunities on the American continent and invoked the provisions of the Emigration Act 1883[8] to prevent Indians leaving for Canada. The Canadian Government itself passed two orders-in-council to deal with the ingress of Indian nationals living abroad. One raised the sum of money required to be in the possession of an intending immigrant from $25 to $200; the other authorised the minister of the interior to prohibit entry of travellers unless they came "from the country of their birth or citizenship by a continuous journey, and on through tickets purchased before leaving the country of their birth or citizenship."[9] Both these orders were specifically directed against the Indians. Chinese and Japanese immigrants were exempted from the provision regarding the possession of $200; the "continuous passage" regulation was even more pointedly aimed at the Indians as it was known that no company ran ships directly from India to Canada (a transhipment at Hong Kong, Shanghai, or

[7] In 1907 he headed the Royal Commission appointed to enquire into methods by which Oriental labour had been induced to migrate to Canada.

[8] The Emigration Act XXI of 1883 was passed to safeguard the interests of indentured labour. Emigration was only allowed to countries which had passed legislation to protect the interests of emigrants and were listed in the schedule. Canada was not listed in the schedule.

[9] The reactions of the Government of India (to which Sikh immigrants naturally looked for protection) to these regulations and enactments can be gauged from the correspondence between the viceroy, Lord Minto, and the Canadian premier. Lord Minto wrote: "We have published the conditions imposed by Canada widely, with the result that emigration has ceased altogether and we consider there is practically no chance of its being reopened . . . we raised no objection to the methods adopted by Canada and we have not any intention of raising any questions regarding them." Letter dated March 1, 1909. Morse, "Immigration and Status of British East Indians in Canada" (unpublished thesis), pp. 40-41.

some other port was necessary) and India had no ships of her own.[10]

The orders-in-council were made substantive law by amending the existing act and then incorporating all the prohibitory clauses in the Immigration Act of 1910. Discriminatory legislation compelled many hundreds of Indians to leave Canada. The Indian population in British Columbia, which had exceeded 5,000 in 1908, fell to less than half in 1911.[11]

Having stopped Indian immigration, the Canadian Government devised means to expel Indians who had come in before the passing of the restrictive measures. The "continuous voyage" and the S200 clauses were invoked to prevent wives and children[12] rejoining their husbands and fathers in Canada.

[10] Mr. H. H. Stevens, M.P. from Vancouver, who took a leading part in mobilising Canadian opinion against Indian immigrants, admitted that the minister who drafted the order "knew, and his government knew, that there was no steamship line direct from India to Canada and therefore this regulation would keep the Hindu out, and at the same time render the government immune from attack on the ground that they were passing regulations against the interests of Hindus who are British subjects." *House of Commons Debates 1914*, No. 1233.

The first victims of the orders-in-council were 200 Indians (mostly Sikhs) who came to Vancouver in March 1908 on the *Monteagle*; 18 who had waited for the boat at Hong Kong were debarred because they had not come by direct passage from India; another 105 who had boarded the ship at Calcutta were turned back because they could not furnish proof that they were not impostors and were the very men who had purchased the tickets at Calcutta. Morse, "Immigration and Status of British East Indians in Canada," p. 36.

[11] The census figure for 1911 was 2,342 Hindus, of which all but 27 were in British Columbia.

[12] The case of Indian wives came up early in 1912 when two Sikh residents of Vancouver, Bhag Singh and Balwant Singh (president and priest, respectively, of the Vancouver gurdwara), returned to British Columbia with their families. The men were allowed to re-enter, but their wives were ordered to be deported. Indians appealed against the order, but before the Supreme Court could pronounce on the case, the Immigration Department allowed the women and children in question to remain in Canada, "as an act of Grace, without establishing a precedent." *House of Commons Debates 1912*, No. 2457.

The Immigration Act of 1910 came up for scrutiny before the Canadian Supreme Court in 1913. A party of 39 Indians (mostly Sikhs) had come to British Columbia by a Japanese ship, the *Panama Maru*, and succeeded in obtaining writ of *habeas corpus* against the Immigration Department's order of deportation.[13] Within a fortnight of the passing of the judgment, the Canadian Government promulgated a new order-in-council forbidding entry of "artisans or labourers, skilled or unskilled . . . at any port of British Columbia.[14] A month later, the "continuous passage" and the $200 clauses were reintroduced through new orders-in-council carefully worded to circumvent the verdict of the Supreme Court. The door to Canada was firmly shut with a notice printed on the outside in invisible ink reading "Indians keep out."

Sikh immigration to the United States was a spill-over from Canada. In the three years from 1904 to 1906 about 600 Indians (mainly Sikhs) crossed over into the United States. As the Canadian Immigration Department became stricter, the number of immigrants to the States increased.[15] Immigrants found employment as farmhands and lumberjacks in Washington, Oregon, and California. Small com-

---

[13] In *Re. Narain Singh et al* No. 18 British Columbia Law Reports 1913. Shortly before Chief Justice Hunter delivered his judgment in favour of the Indians, the Immigration Department—perhaps to forestall the results of a pending appeal—ignored the writ of *habeas corpus* granted temporarily by a judge of the Supreme Court to one Bhagwan Singh Gyani, the leader of Sikh settlers on the Chinese coast, and deported him.

[14] PC 23624 of 1914 and PC 2642 of 1913. Only Orientals entered Canada through British Columbia. Of the Orientals, the Japanese were exempted by virtue of a "gentleman's agreement" with their government; and the act was not invoked in the case of the Chinese. Thus the Canadian Government again succeeded in discriminating against the Indians without having to use the word.

[15] 1,072 in 1907 and 1,710 in 1908. *Report of the Commission General for Immigration 1919-20*, 181-82; quoted by R. K. Das in *Hindustani Workers on the Pacific Coast*.

munities of Sikhs grew up in the San Joaquin and Sacramento Valleys. Some went further south to the Imperial Valley, where the climate was similar to that in the Punjab. On receiving favourable accounts of conditions in the States, other Sikhs began to go directly to California. American whites, however, reacted even more violently than the Canadians. In 1908 a body known as the Asiatic Exclusion League organised pogroms against Orientals. For the next two years few Indians were able to enter the States. When there was a lull in these race riots, immigration started again and by the end of 1910 there were nearly 6,000 Indians in California. Once again racial hatred was whipped up by the local press against the "turbaned tide" and the "ragheads." The United States Immigration Department did not bother with legal niceties; it turned back Indians for one or the other of three reasons: "liable to public charge," "suffering from dangerous contagious disease," or "violates alien contract labour law."[16] Thus the doors of the United States were also slammed in the face of the Sikh immigrants, and those who had succeeded in entering had to face constant harassment from the police and white racists.

Founding of the Ghadr Party

Since the vast majority of Indian immigrants were Sikhs, the earliest immigrant organisations centred on Sikh gurdwaras. In 1907 the Khalsa Diwan Society was organised in Vancouver with branches at Victoria, Abbotsford, New Westminster, Fraser Mills, Duncan Coombs, and Ocean Falls. This Society built a gurdwara in Vancover in 1909. Three years later another temple was erected in Victoria and, somewhat later, smaller ones in other towns. The Khalsa Diwan Society of the United States built a gurdwara at Stockton. Although the objects of the Diwan were religious, educational, and philanthropic, problems con-

[16] *Pacific Monthly*, Vol. 17 of 1907, p. 584.

nected with immigration and incidents of racial discrimination began to loom large in its proceedings.

Alongside the purely Sikh Diwan, there grew other Indian societies to safeguard the economic interests of Indian workers and to fight cases against immigration authorities. The United India League operated in Vancouver; the Hindustani Association of the Pacific Coast was set up in Astoria. Since the only public places where Indians could meet were the gurdwaras, they became storm centres of political activity. The Sikh Diwan and other organisations began to publish tabloid papers in Gurmukhi, Urdu, and English.[17]

A large number of Sikh immigrants were ex-soldiers or policemen to whom loyalty to the British Crown was an article of faith. It was only after they had failed to get any response from Buckingham Palace and the Viceregal Lodge that the words *gorā* (white man) and *gore śāhī* (white man's lawlessness) acquired a pejorative connotation and they began to lend ear to more radical counsel given by men such as Lajpat Rai, who visited them in Canada and the United States. New leaders came to the fore. In California, Hardayal of Delhi,[18] who was a lecturer in Stanford

---

[17] None of these journals had a very long life. The first venture in this line is said to have been started by a Bengali, Tarak Nath Das, and ended on the editor's deportation a few months later. Copies of the following journals are in the library of Berkeley University: *Deś Sewak* published in Gurmukhi and Urdu by Harnam Singh and Guru Datt Kumar from Vancouver; *Khālsā Herald*, a Gurmukhi monthly started in 1911 in Vancouver by Kartar Singh Akali; *Aryan*, an English journal edited by Dr. Sunder Singh with the help of Quakers; *Sansār* (1912), edited by Kartar Singh Akali, was later merged with the *Aryan*; *Hindustani* (1914), an English journal edited by Seth Hussain Rahim. Dr. Sunder Singh later edited *Canada and India* from Toronto which continued appearing till 1917. Kartar Singh Akali also shifted to Toronto and for some years edited *The Theosophical News*.

The author was unable to find any journals published by the Indian immigrants in the United States except the *Ghadr*.

[18] Hardayal (1884-1938) belonged to a Kayastha family of Delhi. He possessed a phenomenal memory and broke many university examination records. He came to be known as the "Great Hardayal." His book, *Hints on Self Culture*, does not betray any signs of genius. He was also

University, became for a short while the political mentor of the immigrants. A dual leadership grew up: effective control remained in the hands of the largely illiterate Sikh workers.[19] Since the immigrants had to deal with lawyers and government departments, they had to have spokesmen who could speak English.[20] Friction between Hindu "intelligentsia" and Sikh workers was inevitable. The Sikhs looked down upon the Hindus as English-speaking babus who did not have the courage of their convictions. The Hindus treated the Sikhs with the contempt with which lawyers generally treat their rustic clientele.

Jwala Singh and Hardayal took the initiative in organising the immigrants at Stockton and set up a body entitled the Hindustani Workers of the Pacific Coast. Sohan Singh Bhakna, (B 1870) who was then working in a lumber mill at Oregon, and Hardayal were elected president and secretary, respectively. (Jwala Singh remained behind the scene but provided most of the funds, including scholarships of Indian students.) The party bought premises in San Francisco and began publishing a weekly paper called *Ghadr* (revolution) in Urdu and later many other Indian languages—the largest issue being in Gurmukhi. Thereafter the organisation came to be known as the *Ghadr* party. The first issue of the paper stated the objective of the party in the following terms:

"Today, there begins in foreign lands, but in our country's language, a war against the British Raj . . . What is our name? Ghadr. What is our work? Ghadr. Where will Ghadr

---

eccentric in his political views. After the first world war he lived in Sweden, taught Indian philosophy at Upsala, and published an apology for British rule in India.

[19] Represented in British Columbia by men such as Bhag Singh; in California by Jwala Singh (a prosperous rancher of Stockton known as the "potato king"), Santokh Singh, Sohan Singh Bhakna, and Bhagwan Singh Gyani.

[20] In British Columbia they sought guidance from Tarak Nath Das and Chagan Lal Verma alias Seth Hussain Rahim; in California from Hardayal.

break out? In India. The time will soon come when rifles and blood will take the place of pen and ink."[21]

Beneath the name of the paper on the front page was the legend: "Enemy of the British Government." This was further elucidated in the third issue of the journal, which dealt with the impending war in Europe: "The Germans have great sympathy with our movement for liberty because they and ourselves have a common enemy (the English). In the future Germany can draw assistance from us and they can render us great assistance also."[22]

Within a few months, the *Ghadr* began to circulate among Indian settlers in Canada, Japan, the Philippines, Hong Kong, China, the Malaya States, Singapore, British Guiana, Trinidad, the Honduras, South and East Africa, and other countries where there were Indian communities. Thousands of copies were also sent to India.[23] Then took place an incident which drew the attention of the world to the plight of Indian immigrants in Canada; this was the arrival of the *Komagata Maru* in Canadian waters.

---

[21] *Ghadr*, November 1, 1913. [22] *Ibid.*, November 15, 1913.

[23] Many articles and poems from the *Ghadr* were reprinted in booklets, of which four became very popular, viz. (1) *Ghadr-dī-Gūnj* (Echoes of the Mutiny), (2) *Ilān-i-Jang* (Declaration of War), (3) *Nayā Zamānā* (the New Age), and (4) *The Balance Sheet of British Rule in India*.

The following extracts are from *Ghadr-dī-Gūnj*.

> No pundits or mullahs do we need,
> No prayers or litanies we need recite,
> These will only scuttle our boat.
> Draw the sword; 'tis time to fight.
> (Vol. 1, No. 4)

> Though Hindus, Mussalmans and Sikhs we be,
> Sons of Bharat are we still,
> Put aside our arguments for another day,
> Call of the hour is to kill.
> (Vol. 1, No. 23)

> Some worship the cow; others, swine abhor,
> The white man eats them at every place;
> Forget you are Hindu, forget you are Mussalman,
> Pledge yourselves to your land and race.
> (Vol. 1, No. 17)

The *Komagata Maru*

On the morning of May 23, 1914, a Japanese passenger ship, the *Komagata Maru*, dropped anchor in the Burrard inlet—a narrow arm of the sea between the mountains and the city of Vancouver. Aboard the vessel were 376 Indians, of whom all but 30 were Sikhs. Their leader was one Gurdit Singh, who had a prosperous business at Singapore. Gurdit Singh had chartered the vessel for six months and collected his passengers from India and ports en route: Hong Kong, Shanghai, Kobe, and Yokohama.

The progress of the *Komagata Maru* was reported in British Columbian papers as a "mounting Oriental invasion." When the ship arrived in Canadian waters, it was cordoned off and only 22 men who could prove their Canadian domicile were allowed to land. The rest were told to go back. Pressure was brought to bear upon Gurdit Singh to pay the charter dues immediately or suffer the ship to be impounded or forcibly returned to Hong Kong. Gurdit Singh's protests that he could only pay the money after he had fulfilled his contract with the passengers by getting them into Canada and had sold the cargo which he had on board were ignored.

Sikh labourers in Canada raised $22,000 to pay for the charter. They appealed to the Canadian people and government for justice, sent telegrams to the king, the Duke of Connaught, the viceroy, and Indian leaders in India and England. There were public meetings in several cities of the Punjab to express sympathy with the passengers of the *Komagata Maru*. Mrs. Annie Besant took up the cause in the British press.[24] Little notice was taken, however, of this

[24] The reaction of the *Times* (London) was typical. In a leader (June 4, 1914): "Phrases like British citizenship cannot be used as a talisman to open doors . . . sophistry and catch logic, the spinning of words or the reading of many books will not help her (India). And she is likely to get little profit out of enterprises like that which has sent the *Komagata Maru* to hurl its shipload of hundreds at the door of Canada."
In a leader, on July 9, 1914, the *Times* said: " 'East is East and West is West,' and though we may hesitate to accept as inevitable the corollary

agitation by the British, Indian,[25] or Canadian governments. The prime minister of British Columbia, Sir Richard MacBride, stated categorically: "To admit Orientals in large numbers would mean in the end the extinction of the white peoples and we have always in mind the necessity of keeping this a white man's country."[26]

The "Shore Committee" of Vancouver Sikhs took the case of the *Komagata Maru* to court. A full bench of the Supreme Court decided that the new orders-in-council barred judicial tribunals from interfering with the decisions of the Immigration Department.[27] The passengers took over control of the ship from the Japanese crew and refused to leave until a cruiser threatened to fire on them. After two months of Canadian hospitality, the *Komagata Maru* slipped out into the Pacific.[28]

---

that 'never the twain shall meet'; it would be futile to deny the immediate difference between them."

[25] Lord Hardinge's subsequent statements show clearly that he was out of sympathy with the Indian immigrants. In a speech to his council on September 8, 1914, he said that the voyage of the *Komagata Maru* had been undertaken without the cognizance or approval of the Indian Government and was in contravention of Canada's immigration laws. He spoke of the generosity of the Canadians in supplying the *Komagata Maru* with 4,000 dollars worth of provisions and summed up his own attitude in the following words: "The development of this incident was watched by the Government of India with the closest attention; but that as the question at issue was of a purely legal character, there was no occasion for intervention." *Gazette of India*, September 19, 1914, p. 973.

[26] The *Times*, London, May 23, 1914.

[27] In *Re. Munshi Singh* No. 20, 1914. British Columbia Law Reports (p. 245) decided on July 7, 1914.

[28] In Vancouver, a trail of violence followed the departure of the *Komagata Maru*. The Immigration Department had engaged the services of a Eurasian policeman, William Hopkinson, to break up the Ghadr organisation. Hopkinson's chief aide was one Bela Singh. Two of Bela Singh's henchmen were found murdered. At the post-funeral service of these murdered men in the gurdwara, Bela Singh killed two and wounded six other men. William Hopkinson volunteered to appear as a witness for the defence in the trial of Bela Singh. On October 21, 1914, Hopkinson was shot and killed by Mewa Singh, the priest of a gurdwara. Mewa Singh was sentenced to death. Prior to his execution he made a confessional statement which ran: "My religion does not

The travails of the *Komagata Maru* were not yet over. None of her passengers was allowed to land at Hong Kong or Singapore (where several had their homes). The boat finally arrived at the mouth of the Hoogly and docked at Budge Budge harbour. It was searched by the police, but no arms were found.[29] War had broken out while the *Komagata Maru* was still at sea, and the government had empowered itself with the right to restrict the liberty of returning emigrants. The passengers were ordered to board a train which was to take them to the Punjab. The Sikhs refused to obey[30] and left the ship in a procession, carrying

---

teach me to bear enmity with anybody, no matter what class, creed or order he belongs to, nor had I any enmity with Hopkinson. I heard that he was oppressing my poor people very much . . . I—being a staunch Sikh—could no longer bear to see the wrong done both to my innocent countrymen and the Dominion of Canada. . . . And, I, performing the duty of a true Sikh and remembering the name of God, will proceed towards the scaffold with the same amount of pleasure as the hungry babe does towards its mother. I shall gladly have the rope put around my neck thinking it to be a rosary of God's name. . . ."

Mewa Singh was hanged on January 11, 1915. The anniversary of Mewa Singh's martyrdom is celebrated every year by the Sikhs of Canada and the U.S.A.

[29] This fact is important in view of the charge subsequently made by the police that the Sikhs of the *Komagata Maru* used firearms. A secret report prepared by senior C.I.D. officers, Messrs F. C. Isemonger and Slattery states: "While there was no obstruction to the search of baggage it was impossible on the crowded ship to make this thorough." *An Account of the Ghadr Conspiracy*, p. 81.

Gurdit Singh himself writes "all the illegitimate things with the passengers were either thrown overboard in the sea or restored to the Japanese. . . . The deck passengers were thoroughly searched. . . . Thank Heaven that nothing incriminating in the eyes of the Lord was found on us." Gurdit Singh, *Voyage of the Komagata Maru*, Part II, pp. 31-34.

[30] Gurdit Singh explained to the police officers who served them with the notice that his dispute with the steamship company had to be settled by arbitration at Calcutta; that the cargo on the *Komagata Maru*, which was his property, had to be disposed of; that he had still to recover $25,000 from the passengers who expected to get the money from friends and relatives in Calcutta; that the men who had spent nearly six months on board wanted time to settle their accounts with each other; and that most of the passengers wished to stay in Calcutta, where they could get employment, rather than return to their villages where they had now no land or tenements. *Ibid.*, Part II, pp. 40-43.

the *Granth* in their midst. The police and a unit of the army barred their progress. A fracas ensued: the police o-pened fire, killing 18 men and wounding another 25.[31] Gur-dit Singh and 28 of his companions escaped. The rest were rounded up and sent to the Punjab, where over 200 of them were interned under the Ingress Ordinance.

"Revolution" in the Punjab

Leaders of the Ghadr party had prepared themselves for the war in Europe. Since Canada was a part of the British Empire, they decided to shift their revolutionary activities to the United States. A week after war was declared, a mass meeting of Indians took place at Sacramento. Several thousand men volunteered for terrorist work in India, and funds were collected to pay for their passage; there was a rush to catch boats leaving for India.[32] At this critical juncture, the Ghadr party was deprived of its leaders. Jwala Singh and Sohan Singh Bhakna enlisted for revolutionary service in India; Hardayal, who had been arrested earlier on a charge of anarchy, jumped bail and escaped to Switzerland. In their absence the control of the party in California fell to Ram Chandra, a Brahmin from Peshawar.

The first band of revolutionaries, led by Jwala Singh, sailed from San Francisco in August 1914 by the *Korea*. Ram Chandra addressed them in the following words:

"Your duty is clear. Go to India. Stir up rebellion in every corner of the country. Rob the wealthy and show mercy to

[31] A Commission of Enquiry appointed by the government exonerated the police and put the blame squarely on the passengers of the *Komagata Maru*. The commission consisted of three Englishmen and two Indians, Sir Bijoy Chand, the maharajah of Burdwan, who had already earned notoriety for his contemptuous remarks about Indian nationalists and Daljit Singh of Kapurthala. Daljit Singh was subsequently knighted for his "services."

[32] The *Portland Telegram* of Oregon had the following caption in its issue of August 7, 1914: "Hindus go home to fight in Revolution."

Astoria (Oregon) August 7, 1914: "Every train and boat for the south carries a large number of Hindus from this city, and if the exodus keeps up much longer, Astoria will be entirely deserted by the East Indians."

the poor. In this way gain universal sympathy. Arms will be provided for you on arrival in India. Failing this, you must ransack the police stations for rifles. Obey without hesitation the commands of your leaders."[33]

At Canton, another 90 volunteers joined the *Korea*. British intelligence received information of the Ghadrites' plans, and, as soon as the *Korea* docked at Calcutta, the ring leaders including Jwala Singh were arrested. Those who were able to evade police surveillance returned peacefully to their villages.

Ghadrites continued to come in batches from Canada, the United States, Hong Kong, Shanghai, China, Straits Settlements, Borneo, Japan, and the Philippines. On their way to India, they approached Indian troops posted abroad: at Hong Kong, contact was made with the 26th Punjabis; at Singapore, with the Malaya State Guides and the 5th Light Infantry; at Penang, with a unit of Sikh sepoys.

Amongst the fleet of Japanese ships which brought the Ghadrites to India, the more important were the *Tosa Maru*, which arrived in Calcutta late in October, and the *Mishima Maru*, which docked in Colombo. The *Tosa Maru* was searched by the police, four of the leaders were arrested, and 179 passengers sent to the Punjab under police escort.

The Indian police did not forestall the possibility of the revolutionaries coming from southern ports; many were thus able to reach the Punjab. It was estimated that, by the beginning of December 1914, nearly 1,000 Ghadrites had come to India. The "Ingress into India Ordinance" (promulgated on September 5) empowered local authorities to detain returning emigrants. The Defence of India Act, passed on March 19, 1915, authorised the governor general to frame rules "to empower any civil or military authority to prohibit the entry or residence in any area of a person

[33] The testimony of approver, Nawab Khan. Isemonger and Slattery, *An Account of the Ghadr Conspiracy.*

suspected to be acting in a manner prejudicial to the public safety, or to direct the residence of such person in any specified area." The act was brought into force in 16 out of 23 districts of the Punjab to restrict the movements of suspicious characters.

The Ghadrites discovered to their chagrin that the atmosphere in India was far from conducive to revolution.[34] Leaders of the National Congress were sympathetic to the British cause. Mahatma Gandhi had volunteered for medical service, and even radicals such as B. G. Tilak expressed strong disapproval of those who wished to exploit the situation. The Punjab was sending the flower of its manhood to the front. The one significant Sikh political party, the Chief Khalsa Diwan, had reiterated its loyalty to the crown, and priests of several important Sikh shrines denounced the Ghadrites as renegades or thugs.[35]

The Ghadrites made desperate efforts to secure a footing amongst the peasantry. They went to religious festivals at Amritsar, Nankana Sahib, and Tarn Taran and openly exhorted the people to rise. There was little response, and the revolutionaries had to fall back on their own resources. They held meeting and made plans to raid arsenals and government treasuries, but all they succeeded in doing by the end of 1914 was to commit a few dacoities and kill a police constable and a village official.[36]

[34] "When the emigrants began to arrive back in September, 1914, they expected to find the Punjab, if not ready for a revolution, at least in a state of uneasiness and it is certain that in this respect, as in the matter of arms, they suffered a disappointment. The vast majority of the people were thoroughly loyal and contented, though of course, somewhat perturbed over the European war which had broken out in the previous month." Isemonger and Slattery, *An Account of the Ghadr Conspiracy.*

[35] "The peasantry saw nothing justifiable in these acts [i.e. acts of violence committed by the Ghadrites] . . . To them the revolutionaries became murderers and plunderers of honest men, the more dangerous for their organisation and arms but to be resisted by all means possible and captured." *Ibid.*

[36] The following revolutionary crimes were listed in the Rowlatt Committee Report, *Sedition Committee Report*, pp. 104-06.

Early in 1915, Ghadrites made contacts with terrorist organisations in other parts of the country. In January, Rash Bihari Bose (leader of the group which tried to assassinate Lord Hardinge in 1912) arrived in the Punjab and took over the general direction of the revolution. Bose pinned his hopes on the defection of the men of the 23rd Cavalry at Lahore and 26th Punjabis at Ferozepur, some of whom had agreed to mutiny; the response of the 28th Pioneers and the 12th Cavalry at Meerut was also encouraging. Bose sent out his agents to other cantonments: Ambala, Agra, Kanpur, Allahabad, Benares, Fyzabad, Lucknow, Multan, Jhelum, Kohat, Rawalpindi, Mardan, and Peshawar. On receiving favourable reports, he fixed the night of February 21, 1915, for a general rising of the Indian troops. Factories to manufacture bombs were set up at Amritsar, Jhabewal (near Ludhiana), and Lohatbadi. The revolutionaries were supplied with instruments to cut telegraph wires and derail railway trains. Tricolour national flags were made, and more copies of the *Ilan-i-Jang* (declaration of war) were cyclostyled for distribution.

These carefully laid plans were foiled by the police, who succeeded in extracting information from one of the captured revolutionaries. Bose advanced the date of the rising from the 21st to the 19th of February. Information of the change was also conveyed to the police by a spy who had wormed his way into Bose's inner council. Disaffected regiments were disarmed; suspects were court-martialled

---

1. October 16, 1914. Attack on Chauki-Man railway station on the Ferozepur-Ludhiana line.
2. November 27, 1914. Attempt to loot the Moga sub-divisional treasury in Ferozepur district resulting in the death of a police sub-inspector and village zaildar. (Two revolutionaries were killed and seven captured.)
3. December 17, 1914. Robbing of a money-lender's house in village Pipli (Ambala district).
4. December 24 & 25, 1914. Dacoities in villages Pharala and Karnama (Jullundur district).
5. December 24 & 25, 1914. Robberies in Ferozepur District.

and executed. The revolutionaries waited in vain for the troops to come out; then they too dispersed—only to walk into the net the police had spread for them. Rash Bihari Bose left the Punjab in disgust.

By the summer of 1915, the Ghadr uprising had been virtually smashed. A few desperate characters who remained at large turned their wrath on informers, crown witnesses, and men who were actively cooperating with the police to hunt down the revolutionaries. By the autumn even these had been apprehended or frightened into inactivity.[37]

Another plot which came to nothing was hatched in Mandi state. Six men were arrested, tried, and sentenced to varying terms of imprisonment.[38]

Rising at Singapore

Ghadrites returning from the States and Canada made contact with the 5th Light Infantry (the "loyal Fifth"), a Muslim unit posted at Singapore.[39] On the afternoon of February 15, 1915, men of the 5th Light Infantry overpowered the local reservists who were on guard duty at the military prison, released German sailors from the coal tug attached to the *Emden*, and took possession of the fort. The mutineers, estimated to be over 700 men, then

[37] "By August 1915, that is within nine months of the first outbreak, we had crushed the Ghadr rebellion. Nearly all the leaders and many of their most active adherents were in our hands awaiting trial or were brought to justice later, internal order was restored and, above all, the Sikh community had again proved its staunch loyalty." Sir Michael O'Dwyer, *India as I Knew It*, p. 206. The last sentence refers to the committees of loyal Sikhs who helped the government against the revolutionaries.

[38] Mandi conspiracy case. See index of Isemonger and Slattery, *An Account of the Ghadr Conspiracy.*

[39] There is no documentary evidence of a connection between the Ghadr party and the Singapore rising, but there is little doubt that the Ghadrites, particularly one Jagat Singh, had been working among the troops. The man who influenced the Muslims of the 5th Light Infantry was a well-to-do businessman, Kassim Mansoor, who was later courtmartialled and shot. Unpublished thesis by R. W. Mosbergen, "The Sepoy Rebellion."

marched towards the town, hoping to rouse the populace. On their way, a party clashed with the Sikhs of the Malaya State Guides and Sikh sentries guarding the local gaol. This gave the rising a communal colour—Sikh versus Muslim. The mutiny was quelled by the joint efforts of the local militia, the police, and the arrival of the British sloop *Cadmus*. In the 48 hours of fighting 44 were killed, of whom eight were senior British officials. There is no record of the number of the mutineers' casualties, but later 126 men were tried by summary court-martial: 37 men were sentenced to death, 41 to transportation for life, and others to varying terms of imprisonment. The condemned men were publicly executed at Singapore.[40]

German Participation in the Ghadr

Indian revolutionaries had active propaganda centres in London, Paris, and Berlin for at least a decade before the formation of the Ghadr party. As tension in Europe grew and it became obvious that war would be between Germany on one side and Great Britain and France on the other, Indian revolutionaries shifted their activities from London and Paris to Berlin. In the spring of 1914, Hardayal arrived in Germany and apprised his countrymen of the Ghadr organisation, which had by then nearly 10,000 active members. The "Berlin-India" Committee approached the German Government and succeeded in persuading the foreign minister, Zimmerman, to send instructions to his ambassador in the United States to provide arms to the Ghadrites and place funds at their disposal. German consuls general in San Francisco, Shanghai, and Bangkok were also instructed to help the revolutionaries.

German participation created factions in the Ghadr party. The rank and file constituted by the Sikh workers and peasants was without a spokesman of its own. Ram Chandra, who had little rapport with the Sikhs, had acquired over-all control of the party. The nominee of the

[40] *Ibid.*

"Berlin-India Committee," Haramba Lal Gupta, had German money in his pocket. Misunderstandings arose between the rival Indian groups and between the Indians and the Germans.

The first attempt to smuggle arms from the United States into India came to nought. Five thousand revolvers were put on board a chartered ship, the *Henry S.* The ship and the crew were captured by the British navy. After the failure of the *Henry S*, Haramba Lal Gupta went to Japan to try and buy arms. British intelligence alerted the Japanese Government, and Gupta had to spend several months in hiding; he returned to the United States without achieving anything.

While Gupta was in Japan, another attempt was made to send arms to India. In March 1915, the *Annie Larsen*, loaded with war material, put out to sea. A few days later, a tanker, the *Maverick*, with five Ghadrites on board dressed as waiters left America. The ships were due to meet at sea, where the *Maverick* was to take over the arms and ammunition submerged in oil tanks and deliver them to the revolutionaries at some remote spot in the Sunderbans in East Bengal. The rendezvous never took place. The *Maverick* was searched by British and American warships, and the revolutionaries had to burn Ghadr literature to avoid detection. The tanker was interned by the Dutch navy and, after being released by the Dutch, captured by the British. The *Annie Larsen* was captured by the United States navy and impounded for carrying contraband.

The Germans had planned to send five other ships with arms to India, but the fate of the *Henry S*, the *Annie Larsen*, the *Maverick*, and the quarrels between Indians dampened their enthusiasm for the Ghadr organisation. Their worst experience was however yet to come. In February 1916 the "Berlin-India" Committee, with the approval of the German foreign office, sent out a Bengali, Dr. Chandra Kant Chakravarty, to take over the conduct of the Ghadr movement and furnished him with large sums of money.

Chakravarty appropriated the money to his own use, and fed the Germans with imaginary reports of the work he was doing. When the Germans discovered the truth, they washed their hands of the Ghadr party and became insulting in their behaviour towards Indians. Ghadrite plans to celebrate 1917, which was the diamond jubilee year of the 1857 Mutiny, as the year of victory were frustrated.

The bickerings between Ghadrites increased. Chakravarty made away with most of the money given by the Germans. Ram Chandra and his friends had control of the donations made by the immigrants, the party journal, and the headquarters. The rank and file, who had staked everything including their lives, were left with nothing. The have-not group was entirely Sikh; the other almost entirely Hindu. Thus religious differences further accentuated the rift.

On April 6, 1917, the United States entered the war. At the insistence of the British Government, the United States police arrested 17 Indian revolutionaries along with 18 Germans of the consulate service and charged them with violating the neutrality of the United States Government.[41] All the accused save one were found guilty and sentenced to various terms of imprisonment and fines. The trial ended on a dramatic note. On the last day one of the accused whipped out a revolver and shot Ram Chandra. The assailant was in turn shot by the marshal of the court and killed instantaneously.[42]

[41] *U.S.A. Vs. Franz Bopp and others* before Judge W. C. Van Fleet was one of the longest and most expensive trials in the history of the United States. It lasted five months; witnesses were summoned from all parts of the world. The estimated cost was about 3 million dollars. *San Francisco Chronicle*, April 22, 1918.

[42] This murder continued to be a cause of friction between Ghadrite factions for many years. The *San Francisco Chronicle* (24.4.1918) gave the following version of the crime: "The motive for Singh's deed is clear. According to the Hindus of Bhagwan Singh faction. Ram Singh (the killer of Ram Chandra) formerly owned hundreds of acres of land in Canada and was accounted a rich man. He had given thousands of dollars to the Hindoo cause—thousands of dollars which were turned over to

The British Defence of India Act of 1915 empowered provincial governments to set up tribunals which could dispense with the usual committal proceedings and whose verdict was final. Special tribunals consisting of three judges (of whom two were invariably English) were set up to try the Ghadrites. In a series of trials held at Lahore, Mandi, Benares, and as far away as Mandalay and Singapore, several hundreds of revolutionaries were tried and convicted. Of those tried in the Punjab, 46 were hanged and 194 sentenced to long terms of imprisonment.[43] Besides these, many soldiers were court-martialled and shot.

The Ghadr rebellion failed for a variety of reasons: lack of arms; lack of experience; bad leadership; the inability of the revolutionaries to keep secrets;[44] tension between the Germans and the Ghadrites; the efficiency of the British Intelligence service, which planted spies in the highest councils of the revolutionaries; the stern measures taken by the Government of India; the brutal methods adopted by the Punjab police, which compelled many of the leaders to inform against their colleagues. Above all, it failed because the Punjabi masses were not ready for it. Rich landowners assured the governor of their loyalty and set up

---

Ram Chandra. In private conversations, the Bhagwan Singh faction freely called Ram Chandra a grafter and has pointed to the many thousands of dollars given to the cause by Ram Singh. Most of this money, according to the Hindoos, was 'retained' by Ram Chandra for his personal use." This version is also supported by the *Un-American Activities, Seventh Report*. Lajpat Raj wrote: "Most of the Bengali revolutionaries I found absolutely unprincipled both in the conduct of their campaign and in the obtaining and spending of funds. . . . Amongst the Punjabis the worst cases were of Ram Chandra and Harish Chandra. The Sikhs on the whole proved to be purer, more unselfish and disciplined. The worst possible case among them was Bhagwan Singh Gyani's but even he was infinitely superior to Ram Chandra or Chakravarty or Gupta." *Autobiographical Writings*, p. 218. Ram Chandra's name is, however, officially listed by the Indian National Congress as one of the heroes of the revolution.

[43] See Appendix to Isemonger and Slattery, *An Account of the Ghadr Conspiracy*.

[44] Isemonger and Slattery, *An Account of the Ghadr Conspiracy*.

committees in the districts to watch the movements of returning emigrants and to bring them back to the path of obedience and loyalty. Even the peasants were more concerned with the war than with the revolution. The story of the heroic stand made by a Sikh battalion against an overwhelming Turkish force at Gallipoli fired the Sikh youth more than the stories of racial discrimination in Canada and the United States.[45]

The Ghadr party aimed to drive out the English from India; but no Englishman lost his life at the hands of the Ghadrites, nor at the time did it pose a very serious threat to the British Raj. Nevertheless, the movement is of considerable importance to the historian. It was the first secular movement which aimed to liberate India by the use of arms. Both in Maharashtra and Bengal, political terrorism was closely connected with the revival of Hinduism: in Maharashtra, with the cult of Sivaji; in Bengal with that of the goddess Kali. And both the Maharashtrians and Bengalis rigorously excluded Muslims from their ranks. Though the vast majority of the Ghadr party was Sikh (and therefore its literature was printed in Gurmukhi and its meetings held in gurdwaras), it had nothing whatsoever to do with the revival of Sikhism. The Ghadr party attracted Hindus and Muslims to its fold and later influenced other revolutionary groups in the country to shed their religious bias.

The eruption of the Ghadr movement brought about a radical change in the political outlook of the Sikh community. It marked the beginning of the end of three quar-

---

[45] "After that [the stand made by a battalion of the 14th Sikhs on June 4, 1915] the rush to the colours in the Sikh districts was extraordinary," wrote Sir Michael O'Dwyer. "In the four years of war the Sikhs who form a total population of two and a half millions—less than 1% of British India—furnished no less than ninety thousand combatant recruits [the number was larger; Leigh, p. 44] or one-eighth of India's total. In fact, so enthusiastic was their response, so gallant were their deeds, and so generous the rewards and appreciation, that many of them have got the idea in their heads that 'we won the war.'" O'Dwyer, *India as I Knew It*, p. 207.

ters of a century of unquestioned loyalty to the British Raj. Though the rebellion was suppressed and submerged in the enthusiasm generated by the war, it continued to ferment and erupted a few years later during the Akali agitation: Akali terrorists known as the *Babbars* were largely recruited from the ranks of the Ghadr party.

The conversion of the Ghadr party from xenophobic nationalism to communism came after the war. In 1924 Bolshevik agents working through an American communist, Agnes Smedley, made contacts with the Ghadr organisation in the United States and Canada. In 1925 a batch of Ghadrites was sent to Russia, where they received instruction at the Lenin Institute and the Eastern University. Two years later this batch was sent to India via Afghanistan. By then many other Ghadrites in India (now known as *Bābās* —venerables) were out of gaol and had renewed association with their erstwhile colleagues. They received funds from British Columbia and California for the relief of political sufferers. These funds were disbursed by the *Deś Bhagat Parivār Sahāyak Sabhā* (committee for the relief of families of patriots). Muscovite Ghadrites joined hands with the *Bābās*, a paper known as *Kirtī* (worker) was started, and in 1926 the party came to be known as the *Kirtī Kisān* (workers and peasants) party; its publications bore the title: "Official organ of the Punjab branch of the Communist Party, affiliated to the Third International."[46] For some years the Kirtis' chief protagonist was Teja Singh Swatantra.[47] The Kirtis and the "official" Communist party

[46] Dr. J. S. Bains in the *Spokesman*, February 9, 1955; also Tilak Raj Chaddha in *Thought*, June 14, 1952.

[47] Teja Singh Swatantra (b.1901), a Jat Sikh of village Aluna (Gurdaspur district), was active in the Akali and Congress movements. He spent five years in a military college in Turkey, and then made contacts with Ghadrites in California in 1929. He was externed by the U. S. government in 1931. Swatantra spent two years in Soviet Russia before returning to India. He was arrested in 1936 and spent the next 6 years in gaol. While in gaol he was returned unopposed to the Punjab Assembly in 1937. On his release in 1942, Swatantra was elected president of the provincial Kisan Sabha and joint secretary of the provincial executive

of the Punjab led by Sohan Singh Josh[48] maintained a united front. With funds liberally supplied by Moscow and Canadian-American Ghadrites, they were able to spread their influence amongst the Sikh peasantry of central Punjab.

Communist infiltration split the Ghadr party. The majority of Ghadrites in the United States and Canada either turned anti-communist or were submerged by the wave of anti-communism which spread across the western world. Their quarrels often led to violence, and at one time over two dozen murders of "Hindus" by "Hindus" were recorded as untraced in the state of California.[49] The bickerings continued through the years till the independence of India. In 1948 the assets of the party were turned over to the Indian ambassador in the United States, thus bringing to an end its 30-year-old turbulent career.

---

of the Communist party of India. He was expelled from the official party and set up his *lāl* (red) Communist group in 1947. He was involved in cases of dacoity and murder and absconded for many years. He reappeared in the winter of 1962 but was never tried for his crimes.

[48] Sohan Singh Josh (b.1898), a Jat Sikh of village Chetanpur (Amritsar district), worked in a textile mill and the censors' office before joining the Akali movement. He was secretary of the Akali Dal in 1922 and was gaoled in the Akali conspiracy case from 1923-26. On his release, he helped to edit the *Kirti* and in 1928 joined the Communist party of India. He was arrested in the Meerut conspiracy case and spent four years (1929-33) in gaol. He was secretary of the Punjab Committee of the Communist party from 1934-50 and was member of the Central Committee of the party from 1943-53. Josh is the most important communist leader of the Punjab.

[49] Listed in the *Un-American Activities Report*.

CHAPTER 13

GURDWARA REFORM: RISE OF THE
AKALI IMMORTALS

THE awakening brought about by the Singh Sabha movement had made the Sikhs conscious of their rights. While the educated began to press for their due in services and administrative bodies (municipalities, district boards, provincial and central legislatures), the masses were more anxious to gain control of their gurdwaras. There were no rules for the administration of Sikh shrines and over many of them priests (*mahants*) who were Hindus as often as Sikh had asserted proprietary rights. The incomes of some of the gurdwaras, such as the Golden Temple in Amritsar and the birthplace of Guru Nanak at Nankana, ran into several lacs per year. For many years, Sikh associations carried on civil litigation against the *mahants*. Then the impatience generated by the Ghadr and the nationalist movement spurred the Sikh masses into jettisoning methods of petition and redress from courts of law followed by the Singh Sabhaites and to adopt instead the non-cooperation (*nā milvertan*) and passive resistance of the newly formed party, the *Akālīs* (Immortals). This brought them into conflict with the Punjabi Hindus, many of whom unwittingly sided with the *mahants* as well as the administration, which felt impelled to support the priests who were in possession of the temples. In order fully to grasp the importance of this movement, one should know something of the evolution of the gurdwara and its importance in Sikh social life.

Gurdwara: Its Income and Management

The first Sikh temple was probably established by Nanak at Kartarpur after his return from his travels. It was then a simple *dharamsāl* (place of worship), where his disciples gathered to listen to his discourses and to sing hymns. The *dharamsāl* soon became a community centre where, apart from worship and religious ceremonial connected with births, baptisms, betrothals, marriages, and obsequies, there was a free kitchen, the *guru-kā-laṅgar*, and a school where children learnt the alphabet and their daily prayers. It also became the *pañcāyatghar*, where the elders met to settle disputes and to deliberate on matters concerning the community. These functions were performed in the smallest village gurdwara as well as in the biggest. The village temple subsisted on the contributions made by the local peasants; the bigger shrines received large sums in offerings, particularly during religious festivals when their *laṅgars* would be called upon to feed as many as 50,000 pilgrims in one day. To meet these obligations, sardars of the misls, and thereafter Maharajah Ranjit Singh, his family, and the Sikh princes, assigned large estates to their favourite shrines. Some like the Golden Temple, the temples at Nankana and Panja Sahib had sizeable jagirs attached to them. With the introduction of canal-irrigation, the income derived from land of the gurdwaras assumed princely proportions.

No rules had been made for the management of the gurdwaras nor were qualifications prescribed for their caretakers. In the days of Mughal persecution, the job of *graṅthī* (scripture reader) was a hazardous one, and many important shrines were entrusted to members of the Udasi order, who did not fully subscribe to the Khalsa creed and, being usually clean-shaven, could disclaim their association with Sikhism when their lives were in danger. Even after Mughal rule, these shrines continued to be looked after by Udasis, and the post of *graṅthī*-cum-manager passed from father to son. The less important gurdwaras were looked after by men who wished to dedicate their life to prayer and the service of the community.

With the establishment of British rule, new settlement records had to be made. In many of these, the lands and properties attached to the gurdwaras were entered against the names of the *mahants*.[1]

Where the congregation was vigilant, the entry remained a nominal one; where the priests were able to have it their own way, they were recorded as owners and began to utilise and alienate the property as they wished. The Udasis, who were as much Hindu as they were Sikh, and anxious to attract Hindu worshippers, installed images of Hindu gods and goddesses in gurdwara premises. There were also some cases of misuse of the sacred precincts.[2]

Management of the Golden Temple had always been of special interest to the community. After the annexation, matters of importance were sometimes looked into by the deputy commissioner of Amritsar; for the rest, the priests had everything their own way. Soon after the suppression of the mutiny, leading Sikh sardars moved the government to reorganise the management of shrines. At a meeting held on December 22, 1859, over which the deputy commissioner presided, it was decided to set up a manage-

---

[1] "On the advent of the British rule, however, the very word of 'possession' acquired special significance and unfortunately very little, if any, distinction at all was made between possession as owners and possession as servants of the public for carrying out the religious and charitable services, connected with the gurdwaras. The result was that the incumbents began to feel and exercise personal rights in the endowments which soon led, as it was bound to lead, to the deterioration of their characters. The Sikhs were too stunned—by the blow depriving them of their empire—to offer much resistance to this encroachment upon their rights." Mehtab Singh, *P.L.C.D.*, March 14, 1921, p. 360.

[2] "In proportion as the properties and incomes of the gurdwaras increased by canal irrigation and offerings, etc., etc. the *mahants* became more and more depraved. Bad characters flocked around them as *celas* to lead easy and immoral lives. Resorting of desperate characters to our gurdwaras and their association with the *mahants* converted these sacred places of virtue and religion to brothels and dens of gamblers, drunkards, robbers and thieves. No man's honour and no woman's virtue was safe. Women of the highest families in the land were led astray from the path of duty and virtue and gave birth to illegitimate children. Maidens were abducted and outraged. *Mahants* kept mistresses and concubines and in doing so did not confine themselves to their own community. From prostitutes they had sons whom they provided with millions worth of properties out of gurdwara funds." *Ibid.*

ment committee of nine members. The committee, however, does not seem to have taken much interest, and the management remained as before in the hands of the head priest under the direct supervision of the deputy commissioner.[3]

Singh Sabha was the first to protest against the exclusion of Sikhs of untouchable castes and the performance of idolatrous ritual in the bigger shrines. The priests of Hazur Sahib in Nanded (Hyderabad state) retaliated by excommunicating members of the Singh Sabha and exhorted the priests of other temples to do the same. The behest could not be carried out as the Singh Sabha had become powerful in the Punjab; on the contrary, as a result of pressure applied by the Sabha, Hindu idols were removed from the precincts of the Golden Temple in 1905. A year later, when the manager died, the Singh Sabha pressed upon the deputy commissioner the need to consult representatives of the community in the appointment of a successor.

Leaders of the Singh Sabha were loyalists who believed in doing no more than making representations to officials or instituting suits. The misuse of gurdwara property required more drastic action. Matters came to a head in 1912, when, in the course of the building of the new capital, the government acquired land attached to gurdwara Rikab Ganj in Delhi and demolished an old boundary wall. Radical elements seized the opportunity to challenge the *mahant's* right to alienate gurdwara property and condemned the demolition of the gurdwara wall as sacrilegious. There was talk of launching a *morcā* (battle front); but it had to be postponed because of the war.

[3] No specific qualifications were ever laid down regarding *granthīs* or priests. The Nizām's government had, however, ruled that in Nanded (in the Nizām's dominion) only a celibate of good character who did not drink could be appointed head priest. In *Narain Singh Vs Bhagat Singh* (Civil Suit 807 of December 3, 1886) the court had ruled that only a *nādī* (a celibate) above the age of 35 years and of unimpeachable character could be appointed as priest of the Golden Temple. *Tribune*, June 20, 1886.

The matter was re-agitated in the autumn of 1918. Disappointment over the Montagu-Chelmsford constitutional proposals (discussed hereafter), followed by large scale terrorism practised by the martial law administration, made the Sikh masses critical of the government. Men of nationalist views broke the monopoly of the Singh Sabha over Sikh affairs and set up in the winter of 1919 the Central Sikh League at Amritsar. At a subsequent meeting at Lahore, the League passed a resolution of non-cooperation with the British and decided to send volunteers to take forcible possession of Rikab Ganj land acquired by the government. It also demanded that the management of the Khalsa College, Amritsar, be taken out of official control and placed in the hands of a Sikh committee.

The government tried to appease the Sikhs. The demolished wall of Rikab Ganj was rebuilt, and the acquired land was restored to a committee of representative Sikhs who had taken over the management of the shrine. Other minor grievances of the Sikhs were also redressed. Sikhs were, in one respect, exempted from the operation of the Arms Act and were allowed to carry kirpans; Sikh prisoners in gaols were permitted to retain their religious emblems and, unlike other inmates who had to wear cloth caps, were allowed to keep their turbans.

These concessions had little bearing on the question of the control of the shrines. On this matter, the authorities were slow to respond to the demands of the Sikhs and somewhat insensitive to the temper of the times. The official attitude was that a person in whose name a piece of land or property was registered was *prima facie* the owner and could be ousted only by means of a suit for possession in the civil court. It did not occur to them that the *mahant* of a gurdwara was exactly in the same position as the vicar of a church in whom no proprietary rights were vested. Many Sikh committees had tried and discovered the futility of civil actions. Court fees had to be paid on the value of the property, and suits could be prolonged interminably by the ingenuity of lawyers. Frustration and anger began to mount.

Meanwhile, Sikhs had been planning a committee of management of their own. On November 15, 1920, a proclamation was made from the Akal Takht, Amritsar, to the effect that a committee of 175 to be known as the *Shiromaṇī Gurdwārā Prabaṅdhak Committee* (Central Gurdwara Management Committee—thereafter referred to by the initials S.G.P.C.) had been set up for the management of all Sikh shrines; Sunder Singh Majithia, Harbans Singh of Attari, and Bhai Jodh Singh, were elected president, vice-president, and secretary, respectively. The more radical elements organised a semi-military corps of volunteers known as the *Akālī Dal* (army of immortals). The Akali Dal was to raise and train men for "action" in taking over the gurdwaras from recalcitrant *mahaṅts*. A Gurmukhi paper, the *Akālī*, was started.[4]

Under pressure of Sikh opinion, backed frequently by demonstrations of strength, the *mahaṅts* began to yield control over gurdwara properties to elected committees and agreed to become paid *graṅthīs*. However, at the gurdwara at Tarn Taran, there was violence resulting in the deaths of two Akalis and injuries to over a dozen; Tarn Taran was only the prelude.

The Nankana Holocaust

The birthplace of Guru Nanak was among the most richly endowed Sikh shrines. At the time, it was being managed by an Udasi *mahaṅt*, Narain Das, who lived in

[4] The editors, Mangal Singh and Hira Singh Dard, later became important figures in Sikh politics. Mangal Singh (b.1896), a Gill Jat of village Gill in Ludhiana district, served a five-year sentence for seditious writing in the *Akālī*. He later joined the Indian National Congress and represented Sikh interests at the All Parties Conference and in the drafting of the Nehru Report. He was a member of the Central Assembly from 1934-45.

Hira Singh Dard (d.1965) was imprisoned several times and later joined the Communist party. He edited the weekly *Phulwārī* and also made his mark as a poet.

the gurdwara with a mistress and was known to have invited prostitutes to dance in the sacred premises. Local Sikhs threatened to eject him by force.[5] The *mahant* asked the police for protection and hired nearly 400 thugs to safeguard and defend his interest.

In the early morning hours of February 20, 1921, a *jathā* (band) of Akalis led by Lachman Singh Dharovalia entered the gurdwara. The gates of the shrine were then closed, and Narain Das's thugs attacked the *jathā* with swords, hatchets, and firearms. The dead and dying Akalis were then dragged to a pile of logs which had been collected earlier, and burnt. By the time the police and local Sikhs came on the scene, 130 men had been consumed by the flames.[6]

The news of the outrage spread like wildfire. Bands of Akalis from distant towns began to converge on Nankana. The commissioner of Lahore[7] hurried to the scene and with great alacrity handed over the keys of the shrine to a representative of the S.G.P.C.

The atmosphere of the days following Jallianwala came again to pervade the Punjab. The districts of Lahore, Amritsar, and Sheikhupura were declared "proclaimed areas"

[5] The situation at Nankana had attracted the attention of the authorities earlier. On February 16, 1921 (four days before the incident narrated in the text), the government had issued a press release announcing the appointment of one Shaikh Asghar Ali to preside over a conference of the Akalis and Lieutenant Kartar Singh Bedi representing *mahants*, *sants* (holy men) and *pujārīs* (priests).

A widely publicised letter written by the commissioner of Lahore to Kartar Singh Bedi which assured the *mahants* of their legal rights was responsible for the hardening of the *mahants*' attitude. *P.L.C.D.*, March 5, 1921, p. 21.

[6] *P.L.C.D.*, 1921, p. 304. For the murder of the 130 Akalis, three men were sentenced to death and two, including Narain Das, to transportation for life (*King Vs. Narain Das and others, Tribune*, March 3, 1922).

[7] The commissioner, Mr. King, made a personal statement on the incident to the Legislative Council on March 15, 1921. He said: "Unfortunately the precipitate action of one party threw out our calculations. Lachman Singh's party went to Nankana quite unexpectedly, and there was no one in authority to prevent the dreadful happenings that occurred." *P.L.C.D.*, March 15, 1921, pp. 380-83.

under the Seditious Meetings Act; the more outspoken leaders were arrested. Resolutions to non-cooperate with the government were passed by several provincial organisations.[8]

The summer of 1921 was one of acute political unrest all over India: the Moplahs rose in Malabar; there were *hartāls* in the wake of the Prince of Wales' visit; foreign liquor shops were picketed and bonfires made of British goods. These demonstrations were met by baton charges and arrests. By an unhappy coincidence, the failure of the winter monsoon had its delayed effect in the summer; in several districts of the Punjab, famine conditions came to prevail.

Repression and economic distress quickened the pace of Sikh agitation.[9] Those who, like members of the Chief Khalsa Diwan, collaborated with the government came to be described contemptuously as *jholī cuks* (toadies). Radical leadership which came to the fore reflected different shades of political opinion and religious enthusiasm. Baba Kharak Singh,[10] Mehtab Singh,[11] and Teja Singh Samundari were largely motivated by religious considerations. Master Tara Singh[12] and three brothers—Amar Singh,

[8] Mahatma Gandhi visited Nankana. He said, "Everything points to a second edition of Dyerism, more barbarous and more fiendish than the barbarism at Jallianwala Bagh." The *Times*, March 11, 1921.

[9] "Moreover, it is believed that the awakening of national consciousness is to a certain extent responsible for the spirit of restlessness and dissatisfaction with the management of shrines and gurdwaras." Statement by Mian Fazl-i-Husain. *P.L.C.D.*, March 14, 1921, p. 350.

[10] Kharak Singh (1867-1963) Ahluwalia was the son of an army contractor of Sialkot. He was for some years, the most powerful leader of the Sikhs—their *betāj bādsāh* (the uncrowned king). Though called a Baba, he has no connection whatsoever with the Communists.

[11] Mehtab Singh (1879-1938), an Arora of Shahpur district, qualified as a barrister and had a lucrative practice.

[12] Tara Singh (b. June 24, 1885) of village Harial (district Rawalpindi), was the son of a Hindu of the Malhotra caste. He was converted to Sikhism while at school, educated at Rawalpindi and then at the Khalsa College, Amritsar. After taking his degree in 1907, he took a diploma in teaching and became a teacher in the Khalsa High School, Lyallpur: the title "master" has attached to his name ever since. He joined the Akali move-

Sarmukh Singh, and Jaswant Singh of Jhabal—who were more representative of majority opinion, were equally religious and nationalistic. There were also fanatics believing in the militant tradition of the Nihangs who wanted to meet force with force. This group organised itself into bands of terrorists known as *Babbar Akālīs* (immortal lions).

The new leaders exploited the inflamed sentiments of the people to the full. The Sikhs were asked to wear black turbans in honour of the martyrs of Nankana. A *śahīdī* (martyrs) fund was opened to provide for the families of the deceased, to set up a school and a hospital at Nankana and a missionary college at Amritsar as memorials to the victims. Collections for the purpose were made all over the province. The effects of this propaganda were visible at the birthday celebrations of Guru Nanak that autumn. Over 50,000 Sikhs congregated at Nankana, of whom 20,000 professed to be Akalis and 12-15,000 belonged to *jathās*.[13]

The Keys Affair

Into this highly inflammable atmosphere the deputy commissioner of Amritsar threw a lighted match. Being suspicious of the bona fides of Baba Kharak Singh, the new president of the S.G.P.C., he took the keys of the treasury of the Golden Temple and planned to hand them over

---

ment at its inception and became the dominant figure in Sikh affairs in the 1930's. Master Tara Singh has published many works on religion, politics, and fiction of which the better known are *Bābā Tegā Singh* and *Prem Lagan*. Two papers, *Prabhāt* (dawn in Urdu and *Jathedār* in Gurmukhi publicise his views.

[13] A police report stated that "A strong national spirit and contempt for authority pervaded the assembly." *The Akali Dal* (C.I.D. Report, pp. 6-7).

The fair was made memorable by the dramatically stage-managed appearance of Gurdit Singh of *Komagata Maru* fame, who surrendered himself to the police. Master Mota Singh, who had been declared an absconder some months earlier, arrived with an escort of armed Akalis, delivered a violent speech to the assemblage and then disappeared.

to his own nominee. He clamped down the Seditious Meetings Act and arrested 193 of the leading Akalis. The leaders were sentenced to varying terms of imprisonment and fines.

The seizure of the shrine keys aroused considerable excitement in India. The government realised that the deputy commissioner of Amritsar had disturbed a hornet's nest, and, a few days after the passing of the sentences, the governor of the Punjab announced his decision to release the prisoners and hand over the keys to Kharak Singh's committee. Mahatma Gandhi described it as the "first decisive battle won."

The lieutenant governor, Sir Edward Maclagan, tried to push through legislation to transfer gurdwaras to their rightful owners, the Sikh congregation. In March 1921, the education minister, Mian Fazl-i-Husain, introduced a bill to set up a Board of Commissioners which would take over the management of Sikh shrines. The bill was opposed by the Sikh legislators, who objected to having non-Sikhs on a board whose sole function was to manage Sikh places of worship. Nor could the members agree on what constituted a gurdwara; a large number of Udasis declared their shrines to be Hindu temples and so gained the backing of Hindu and anti-Akali Sikh members.[14] Mian Fazl-i-Husain had the bill passed into law as the Sikh Gurdwaras and Shrines Act VI of 1922. The Sikhs ignored the legislation.

The S.G.P.C. passed a resolution (May 21, 1921) not to cooperate with the government and exhorted Sikhs to

14 Mehtab Singh retaliated by a vitriolic attack on the *mahants*: "The *mahants* are a class of parasites. They have become infected with the poison, which in accordance with a saying of our guru, is contained in the income derived from the alms of the worshippers, and this poison has made devil of a man. . . . If the government is honestly prepared to help us in this matter we have no objection to receiving this aid, but we are not prepared to admit that sadhus belonging to the Nirmala or Udasi sects possess the right of interfering in our religious affairs and of wounding our religious susceptibilities." *P.L.C.D.*, April 5, 1921, pp. 544-45.

boycott British goods. The moderates quit the S.G.P.C. About the same time Mehtab Singh resigned his post as deputy president (speaker) of the Punjab Council and thus deprived the legislature and the government of the benefit of the Akali point of view. District officers who had been piqued by the lieutenant governor's decision in the keys affair began to conduct themselves in a harsh and uncompromising manner with the Akalis. Over 1,200 arrests were made in 13 districts of the province.[15] Among the most headstrong was the deputy commissioner of Amritsar who precipitated a showdown with the Akalis.

Guru ka Bagh

Guru kā Bāgh (the garden of the Guru), a small shrine thirteen miles from Amritsar, had been erected to commemorate the visit of Guru Arjun. Adjacent to the shrine was a plot of land on which acacia trees were planted to provide firewood for the gurdwara kitchen. The Udasi *mahant* accepted baptism and submitted himself to the authority of an elected committee. Then without any apparent cause, in the first week of August 1921, he lodged a complaint that Akalis were cutting timber from the gurdwara land. The police arrested the Akalis and charged them with criminal trespass. Akali leaders held a meeting at the Guru ka Bagh in contravention of the order under the Seditious Meetings Act. The police dispersed the meeting and arrested the leaders, including Mehtab Singh and Master Tara Singh. The S.G.P.C. took up the challenge.

Jathās of 100 Akalis each were formed. They first took an oath at the Akal Takht to remain non-violent, then proceeded towards Guru ka Bagh. The police stopped them at various points far removed from the land in dispute, ordered them to disperse, and, on their refusal to do so, beat them mercilessly with their lathis, jack-boots, and

---

[15] Sir John Maynard put the figure at 1,286, excluding persons who were arrested and subsequently released. *P.L.C.D.* August 9, 1922, p. 1698.

fists. For nineteen days the encounters between the police and the passive resisters continued and were observed by many Indian leaders. The Indian National Congress appointed a committee of enquiry, which lauded the Akalis and censured the police for the atrocities committed by it.[16] When C. F. Andrews visited the scene, he was deeply moved by the noble "Christ-like" behaviour of the Akalis. He apprised the lieutenant governor of the brutality of the police and persuaded him to see things for himself. Sir Edward Maclagan arrived at Guru ka Bagh (13th September) and ordered the beatings to stop. Four days later the police retired from the scene. By then 5,605 Akalis had been arrested, and 936[17] were hospitalized. The Akalis took possession of Guru ka Bagh along with the disputed land.[18] It was the second decisive battle won.[19]

Guru ka Bagh excited religious fervour to a degree which had not been seen among the Sikhs since the annexation of their kingdom. The trial of the leaders was followed with close interest, and, when the convicted leaders were being removed to gaols to serve their sentences, mammoth crowds greeted them on the route.[20]

[16] The committee stated: "We are all clearly and emphatically of opinion that the force used was excessive on all occasions and on some was cruelly excessive. Divesting ourselves of all political bias, we consider that the excesses committed reflect the greatest discredit on the Punjab Government and are a disgrace to any civilised government." The committee included an American missionary, Rev. S. E. Stokes. It examined over 100 witnesses and submitted its report on January 3, 1924. *Congress Enquiry Committee Report on the Guru-ka-Bagh.*

[17] The official figure given by H. D. Craik in the Punjab Legislative Council was 1650 against whom force was used. *P.L.C.D.* November 1, 1922, p. 468.

[18] The Guru ka Bagh land was purchased by the Hindu philanthropist, Sir Ganga Ram, and given to the gurdwara. This was obviously a government device to save face.

[19] The Indian National Congress, meeting at its annual session at Gaya in December-January, passed a resolution recording "with pride and admiration its appreciation of the unexampled bravery of the Akali martyrs and the great and noble example of non-violence set by them for the benefit of the whole nation."

[20] On October 30, 1921, thousands of men and women laid themselves

Babbar Akali Terrorists

Not all Sikhs accepted the cult of non-violence which the S.G.P.C. had adopted. The behaviour of the police at Guru ka Bagh induced some to organise an underground terrorist movement.[21] These terrorists were largely drawn from the Ghadr party and soldiers on leave. Two of the most active members were retired Havildar Major Kishen Singh Bidang and Master Mota Singh. To get arms, the Babbars sent agents to the North West Frontier Province and to the Indian states. They also tried to persuade soldiers to steal them from army arsenals. They acquired a couple of duplicators and began to issue a bulletin entitled the *Babbar Akālī Doābā.*

The Babbars were no more successful than the Ghadrites in securing arms; and their organisation, like the Ghadr party, was rendered ineffective by the members' inability to remain secretive and by allowing personal spite to mingle with revolutionary zeal. The Punjab C.I.D. did not have much difficulty in infiltrating the Babbars' inner circles.

Babbar violence was of short but intense duration. For a few months they terrorized the Jullundur Doab and Hoshiarpur. Encounters with the police redounded to the credit of the Babbars, most of whom displayed a contemptuous disregard for their lives.[22] But by the summer

---

on the rail track at Panja Sahib in an attempt to stop a train to give refreshments to the prisoners being escorted to Naushera gaol. Two men were crushed to death before the engine driver could pull up.

[21] A nebulous terrorist group had been formed earlier. At the Sikh Educational Conference, which met at Hoshiarpur in March 1921, a band of terrorists resolved to assassinate people they believed responsible for the Nankana outrage. Seven men were convicted for conspiracy to murder and five declared absconders.

[22] Two instances are worthy of record. On August 31, 1923, four Babbars led by Karam Singh, acting editor of the *Babbar Akālī Doābā*, were surrounded in village Babeli by a large force of police and armed constabulary. The Babbars refused to surrender and when the hut in which they were hiding was set on fire, they emerged with drawn kirpans

of 1923 the wave of violence was spent, and most of the Babbars had been apprehended. Of the 62 Babbar Akalis put up for trial, 22 turned witnesses for the Crown. The trial was conducted in camera in Lahore gaol and was presided over by an English judge. Six men, including Kishen Singh Bidang, were condemned to death, and, apart from 34 who were acquitted, the rest were sentenced to varying terms of imprisonment. The condemned men declined to appeal or petition for mercy and were hanged.[23]

The attitudes of both the government and the Akalis hardened. The Akalis became more obstreperous and forcibly occupied more gurdwaras: one notable take-over was the historic shrine at Muktsar (February 17, 1923). The police became harsher in their treatment of Akali prisoners. There were complaints of dragging men by their long hair,[24] beating them, keeping them hungry, and forcing them to sleep out in the open on cold winter nights.[25]

A resolution urging the release of Akali prisoners was

(they had no firearms) and fell under a hail of rifle-shot while charging the police.

Even more dramatic was the conduct of Dhanna Singh of Behbalpur on October 25, 1923. He was betrayed by one of his comrades and captured at night while asleep. With his manacled hands he was able to explode a hand-grenade under his armpit. The blast killed Dhanna Singh, nine policemen, and a buffalo.

23 The Babbar Ghadrite combination was responsible for some notable crimes in later years. S. G. M. Beatty, who earned notoriety at Guru ka Bagh, was murdered in a village of Patiala (a Babbar was hanged for the murder). Bela Singh of Jaina, who had fled Vancouver after murdering and betraying his co-religionists, was hacked to death in his village in 1933.

24 *P.L.C.D.*, November 9, 1922, pp. 57-59.

25 Conditions in Attock fort gaol were investigated by Raja Narendra Nath and Sewak Ram, both members of the Punjab Council. Over 80 Akali prisoners were found to be in the hospital suffering from bronchitis, asthma, pneumonia, etc. *P.L.C.D.*, March 6, 1923, p. 989.

To protest against the treatment of his fellow Akalis and the ban on Gandhi caps for non-Sikh prisoners, Baba Kharak Singh serving his sentence of four years' rigorous imprisonment refused to wear anything more than his *kach* even on the coldest days. He was kept in solitary confinement for over six months.

moved in the Legislative Council and passed with the strong support of non-officials, both Hindu and Muslim. The official spokesman admitted that, in the Hindu-Muslim communal riots in March 1923, the Akalis "rendered useful assistance to the authorities in maintaining order pending the arrival of military reinforcements." In recognition of these services the lieutenant governor ordered the release of over 1,000 Akalis arrested in August and September 1922 at Guru ka Bagh.[26]

It was with a sense of triumph that the Akalis arranged the cleansing of the tank (*kār sevā* of the Golden Temple. The operation, which is performed after every two or three decades to remove the accumulation of sediment left by millions of pilgrims who bathe in the holy waters, took one month to complete, during which hundreds of thousands of Sikhs from all over India and abroad came to Amritsar. The Akalis made full use of this opportunity to disseminate propaganda and work up feelings against the government.[27] They began to look upon themselves as the sole representatives of the community. A decision of the S.G.P.C. became like a proclamation of the guru.

While the *kār sevā* was in progress, the Central Sikh League held a session at Jallianwala Bagh. At this meeting, rumours began to circulate that the government meant to remove Maharajah Ripudaman Singh of Nabha from his state. A few days later came an official announcement that the maharajah had abdicated.

[26] This was the second attempt to secure the release of Akalis. The first resolution moved in November 1922 was defeated by supporters of the government; *P.L.C.D.*, March 8, 1923, p. 1100. According to the government, the total number of Akalis in gaol on January 1, 1923 was 3,597; of these 3,148 were convicted at Guru ka Bagh. On the 25th of October 1923 Sir John Maynard gave the figure of Guru ka Bagh prisoners as "over 4,400" Sikhs. The final figure was 5,554. *P.L.C.D.*, January 2, 1924, p. 124.

[27] It was commonly believed that a hawk which occasionally appeared and sat on the central pinnacle of the Golden Temple was a messenger of Guru Gobind Singh. The legend generated enormous religious fervour and further added to the popularity of the Akalis, to whose activities the "miracle" came to be ascribed.

Jaito

The maharajah of Nabha's dispute was with the maharajah of Patiala, not with the Government of India. But he had taken interest in the affairs of the community and the government was aware of his sympathies with the nationalist and Akali movements.[28] The government appointed Justice Stewart of the Allahabad High Court to enquire into the dispute. His finding was adverse to the ruler of Nabha.[29] The political agent "persuaded" Ripudaman Singh to abdicate in favour of his minor son. The S.G.P.C. passed a resolution exhorting the Sikhs to observe the 9th of September, 1923, as "Nabha Day." The Sikhs of Nabha organised a non-stop recitation of the *Granth* in their gurdwaras. One such ceremonial held at the tem-

[28] "The Shiromani Committee received thousands of telegrams from the people demanding that full investigation be made into this (Nabha) affair. The committee addressed a telegram to this effect to the viceroy. The maharajah of Nabha had great sympathy with the Gurdwara Reform movement and had rendered good service in the agitation over the wall of Rikab Ganj." Statement by Mehtab Singh in the *Akali Leaders Case*, I, 711.

[29] Justice Stewart conducted the enquiry at Ambala from January 3 to May 2, 1923. His findings were never disclosed to the public; only the parties concerned and the government received copies of the judgment. Details of the charges and counter-charges by one maharajah against the other were known only after the Akalis and, following them, the Indian National Congress had formally pledged support to Ripudaman Singh. At a meeting of the Central Sikh League in June 1923 at Amritsar, the president, Sunder Singh Lyallpuri, while supporting Nabha, admitted that "both maharajahs had earned a bad name." At the Indian National Congress Session at Coconada in December 1923, the president, Maulana Mohammad Ali said: "We hold no brief for the maharajah sahib; but this much is certain, that even if all that his detractors say of him be true, he was not deposed for any such shortcomings, but for his virtues." The Akalis published their version of the affair in a pamphlet entitled *Truth about Nabha*, wherein they stated that the hostility towards Ripudaman Singh was due to his association with nationalist leaders.

The name of Bhupendra Singh of Patiala (d.1937) had become a legend because of his gargantuan appetite for women. Ripudaman Singh of Nabha was no saint either. Among the many charges and counter-charges hurled by the two maharajahs at each other, one related to the murder of one Lal Singh and another to the disappearance of a woman, Ishar Kaur.

ple at Gangsar in village Jaito was interrupted by the police. A new *morcā* was thus launched; batches of passive resisters began arriving every day at Jaito. The government took up the challenge. The S.G.P.C. and the Akali Dal were declared illegal, and 59 Akali leaders were arrested.[30] They were charged with conspiracy to wage war against the king and were taken to Lahore fort for trial.

The incarceration of all the top leaders of the party did not kill the Nabha agitation; on the contrary, it became a mass movement in the real sense of the term. The sizes of *jathās* going to Jaito increased from twenty-five each to a hundred and then from one hundred to five hundred. They came from all parts of the Punjab, and through every village they passed, Sikh, Hindu, or Muslim, they were fêted, garlanded, and sent off with good wishes. The Indian National Congress declared its full sympathy with the *morcā*; among those arrested at Jaito was Jawaharlal Nehru.

While the Jaito *morcā* was going on, a second front was opened at Bhai Pheru in Lahore, where the *mahant* had resiled from an earlier agreement with the Akalis and charged them for trespass. Batches of 25 Akalis began to present themselves for arrest every day at Bhai Pheru.

The unending stream of passive resisters that continued to arrive at Jaito and Bhai Pheru exasperated the government, and it made a desperate bid to smash the movement. In the first week of January 1924, Amritsar police raided the Akal Takht, seized documents of the S.G.P.C., and arrested another 62 men. Measures taken by the Punjab police encouraged Nabha state authorities to go a step further. The English administrator ordered the confisca-

---

[30] They included Mehtab Singh, Teja Singh Samundri, Teja Singh Akarpuri, Bhagat Jaswant Singh, Master Tara Singh, Bawa Harikishen Singh, Gyani Sher Singh, Professor Teja Singh, Professor Narinjan Singh, Sarmukh Singh Jhabal, Sohan Singh Josh, Gopal Singh Qaumi, and Seva Singh Thikrivala. This trial had the most decisive influence on the future of Sikh politics. It went on for two years and three months without any result.

tion of properties of the Akalis in the state, restricted many thousands to their villages, and authorised use of greater violence against *jathās* coming to Jaito. On February 21, 1924, one such *jathā* of 500 Akalis arrived at Jaito and on its refusal to disperse was fired on by the state police resulting in considerable loss of life.[31] The shooting aroused sympathy for the Akali cause throughout India,[32] and the Sikhs were drawn closer to the freedom movement.

The government tried to isolate the Akalis by giving wide publicity to the story that they (the Akalis) wished to restore Sikh rule in the Punjab. This propaganda had the reverse effect. Even Sikhs who had kept aloof from the movement felt that it was their duty to support a party which intended to restore their kingdom. And since there was no substance in the charge, Sikh leaders as well as Congress were able to accuse the government of deliberate perfidy. Meanwhile *jathās* continued marching triumph-

[31] According to the government version, 21 men were killed and 33 injured; according to Akali sources the number of dead was over a hundred and of the injured over two hundred.

Pressure of public opinion forced the government to hold an enquiry into the Jaito firing. A subordinate magistrate of the provincial civil service exonerated the state police from charge of excessive use of force. *India in 1923-24*, pp. 325-31. Although the Akalis exaggerated the figures of killed and wounded, their plea that the police fired without provocation is convincing. It was corroborated by men such as Professor Gidwani and Dr. Kitchlew, who were arrested at the time, and an independent witness, Mr. Zimand, correspondent of the *New York Times*, who was present throughout the incident. In a letter dated February 9, 1924, written to Mahatma Gandhi, Mr. Zimand stated: "I had every opportunity to see the *jathā* and the crowd; I did not see any one person in the *jathā* or the crowd carrying firearms or any other weapon . . . members of the *jathā* wore kirpans and the crowd had lathis. As far as I know no one had any other weapons."

[32] On February 27, 1924, 47 members of the Central Legislative Assembly moved an adjournment to discuss the Jaito firing. Among the movers were Mr. M. A. Jinnah and Madan Mohan Malaviya. The speaker refused to allow the motion. A day later the working committee of the All India Congress Committee met in Delhi under the presidentship of Maulana Mohammad Ali and passed a resolution of sympathy with the victims of Jaito and promised assistance to the sufferers. A "Congress-Akali bureau" was set up in Amritsar.

antly across the Punjab to Amritsar and onwards to Jaito or Bhai Pheru.

Sikh Gurdwaras Act

Army authorities were seriously perturbed by the sympathy for the Akalis in the services. In March 1924, General Sir William Birdwood opened negotiations with the Akali leaders. By then the S.G.P.C. had declared that the Jaito *morcā* was not a protest against the removal of Ripudaman Singh but was intended solely to affirm the right to perform religious ceremonial in their temples without outside interference.[33] General Birdwood's efforts bore fruit later, when Sir Malcolm Hailey became lieutenant governor (May 1924). Hailey was a skilful operator. He kept up police repression against Akali passive resisters and at the same time opened negotiations with moderate elements among the Sikhs. He encouraged the latter to set up *sudhār* (reform) committees of loyal Sikhs in the Sikh districts. He toured the province and made speeches warning the Sikhs that continued agitation would affect their future in the armed services.

Hailey's tactics paid off. Although *jathās* continued to march (the number of men arrested in Jaito and Bhai Pheru had risen to nearly 10,000), the unity of the community was effectively undermined. A *jathā* consisting of members of Sikh Sudhar Committees was allowed to enter the gurdwara at Jaito and to perform the *akhaṅd pāth* without interference (October 1924). By this move, Hailey put the onus of proving that the object of the *morca* was religious on the Akalis. Through a five-member committee constituted by the Sikh members of the Legislative Council, Hailey presented a draft of a new gurdwara bill to the

[33] Vide Proclamation No. 1541. The Chief Khalsa Diwan had by now come round to the view that the Akalis were deliberately protracting the *morcā* for political ends. The *Khalsa Advocate* wrote: "There is a faction amongst the Sikhs, which is using the gurdwara reform movement to mislead the Sikhs and which is preventing an agreement because it does not want the agitation to end." (Quoted by the *Akali*, March 26, 1924.)

Akali leaders imprisoned in Lahore fort. The bill met all the Akali demands and was passed into law in 1925.[34] Hailey, however, made it appear that only those who recanted their past deeds would be freed to take over the S.G.P.C.[35] One group led by Mehtab Singh agreed to cooperate and was released. The larger number, which included Baba Kharak Singh and Master Tara Singh, considered the conditional release derogatory to their self-respect and refused to give any undertaking. They also in-

[34] The Sikh Gurdwaras Act of 1925 had two schedules; the first listed 232 shrines. Another 28 were added to the list which were recognised as Sikh gurdwaras without further enquiry. The second schedule listed 224 *akhārās* of Udasis or Nirmalas which were not to be declared gurdwaras unless they fulfilled certain conditions. Any Sikh could put in a petition within one year to have any institution (except those listed in the second schedule) declared a gurdwara.

A tribunal of three judges was set up to determine whether an institution was or was not a gurdwara and the compensation, if any, to be paid to any one deprived of possession. The tribunal's findings were subject to appeal to the High Court.

The act provided for elected bodies to replace the *mahants*. The central body, the S.G.P.C., was to consist of 151 members, of whom 120 were to be elected, 12 nominated by the Sikh states, 14 to be co-opted, and 5 to represent the four chief shrines of the faith.

Local gurdwaras were to have their own elected bodies of management with one nominee of the S.G.P.C. on its committee. The act also indicated in what way incomes of gurdwaras were to be utilised.

The most important part of the act was to define a Sikh as "one who believed in the ten gurus and the *Granth Sāhib* and was not a *patit* [apostate]." This last proviso was particularly odious to the Hindu members of the Legislative Council.

[35] "I read to you the precise terms of our decision. The Punjab government will release (or will withdraw from the prosecution of) any person (other than those persons who have been convicted of or are under trial for crimes of violence or incitement to such crimes) who has been convicted by the criminal courts, or is under trial in such courts on charges arising out of the recent agitation in the Sikh community or on charges involving offences against the Criminal Law (Amendment) Act, provided that (and this is important) such release will be conditional on such persons signing and undertaking that they will obey the provisions of the law recently enacted securing to the Sikh community the control and management of shrines and their endowments and will not seek by means of force, or show of force, or by criminal trespass to gain control or possession of any shrine or the property attached to it or its endowments." *P.L.C.D.*, July 9, 1925, p. 1304.

sisted that all Akalis be freed before they would operate the act. A few months later they too were released and, as could have been anticipated, condemned Mehtab Singh's party as collaborators and ousted it from control of the S.G.P.C. Akali unity was shattered, and the agitation at Jaito petered out.[36] Akalis, who had won their bitter struggle against the *mahaṅts* and the government over control of their shrines, now turned their venom against each other.

The number of men and women who were jailed or lost their lives in this movement cannot be stated with precision; the government's figures and those of the Akalis never tallied. However, the following statement made by Tara Singh of Ferozepur, who took a leading part in the debate on the Gurdwara Act in the Punjab Legislative Council, was never challenged by the official members and may be taken to approximate the truth: "Briefly summarising, these sacrifices (at Tarn Taran, Nankana Sahib, Guru-ka-Bagh, Bhai Pheru and Jaito) amount to 30,000 arrested, 400 killed and 2000 wounded, Rs. 15 lacs of fine inflicted, including forfeiture of pensions of retired soldiers. In addition to this, a ban has been placed on civil and military recruitment of Sikhs."[37]

The most significant outcome of the four years of intense agitation, in which the Hindus supported the Udasi *mahaṅts* against the Akalis, was to widen further the gulf between the two communities. The breakaway from Hinduism, to which Kahan Singh of Nabha had given expression in his pamphlet *Ham Hiṅdū Nahīṅ Haiṇ*—We are not

---

[36] Another pointless *morcā* was launched by Baba Kharak Singh at Daska in district Sialkot. This was subsequent to a dispute with Hindus over property attached to a gurdwara.

[37] *P.L.C.D.*, May 7, 1925, p. 1105. According to Dr. B. R. Ambedkar, because of the Akali agitation the proportion of Sikhs in the army was reduced from 20% in 1914 to 13% in 1930 while that of Punjabi Mussalmans and Pathans rose from 26% in 1914 to 34% in 1930. B. R. Ambedkar, *Pakistan and the Partition of India*, p. 84.

Hindus (discussed in the chapter on Singh Sabha), was even more emphatically stated by Mehtab Singh in a speech he delivered on the first gurdwara bill.

"I, for one, say that if the Sikhs do not wish to remain in the fold of Hinduism, why should the Hindus seek to force them to do so. What benefit can they obtain by keeping an unwilling people as partners in their community? Why not let them go? That, Sir, is at the bottom of the whole excitement. The Hindus say, we will manage your affairs for you as your gurdwaras are partly yours and partly ours. We say that we wish to manage our own affairs and look after our own gurdwaras and are determined to do so."[38]

Hindus, despite their opposition to the Akalis, continued to protest that Sikhs were Hindus. "I look upon Sikhism as higher Hinduism," said a leader of the Punjab Hindus.[39] Another, who came to the support of the gurdwara legislation, referred to the Sikhs as "the flesh of our flesh, and the bone of our bone."[40] Whether the Sikhs were a separate people or a branch of the Hindu social system became a major issue in the years that followed.

The S.G.P.C. became a sort of parliament of the Sikhs: its decisions acquired the sanctity of the ancient *gurūmatā*; the Dal became its army; and the income from gurdwaras (over ten lacs of rupees per year) gave it financial sustenance. Disbursement of this income in the management

[38] *P.L.C.D.*, April 8, 1921, p. 583.

[39] Raja Narendra Nath said: "The *Granth Sāhib* is nothing more nor less than the higher teachings of the Vedas and Upanishads in popular language. . . . I need not dilate upon the close connection between the Hindus and Sikhs. It is well known that of two brothers, one may be a Hindu and the other a Sikh, and that the Sikhs and Hindus intermarry freely. Khatri and Arora Sikhs living in towns are supposed to follow Hindu law. In this connection it would be interesting to peruse the Privy Council ruling reported as No. 84, P.R. 1903, in which the learned judges of the Privy Council held that Sikhs were Hindus." *P.L.C.D.*, April 5, 1921, p. 539.

[40] *P.L.C.D.*, July 6, 1925, p. 1214. Sir Gokul Chand Narang, later minister in the Punjab Government and author of *Transformation of Sikhism*.

of shrines, patronage in the appointment of hundreds of *granthīs, sevādārs* (temple servants), teachers, and professors for schools and colleges which were built, arrangements for the training of *granthīs* and for missionary activity outside the Punjab, all made the S.G.P.C. a government within the government. Its control became the focal point of Sikh politics. The Akalis automatically took over control and have never relinquished it. The struggle for power has been between different factions of the same party. Of these, the one controlled by Master Tara Singh remained (except for brief periods) dominant for the following four decades.

The Akali movement was indirectly responsible for the political awakening in the princely states. After the settlement of disputes over the gurdwaras, the Akalis from the states began to agitate against the autocratic misuse of power by the maharajahs, chiefly Bhupendra Singh of Patiala. Bhupendra Singh retaliated by having the leading agitator, Seva Singh Thikrivala, transferred from Lahore gaol and interned in Patiala on a palpably false charge of theft. The Akalis took up the case of Thikrivala and let loose a campaign publicising Bhupendra Singh's amorous escapades and the sadistic behaviour of his police. The maharajah was able to win over a section of the Akalis,[41] but could not silence the Punjabi and Urdu press.

In 1928 Akalis from the states joined with Hindu nationalists and founded the *Prajā Maṇḍal* (States People's Association); the *maṇḍal* was later affiliated to the All India States People's Congress (in its turn associated with the Indian National Congress). Seva Singh Thikrivala was the moving spirit behind the Mandal. He was arrested several times and in 1935 succumbed to third degree methods practised on him by the maharajah's gaolers. As

[41] The pro-Patiala group was led by Gyani Sher Singh and Jaswant Singh Jhabal. They condemned the agitation against Bhupendra Singh as a *bhrā mārū jang*—murderous war against a brother.

a result of the murder of Thikrivala,[42] the anti-maharajah, anti-British movement gained momentum in all princely states of the Punjab.

[42] A statue of Seva Singh Thikrivala (1878-1935) stands on the main thoroughfare leading to the palace. It was erected at the instance of Brish Bhan when he was chief minister of Patiala and the Punjab States Union in 1955.

Prominent among the men associated with Thikrivala were Bhagwan Singh Lohnguvalia, Gyani Zail Singh (later minister in the Punjab Government), Pritam Singh Gojran (later protagonist of the Sikh state), and Jagir Singh Joga (communist).

CHAPTER 14

CONSTITUTIONAL REFORMS AND THE SIKHS

Sikh Indifference towards Politics

◈◈◈◈ OF all the provinces of British India, the Pun-
◈◈◈◈ jab was the slowest to respond to schemes of
◈◈◈◈ self-government; and of the three communities of the Punjab, the Sikhs were the least responsive.
Punjabi Hindus and Muslims had the benefit of the guidance of enlightened Hindus and Muslims from other parts
of India. The Sikhs had no political teachers. The Mal-
wais, who had long been under British protection, had remained under the unenlightened autocracies of princes
and jagirdars who were singularly ill-equipped for leadership.

The formation of the Indian National Congress in 1885
and Sir Syed Ahmed's United Patriotic Association in
1887 began a ferment in the Indian body politic. At the
same time communal bodies became active: Muslim organisations began to press for special rights and protection of Urdu; Hindu associations began to demand the
prohibition of the slaughter of cows and the recognition of
Hindi as the national language. Educated members of the
Chief Khalsa Diwan felt that they should also press for
the rights of Sikhs: separate representation, special privileges and safeguards in services, and facilities for develop-
ing their language and preserving their way of life.

The Punjab Legislative Council was established in
1897.[1] It consisted of nine members nominated by the lieu-

[1] Although the Indian Council Act of 1861 had authorised the setting
up of provincial legislatures (and the Act of 1892 further increased their
powers), the Punjab did not have a council till 36 years later. The same
indifference was shown towards municipal and district board administration. Although the Municipal Act was passed in 1862 and the District
Board Act in 1883, people took little interest in the elections; and those
who were elected or nominated strictly toed the official line. The *Tribune*
described Punjab's city fathers as men who knew no more than to say

tenant governor and was more in the nature of a durbar than a body of representative citizens. The governors, like their oriental predecessors, wished to be surrounded by men of proven loyalty from rich zamindar families or heads of religious organisations. In the early years, Sikh durbaris were chosen from the top layer of Sikh society.[2] These worthy gentlemen distinguished themselves by observing throughout their tenures a respectful reticence.[3]

Minto-Morley Reforms, 1909

The first time the elective principle (alongside nomination) was introduced to select representatives for legislative bodies was with the introduction of reforms which went under the joint name of the governor general and the secretary of state as the Minto-Morley reform scheme of 1909. By then the Muslims had succeeded in persuading the not-too-reluctant Minto (who in turn persuaded Morley) that the best way of getting proper Muslim representation was to have separate electorates, in which only Muslims could vote for Muslims and that the Muslims should be given "weightage" to offset the Hindu preponderance in numbers. The Chief Khalsa Diwan asked for similar concessions for the Sikhs. The lieutenant governor supported the Diwan and wrote to the viceroy that "in the Punjab the Sikh community is of the greatest importance and it should be considered whether any and what measures are necessary to ensure its adequate representation."

---

jo hukam khudāwaṅd—Your Lordship's orders will be obeyed. *Tribune*, April 14, 1883.

[2] Sikh members of the Punjab council were Baba Sir Khem Singh Bedi. Bhagat Singh, chief secretary of Kapurthala state, Sir Ranbir Singh, and Pratap Singh Ahluwalia. Yuvraj Ripudaman Singh of Nabha and Arjan Singh of Bagarian were nominated to the governor general's council. The prince initiated the Anand Marriage Bill legalising the Sikh form of marriage (thus excluding Hindu ritual from Sikh weddings). The bill was passed in 1909 when Nabha had been replaced by Sunder Singh Majithia.

[3] The silence was broken by Pratap Singh Ahluwalia on February 28, 1907, when he uttered a few carefully prepared sentences on the Colonisation Bill. *P.L.C.D.*, February 28, 1907.

No notice was taken of the Khalsa Diwan's representation nor of the lieutenant governor's recommendation. Under the Minto-Morley scheme, the Muslims were conceded separate representation and weightage in the states in which they were a minority as well as at the centre; similar privileges were extended to neither the Hindus nor the Sikhs of the Punjab. Consequently, in the elections that followed, the Sikhs were muscled out by the Muslims or the Hindus[4] and the lieutenant governor had to complete the Sikh quota by nomination.[5]

The Lucknow Pact; Montagu-Chelmsford Reforms and the Government of India Act, 1919

The next scheme of constitutional reforms was mooted while the outcome of the first world war was still uncertain. At the time the Sikhs' major preoccupation was with the fortunes of battle and with the proceedings of the Mesopotamia Commission (an enquiry into the breakdown of medical and other facilities for the Indian—substantially Sikh—expeditionary force). Meanwhile representatives of the Indian National Congress and the Muslim League met at Lucknow and drew up an agreement by which Muslims were conceded separate electorates in seven states in which they were in a minority, given half the elected seats in the Punjab and one third of the elected seats in the central legislature (elected by a purely Muslim electorate).[6]

[4] In 1909, the three seats open to election were all carried by Muslims; in 1912, of the six elected, four were won by Hindus, one by a Muslim and one by a Sikh; in 1916, out of eleven elected seats, the Hindus and Muslims obtained five each, a European got the eleventh; the Sikhs were not represented at all.

[5] Sunder Singh Majithia was nominated as representative of the Chief Khalsa Diwan, in addition to Pratap Singh Ahluwalia and Gurbaksh Singh Bedi, nominated earlier. In 1913 Daljit Singh of Kapurthala replaced Pratap Singh Ahluwalia, and a fourth man, Gajjan Singh, a lawyer from Ludhiana, was added to the Sikh quota.

[6] A group of members of the Central Assembly had earlier addressed a note on constitutional reforms to the viceroy, Lord Hardinge; this also contained no safeguards for the Sikhs. The Lucknow Pact was a sequel o this 19-member memorandum.

No Sikh was invited to these confabulations, nor was the Sikh point of view given adequate consideration. To forestall any political change based on the Lucknow Pact the Chief Khalsa Diwan addressed a memorandum to the lieutenant governor stating that they would not accept a constitution "which did not guarantee to them [the Sikhs] a share in the provincial and imperial councils as well as in the civil administration of the country, with due regard to their status before the annexation of the Punjab, their present state in the country and their past and present services to the empire. In order that such representation be adequate, effective and consistent with their position and importance, the Sikhs claimed a one-third share in all seats and appointments in the Punjab as their just share; they demanded that their share in the viceroy's and the secretary of state's council should be adequate and fixed on principles of the like nature."[7]

In August 1917, the secretary of state, Mr. Montagu, made his momentous declaration that the aim of British policy was "the increasing association of Indians in every branch of the administration" and "the gradual development of self-governing institutions with a view to the progressive realisation of responsible government."[8] When Mr. Montagu visited India that autumn, Maharajah Bhupendra Singh of Patiala conveyed the Sikhs' views to him. A deputation of Sikh leaders also waited on the viceroy (November 22, 1917) and pressed their claim to a one-third representation in the Punjab on the basis of their services in the war.

The Montagu-Chelmsford Report issued in the spring of 1918 reassured the Sikhs. Its authors disagreed with the principle of separate representation conceded to the Muslims and expressed regret that it could not be altered. But

[7] Chief Khalsa Diwan's communication No. 5075 of December 26, 1916 addressed to the chief secretary, Punjab Government.

[8] Many British officials were critical of this step towards self-government. Sir Michael O'Dwyer was outspokenly hostile.

they felt that what had been given to the Muslims could not in any fairness be denied to the Sikhs. They wrote: "The Sikhs in the Punjab are a distinct and important people; they supply a gallant and valuable element to the Indian army; but they are everywhere in a minority and experience has shown that they go virtually unrepresented. To the Sikhs therefore, and to them alone we propose to extend the system already adopted in the case of Muhammadans. . . ."[9]

The Chief Khalsa Diwan expressed its appreciation, adding to its resolution the words: "A minority community cannot allow itself to be swamped by the majority vote, purely on a numerical basis."[10]

The Montagu-Chelmsford proposals were debated in the joint committee of the Punjab Legislative Council. Mian Fazl-i-Husain tried to push through a resolution that the Muslim proportion in the Punjab Legislative Council be based on the Lucknow Pact. Gajjan Singh proposed that the words "subject to the just claims of the Sikhs"[11] be added to the resolution. The innocuous amendment was

[9] Montagu-Chelmsford Report, *Indian Constitutional Reforms Report*, p. 150.

[10] C.K.D. Resolution, September 18, 1918. Also quoted by Gajjan Singh in the *P.L.C.D.*, November 21, 1918, p. 527.

[11] Gajjan Singh elucidated what he meant by "just claims." He said: "According to the census figures of 1911 the Sikhs numerically form very nearly 12 per cent of the population of the Punjab (the actual figures being 2,883,729 out of 24,187,750). With regard to the status and importance in the country and the services and sacrifices in the cause of the Empire, however, we occupy a unique position, unapproached and unapproachable by any other community in India. Our strength in the entire Indian Army is 20 per cent, while among the units recruited from the Punjab, which supplies no less than 60 per cent of the Indian combatants in His Majesty's Army, we supply no less than a third of their entire man-power. . . . Nearly one-third of the awards made to the entire Indian army during the present war have been won by members of our community. Proportionately the largest numbers of recruits to keep up the fighting strength of the Indian Army have been supplied by us. . . . It has not been our habit to talk loudly of our services to the Empire or to demand rights and privileges for ourselves from the government, and that may be the reason why hitherto in all the schemes of reform and development of the administrative machinery in this country the Sikhs have

vigorously opposed by both Muslims and Hindu members. The chairman drew their attention to the injustice they were doing to the Sikhs. He said: "You will have justified those among ourselves who contend that Indians are not really fit to manage their own affairs because they cannot consider sectarian questions in an unbiased spirit. . . . It is perfectly obvious that if this amendment of Sardar Gajjan Singh is laid before this Council, simply because there are only two Sikhs, that it will be lost. Nevertheless it is equally obvious that whatever it may be in form, it is in substance and spirit a perfectly just and fair claim."

The amendment was put to vote and, as anticipated, lost by six votes to two—the two being Sikhs.[12] Gajjan Singh then moved the resolution that one-third of the seats in the council be reserved for the Sikhs. This resolution met the same fate—the Hindu-Muslim block voting against the Sikhs. Sunder Singh Majithia fared no better in the Imperial Legislative Council: non-official Hindus and Muslims turned a deaf ear to Sikhs' pleadings.

The Chief Khalsa Diwan continued to press for Sikh rights.[13] The only support it received was from the Punjab Government, which addressed the Franchise Committee in the following words: "Their [the Sikhs] influential position in the province, which is partly based on historical and political factors, partly on their military prestige and partly on their high educational level and economic importance in the central and colony districts, entitles them to a considerably greater degree of representation than is indicated by numbers alone. The number of Sikhs in the army is now believed to exceed 80,000, a proportion far higher than in the case of other communities, and the

---

suffered considerably in comparison with the more articulate sections of their countrymen." *P.L.C.D.*, November 21, 1918, p. 528.

[12] Mian Fazl-i-Husain aimed another barbed shaft at the Sikhs. The Sikhs, he said, had kept aloof from the Lucknow pourparlers because they relied not so much on their rights as upon hopes of favouritism.

[13] C.K.D. Resolution 7575 of November 24, 1918.

amount which they pay in the form of land revenue and canal charges is out of all proportion with their numerical strength."[14]

The Punjab Government's note also drew attention to the fact that the proportion of voters was highest among Sikhs and suggested that they be given 5 out of 26 of the non-official seats, i.e. 19 percent representation. The Franchise Committee ignored the suggestion and conceded only "a separate electoral roll and separate constituencies for the Sikhs"; it was recommended that the Sikhs be given 8 out of 54 (15%) non-official seats. The Chief Khalsa Diwan expressed "feelings of grave and serious apprehension" at the Franchise Committee's recommendations.

The Government of India Act of 1919 did not give the Sikhs the 33 percent that they had expected as a reward for their service rendered and their economic importance in the Punjab; in fact it gave them less in the Punjab than it gave to the Muslims in provinces in which they (the Muslims) were a minority.[15] Under the new constitution, the Punjab Legislative Council would comprise 93 members, of whom 15 were to be Sikhs elected by Sikh constituents;[16] the Central Assembly was to have 145 members, of whom three were to be Sikh; the Council of States would have 60 members, of whom one was to be a Sikh.

Provincial governments were to have two kinds of executives; one consisting of nominated members to deal with "reserved subjects" (such as law and order and land revenue) and the other chosen from among the elected members to handle "transferred subjects."[17] The governor was

[14] Home-Judicial No. 2120 of November 23, 1918. The Sikhs paid 25% of the Punjab's land revenue and 40% of the land revenue and water tax combined.

[15] The Sikhs, who formed 12% of the Punjab, received 18% representation; Muslims, who formed 11% of the population of Bihar and Orissa, received 25% representation.

[16] There was provision for nomination by the governor. Three additional Sikhs were nominated to the Council in 1920.

[17] "Subjects which afford most opportunity for local knowledge and social service, those in which Indians have shown themselves to be keenly

to preside over both the executives. The system was described as the double dyarchy of the executive.

The Chief Khalsa Diwan made a last effort (almost six months later than it should have) to influence the British Government to revise its decision. A delegation of four Sikhs[18] arrived in London a week after the joint Parliamentary Committee had made its report. The only satisfaction they could derive was the knowledge that the Committee had on its own initiative increased Sikh representation in the Punjab by two.

The first elections under the new act took place in 1920. The treatment of the Ghadrites, the shooting at Jallianwala, and the tyranny of the martial law regime were fresh in the minds of the people. The nationalists boycotted the elections. The Chief Khalsa Diwan had begun to lose credit in the eyes of the Sikh masses, but no other political party had yet taken its place. With the limited franchise only the well-to-do had a vote and could afford to contest. These men were largely independents.[19] The lieutenant governor nominated three others, including Sunder Singh Majithia, as representatives of the Chief Khalsa Diwan. Majithia was nominated to the governor's executive council and entrusted with the care of revenue matters. None of the three Sikhs elected to the Central

---

interested, those in which mistakes that occur, though serious, would not be irremediable, and those which stand most in need of development—e.g. education, agriculture, public health, local government. Over these functions the governor was to exercise powers of 'superintendence, direction and control.' "

[18] The delegates were Shiv Dev Singh Oberoi, Sohan Singh, Sewaram Singh, and Ujjal Singh—the last named became the chief exponent of Sikh views on constitutional matters.

[19] Of the elected Sikhs only two could be described as having a semblance of popular support in the community: Mehtab Singh, the Akali leader, who was elected from Lahore and became deputy president of the council, and Dasaundha Singh, a Jat from Ludhiana. Both men were lawyers.

Assembly had any political affiliations. Jogendra Singh,[20] who was elected to the Council of States, was also a non-party man.

The 1920 elections saw the emergence of the Unionist Party headed by Mian Fazl-i-Husain and Chaudhri Chhotu Ram. The party consisted largely of Muslim landowners and Hindu Jats of Hariana—united in their loyalty to the British and their aversion to urbanite Hindus and Sikhs. Its composition was entirely "agriculturist," and its policy was to forward the interest of the "agricultural" classes. Although the majority of Sikhs were Jats and agriculturists, leaders of the Chief Khalsa Diwan found the racial basis of the Unionists repugnant to the tenets of Sikhism and refused to join the party. Nevertheless a few years later a section of Sikh Jats realised that their Khatri and Arora co-religionists, being more educated, were getting away with the best jobs and threw in their lot with the Unionists. Under Unionist dispensation it was no longer good enough for a Punjabi to be Muslim, Hindu, or Sikh, or to be better qualified for a post; he had to prove that he belonged to an agricultural tribe.

The Sikh Akalis and Nationalists made headway among the masses, and in 1923 they were able to capture some seats in the Punjab Legislature. Nevertheless Sunder Singh Majithia was renominated to the lieutenant governor's executive council and reappointed minister of revenue.

[20] Jogendra Singh (1877-1946), a Jat of the Baath sub-caste, was a landowner with estates in Uttar Pradesh and in the Montgomery district. He served in Patiala state for some years before coming to the Punjab. In 1926 he became minister of agriculture in the Punjab and thereafter held different ministerial posts for ten years. In July 1942 he was nominated to the governor general's executive council and became member for health, education, and lands. Jogendra Singh wrote a number of books in English. His publications include *Kamla* and *Nur Jehan* (both fiction) and some on Sikh religion.

The Round Table Conferences and the Government of India Act of 1935

THE SIMON COMMISSION AND THE NEHRU REPORT

In the autumn of 1927 the British Government announced that a commission under the chairmanship of Sir John Simon would be sent to India to review the working of the Government of India Act of 1919. Since no Indians were associated with the commission, both the National Congress and the Muslim League resolved to boycott its deliberations. Consequently when the Commission arrived in India it was greeted with black flags and mobs shouting "Simon, go back."[21]

The Punjab Legislative Council nominated a committee under the chairmanship of Sikandar Hayat Khan with Ujjal Singh[22] as secretary to furnish evidence to the commission. A memorandum on Sikh representation[23] was presented to the commission. It said: "While anxious to maintain their individuality as a separate community they [the Sikhs] are always ready to cooperate with their sister communities for the development of a united nation.

[21] In many places, the police had forcibly to disperse mobs; at one such melee in Lahore Lajpat Rai was injured. It was popularly believed that the Lala had been assaulted by Inspector Saunders of the Punjab police. Later Saunders was shot dead. Three young men, Bhagat Singh, Rajguru, and Sukhdev, were convicted of the murder and executed on March 23, 1931. Bhagat Singh became the most famous of all terrorists in the annals of Indian revolutionary history. Mahatma Gandhi wrote, "there has never been, within living memory, so much romance round any life as had surrounded that of Bhagat Singh."

[22] Ujjal Singh (b. 1895), an Arora of Shahpur district, owned large estates in Multan district. He was elected to the Punjab Legislative Council in 1926, was finance minister in the Sachar government, and remained in the hub of Sikh politics till 1955. In 1965 he was nominated governor of the Punjab.

[23] The signatories to the memorandum were Shivdev Singh Oberoi (president of the Chief Khalsa Diwan and member of the Council of States), Harbans Singh of Attari (secretary, Chief Khalsa Diwan), Raghbir Singh Sandhawalia, Sunder Singh Majithia and Mohan Singh Rais of Rawalpindi. *Memorandum on Sikh Representation* to be placed before the Indian Statutory Commission, May 1928.

They would, therefore, be the first to welcome a declaration that no considerations of caste or religion shall affect the matter of organisation of a national government in the country. They are prepared to stand on merit alone, provided they, in common with others, are permitted to grow unhampered by any impediments, in the way of reservation for any other community."[24]

If, however, separate representation was to continue, the memorandum demanded that in the Punjab Legislature communal proportions should be fixed as follows—40 percent Muslim, 30 percent Hindu, and 30 percent Sikh. Claim was made for Sikh representation in Sindh (if it was made into a separate province), Delhi, and the North West Frontier Province.

While the commission was at work, the Indian National Congress tried once more (as in 1916) to present the British Government with a draft constitution agreeable to Indians. In February 1928 it called a conference of members of all important Indian parties "to consider and determine the principles of the constitution for India." The moving spirit behind the conference was Motilal Nehru; his son, Jawaharlal, was secretary. The Sikhs were represented by Mangal Singh Gill. The Nehru Report recommended the abolition of separate electorates but agreed to reservation of seats for Muslims at the centre and in the provinces in which they were a minority; the only other people for whom this concession was recommended were non-Muslims of the North West Frontier Province. Mangal Singh did not press for special rights for his community in his home state or at the centre.[25]

24 *Ibid.*, p. 2.
25 The committee met for over two months. At first Mangal Singh insisted that, if the Muslims were given separate rights, the Sikhs would ask for one-third representation in the Punjab and 5% at the centre. And, if weightage was abolished, he would accept representation on the basis of population with the right to contest other seats. The final decision to give up all communal representation was taken under the inspiration of Dr. Ansari. (Author's interview with Mangal Singh Gill.)

The Nehru Report was an impressive exercise in political bargaining. But the Muslims took scant notice of it, and the Sikhs rejected it. One group led by Baba Kharak Singh was so angered by the report that it severed its connection with the Indian National Congress. Others led by Master Tara Singh were equally emphatic in their rejection of the proposals but decided to continue their association with the Congress and so remained in the mainstream of national politics. The Nehru Report found honourable burial in the archives of the National Congress.

The Simon Commission was still drafting its proposals when Lord Irwin announced that a conference of representatives from British India and the Indian States would be convened in London to discuss the question of granting Dominion status to India. The Indian National Congress asked for a declaration that the conference would frame a Dominion constitution for India and not merely discuss when or how it was to be granted. As no such declaration was forthcoming, the Congress decided to abstain from the conference and, at its session in December 1929 at Lahore, passed a resolution in favour of complete independence (instead of Dominion status) for India. Political opinion in England hardened against the nationalists.

In March 1930, the Mahatma launched a campaign to break the law by manufacturing salt, which was a government monopoly. He and most other national leaders were imprisoned. Thus the most important Indian political party was unrepresented at the first London Conference.

In May 1930, the Simon Commission made its report proposing a federal constitution with two houses of legislature at the centre and autonomy for the constituent provinces and the princely states. The recommendations were a step forward in regard to the provinces, where dyarchy was abolished and they became masters of their own homes. But the report did not recommend wider powers for central government. It gave a certain measure of reassurance to the Sikhs: "It would be unfair that Mohammedans should retain the very considerable weightage they now enjoy in the six provinces and that there should at the same time be imposed, in face of Hindu and Sikh opposition, a definite Muslim majority in the Punjab and in Bengal unalterable by any appeal to the electorate."[26]

The recommendations disappointed progressive opinion both in India and in England. In September, the viceroy issued invitations to 66 Indians (50 from British India and 16 from the states) to proceed to London to deliberate on the recommendations. The Sikh invitees (in addition to Bhupendra Singh of Patiala, who was invited as the chancellor of the Chamber of Princes) were Sampuran Singh and Ujjal Singh. The Akalis, the party that really mattered, consisted largely of *jathedārs* incapable of grasping the niceties of constitutional practice; the Akalis tacitly acquiesced in the selection.

THE FIRST ROUND TABLE CONFERENCE

The First Round Table Conference opened in London in November 1930, with Prime Minister Ramsay MacDonald in the chair. He outlined the Simon Commission scheme for a federal India; the princes (except Bhupendra Singh of Patiala) expressed willingness to join the federation. The biggest hurdle was communal representation. Sikh delegates agreed to joint electorates with the reservation of seats for minorities, but they strongly opposed communal majorities based on separate electorates.[27] The Muslims were unwilling to accept joint electorates on any terms. Separate electorates won the day—not only for Muslims but also for Sikhs, Indian Christians, Anglo-Indians, and the untouchables.

The First Round Table Conference achieved more than either the British Government or the participants had an-

[26] Simon Commission Report, *Indian Statutory Commission Report*, II. 71.
[27] The Sikhs' demands were tabulated in 17 points.

ticipated. It encouraged Lord Irwin to extend the hand of friendship to the Mahatma. On March 5, 1931, they signed a pact (known thereafter as the Gandhi-Irwin Pact) whereby nationalists were released from gaol, the passive resistance movement was called off, and Mahatma Gandhi accepted an invitation to go to London for the Second Round Table Conference. He was to be the sole representative of the Indian National Congress. The delegates to the first conference were re-invited.

SECOND ROUND TABLE CONFERENCE

The Second Round Table Conference met under adverse circumstances. The progressive labour government had been defeated in the elections, and Ramsay MacDonald now presided over a coalition which was largely conservative. Wedgwood Benn had been replaced by the reactionary Samuel Hoare as secretary of state; and, at home, the gentle Irwin had been succeeded by the blimpian Willingdon as viceroy.

The conference bogged down on the question of communal representation. Mahatma Gandhi tried to resolve the issue by private talks outside the conference hall. His efforts were unsuccessful because Mr. Jinnah refused to give up separate electorates for the Muslims. On behalf of the Sikhs, Ujjal Singh reiterated their offer to accept joint electorates; but if separate representation was conceded to any community, particularly the Muslims, the Sikhs would insist on getting it as well. He added: "Unless the communal question, which in the Punjab means the Muslim-Sikh question, is settled, it is not possible for the Sikhs to commit themselves to a federal scheme in which the Punjab would be an autonomous province."[28]

Ujjal Singh and Sampuran Singh demanded for the Sikhs 30 percent representation in the Punjab[29] and 5

[28] *Second Round Table Conference*, Minorities Committee, 1, 89.
[29] In Bihar and Orissa, the Muslims, who constituted 11% of the popu-

percent at the centre, with at least one Sikh member in the central cabinet. Ujjal Singh presented as an alternative a scheme for a territorial readjustment of the Punjab. He proposed that the Rawalpindi and Multan divisions (excepting the districts Lyallpur and Montgomery) should be separated from the Punjab and attached to the North West Frontier Province, which would make the communal proportions in the Punjab 43.3 percent Muslims, 42.3 percent Hindu, and 14.4 percent Sikhs. In this Punjab, the Sikhs would not ask for any weightage, and would only ask for it in the North West Frontier Province and Sindh if the Muslims received it in other provinces. This eminently sensible and constructive proposal[30] received scant consideration from the conference and was rejected along with a similar, but from the Sikh point of view less satisfactory, proposal by S. W. G. Corbett, to detach Ambala division from the Punjab and join it to the United Provinces.

In the absence of agreement among the Indian delegates, Ramsay MacDonald assumed the right to adjudicate on joint versus separate electorates and the proportions of communal representation. The Second Round Table Conference was a dismal failure.

The Mahatma returned home to find many of his colleagues in prison. A "no-rent" campaign had started in the United Provinces; the Red Shirt movement was active in the North West Frontier Province; and terrorists had renewed their activities. The Mahatma protested against Willingdon's repressive measures; Willingdon promptly clamped the Mahatma in gaol.

---

lation had 25% representation, i.e. 130% weightage; in the U.P. they formed 14.8% of the population and had 30% representation, i.e. 100% weightage; in the C.P. they had 4.4% population and had 15% representation, i.e. 250% weightage. Anglo-Indians with .02% population of the Punjab had 4000% weightage. The Europeans had even greater weightage.

30 For details see *Second Round Table Conference*, Minorities Committee, III, Appendix XVII, pp. 1435-37.

THE COMMUNAL AWARD

On April 16, 1932, Ramsay MacDonald made his award on communal representation. Separate electorates were given to all minorities: Muslims, Christians, Sikhs, as well as the untouchables.[31] The Muslims were given 33.1/3 percent weightage in the centre and 86 out of 175 seats in the Punjab. The Sikhs were also given weightage but not in the same measure as the Muslims; their position was as follows:

> 33 out of 175 in the Punjab Assembly;
> 3 out of 50 in the North West Frontier Province;
> 6 out of 250 in the Federal Legislative Assembly; and
> 4 out of 150 in the Council of States.

The Sikhs got nothing in the United Provinces and Sindh, where they had by then sizeable populations.

The award was a bitter blow to the Sikhs. It gave the Muslims a permanent communal majority in the Punjab. Sampuran Singh and Ujjal Singh issued a joint statement strongly criticising the award and, as a protest, withdrew from the conference.

THIRD ROUND TABLE CONFERENCE

The third conference was called to consider the reports of the committees which had been deliberating during the previous months. Only 46 Indians were invited. The Sikh nominee, Tara Singh of Ferozepur, protested against provincial autonomy under a permanent and dominant Muslim majority in the Punjab. He supported safeguards which would provide that measures affecting minorities should not be passed without the consent of three-fifths of the community concerned and be subject to the veto of the governor. He pleaded for weightage in services, a 5

[31] This was later withdrawn under the "Poona Pact" between the Mahatma and Dr. Ambedkar. The untouchables were given heavy weightage in mixed Hindu seats.

percent representation in the Federal Legislature, and Sikh representation in Sindh.[32]

The results of the conference were published in the form of a White Paper in March 1933. A joint committee of the two Houses of the British Parliament was set up under Lord Linlithgow (later viceroy of India) to work out the details of the future administration of India.[33]

THE GOVERNMENT OF INDIA ACT, 1935

On August 4, 1935, the Government of India Act received royal assent. It provided for a Federation of Indian Provinces and Princely States with two Houses of Parliament in the centre: the Central Legislative Assembly and the Council of States. Six of the larger provinces were to have two legislatures of their own; the rest, including the Punjab, only one. About 11.5 percent of the population was enfranchised, giving 30 million people the right to vote. While the provinces were made masters in their homes (subject to the reservation of special powers of intervention by governors), the Central Government remained as before under the control of the governor general. Dyarchy, which had been abolished in the provinces, was introduced in the centre. Subjects such as defence and foreign affairs were to be "reserved" and therefore the prerogative of the governor general.

The Indian National Congress rejected the Government of India Act of 1935, because of the powers of intervention given to governors in the provinces and the dyarchy in the centre. It resolved to capture power and then destroy the constitution. The Muslim League followed suit but reserved the right to try out the provincial scheme "for what it was worth." The princes who had shown such alacrity in accepting federation got cold feet when they realised it

---

[32] *Third Round Table Conference*, pp. 99-102.
[33] Some Indians were invited to collaborate with this committee's deliberations. The Sikhs were represented by Buta Singh Virk, a lawyer from Sheikhupura who was also a member of the Punjab Legislative Council.

would mean surrendering some of their "sovereignty." Sikh political parties had already condemned the communal award; they added their voice to the chorus of denunciation. For all practical purposes, the Government of India Act of 1935 was a still-born child.

The first elections under the new act were held in the winter of 1936-1937. The Sikhs had the choice of backing either the Congress or the Unionists. They rejected both: the Congress because of its predominantly anti-Sikh Arya Samaj leadership; the Unionists because, despite their championing the cause of the agriculturists (which found favour in the eyes of Sikh agriculturists), their primary interest was the Mussulman Jat; the Sikh and Hindu Jat was of secondary importance. They could have formed alliances with one or the other political party, but none of the leaders had the foresight or the following to do so. Instead they split their forces into the Akali and the anti-Akali group (known as the Khalsa National party), both of minor importance in provincial affairs and of none whatsoever on the national scene.

In all provinces except Bengal, Sindh, and the Punjab, the Indian National Congress swept the polls. Its poorest performance was in the Punjab, where it got a bare 10 percent of the vote. Out of the total of 175 seats, the Unionists won 96 and the Khalsa Nationalist party won 15-20 (some members constantly changed their allegiance); the rest were shared by the Congress, Muslim League, Communists, and Independents. Sikandar Hayat Khan chose his cabinet of three Muslims, two Hindus, and one Sikh (Sunder Singh Majithia). The rural-Jat bias was in evidence as before; of the six ministers only one of the Hindus was an urban non-agriculturist.

The Unionist ministry did not have an easy time. Rumours of an impending war with Hitlerite Germany and the increased tempo of the nationalist movement indicated a change in the political barometer. People knew

India would soon be free; but who would be masters of the Punjab—the Muslims or the Sikhs?[34]

[34] The uncertainty bred suspicion and hate; occasionally the hate exploded into violence. The most serious example of this was in 1938 over the possession of Shahidganj—the martyrs' market (the notorious *nakhās* referred to in Volume I—claimed by Muslims to be a mosque, by the Sikhs to be a gurdwara. The Sikhs won their case in the High Court but not before many Muslims had been shot by the police and a few thousand imprisoned for defying the law.

PUNJABI SUBA

PART V
POLITICS OF PARTITION
INDEPENDENCE AND THE
DEMAND FOR A
SIKH HOMELAND

In March 1940 the Muslim League passed a resolution demanding a sovereign Muslim state which
would comprise the predominantly Muslim areas
of India including most of the Punjab. The Sikhs
were deeply disturbed by this demand: the course
of Sikh-Muslim relations over the centuries had
created distrust of Muslim intentions in their
minds. The only alternatives for the Sikhs were
either to align themselves with the Indian National
Congress and resist the Muslim demand for the partition of India or to strive for a state of their own.

During the war years (1939-1945) Sikh politicians
waged a losing battle against the movement for the
formation of Pakistan. When the Muslims won, the
Sikhs of western Punjab had to abandon their
homes, lands, and shrines, and migrate to India.
Dissatisfaction with the treatment they received
from the Government of India and the resurgence
of Hinduism gave an impetus to the demand for
a Sikh homeland.

CHAPTER 15

SIKHS AND WORLD WAR II
(1939-1945)

Indian Politics during the "Phony War," 1939-1940

◆:◆:◆: ON September 3, 1939, Great Britain declared
◆:◆:◆: war on Nazi Germany. The viceroy issued a
◆:◆:◆: proclamation to the same effect on behalf of
India. Although the Indian National Congress expressed
repugnance for Fascism, it protested that Indians had not
been consulted before being committed to the war. The
Muslim League was also critical of the viceroy's declaration. But Sir Sikandar Hayat Khan and the Unionist Muslims—who were technically members of the League—expressed their unreserved support for Britain. For the Sikh
leaders, the war created a crisis of conscience; their loyalty
to the Raj had been diluted by the events of the preceding
twenty years, but they did not wish their community to lose
its coveted position in the armed forces. Unlike the Congressite or the Muslim Leaguer who had no influence over
the martial sections of the populace, the Sikh politician
had to be both a political guide and a recruiting agent.

The titled gentry of the Chief Khalsa Diwan promptly
declared their support for Britain. Congressite Sikhs followed the Congress line of sympathy-but-no-support. Communists, who had acquired influence in the central districts, adhered to the party line of regarding the war in
Europe as imperialist; their agents busied themselves dis-
seminating anti-war propaganda among Sikh soldiers. The
Akalis, who mattered more than all the other parties put
together, were the most confused. The leaders, most of
whom had served terms of imprisonment during the
gurdwara agitation, had little love for the British. They
were equally hostile to the Muslim Leaguers and to the
pro-British Unionists. But they wished to preserve the nu-

merical strength of the Sikhs in the armed services so that when the day of reckoning came, the Khalsa would have an army of its own. The Akali party agreed to help the government and pressed for more Sikh recruitment; at the same time it carped at the administration over matters of little import, e.g. non-availability of *jhatkā* (non-kosher) meat at railway stations, refusal of gaol authorities to allow Sikh convicts to wear kirpans, etc.

The unenthusiastic support of the Akalis and the antagonism of the Communists during the "imperialist" phase of the war was reflected in the reluctance of Sikh peasants to enlist and disaffection in some regiments. A Sikh squadron of the Central India Horse refused to go overseas; over a hundred were court-martialled, and a few executed. Some Sikhs of the 31st Punjab regiment deserted. Sikhs of the Royal Indian Army Supply Corps, serving in Africa, refused to load stores on the plea that they were not "coolies." These and similar incidents compelled the authorities to put a temporary ban on the recruitment of Sikhs. A committee was appointed to look into the situation. It found evidence of Communist infiltration in the ranks and also a pervading sense of uneasiness among the Sikhs concerning the Unionist Ministry's alignment with the Muslim League, which had begun to talk of a Muslim state in the Punjab. Sikh "grievances" were redressed; assurances were given to the leaders that Sikh interests would not be sacrificed to appease the Muslims. A Khalsa Defence of India League under the chairmanship of the maharajah of Patiala was organised to step up recruitment. The ban on the enlistment of Sikhs was lifted.[1]

[1] The enquiry was suggested by the secretary of the Defence Ministry, Sir Charles O'Gilvy, who had served in the Punjab. It consisted of officers well acquainted with the Sikhs: Brigadier General A. E. Barstow (Chairman), Major A. J. M. Kilroy (36th Sikhs), Major A. E. Farwell (Ludhiana Sikhs), Major "Billy" Short (47th Sikhs), and Captain Narinjan Singh Gill, who later joined the Japanese-sponsored Indian National Army. Members of the commission individually toured Sikh districts and discussed the difficulties of soldiers with retired Sikh officers. They also had meetings with political leaders.

The issue was, however, more complicated than a simple "for" or "against" the British war effort. The Sikhs had also to make terms with their fellow Indians—the Hindus, most of whom supported the Congress, and the Muslims, most of whom were emotionally aroused by the notion of an independent Muslim state. It was in the negotiations with their own countrymen that Sikh leaders betrayed confusion and the absence of a precise Sikh point of view.

The Viceroy's efforts to elicit cooperation of Indian political parties in the prosecution of the war failed. On the resignation of Congress ministries, the governors took over the administration in seven provinces. Only in four provinces was the Muslim League (in the Punjab, the Unionists) able to carry on the business of government through elected representatives. While the Muslim League eagerly filled the power vacuum, the Congress reaffirmed its decision to non-cooperate with the war effort and went further into the wilderness. A group led by Subhas Chandra Bose and Sardul Singh Caveeshar (d. 1963) broke away from the parent body to organise more active opposition to the British. A few days later, the Muslim League in a session at Lahore formally resolved that its aim was an independent Muslim state.[2]

Mr. Jinnah assured the Sikhs that they had nothing to fear. Sir Sikandar Hayat Khan, who had sponsored the original draft of the Lahore resolution, tried further to

[2] The Lahore resolution did not use the word *Pakistan* but the intention was abundantly clear: "that no constitutional plan would be workable in this country or be acceptable to the Muslims unless it is designed on the following basic principles, namely, that *geographically contiguous units are demarcated into regions which should be so constituted, with such territorial adjustments as may be necessary*, that the areas in which the Muslims are numerically in a majority as the northwestern and eastern zones of India should be grouped to constitute 'independent states,' in which the constituent units should be autonomous and sovereign." (Emphasis added.)

The words in italics were rightly interpreted by non-Muslims to indicate that the Muslim League did not want the whole of the Punjab but was willing to exclude the eastern half, which was predominantly non-Muslim.

allay the suspicions of non-Muslims. He said: "We do not ask for freedom that there may be Muslim Raj here and Hindu Raj elsewhere. If that is what Pakistan means I will have nothing to do with it. . . . If you want real freedom for the Punjab, that is to say a Punjab in which every community will have its due share in the economic and administrative fields as partners in a common concern, then that Punjab will not be Pakistan, but just Punjab, land of five rivers; Punjab is Punjab and will always remain Punjab whatever anybody may say. This then, briefly, is the political future which I visualise for my province and for my country under any new constitution."[3]

This verbal jugglery did not impress the Sikh leaders. On the contrary, they were convinced that the Muslim Unionist was only the Dr. Jekyll aspect of the Muslim League's Mr. Hyde, and that Sir Sikandar Hayat Khan was just another double-faced politician.

The Sikhs found themselves in a tricky situation. They were faced with two rival freedom movements: one led by the National Congress for the freedom of the country as a whole; the other led by the Muslim League for an independent Muslim state involving a division of the country which would inevitably cut across the land in which the Sikhs lived. Congress leaders, much as they desired to have the Sikhs on their side, were unwilling to concede to them the privileges they enjoyed under British rule. On the contrary, in the shape of things envisaged by the nationalists, separate electorates and privileges based on race or religion were to be abolished. The League promised little; and even in that little the Sikhs placed no faith. What course of action could the Sikhs follow? Obtain the best terms they could from the Congress and support a free, united India? Exploit Congress-League differences and extract concessions from both? Or, ignore both the Congress and the League and strive for an autonomous state of their own? Some politicians advocated one line of policy; others the

[3] *P.L.C.D.*, March 11, 1941.

absolute opposite. Events began to move so fast that they had little time to sit back, take stock of the situation, and then present a united front of Sikh political opinion.

The political stalemate in India ended with the conclusion of the "phoney war" in Europe. In April 1940 the Nazis overran Norway, Denmark, Holland, Belgium and smashed through the Franco-British defences. French resistance collapsed; Britain avoided a near disaster at Dunkirk. In May, Winston Churchill took over as prime minister with L. S. Amery as his secretary of state for India.

Lord Linlithgow resumed his efforts to resolve the Indian deadlock. In August he offered to expand his Executive Council and establish a War Advisory Council with Indian members; he proposed a new constitution with appropriate safeguards for minorities on the successful termination of the war. Both the Congress and the Muslim League rejected the "August offer." The Congress went further and started another civil disobedience movement. In January 1941, Subhas Chandra Bose disappeared from his home in Calcutta. Some weeks later his voice was heard over Berlin radio exhorting his countrymen to rise against the British.

In the summer of 1941, the war entered a critical phase. Fascist powers invaded Yugoslavia and Greece. Germany attacked Russia, and Nazi armour smashed its way towards Moscow. General Rommel threatened the Middle East; Arab followers of the Mufti of Jerusalem declared for the Axis powers.

The succession of reverses suffered by the Allies cast gloom over India. How long would it be before the British capitulated? Would the Fascists take over India? Would there be a civil war between the Hindus and the Muslims? These were the sort of questions people asked each other. The Sikhs became restive. There were rumours of a Khalsa uprising against the Unionist administration. At a largely attended meeting in Amritsar, resolutions were passed denouncing the Unionist Ministry's Muslim Raj. Having thus let off steam, the leaders relapsed into a sullen and confused silence.

Lord Linlithgow abandoned his efforts to bring round the Congress and the League. In July 1941, he announced that he would enlarge his Executive Council from seven to twelve members, of whom eight would be Indians. He also set up a National Defence Council of 30 members. Two Sikhs[4] were nominated to the Defence Council and a year later Sir Jogendra Singh was invited to take over the education portfolio in the Executive Council.

Sikh Attitude to the War in Asia: The Indian National Army

Some months before Pearl Harbour (December 7, 1941), Japanese agents had established contacts with leaders of Indian communities in Thailand, China, Hong Kong, Cambodia, the Philippines, Burma, Malaya, and Singapore. The Indian population of these countries was estimated to be well over two million and known to be hostile to the British. The Japanese chose Rash Bihari Bose to win Indian collaboration. Bose's name commanded the respect of patriotic Indians and, because of his earlier association with the Ghadr rebellion, he was held in special esteem by the Sikhs. Since 1915 he had lived in Japan and had married the daughter of the chief of the Black Dragon Society. Rash Bihari had persuaded the Japanese Government to agree that, in the event of a war with England, Indians would not be treated as enemy subjects and captured but that Indian army personnel would be turned over to him. Major Fujiwara of the Japanese intelligence was appointed liaison officer; his bureau came to be named after him as the Fujiwara Kikan.

Rash Bihari Bose showed a marked preference for Sikhs.[5]

---

[4] The maharajah of Patiala and Naunihal Singh Mann were nominated to the Defence Council.

[5] In Thailand his collaborators were Amar Singh (who had spent nearly

He established contacts with Sikh organisations in Thailand and Malaya and with *granthīs* attached to Sikh regiments.[6]

Rash Bihari Bose followed in the wake of the advancing Japanese armies. Wherever he went, he set up branches of his Indian Independence League.

Japanese armies pushed across the Thai-Malayan border and defeated the British-Indian forces opposing them. Among the thousands of Indians captured was Captain Mohan Singh[7] of the 1st/14th Punjab Regiment. Mohan Singh offered his services to the Japanese commander.

Indian prisoners of war in the camp at Alor Star were placed at the disposal of Mohan Singh. He was elevated to the rank of general and made commanding officer of the newly raised Indian National Army (hereafter referred to by its initials as the I.N.A.). The first brigade of the I.N.A. spearheaded the Japanese assault on Singapore, which was captured on February 15, 1942.

At Singapore 45,000 Indian prisoners of war were assembled. Of the 20,000 who volunteered to join the I.N.A., a high proportion were Sikhs.[8] General Mohan Singh set

---

twenty years in British gaols), Gyani Pritam Singh, who was the *granthī* of the gurdwara at Bangkok, and Chanda Singh, a rubber planter in Yala. These men were members of the "Bharat Culture Lodge" of Bangkok run by Swami Satyanand Puri. In Malaya, Bose's chief supporter was Budh Singh, known popularly as the "Malayan Gandhi."

[6] Members of the Shanghai Revolutionary Party—all Sikhs—had succeeded in converting *granthīs* of Sikh regiments posted at Hong Kong. Three *granthīs* attached to a Sikh infantry battalion were deported to India early in 1941.

In April 1941, Gyani Pritam Singh and Chanda Singh sent three Sikh agents into Malaya. These men were apprehended and sentenced to ten years' imprisonment by the Supreme Court of Kotah Baru. They were later released from Singapore by the Japanese.

[7] Mohan Singh (b. 1909) of village Ugoke (Sialkot district), a Jat of Ghuman sub-caste, joined the army in 1927 as a common sepoy.

[8] Among the Sikh officers were Colonel Narinjan Singh Gill, Major Mahabir Singh Dhillon, Major Nripendra Singh Bhagat, Captain Gurbaksh Singh Dhillon, and Captain Thakar Singh. According to Ishar Singh Narula, later finance minister of the provisional government, more than 50% of the I.N.A. were Sikh; according to General Mohan Singh,

up his headquarters at Singapore, next door to the offices of the Fujiwara Kikan. He called on Field Marshal Count Terauchi at Saigon to find out the precise role that the Japanese had in mind for the I.N.A. He was told that Rash Bihari Bose had called a meeting in Tokyo, where the matter would be discussed.

The Tokyo Conference[9] (March 28, 1942) resolved that "independence, complete and free from foreign domination and control of whatever nature, shall be the object of the movement." Another resolution stated that "military action against India was to be taken only by I.N.A. together with such military, naval and air cooperation and assistance as may be requested from the Japanese authorities by the Council of Action of the Indian Independence League." The prime minister of Japan, General Tojo, took personal interest in the deliberations of the conference. The delegates agreed to meet again at Bangkok. (The choice of Thailand, an independent neutral country, as venue of the next conference was deliberate.)

The Bangkok Conference (June 15, 1942) was attended by representatives of Indian communities of Asian countries. General Mohan Singh was accompanied by 30 officers. Representatives of the Axis powers and the Thai foreign minister were also present. The conference reiterated the demand that the Japanese Government make a firm declaration of its policy towards India.

The Japanese Government did not react favourably to

---

only one-third—the remaining two-thirds being Pathans, Dogras, and Hindu Jats. (Author's interview with Ishar Singh Narula and General Mohan Singh, June 24, 1962.)

Narinjan Singh (b. 1906), a Jat of the Gill sub-caste from village Majitha (district Amritsar), was educated at Sandhurst and received the King's Commission in 1925. After the events narrated in the text, Gill was appointed Indian ambassador to Ethiopia (1955) and then to Thailand.

[9] The conference had an inauspicious beginning. The plane carrying Swami Satyanand Puri and Gyani Pritam Singh crashed, and all its passengers were killed.

the Bangkok resolutions. On the contrary, Colonel Iwaguro, who had succeeded Colonel Fujiwara as liaison officer, said quite bluntly that his government did not intend to make any more statements. Other things caused Mohan Singh to doubt the good faith of the Japanese: they censored I.N.A.'s radio broadcasts; their treatment of Indian prisoners had become harsh; despite promises to the contrary, they had taken over Indian evacuee property in Burma; the Japanese commander of Singapore assumed direct control of I.N.A. personnel; and attempts were made to "nipponize" the 1st Division of the I.N.A. Mohan Singh's relations with the too-nipponized Rash Bihari Bose cooled. The Council of Action again submitted a memorandum to Colonel Iwaguro demanding official recognition of the Indian Independence League, the Council of Action, the I.N.A., and an unequivocal statement on Japanese policy towards India. Iwaguro lost patience. "When work is to be done, there is no time to think of legal quibbles," he retorted.

Mistrust grew on either side. The Japanese had reason to suspect some of Mohan Singh's colleagues, particularly Narinjan Singh Gill, who had been put in charge of Burma. The climax came in December 1942, when Gill was arrested. Mohan Singh dissolved the I.N.A. and resigned. He too was put under arrest.[10] With the disappearance of these men, Sikh enthusiasm for the I.N.A. waned.

Rash Bihari Bose tried to reconstitute the I.N.A.; but the spirit had gone out of the men. He retired from the scene in June 1943, when Subhas Chandra Bose arrived from Germany: Subhas took over the presidency of the Indian Independence League and became supreme commander of the I.N.A.

[10] After two months of detention in a bungalow, the general was taken to an island where he was kept till December 1943 and then sent to Sumatra, where the British re-arrested him. He was brought to Delhi in November 1945 and released unconditionally in May 1946. In 1962 he was elected member of the Rajya Sabha.

Subhas Bose[11] held a rally at Singapore, where he announced the establishment of the Provisional Government of Azad Hind (Free India), consisting of himself as the head of state with four ministers and eight representatives of the armed forces.[12] The Provisional Government of Azad Hind was recognised by the Axis powers and their satellites. It declared war on Britain and the United States of America.

As the tide of war turned, the Japanese became more co-operative with Subhas Bose's I.N.A. than they had been with Mohan Singh's. *Netāji* (beloved leader), the title by which Subhas came to be addressed, was treated with marked distinction when he arrived in Tokyo in November 1943 to attend the Great East Asia Nations Conference. The Andamans and the Nicobar Islands were transferred to the Azad Hind Government.

Subhas Bose moved his headquarters to Rangoon, and the I.N.A. was sent to the Burma-India front. Early in February 1944 it fought the British forces and succeeded in forcing its way into Indian territory. There was great jubilation at Netaji's headquarters.

For the next two months, the I.N.A. kept up its offensive on the Arrakan front aimed at the capture of Imphal. By May the offensive had slowed to a standstill. And by the time the monsoons broke, the British had wrested the initiative, and the I.N.A. was on the retreat. It was badly

---

[11] Subhas Chandra Bose (1897-1945) was born in Cuttack in Orissa. After graduating from Calcutta University, he took a tripos from Cambridge and entered the Indian Civil Service. He resigned the service on his return to India and joined the civil disobedience movement under Mahatma Gandhi. He was elected president of the National Congress in 1938 and again in 1939 against Mahatma Gandhi's wishes. He disagreed with the Mahatma's pacifism and formed the "Forward Bloc" of radicals. He was arrested in July 1940. He escaped from house arrest and made his way to Germany by the overland route. For an excellent biography, see *The Springing Tiger* by Hugh Toye.

[12] In the Provisional Government two officers, Nripendra Singh Bhagat and Lieutenant Colonel Gulzara Singh, and one civilian, Ishar Singh Narula of Bangkok, were Sikhs.

fed, ill-equipped, and outnumbered. The Japanese did not provide it with heavy armour, artillery, or air support. Of the force of 6,000 that had set out to capture Imphal, over 1,500 either deserted to the British or surrendered without a fight; only 400 fell in battle; 1,500 more died of disease or starvation. The majority of those who returned to base had to be hospitalised.

The poor performance of the I.N.A. was a great disappointment for Netaji, but he did not give up hope. By the time the monsoon was over, he had another two brigades trained for battle. In January 1945, the I.N.A. fought its second round with the British 14th Army on the Irrawady. The performance of the second I.N.A. force was poorer than that of the first. Desertions and surrenders depleted its number. By the middle of May, the "heroic" epic of the I.N.A. came to an inglorious end.

Netaji Subhas Chandra Bose retreated from Rangoon to Singapore and from Singapore to Bangkok. On August 18, 1945, the plane carrying him to Tokyo crashed in flames, ending his flamboyant career.

Cripps Mission, March-April, 1942

While Japanese armies were storming across Asia, the political barometer in India continued to register "no change." The viceroy freed the Congress leaders but failed to win their hearts. Even in the spring of 1942 when Japanese and I.N.A. brigades were poised on the Indo-Burmese border and Japanese planes dropped bombs on Calcutta and Madras, neither the Congress nor the Muslim League realised the peril to the country. The British Government did; it sent out Sir Stafford Cripps, who was much admired in India, to persuade the Indians to cooperate.

Master Tara Singh, Baldev Singh,[13] Sir Jogendra Singh

---

[13] Baldev Singh (1902-1961), a Jat of Chokar sub-caste of village Dumana (district Ambala), was the son of a wealthy steel magnate. He made his debut in Sikh politics in 1937, when he was elected to the Punjab Assem-

and Ujjal Singh were chosen to represent the Sikh community. An All Parties Sikh Conference was convened in Delhi (March 26) to brief the representatives. Sir Stafford's draft of proposals had already been circulated. It contained an undertaking on behalf of his government that as soon as the war was over a body of elected Indians would be invited to frame a new constitution for India. There was provision that if any province wished to opt out of the Indian Union it could do so. The Congress party declined to accept the offer on the issue of the apportionment of control of the Defence Department. Mr. Jinnah rejected it because, according to him, Pakistan was not conceded.

Sikh spokesmen, on the other hand, construed the proposals as conceding Pakistan.[14] In their note they stated that the cause of the Sikh community had been lamentably betrayed "by the provision for separation of provinces and the constitution of Pakistan. The note continued: "We have lost all hope of receiving any consideration. We shall, however, resist by all possible means separation of the Punjab from an all India Union."[15]

The Sikhs began to pin their faith in the Congress because Congressites ranging from Mahatma Gandhi down to the humblest volunteer had sworn that they would never suffer the dismemberment of the country. A few days after Sir Stafford Cripps' departure, Sikh faith was rudely shaken. A group of members of the Madras Legislative

---

bly. He financed many ventures of the Akali party, including the Sikh National College at Lahore. In June 1942 he entered into an agreement known as the "Sikander-Baldev Pact" with the Unionists, whereby the Akalis called off their agitation against Sikander Hayat's government. One of the terms of the agreement provided his replacing Dasaunda Singh in the Punjab Cabinet. Baldev Singh was the Sikh representative in the negotiations for the transfer of power and became the first defence minister of Nehru's government. He remained at the helm of Sikh affairs till 1957, when he was replaced by Swaran Singh.

[14] At a press conference (March 29), Sir Stafford was asked whether the proviso enabling a province to opt out of the Indian Union meant that Pakistan had been conceded; his reply was a categorical "no."

[15] Master Tara Singh's letter to Sir Stafford Cripps, March 31, 1942.

Assembly belonging to the Congress party passed a resolution that the Muslim claim for a separate state should be conceded. The leader of this group was C. Rajagopalachari, one of the most respected elders of the organisation who also enjoyed the confidence of Gandhi. The working committee of the Congress disapproved of the resolution and compelled Rajagopalachari to resign. The wedge had however been driven; it only needed hammering by the Muslim League to split the unity of India.

The National Congress climaxed its obduracy by launching in August 1942 a campaign to force the English to "Quit India." Mahatma Gandhi and all leading Congressmen were arrested; the Congress party was declared illegal. Attempts were made in eastern Uttar Pradesh and Bihar to pull up rail lines in order to sever communications with the eastern front. The government had little difficulty in suppressing the movement. The Punjab remained peaceful; the arrests of Congressmen went practically unnoticed.

The viceroy turned to other parties willing to collaborate in the war effort. The ban on the Communist party was lifted. An overwhelming majority of Punjabi Communists were Sikhs. They took over a large building in Lahore, and began to publish propaganda literature in many languages, including Gurmukhi. Their weekly *jaṅg-i-azādī* (war for freedom) and pamphlets supported the Muslim demand for Pakistan.

The Muslim League had the field to itself. The last obstacle to Mr. Jinnah's ambition of unquestioned leadership of the Muslims was removed by the death of Sir Sikander Hayat Khan (December 1942). In the summer of 1943 yet another blow was struck for Pakistan when the Muslim League succeeded in forming a ministry in the North West Frontier Province.[16] Only in the Punjab, Sir Khizr Hayat Khan Tiwana (who succeeded Sir Sikander Hayat) qualified his subscription to the aims of the Mus-

[16] The Congress party ousted the League on March 12, 1945, but its position was never secure.

lim League by adhering to the notion of a united Punjab. Mr. Jinnah brought the full pressure of his organisation to bear on the Unionists. He came to Lahore and demanded that Khizr Hayat Khan abandon the title "Unionist" and describe his government as a "Muslim League coalition." Khizr refused. His Muslim following began to dwindle till the ministry was reduced to relying on the support of a handful of Unionists backed by Congressites and Akalis.

Meanwhile C. Rajagopalachari drove the Pakistani wedge further into the heart of United India. On July 10, 1944, he published his famous "formula" by which, if the Muslim League supported the demand for immediate independence, a commission would be appointed to demarcate those contiguous districts in the northwest and northeast of India where Muslims were in an absolute majority; in those areas a plebiscite would determine whether the people wanted a separate state or to remain in India. It was claimed by Rajagopalachari that Mahatma Gandhi (released in May 1944) agreed with him. Considering the position occupied by these two men in Congress circles, the Sikhs assumed that Congress had conceded Pakistan.

The Sikhs reacted violently to the Rajagopalachari-Gandhi acquiescence. At a meeting (August 20, 1944) at Amritsar attended by leaders of all Sikh parties, speeches were made strongly criticising Mahatma Gandhi's leadership ("Let us give up now the practice of looking up to Mr. Gandhi for the protection of our interests"—Gyani Kartar Singh).[17] Master Tara Singh stated for the first

[17] "If Pakistan is foisted upon the Sikhs with the help of British bayonets, we will tear it into shreds as Guru Gobind Singh tore up the Mughal Empire." Gyani Kartar Singh, *Civil and Military Gazette*, August 21, 1944.

Gyani Kartar Singh (b. 1905), a Dhillon Jat born in village Nagoke (Amritsar) but settled in Chak 40 (Lyallpur), joined the Akali movement at the age of 19. He was elected to the Punjab Assembly in 1937; and president of the Akali Dal in 1946. He was considered the brains behind the Akali party and the propounder of the Akali concept of the Sikh

time that the Sikhs were a separate nation.[18] Nevertheless, a resolution demanding "a Sikh independent sovereign state" was rejected as an "impossible demand." Ujjal Singh and Gyani Kartar Singh said explicitly that the "Azad Punjab" scheme was only a counterblast to Pakistan. Master Tara Singh was empowered to organise Sikh opposition to the division of the Punjab and September 3rd was fixed as "protest day."[19] Tara Singh appointed a subcommittee to create effective liaison with other Sikh groups to form a united front.[20]

End of War

On May 7, 1945, Nazi Germany laid down arms. The Japanese were retreating on all fronts. The Government of India felt the time had come to make another attempt to win over Indian politicians to its side. Congress leaders were released. Lord Wavell, who had taken over as vice-

---

state. He was a close collaborator of Master Tara Singh—and often his bitterest opponent. After independence, the Gyani was often a member of the Punjab Government. There will be frequent references to him in the text.

[18] "Azad Punjab" had, however, been mentioned earlier in Akali conferences in September 1942 and March 1943. Master Tara Singh, addressing a conference of the Akali Dal in June 1943, said: "In the Azad Punjab the boundaries should be fixed after taking into consideration the population, property, land revenue and historical traditions of each of the communities. . . . If the new demarcations are effected on the above principles then the Azad Punjab comprises of Ambala, Jullundur, Lahore divisions and out of Multan division Lyallpur district, some portion of Montgomery and Multan districts." *Indian Annual Register*, 1943, Vol. I, p. 298.

[19] *Civil and Military Gazette*, August 21, 1944. Protest Day was marked by closure of business, processions and meetings where resolutions condemning the Pakistan demand were passed.

[20] Sir Tej Bahadur Sapru and Mr. Jayakar made yet another attempt to solve the communal issue. Since the Muslims refused to co-operate, the Sapru Committee's labours were of little practical importance. A memorandum of the Sikh case was prepared by Ujjal Singh, and a delegation consisting of Master Tara Singh, Sampuran Singh, Gyani Kartar Singh, Ishar Singh Majhail, and Udham Singh Nagoke argued the Sikh case.

roy, invited twenty-one Indian leaders, including Master Tara Singh, to meet him. The Cripps proposals were renewed in case it was found that they facilitated a longterm solution, but the immediate plan was to form a new Executive Council composed (except for the viceroy and the commander-in-chief) entirely of Indians—external affairs relating to British India to be handled in future by an Indian.

The leaders met at Simla in the last week of June 1945, but the conference broke down on the insistence of Jinnah that Leaguers only should represent Indian Muslims on the Executive Council—a claim which was untenable.

Jinnah's stand at Simla convinced many Congress leaders of the futility of trying to collaborate with the Muslim League. Nevertheless some of them recognised that Muslim Leaguers would have to be given the right to secede if they so desired, "provided they did not drag others who did not want to do so."[21] In other words, if this were conceded, the Punjab (and Bengal) would have to be divided; the carving knife was firmly placed on the Sikhs' jugular vein.

[21] Jawaharlal Nehru at a press conference on August 29, 1945. *Tribune*, August 30, 1945.

CHAPTER 16

PRELUDE TO THE PARTITION OF INDIA

General Elections of 1945-1946

◆:◆:◆: THE elections of the winter of 1945-1946 were
◆:◆:◆: the most momentous in the history of India.
◆:◆:◆: The socialist government of England was determined to give India independence and was eager to
find a body of men to whom power could be transferred.
Members of the existing legislatures did not qualify for
this role as they did not reflect the views of the people
on the vital issue of whether India was to remain united
or divided: the central assembly had been elected in 1934,
the provincial legislatures in 1936. Consequently, the British Government decided to have fresh elections and from
the men returned form a Constituent Assembly to frame
a constitution for free India.

The Congress party sensed the importance of this election and made an all-out bid to persuade the electorate to
vote for a free and united India. It was confident of winning the non-Muslim vote; but did not want to take any
chances. It knew that the "feats" of the I.N.A. had excited
the imagination of the people. Consequently, Mr. Nehru,
despite his earlier differences with Subhas Chandra Bose
and his reservations regarding collaboration with fascist
powers, acclaimed men of the I.N.A. as fighters for freedom.[1] The government unwittingly played into the hands

[1] "I was of the opinion three years ago and am still of the opinion that
the leader and others of this army had been misguided in many ways
and had failed to appreciate the larger consequences of their informal
association with the Japanese." Jawaharlal Nehru, *Statesman*, August 20,
1945.
Lord Wavell did not mince his words in describing the I.N.A. as a body
of renegades who had proved false to their oath. "Whatever your political
views, if you cannot acclaim the man who prefers his honour to his ease,
who remains steadfast in adversity to his pledged faith, then you have a
poor notion of the character which is required to build up a nation. I

of the nationalists by charging with treason three officers —a Hindu, a Muslim, and a Sikh—and trying them in the historic Red Fort of Delhi, the hub of the Indian Mutiny of 1857. Nehru personally organised the defence and, after the officers were acquitted, arranged for them to tour the country. Wherever they went they were greeted by mammoth crowds shouting the I.N.A.'s war cries— *"Jai Hind"* (Victory to India) and *"Delhi calo"* (onward to Delhi). Elections followed a few weeks later.

Although the Congress party won a spectacular victory at the polls, it failed to dislodge the Muslim League's hold on the Muslim masses. The League went to the polls on the issue of Pakistan and won every single Muslim seat in the Central Legislature. Even in the provinces (except in the North West Frontier Province) it carried 90 percent of the Muslim electorate with it. The position could be summarised simply: the non-Muslims wanted a united India; Muslims wanted India to be divided to make Pakistan.

The Sikhs had gone to the polls to register their opposition to Pakistan. A *Panthic Pratinidhi* board representing all parties save the Communists was constituted to fight the elections. The Panthic party carried the Sikh electorate with it.[2] Communists, who were the only Sikh group supporting Pakistan, were completely eliminated.

The situation that emerged in the Punjab was as follows: out of a total of 175 seats, the Muslim League secured

---

say to you that amongst all the exploits of the last five or six years for which the world rightly extols the Indian soldier, the endurance of those men in captivity and hardship stands as high as any. As a proof of what they endured as the price of their loyalty to their ideals of a soldier's duty, I will tell you this: the 45,000 Indian prisoners of war who stood firm are estimated to have lost about 11,000 or one quarter of their numbers from disease, starvation and murder; the 20,000 who went to our enemy's side lost only 1,500 or 7½ per cent." Lord Wavell, *Statesman*, December 11, 1945.

[2] The elected men formed a Panthic party in the Punjab Assembly. Baldev Singh (development minister) was elected leader; Ujjal Singh and Swaran Singh, deputy leaders, and Ajit Singh, secretary.

79, the Congress 51, Panthic candidates 22, Unionists and Independents 10 each (there were by-elections in the remaining three). Negotiations between the Muslim League, the Congress, and the Panthic Sikhs failed chiefly on the issue of Pakistan. Ultimately, Sir Khizr Hayat Khan reformed the government with Congress and Panthic support.

Cabinet Mission

In the spring of 1946, Mr. Attlee, the Labour prime minister, announced that a team of cabinet ministers would visit India to discuss the next step towards Indian independence. In a debate on the subject a month later, he stated: "We are mindful of the rights of minorities and the minorities should be able to live free from fear. On the other hand, we cannot allow a minority to place their veto on the advance of the majority." (Mr. Jinnah's rejoinder to these words was that the Muslims of India were not a "minority" but a "nation.") Nine days after the announcement the Cabinet Mission consisting of Lord Pethick-Lawrence, Sir Stafford Cripps, and A. V. Alexander arrived in New Delhi. With the Mission was Major Short, who had earned the reputation of being a friend and adviser of the Sikhs.

The Cabinet Mission first interviewed Indian leaders and elicited their views on the sort of constitution they desired for India: the main purport was to ascertain their reactions to the Muslim demand for Pakistan.[3] The

[3] The Muslim League held a convention from the 7th to the 9th of April 1946 in Delhi, where speeches were made warning the people of what was in store for them if Pakistan was not conceded. The most outspoken orator was Sir Feroze Khan Noon. He said "Neither the Hindus nor the British know yet how far we are prepared to go in order to achieve Pakistan. We are on the threshold of a great tragedy . . . if the British force on us an *akhaṇḍ* (united) government, the destruction and havoc which Muslims will cause will put to shame the deeds of Halaku Khan and Chengiz Khan and the responsibility for this will be Britain's." Ashraf, *Cabinet Mission and After*, pp. 32-34. Gyani Kartar Singh attended the convention as an observer.

Sikhs[4] were represented by Master Tara Singh, Gyani Kartar Singh, Harnam Singh (a lawyer from Lahore), and later by Baldev Singh, then development minister in the Punjab Government.

The Sikh delegation was united in its opposition to Pakistan. The delegates marshalled all the arguments they could to impress the Cabinet Mission of the utter impossibility of the Sikhs either living in a Muslim state or having territory inhabited by them handed over to the Muslims. The Sikh spokesman, Master Tara Singh, said that he was for a united India; but if Pakistan was conceded, he was for a separate Sikh state with the right to federate either with India or Pakistan. Gyani Kartar Singh elaborated the latter alternative as a "province of their [Sikhs'] own where they would be in a dominant, or almost dominant position"; this province would comprise the whole of Jullundur and Lahore divisions, together with Hissar, Karnal, and Simla districts of the Ambala division, and the districts of Montgomery and Lyallpur. Baldev Singh defined the Sikh state, Khalistan, in somewhat the same terms, as consisting of "the Punjab excluding Multan and Rawalpindi divisions, with an approximate boundary along the Chenab, an area comprising the Am-

4 The Central Akali Dal (Baba Kharak Singh's group) presented a separate memorandum on behalf of their party. It drew attention to the faulty compilation of census figures which made the Muslims a majority community in the Punjab. It opposed the partition of the Punjab and reiterated the demands that had been made by the Chief Khalsa Diwan many times since the introduction of democratic institutions, viz. 33% representation in the Punjab, 5% in the centre, one Sikh member in the central cabinet. In addition, it demanded an 8% representation in the Constituent Assembly (as recommended by the Sapru Committee); a permanent 14% Sikh quota in the defence services; Sikh representation in U.P., Sindh, Bihar, Bengal, and Bombay, and an increase in Sikh representation in the North West Frontier Province. The Central Akali Dal supported joint electorates with reservation of seats for minorities and the setting up of special tribunals for the protection of minorities. *Memorandum of the Central Akali Dal* presented to the British Cabinet Mission, April 1946 by Amar Singh, working president.

bala division, the Jullundur division and the Lahore division."[5]

The way the Sikh spokesmen worded their demand for a Sikh state—not as something inherently desirable, but simply as a point in an argument against Pakistan—robbed the suggestion of any chance of serious consideration. As a result, the Cabinet Mission took no notice of Sikhistan, Azad Punjab, or Khalistan and treated the idea, as well as the Sikhs' exaggerated claim to weightage, as something that had been put up (by the Indian National Congress) to thwart Muslim aspirations.

After discussions with Indian leaders, the Cabinet Mission presented a tentative scheme for discussion at a conference at Simla in an effort to find a basis of agreement between the Congress and the League. The scheme envisaged a central government controlling defence, foreign affairs, and communications, and two sets of provinces—one consisting of predominantly Muslim, the other of predominantly non-Muslim areas—competent to deal with subjects not dealt with by the centre. The princely states were to negotiate with the centre. As the gulf between the two parties proved too wide to be bridged by discussion, the Cabinet Mission issued a statement on May 16 setting forth proposals based on the widest area of agreement between the two main parties and which,

[5] V. P. Menon, *Transfer of Power in India*, p. 242. On March 22, 1946, the Shiromani Akali Dal passed a resolution stating "Sikhistan" to be its political objective. It said: "Whereas the Sikhs being attached to the Punjab by intimate bonds of holy shrines, property, language, traditions and history claim it as their homeland and holy land which the British took as a trust from the last Sikh ruler during his minority and whereas the entity of the Sikhs is being threatened on account of the persistent demand of Pakistan by the Muslims on the one hand and of danger of absorption by the Hindus on the other, the executive committee of the Shiromani Akali Dal demands the preservation and protection of the religious, cultural and economic and political rights of the Sikh population and their important sacred shrines and historical gurdwaras with provision for the transfer and exchange of population and property." *Tribune*, March 23, 1946.

they hoped, would constitute a basis on which Indians themselves might decide the future constitution of India. This took some account of the Sikh opposition to forcible inclusion in Pakistan.[6] It envisaged a three-tiered constitution consisting of a union (empowered to deal with foreign affairs, defence and communications), of groups of provinces dealing with such subjects as may be delegated to them, and of individual provinces vested with residuary powers. The provinces could, if they desired after ten years, demand reconsideration of the constitution.

The May 16 proposals further provided for a Constituent Assembly elected by members of the provincial legislatures to draft a constitution along the lines envisaged. After a formal plenary session, the Constituent Assembly was to break up into three sections—section A consisting of representatives of non-Muslim majority provinces; section B of representatives from the Punjab, the North West Frontier Province, and Sindh; and section C of representatives from Bengal and Assam.

The Cabinet Mission suggested that, while the constitution was being drafted, the business of administration should be completely transferred to Indian hands.

The new proposals were cautiously received by the Congress as well as the Muslim League. Jinnah accepted them in the hope that they would ultimately result in the establishment of an independent Muslim state. The Sikhs, how-

---

[6] "Nor can we see any justification," the statement said, "for including within a sovereign Pakistan those districts of the Punjab and of Bengal and Assam in which the population is predominantly non-Muslim. Every argument that can be used in favour of Pakistan can equally, in our view, be used in favour of the exclusion of the non-Muslim areas from Pakistan. This point would particularly affect the position of the Sikhs. . . . We ourselves are also convinced that any solution which involves a radical partition of the Punjab and Bengal, as this would do, would be contrary to the wishes and interests of a very large proportion of the inhabitants of these provinces. . . . Moreover, any division of the Punjab would of necessity divide the Sikhs, leaving substantial bodies of Sikhs on both sides of the boundary." V. P. Menon, *Transfer of Power in India*, p. 468.

ever, rejected the proposals outright[7] and refused to be persuaded that with dexterous manoeuvring they could hold the balance of power in the Punjab.[8]

On June 10, a joint meeting of Sikh political parties was held in Amritsar. A "Council of Action" was set up with Narinjan Singh Gill as "dictator"[9] to direct Sikh opposition to the Cabinet proposals. When the viceroy announced the personnel of the interim government—his fourteen-man executive council—the Sikh nominee, Baldev Singh, was prevailed upon to turn down the invitation. Baldev Singh addressed Prime Minister Attlee on the injustice done to the Sikhs. Mr. Attlee replied that the

[7] Mahatma Gandhi, who had earlier lauded the scheme now supported the Sikhs. He wrote in his *Harijan*: "Are the Sikhs for whom the Punjab is the only home in India, to consider themselves, against their will, as a part of the section which takes in Sind, Baluchistan and the Frontier Province?"

[8] Sikh reactions to these proposals were voiced at a mass meeting held in Lahore (May 26), where Britain was accused of betraying the Sikhs and presenting proposals "designed to strengthen the hands of the British so that their hold may continue to last in India." There was talk of launching a *morcā*.

Master Tara Singh wrote to the secretary of state for India of the "wave of dejection, resentment and indignation" that had run throughout the Sikh community on account of the proposals. He continued: "If the first consideration of the Cabinet Mission's recommendations is to give protection to Muslims, why should the same consideration be not shown for Sikhs?" (Tara Singh to secretary of state, May 25, 1946.)

The secretary of state replied that "the anxieties of the Sikhs were kept prominently in mind when we were drafting the Cabinet Mission's statement and I can certainly claim that of the various alternatives open to us the best one from the Sikh point of view was chosen.

"You will, I am sure, admit that if India had been divided into two sovereign states or if the Punjab had been partitioned, either of these decisions would have been far less acceptable to the Sikhs than the one which was actually reached." (Secretary of state to Tara Singh, June 1, 1946.) From Master Tara Singh's personal files.

[9] Other members of the Council of Action included Master Tara Singh, Baldev Singh, Basant Singh Moga, Ujjal Singh, Inder Singh, Darshan Singh Pheruman, Ajit Singh, Pritam Singh Gojran, Ishar Singh Majhail, Bhai Jodh Singh, Sarmukh Singh Chamak, Nidhan Singh Alam (Namdhari), Gyani Kartar Singh, and Bawa Harkishan Singh.

scheme could not be altered to suit the Sikhs[10] and that they should safeguard their interests by electing representatives to the Constituent Assembly and collaborating in the drafting of the constitution.

The Congress party's willingness to work out the Cabinet Mission's proposals was more apparent than real. Despite ratification by its working committee, Nehru, who had become president, admitted that, although the Congress had agreed to the scheme of May 16, it was not likely to accept the grouping of provinces. He was more anxious to get on with the drafting of a new constitution but was not prepared to join the interim government on the basis suggested. Jinnah construed this as a rejection of the May 16 plan. He offered to form an interim government and, on the viceroy's unwillingness to invite him to do so, had the Muslim League reject the May 16 plan *in toto*. The Muslim League called upon its members to express their resentment against the British Government by renouncing their titles and drew up a plan for "direct action."[11] Direct action (dealt with in the next chapter) resulted in the outbreak of violence in different parts of the country.

Reluctantly, the viceroy invited the Congress party to form a government in the hope that it would win over the

[10] On July 18, 1946, Sir Stafford Cripps made a lengthy statement in the British Parliament on the Cabinet Mission's work in India. Regarding the Sikhs he said: "It was a matter of great distress to us that the Sikhs should feel they had not received the treatment which they deserved as an important section. The difficulty arises, not from anyone's underestimation of the importance of the Sikh community, but from the inescapable geographical facts of the situation. What the Sikhs demand is some special treatment analogous to that given to the Muslims. The Sikhs, however, are a much smaller community, 5,500,000 against 90,000,000, and are not geographically situated so that any area as yet desired . . . can be carved out in which they would find themselves in a majority." *Statesman*, July 19, 1946.

[11] Jinnah indicated what he meant by "direct action." He said: ". . . This day we bid goodbye to constitutional methods. . . . Today we have also forged a pistol and are in a position to use it." August 16, 1946, was to be celebrated as "direct action day."

League. The Congress failed to win over Jinnah but succeeded in persuading the Sikhs to give up their opposition.[12] On September 2, 1946, Mr. Nehru's cabinet was sworn in. Baldev Singh took over the defence portfolio.

A few weeks later, when Hindu-Muslim riots flared up, the League decided to join the government. It was reconstituted on October 26, 1946. The viceroy redoubled his efforts to re-establish peace and enlarge the area of agreement between the major political parties. Leaders of the Congress, the League, and Baldev Singh were invited to London. The main object of this meeting was to obtain the co-operation of all parties in the Constituent Assembly, the League having indicated its unwillingness to participate. The issue in dispute was the interpretation of the clauses dealing with the grouping of provinces. The Congress felt unable to accept the Cabinet Mission's interpretation, which had been accepted by the Muslim League. A statement was therefore issued by the British Government at the conclusion of the discussions stating that these clauses were an essential part of the scheme and expressing the hope that, should the Muslim League see its way to participate in the Constituent Assembly, it would agree, as had the Congress, to refer matters of interpretation to the Federal Court. When the Constituent Assembly met three days later it was without members of the League. These events increased the nervousness of minorities in the "Pakistan group" of provinces, and they began to organise themselves in Assam, Bengal, and the Punjab. The Sikhs asked for safeguards in the Punjab similar to those extended to Muslims in the Constituent Assembly, and they resolved to demand anew the partition of their province.[13]

[12] A meeting of the Panthic Board on August 14, 1946, decided to respond to the appeal of the Congress party to accept the statement of May 16. It did so but without giving up its strong reservations against the Mission's proposals. The Board advised Sikh members of the Punjab Assembly to elect representatives to the Constituent Assembly.

[13] Four Sikhs elected to the Constituent Assembly, who at first had decided to keep away from its deliberations, agreed to take their seats after

Meanwhile the Congress Working Committee had passed a resolution on January 5, 1947, agreeing to advise action in accordance with the British Government's interpretation of the disputed clauses. The qualifying clauses of the remainder of the resolution led the Muslim League to conclude that Congress had no intention of implementing their so-called agreement. The Muslim League accused Congress of making the Constituent Assembly a "rump" parliament and demanded its dissolution. The Congress, in view of the League's non-participation in the Constituent Assembly, demanded the resignation of the members of the Muslim League from the interim government. Lord Wavell warned the Indian leaders that civil strife had assumed such proportions that neither the police nor the army could be relied on to act impartially.

In view of the impasse which had been reached, on February 20, 1947, Attlee announced in Parliament that the British Government would relinquish power in India by June 1948 at the latest; Lord Mountbatten would replace Lord Wavell as viceroy and arrange the transfer of power. Attlee hoped that the sense of urgency would engender responsibility and compel the rival parties to come to an understanding.

While the political *pourparlers* were going on, intercommunal violence in India assumed the proportions of a civil war. We must retrace our steps to see how this came to pass.

---

assurances from Congress leaders. On January 17, 1947, Gyani Kartar Singh and Ujjal Singh explained to pressmen that the right of veto which they were seeking would mean that "nothing affecting the Sikhs should be decided upon without the consent of the Sikhs themselves." Five days later, Gyani Kartar Singh, Ujjal Singh, and Harnam Singh met Lord Wavell and asked for the right to veto legislation affecting them in Section B of the proposed groups of provinces (*Tribune*, January 23, 1947). On January 5, 1947, the Congress, at its session in Delhi, repeated the assurance of its support to minorities, particularly the Sikhs.

CHAPTER 17

CIVIL STRIFE, EXODUS, AND RESETTLEMENT

The Prelude

◆❖◆❖◆ IN a poor and overpopulated country such as
◆❖◆❖◆ India, whose peoples are sharply divided by
❖❖❖❖❖ faith, cultures, and ways of living, tensions
between groups are to be expected. In the north, from the
days of the earliest Islamic invasion, communal tensions
developed between invaders and their supporters on the
one side and indigenous inhabitants on the other. Some
enlightened rulers tried to minimise the differences, and a
few, such as Ranjit Singh, temporarily succeeded. But most
either imposed domination of their own creed, or, like
the British, dexterously exploited differences to their own
advantage. If the festival of *bakr id*, when Muslims chose
to sacrifice cows instead of lambs or goats, passed without
violent protest from cow-venerating Hindus or Sikhs, it
was fortunate. And seldom did a noisy procession of
Hindus or Sikhs deliberately routed to pass along mosques
fail in its object of irritating Muslims and being pelted
with brick-bats.

The 1920's and 1930's were particularly bad decades of
communal bitterness in the Punjab. The Arya Samaj
Śudhi (conversion) movement was matched by the *tanzim*
of the Muslims. Sikh-Muslim relations were embittered by
dispute over Shahidganj claimed by the Muslims to be a
mosque and by the Sikhs to be a gurdwara. Sikhs won
their case and demolished remnants of the old mosque
causing much heartbreak to the Muslims. Sikh insistence
on wearing long kirpans further irritated the Muslims.
These decades also witnessed the increase of communal
militias, the Hindu R.S.S.S., the Muslim Khaksars and
the Sikh *dal*.

Communal violence was, understandably, more an

urban than a rural phenomenon. Villages were predominantly one community or the other, the open countryside less corrosive than the cheek-by-jowl living of congested bazaars. Despite the tradition of distrust, village communities were able to co-exist in peace and even to assume a façade of amity, often simulating kinship. But even the villagers' suspicions of each other's motives and intentions were never completely eradicated. In the clasp of a fraternal embrace often lurked the fear of the dagger. It was this kind of mentality which compelled Jinnah to posit his theory that Indians were not one nation but two: Muslims and non-Muslims. And it was this kind of thinking which came to obsess the minds of Indians in the 1940's.

The communal riots of 1946-1947 were in every way different from those that had taken place earlier. Up till then the riots had been minor affairs: an exchange of lathi-blows, a stab in the back, or a bottle of acid hurled from a balcony. Seldom, if ever, were firearms used. People were hurt, occasionally someone succumbed to his injuries. Women were rarely molested; the aged and the children were always spared. The fracas (a stronger word would be too violent) were always followed by periods of contrition when solemn vows were taken never to hurt each other again.

By contrast, what took place in 1946 and 1947 can only be described as a general massacre. No one was exempted on grounds of age or sex. In the past rioting had been the monopoly of the guṅḍā (thug). The killings of 1946-1947 were master-minded by politicians and executed by gangs drawn from all sections of society, armed with modern weapons such as sten-guns and hand-grenades. The explanation was invariably the same. The antagonists accused each other of starting the riot and exonerated themselves by pleading that they had acted only in retaliation.[1]

[1] The future historian sifting the documents on the partition riots will be faced with a mass of contradictory statements. The only course

The Sikhs were in a peculiar position in the Hindu-Muslim conflict. They professed a neutral creed but were a part of the Hindu social system. They were much the most prosperous section of the Punjab peasantry and, having been nurtured in a martial tradition, more ebullient than their numbers (13 percent in the Punjab) would warrant. The Sikhs often tried to play the role of peacemakers, but since their sympathies were manifestly Hindu, as the rioting increased in intensity, the Muslims quite rightly began to look upon them as an aggressively anti-Muslim element. In any case the Muslims felt that if Pakistan was to bring prosperity to their people, Sikhs who owned the best wheatlands of the Punjab would have to be dispossessed. Chaudhri Rahmat Ali, who first conceived Pakistan, stated this categorically:

"Avoid minorityism, which means that we must not leave our minorities in Hindu lands, even if the British and the Hindus offer them the so-called constitutional safeguards. For no safeguards can be substituted for the nationhood which is their birthright. Nor must we keep Hindu and/or Sikh minorities in our lands, even if they themselves were willing to remain with or without any special safeguards. For they will never be of us. Indeed, while in ordinary times they will retard our national reconstruction, in times of crisis they will betray us and bring about our redestruction."[2]

---

is to peruse both the Hindu-Sikh and the Muslim literature on the subject and then consider "neutral" English opinion. For the Hindu-Sikh point of view, see G. D. Khosla's *Stern Reckoning* (which is also the Government of India's version of the riots) and *Muslim League Attack on Sikhs and Hindus in the Punjab 1947* published by the S.G.P.C. For the Muslim-Pakistani version, see *Intelligence Reports concerning the Tribal Repercussions on the Events in the Punjab, Kashmir and India, Note on the Sikh Plan, The Sikhs in Action* and *The R.S.S.S.* For neutral opinion see Campbell Johnson's *Mission with Mountbatten*, Penderel Moon's *Divide and Quit*, Leonard Mosley's *The Last Days of the British Raj*, General Sir W. Francis Tuker's *While Memory Serves*, and Ian Stephens' *Pakistan*.

[2] Rahmat Ali, *The Millat and its Mission; Muslim League Attack on Sikhs and Hindus*, p. 8.

It is not surprising that the Sikh attitude to Pakistan was one of uncompromising hostility. Since the vast majority of Muslims wanted Pakistan, Sikh opposition to the state was construed as animosity towards Muslims.

"Direct Action Day" and its Sequel

The first shot in the series of riots was fired on the "direct action day" organised by the Muslim League in Calcutta on August 16, 1946. The chief minister of Bengal, Suhrawardy, had declared it a public holiday, and a meeting of the Muslim League took place in the afternoon. Muslim crowds returning home clashed with the Hindus. For four or five days the ensuing violence brought life in the metropolis to a standstill. The official estimate of casualties in these few days was 5,000 killed, 15,000 injured, and 100,000 rendered homeless.[3] The riots continued intermittently for many months.

The Muslim League made no attempt to reassure the Sikhs nor tried to win them over in support of Pakistan. On the contrary, Jinnah himself made it quite clear that Pakistan was to be a purely Muslim state. In a speech delivered in London in October 1946 in which he explained his claim for partition he said: "What would Hindus lose? Look at the map. They would have the best parts. They have a population of nearly 200,000,000. Pakistan is certainly not the best part of India. *We should have a population of 100,000,000 all Muslims." Muslim League Attack on Sikhs and Hindus*, p. 13.

[3] The British-owned *Statesman* of Calcutta put the blame for the Calcutta killings squarely on the Muslim League. "Where the primary blame lies is where we have squarely put it—upon the provincial Muslim League Cabinet which carries the responsibility for law and order in Bengal, and particularly upon the one able man of large administrative experience, the chief minister, Suhrawardy." (This opinion was not as categorically repeated by the editor, Ian Stephens in his book *Pakistan* published in 1963, Chapter VIII.) The view is shared by other English writers: Penderel Moon, *Divide and Quit*, p. 58; Leonard Mosley, *The Last Days of the British Raj*, p. 33; and even General Sir Francis Tuker, whose *While Memory Serves* is notoriously anti-Indian (p. 158).

The Muslim League paper, *Dawn*, castigated the *Statesman's* "diabolically planned one-sided propaganda" and maintained that the Hindus launched a well-planned attack on peaceful Muslims. According to *Dawn*, the casualties in the first week's killings were four Muslims to one Hindu.

In 1946 there were no more than 10-20,000 Sikhs in Calcutta—the majority of them taxi drivers or small businessmen. Although the Muslims regarded them as a militant wing of the Hindus and, as such, marked them out for destruction (many were killed in the first few days), the Sikhs of Calcutta succeeded in winning the confidence of both Hindus and Muslims; they rescued the beleaguered of both communities and offered them asylum in their gurdwaras. Chief minister Suhrawardy issued a statement to the press completely exonerating the Sikhs of Calcutta of the charge of being anti-Muslim and complimenting them on the part they had played in rescuing Muslims.[4]

The killings of Calcutta were a signal for riots to break out in other parts of India, notably Bombay and Ahmedabad. The Muslim League now realised the hazards of allowing power to remain exclusively in the hands of the Congress and agreed to join the government. On October 15, 1946, the central cabinet was reconstituted with four Muslim Leaguers and one scheduled caste nominee of the League. This did not abate the violence; on the contrary, rioting broke out in east Bengal. The two districts chiefly affected, Noakhali and Tipperah, were predominantly Muslim (81.35 percent and 77.09 percent); the victims were mainly Hindus. The news of the killing of Hindus triggered off rioting in distant cities; then it exploded with unprecedented fury in Bihar, where the Hindus vastly outnumbered the Muslims. Loss of Muslim life in Bihar was

Liaqat Ali Khan, general secretary of the Muslim League (and later prime minister of Pakistan) issued a statement to the press on August 28 saying "The Hindu elements whose activities plunged Calcutta into the orgies of violence did so to discredit the Muslim League ministry." He said that hospital records of admissions on the evening of August 16 showed that an overwhelming majority of the wounded and dead were Muslims. Jinnah also stated, "We were attacked by the Congress followers because they wanted to stamp out our propaganda and discredit our cause by creating disturbance and then throwing the blame on us." M. Ashraf, *Cabinet Mission and After*, p. 410.

[4] See Appendix 5.

estimated at over 10,000. Equally fierce was a pogrom in Garhmukhteshwar, where several hundred Muslim peasants were massacred in a day.

Few Sikhs were involved in the riots in Calcutta, east Bengal, Bihar, U.P., or central India. The first time the Sikhs were drawn into the vortex of violence was in the winter of 1946-1947 in Hazara (North West Frontier Province), where Muslims formed 95 percent of the population. Muslims who had been inflamed by the slaughter of their co-religionists in Bihar wreaked their vengeance on the Sikhs. Sikhs of the North West Frontier Province (as well as of the districts of Rawalpindi, Cambellpur and Multan, where the riots spread later) were pusillanimous Khatri and Arora shopkeepers with no pretensions to the militancy which distinguished their Jat co-religionists. In December 1946 a large number of Sikh villages in the Hazara district were destroyed. Sikh refugees began to pour into central and eastern Punjab carrying with them evidence of murder, rape, abduction and forcible conversion.

Prime Minister Attlee made personal appeals to Nehru and Jinnah to co-operate in restoring peace, to facilitate the setting up of the Constituent Assembly and a smooth transfer of power. Indian leaders, in their turn, appealed to the people to abstain from violence. The appeals fell on deaf ears. On the contrary, the announcement that Britain would soon relinquish power added fuel to the flames and rioting was resumed with greater frenzy.

Civil Strife in the Punjab

Till 1946 Khizr Hayat Khan (expelled from the Muslim League in June 1944) had been able to walk the razor's edge with a slender majority comprising Unionist Muslims and Hindus and Sikhs of other parties. But the Punjab Government fought a losing battle against the mounting tide of communal passions and on January 24, 1947, passed an order banning private armies, including the Hindu R.S.S.S. and the Akali Dal, as well as the Muslim League's National Guards. The League seized the opportunity and organised a massive defiance of the order. After a few days the order was withdrawn and the Muslim leaders who had been seized for their defiance were released. It was an ignominious retreat ending in abject surrender. On March 2, 1946, Khizr Hayat Khan submitted his government's resignation. There were scenes of great excitement outside the Punjab Legislative Assembly building in Lahore. Master Tara Singh (not a member of the Assembly) unsheathed his kirpan before the assembled crowd and shouted, "Death to Pakistan." Two days later, a procession of Sikh and Hindu students parading the streets of Lahore clashed with a Muslim mob. News of the outbreak in the capital was a signal for rioting in Amritsar, Rawalpindi, Gujarat, Multan, and Cambellpur.

The largest number of victims of the March riots were Sikhs. The murderous game of stealthily creeping up, quickly stabbing the victim, and running away could best be played against the easily identifiable Sikh rather than the Hindu or the Muslim, who, unless attired in his special dress, had to be stripped naked to see whether or not he was circumcised before his fate could be decided. The Sikhs took a terrible beating.[5] The March riots proved

[5] One of the worst cases of destruction was the Sikh village Kahuta in Rawalpindi district. Lord Mountbatten visited it with his party in April. His press officer records: "Picking our way through the rubble, we could see that the devastation was as thorough as any produced by fire-bomb raids in the war. This particular communal orgy involved the destruction of Sikhs and their livelihood by Moslems who were proving difficult to track down. The Moslems in the area seemed to be quite pleased with themselves." Campbell Johnson, *Mission with Mountbatten*, p. 79.

On March 6, 1947, a deputation led by Ujjal Singh waited on the governor, Sir Evan Jenkins, and asked for the posting of military personnel in towns and cities for the protection of urbanite Hindus and Sikhs. *Tribune*, March 7, 1947.

On April 12, 1947, Bhim Sen Sachar and Swaran Singh asked for a division of the Punjab with two separate ministries—one for Muslim and the other for non-Muslim zones. *Tribune*, April 13, 1947.

that their so-called armies—the Akali Dal, Akal Fauj, or Akal Sena—were paper organisations and their leaders paper tigers.

The communal bent of the police was an important factor in the killings. Over 74 percent of the Punjab force was Muslim.[6] In addition to the regulars, there were 6,000 men in the additional police force which had been raised in the early years of the war by Sikandar Hayat Khan. The additional police was armed, overwhelmingly Muslim, and suspected by non-Muslims as the nucleus of the army for Pakistan.

The riots were a rude awakening to the Sikhs. The fear that their name had at one time aroused had evaporated; their talk of martial prowess was dismissed as the bombast of a decadent race. Humiliation steeled the hearts of the Sikhs against the Muslims; their mood was not one of compromise but of settling scores. The chief secretary's report described the Sikhs without "a vestige of a wish to settle the communal problem without partition" and as "organising for strife." The report continued:

"Their plans embrace the whole community in the Punjab and it is said that they also involve the Sikh states. The Sikhs are being regimented, they are being armed, if they are not armed already and they are being inflamed by propaganda both oral and written. With deliberate purpose their hatred is being increased by the stories related to them by their co-religionists who have suffered at Muslim hands. The important question about the Sikhs is not if and when they intend to fight; it is whether if the Sikh leaders continue as they are doing, they will be able to hold their following in check and maintain their discipline.[7]

On Baisakhi day (April 13, 1947) Master Tara Singh and 280 *jathedārs* vowed at the Akal Takht to sacrifice

---

[6] The total police force in the Punjab was 24,095, of which 17,848 were Muslims, 6,167 Hindus and Sikhs, and 80 Europeans or Anglo-Indians.
[7] *Note on the Sikh Plan*, pp. 7-8.

their lives for the community. From then onwards, the Sikhs began to reorganise their defunct *jàthãs* in towns and villages, to arm them with swords and, if possible, guns.[8] The number of Nihangs increased suddenly. Contacts were made with the R.S.S.S. and Sikh princely states; members of the I.N.A. were recruited to guard the Golden Temple and other historic gurdwaras. A drive was made to collect Rs. 50 lacs for a defence fund.[9]

On March 22, 1947, Lord Mountbatten took over as viceroy from Lord Wavell. His brief was to arrange the transfer of power from British to Indian hands as expeditiously as possible. He started by meeting leaders of the different parties and ascertaining their views on the alternatives—united India or Pakistan. He consulted the governors of the provinces. Sir Evan Jenkins warned him that division of the Punjab on communal lines would be disastrous because in every district the Muslims, Hindus, and Sikhs were inextricably mixed.

Public opinion in the country was, however, in favour of division. Sikh and Punjabi Hindu members of the Central Legislature, the Punjab Assembly, and the Constituent Assembly met in Delhi and passed a resolution demanding a "just and equitable" division of the province on the basis of numbers and property. Akalis and Communists

[8] The chief figures in this "Sikh Conspiracy," as it has often been described, were Master Tara Singh, Gyani Kartar Singh (who took over as president of the Akali Dal on April 16), Udham Singh Nagoke, Ishar Singh Majhail, Jathedar Mohan Singh, Sohan Singh Jalal Usman, Sarmukh Singh Chamak, Amar Singh Dosanjh, "General" Mohan Singh, and Colonel N. S. Gill. In the initial stages Sikh bands were organised by Gyani Harbans Singh of Anandpur, who had been absconding on a charge of murder. (The Gyani was later apprehended and hanged.)

The I.N.A. Sikhs set up their headquarters at Majitha House (the residence of Surjit Singh Majithia) in Amritsar. Surjit Singh, son of Sunder Singh Majithia was later Indian ambassador to Nepal and then a member of Parliament (Congress) and deputy minister of defence.

[9] The Akalis did in fact raise 10-12 lacs. Baldev Singh was confronted by Lord Mountbatten in the presence of the Punjab governor and asked whether he was treasurer of the Sikh defence fund. He denied all knowledge of it. Campbell Johnson, *Mission with Mountbatten*, p. 66.

(who supported Pakistan) put forward the claim to a Sikh state, Khalistan.

Lord Mountbatten returned to England to apprise his government of the Indian situation and to renew his brief. The British Government agreed that if the Indians so desired, they should divide India. For the Punjab and Bengal, the procedure recommended was that their respective legislatures be divided into two groups: one representing Muslim majority districts, and the other the rest of the province. Each group would vote for or against partition. If any one group voted for partition, a commission would be appointed to draw the line of demarcation.

Lord Mountbatten came back to India and placed the plan for voting on partition before the Indian leaders. In an introductory speech, he made special reference to the position of the Sikhs, whose future (according to Mountbatten) had been of the greatest concern to the members of the British Parliament.[10] The viceroy affirmed that he had questioned Sikh leaders many times whether they really wanted a partition of the Punjab which would inevitably split their population into two and had been assured by every one of them that he would rather have the Punjab divided than live in Pakistan.

The Congress and the Muslim League agreed to the proposals in principle. Baldev Singh's views had already been ascertained. All he had to add at this stage was that the Sikh position should be borne in mind in drafting the terms of reference of the Boundary Commission.[11]

[10] The plight of the Sikhs aroused the sympathy of many British parliamentarians. On July 15, R. A. Butler said in the House of Commons: "The British had the happiest possible relations with the Sikh community and, of all the martial races of the world, the Sikhs probably had built up the greatest reputation. The only situation which could mitigate the plight of the Sikhs was that the Boundary Commission should so define the boundary that the maximum portion of the Sikhs should be included within one conglomerate whole." *Tribune*, July 16, 1947.

[11] Sikh leaders were in constant consultation with each other. The Akali Dal Working Committee met in Delhi on June 2, 1947. The meet-

In his broadcast on the night of June 3, the viceroy again spoke feelingly of the fate that awaited the Sikhs.

"We have given careful consideration to the position of the Sikhs. This valiant community form about an eighth of the population of the Punjab, but they are so distributed that any partition of this province will inevitably divide them. All of us who have the good of the Sikh community at heart are very sorry to think that the partition of the Punjab, which they themselves desire, cannot avoid splitting them to a greater or lesser extent. The exact degree of the split will be left to the Boundary Commission on which they will of course be represented.[12]

At a press conference the following day he said:

"There are two main parties to this plan—the Congress and the Muslim League—but another community much less numerous but of great importance—the Sikh community—have of course to be considered. I found that it was mainly at the request of the Sikh community that Congress had put forward the resolution on the partition of the Punjab, and you will remember that in the words of that resolution they wished the Punjab to be divided between predominantly Muslim and non-Muslim areas. It was therefore on that resolution, which the Sikhs themselves sponsored, that this division has been provided for. I was not aware of all the details when this suggestion was made but when I sent for the map and studied the distribution of the Sikh population under this proposal, I must say that I was astounded to find that the plan which they had produced divided their community into two almost equal parts. I have spent a great deal of time both

---

ing was attended by Gyani Kartar Singh (president), Master Tara Singh, Amar Singh Dosanjh, Pritam Singh Gojran, Mangal Singh Gill, Swaran Singh, Ujjal Singh, and Baldev Singh. Baldev Singh reported on his talks. The leaders resolved to press for a partition of the Punjab but to maintain the integrity of the community by demanding that the boundary be drawn at the Chenab. (*Hindustan Times*, June 3, 1947.) Similar meetings were convened at Lahore.

[12] Lord Mountbatten's broadcast at All India Radio, June 3, 1947.

out here and in England in seeing whether there was any solution which would keep the Sikh community more together without departing from the broad and easily understood principle, the principle which was demanded on the one side and was conceded on the other. I am not a miracle worker and I have not found that solution."[13]

Lord Mountbatten was asked whether in drawing the boundaries of provinces to be partitioned the basic factor would be religion or whether other considerations such as property and economic viability, would be included in the terms of reference. Mountbatten replied that it could hardly be expected that a Labour Government would subscribe to partition on the principle of property.[14]

Any notion that the Sikh leaders might have had of pressing their case in terms of the land they owned or the revenue they paid should have been dispelled by this statement. But they persisted in holding to their cherished illusions. A few days later an All Parties Sikh Conference met in Lahore and passed a resolution that the Sikhs would not accept a boundary which did not preserve the solidarity and integrity of the community.[15]

The procedure for partitioning the Punjab (and Bengal) was put into effect straightaway. The Punjab Legislative Assembly was convened, and in the series of votings

[13] It cannot be too often repeated that the Sikhs chose the lesser of two evils—partition or Muslim domination.

[14] Campbell Johnson, *Mission with Mountbatten*, p. 109.

[15] The Sikh reaction to the plan and their temper can be gauged from the chief secretary's report: "The partition plan envisaged divides their [the Sikhs] strength and leaves them in a minority in both areas. . . . They have therefore, been driven back on reiterating their demands and perfecting the organisation of their forces. Their endeavour in both directions is positive in character. The Sikhs are pinning their hopes upon the Boundary Commission and the Congress, but their latest circular issued by the Shiromani Akali Dal shows that the confidence in the strength of the *Panth* has neither been undermined nor surrendered. The circular states that Pakistan means total death to the Sikh *Panth* and that the Sikhs are determined on a free sovereign state with the Chenab and the Jumna as its borders, and it calls on all Sikhs to fight for their ideal under the flag of the Dal." *Note on the Sikh Plan*, p. 25.

all Muslim members voted against while all Sikhs and Hindus voted for partition of the province.[16]

Boundary Commissions were appointed with Sir Cyril Radcliffe as chairman. Each commission included four judges, two Muslims and two others. The Sikh member of the Punjab Commission was Teja Singh, a judge of the Punjab High Court. The terms of reference of the commissions were to demarcate contiguous Muslim majority areas and in so doing to take into account "other factors."

The Sikhs built their hopes of salvaging their shrines, homes, and lands in western Punjab on the commission taking into account "other factors" besides the incidence of population. A memorandum signed by 32 Sikh members of the legislature was presented to the Punjab Boundary Commission. It drew attention to the inaccuracy of the census reports; the floating character of a sizeable section of the Muslim population (i.e. nomadic tribes); the colonisation and ownership of the richest lands in western Punjab by the Sikhs; the location of some of their important historical shrines. The memorandum demanded that the dividing line be drawn along the Chenab River which would, with some modifications, keep over 90 percent of the Sikhs in a compact unit in eastern Punjab.[17]

Representations on behalf of the Muslims claimed not only the Lahore, Multan, and Rawalpindi divisions but also a number of tehsils in the Jullundur and Ambala divisions.

The points of view of the Muslim and the non-Muslim judges on the location of the line of partition were completely at variance; the decision was in fact solely that of Sir Cyril Radcliffe. To East Punjab he gave 13 districts,

[16] In the plenary meeting, 91 votes were cast for and 77 against joining a new Constituent Assembly. Then members from the Muslim majority areas of west Punjab voted by 69 to 27 against the partition of the province. And finally members from the non-Muslim districts of east Punjab voted in favour of partition by 50 for and 22 against.

[17] *The Sikh Memorandum to the Boundary Commission*, July 1947. The Indian National Congress presented a separate memorandum to the Punjab Boundary Commission.

viz. the districts of Ambala and Jullundur divisions, the district of Amritsar and some tehsils of Lahore and Gurdaspur. He also gave the upper reaches of the Sutlej, Beas, and Ravi to East Punjab. The rest, comprising of 62 percent of the total area of the province and 55 percent of the population, was given to Pakistan.

The Radcliffe award was as fair as it could be to the Muslims and the Hindus. The one community to which no boundary award could have done justice without doing injustice to others were the Sikhs. Their richest lands, over 150 historical shrines, and half of their population were left on the Pakistan side of the dividing line.

While the Boundary Commission was holding its deliberations, law and order in the Punjab continued to deteriorate. Ever since the flare up in March, militant organisations had been busy recruiting and procuring weapons. While Muslims[18] got arms from the tribal areas

---

[18] The Muslim League had begun to build up a stock of arms for use in riots as early as December 1946. A secret fund (secret *sandūq*) was raised and arms procured from the North West Frontier Province. This was proved in the enquiry against the Khan of Mamdot ordered by the Pakistan Government in 1949. The following extract from the proceedings of the enquiry amply proves this contention:

Answering questions by defence counsel in the Mamdot Enquiry, Chaudhri Mohammed Hassan, ex-M.L.A., affirmed that in October 1946 members of the working committee of the Punjab Provincial Muslim League and prominent Muslim League leaders met in a secret meeting at Mamdot Villa. Among those who attended were the Khan of Mamdot, Mian Abdul Bari, and the witness.

"The meeting was held at a time when communal riots in Calcutta and Bombay had not yet completely ended. It was decided at the meeting to raise secret funds to be called 'secret *sandūq*' for the purchase of jeeps, trucks, iron jackets, arms and ammunition, and blankets.

"Consequently," witness continued, "another secret meeting was called and the Khan of Mamdot directed Rana Nasrullah Khan to arrange for the purchase of one hundred iron jackets through his brother Rana Zafrullah Khan. At the same meeting Begum Shah Nawaz was asked to arrange for the purchase of hand grenades through her daughter, the late Miss Mumtaz Shah Nawaz.

"Replying to further questions, witness deposed it was true that Sardar Rashid Ahmad and Mohammed Akbar Khan, who is the son-in-law of Begum Shah Nawaz, were also directed to purchase arms and

of the North West Frontier Province and Bahawalpur, Sikhs obtained them from the Sikh states, chiefly Patiala. Kapurthala, and Faridkot. The real build-up of Sikh militarism was the formation of *jathās* in villages armed with the traditional kirpan and the spear.[19] It became obvious that as soon as the dividing line was drawn, the communities would be at war against each other and there would have to be an exchange of population.[20] A Partition

---

ammunition from the Frontier Province and to bring them here for distribution. . . . The respondent provided the requisite money with which seven thousand steel helmets were purchased directly from military stores." *Dawn*, October 22, 1949.

The nawab of Mamdot was able to prove that the money had in fact been spent in buying weapons and equipping Muslims with them. He was acquitted of the charge of misuse of funds.

[19] On June 14, 1947, Lord Mountbatten's press attaché wrote: "We are in the heart of Sikh country here, and the prevailing atmosphere is one of tension and foreboding . . . they [the Sikhs] see that the partition of India means substantially and irrevocably the partition of the Sikhs, and they feel themselves to be sacrificed on the altars of Muslim ambition and Hindu opportunism. . . . No juggling of the Boundary Commission can prevent their bisection. They react accordingly and their leaders hopelessly outmanoeuvred in the political struggle, begin to invoke more primitive methods . . . power is passing to the wilder men, such as Master Tara Singh and some of the younger I.N.A. officers. Rough weather lies ahead of us. . . ." Campbell Johnson, *Mission with Mountbatten*, p. 118.

[20] Sir Evan Jenkins' letter to Lord Mountbatten dated July 10, 1947, regarding his meeting with Gyani Kartar Singh is illuminating. "The Gyani was extremely frank about the intentions of the Sikhs. What he said confirms my view that they mean to make trouble if the decision based on the Boundary Commission is not to their liking, or if the new governments of Pakistan and India are set up before the decision is given."

Sir Evan appended another note to the letter saying: "Gyani Kartar Singh came to see me today. . . . He said he had come to see me about the Indian Independence Bill and the Boundary Commission. . . . He said that in the Punjab there would have to be an exchange of populations on a large scale. Were the British ready to enforce this? He doubted if they were, and if no regard was paid to Sikh solidarity a fight was inevitable. The British had said for years that they intended to protect the minorities and what had happened? The present situation was a clear breach of faith by the British.

"I replied that I realised that the Sikhs were dissatisfied, but when independence came to any country some classes, who had formerly regarded themselves as protected, inevitably suffered. At the same time,

Council was set up to handle the problem. A Boundary
Force under Major General Rees assisted by Brigadier
Digambar Singh Brar (India) and Colonel Ayub Khan
(later president of Pakistan) consisting of two and a half

I thought that the Sikhs had only themselves to blame for their present
position. The Gyani himself had insisted on partition and Baldev Singh
had accepted the plan.

"Gyani then said neither had viewed partition as being based on
population alone. The Sikhs were entitled to their own land just as
much as the Hindus or the Muslims. They must have their shrine at
Nankana Sahib, at least one canal system, and finally arrangements must
be made so as to bring at least three-quarters of the Sikh population
from West to East Punjab. Property must be taken into account as
well as population in the exchange as the Sikhs on the whole were better
off than the Muslims. Gyani said that unless it was recognised by His
Majesty's Government, the viceroy and the Party leaders that the fate
of the Sikhs was a vital issue, there would be trouble . . . they would be
obliged to fight . . . that the Sikhs realised that they would be in a
bad position, but would have to fight on revolutionary lines by murdering officials, cutting railway lines, destroying canal headworks and so on.

"I reiterated that this would be a very foolish policy, to which Gyani
replied that if Britain were invaded, no doubt my feelings would be
much the same as his. . . . The Muslims were now putting out some
conciliatory propaganda about their attitude towards the Sikhs in their
midst, but their intention was that of a sportsman who is careful not
to disturb the birds he means to shoot. He believed the Muslims would
try to make the Sikhs of West Punjab feel secure and then set about them
in earnest."

Sir Evan Jenkins ended his dispatch: "Finally the Gyani appealed to
me to do all I could to help the Sikhs during a period of great trial.
He said I surely could not wish to abandon the Punjab to tears and
bloodshed. There could be tears and bloodshed here if the boundary
problem was not suitably solved. The Gyani was matter of fact and
quiet throughout our conversation but wept when he made his final
appeal. This is the nearest thing to an ultimatum yet given by the
Sikhs. They are undoubtedly puzzled and unhappy. I see no reason to
suppose that they have lost the nuisance value they have in the past
possessed over a century."

On July 13, Jenkins wrote yet another letter to Mountbatten, rein-
forcing his warning of the dangers of the situation. 'The communal feeling is now unbelievably bad,' he said. 'The Sikhs believe that they will
be expropriated and massacred in West Punjab and smothered by the
Hindus and Congress generally in East Punjab. They threaten a violent
rising immediately.' " Leonard Mosley, *The Last Days of the British Raj*,
pp. 205-7.

divisions was entrusted with the control of movements of populations in the districts of Sialkot, Lyallpur, Montgomery, Lahore, Amritsar, Gurdaspur, Hoshiarpur, Jullundur, Ferozepur, and Ludhiana.

On August 15, 1947, as India celebrated its independence, nearly ten million Punjabis were at each other's throats. In East Punjab, the Muslim police were disbanded and the Muslims left to the mercy of marauding bands of Sikhs and R.S.S.S. militia. Sikh violence attained its peak in September 1947.[21] General Rees of the Boundary Force reported:

"*Jathās* were of various kinds in strength from twenty to thirty men up to five or six hundred or more. When an expedition was of limited scope the *jathās* did not usually increase beyond the numbers which had originally set out; but if the projected operation was to attack a village, a convoy or a train, the local villagers would join and swell the assailants to several thousands. They had recognised leaders, headquarters which constantly shifted about, and messengers who travelled on foot, on horseback and even by motor transport. The usual method of attack, apart from assaults on villages, was from ambush. Information as to the movement of convoys or trains was relatively easy to obtain. As the crops were high, it was simple to ambush marching columns of refugees. The attackers would remain concealed until the last moment and then would pour in a stampeding volley, usually in the northwest frontier fashion, from the opposite side from where the shock assailants lay in wait. In spite of the best efforts of the escorts to hold them together, the refugees would scatter in panic; whereupon the ambush parties would dash in with sword and spear. With attackers and attacked

---

[21] "Mountbatten asked about Sikh motives. Was the object to set up a Sikh State? V. P. [Menon] replied no. Politically they had lost out, and had not even gained the Jullundur division. Their motive was almost entirely revenge." September 15, 1917. Campbell Johnson, *Mission with Mountbatten*, p. 191.

inextricably mixed, the escort was usually unable to protect its charges."[22]

On both the Indian and Pakistan sides horrible atrocities were committed. Foot-weary convoys of refugees were attacked till the roads were clogged with corpses; trains were attacked and sent across the borders with bogies jammed with slaughtered passengers. No quarter was given to the sick or the aged or even to infants. Young women were occasionally spared only to be ravished. Never in the history of the world was there a bigger exchange of populations attended with so much bloodshed.[23]

Then the monsoon burst in all its fury: rivers rose; roads were submerged; bridges collapsed; rail-tracks were washed away. In refugee camps cholera broke out. The floods wiped the bloodstains off the face of the land.

The Exodus and Resettlement in East Punjab

In the winter of 1946-1947 Sikh refugees from the North West Frontier Province had started trekking to the central districts of the Punjab. The second round of violence in March 1947 showed that, even in cities such as Lahore and Amritsar, the Muslim thug could get the better of the Hindu or Sikh hoodlum. The refugees resumed their trek southeastwards into districts where a preponderance of their coreligionists gave them a sense of security.

In August when rioting assumed the proportion of civil war, people again packed up their belongings and awaited directions from their leaders for the next move. Master Tara Singh and Gyani Kartar Singh (both authors of the

[22] Lt. Col. G. R. Stevens, *History of the 4th Indian Division.*

[23] There are various estimates of the number of people killed in the Punjab during these riots. Penderel Moon, who claims to have had a "pretty accurate knowledge of the casualties" in Bahawalpur and adjacent Pakistani districts and who compared notes with Sir Francis Mudie, governor of West Punjab, came to the conclusion that it was 60,000 dead in Pakistan and a little more in East Punjab. He qualified his first computation of a total of 200,000 dead on both sides as "somewhat inflated." Penderel Moon, *Divide and Quit*, p. 293.

partition plan) first exhorted the Sikhs in western Punjab to stay where they were and make their terms with Pakistan. Mahatma Gandhi made similar appeals to the Muslims of eastern Punjab to stay on in India. But the wave of hatred that swept the province compelled the Hindus and Sikhs in Pakistan to leave for India and Muslims in eastern Punjab to seek asylum in Pakistan; the two-way traffic assumed mammoth proportions.[24] A Military Evacuation Organisation (M.E.O.) was set up in the first week of September. There were four main routes from Pakistan Punjab to Indian Punjab: Narowal-Dera Baba Nanak, Lahore-Amritsar, Kasur-Ferozepur and Montgomery-Fazilka. The M.E.O. and the Boundary Force tried to minimise collisions between the convoys moving in opposite directions and to fight off gangs which preyed on them. The Indian Government organised camps for non-Muslim refugees, the biggest one being at Kurukshetra. In October 1947, the refugee population from West Punjab in Indian camps was well over 720,000.

The new governments were not sure of the exact nature of the problem. Was the migration permanent? Or would the people return to their ancestral homes? Even with this uncertainty Indian authorities showed commendable expedition in tackling the task of rehabilitation. A Resettlement Department with a staff of nearly 8,000 *patwārīs* and rural officers was established at Jullundur. Two young Sikh civilians, Tarlok Singh and M. S. Randhawa, were appointed to tackle the problem. Tarlok Singh drew up a Land Resettlement Manual which outlined the policy to be followed. The government took over the houses and

24 Sir Francis Mudie, governor of west Punjab (Pakistan), wrote to Jinnah on September 5, 1947, regarding the desirability of evicting Sikh colonists from Lyallpur: "I am telling everyone that I don't care how the Sikhs get across the border; the great thing is to get rid of them as soon as possible. There is still little sign of three lakh Sikhs in Lyallpur moving, but in the end they too will have to go." G. D. Khosla, *Stern Reckoning*, pp. 314-16; *Muslim League Attack on Sikhs and Hindus*, p. 138.

lands of Muslim evacuees. Hindu and Sikh peasant refugees crossing the frontier as well as those in refugee camps were directed to specified towns and villages. Each family, irrespective of what is left behind in Pakistan, was temporarily allotted a "plough unit" of ten acres of land and given loans to buy seed and agricultural equipment.

By the time the winter harvest had been garnered it became apparent that the migration was in fact a permanent transfer of population. The temporary allotments had to be made permanent and the refugees compensated out of what the Muslims had left behind. This was not easy as not only was the number of Hindus and Sikhs who had come out of West Punjab and the North West Frontier Province somewhat larger than the number of Muslims who had left East Punjab (4,351,477 against 4,286,755), but there was also a considerable difference, both quantitative and qualitative, in the land left behind by the Muslims: the Hindus and Sikhs had left behind 67 lac acres of the very best agricultural land; the Muslims of East Punjab left behind only 47 lac acres of comparatively poor soil. Added to the complications was the fact that in districts such as Karnal, Muslim-owned land was in the possession of Hindu tenants, who were naturally reluctant to let refugees take over cultivation.

Tarlok Singh produced an elaborate scheme for permanent resettlement. Since the productive capacity of land varied, to compute the amount of compensation due, he evolved a "standard acre," i.e. an acre which could yield between 10 to 11 maunds of wheat. The standard acre was equated to one rupee, and land was assessed in terms of annas fraction of the standard acre. In terms of this standard acre, the Hindu-Sikh refugees who had left behind nearly 4,000,000 units had to be compensated with less than 2,500,000 units. In order to make the distribution of land equitable, a scheme of graded cuts was introduced by which the small landholder suffered very little loss but the rich zamindar was reduced to modest proportions.

Partition brought about revolutionary changes in the economic, social, and political structure of the Punjab. From having been the most prosperous community the Sikhs were reduced to the level of other Indian communities. This applied both to the agriculturist as well as the trading classes. Sikh farmers of western Punjab who owned large estates were reduced in the process of resettlement; those of eastern Punjab were levelled by legislation fixing 30 acres as the maximum holding of land. The urbanite Sikh was worse hit than the peasant. Urban property left behind by Muslims was infinitesimal compared with what the Sikhs left in Pakistan. In addition the Sikh merchant had to compete both with the Hindu refugee as well as established Hindu tradesmen.

Class barriers were lowered. The temporary allotments of 1947 had, by giving them the same amount of land, elevated menial classes—sweepers, cobblers, potters, and weavers—to the level of the Jat and Rajput agriculturists. The 30-acre ceiling and cooperative farming carried the levelling process further.

Adversity had its redeeming features. Reduction in the size of agricultural holdings forced owners to cultivate their lands themselves rather than rent them out to tenants. Absentee landlordism virtually disappeared. Farmers invested their savings in tractors, sinking tube-wells, and introducing modern methods of cultivation. Agricultural cooperatives, improved seed, and fertiliser stores became a common feature in villages. More attention began to be paid to animal husbandry. With the advent of the community project movement, "key" villages with facilities for artificial insemination, castration of poorer breeds of bulls, veterinary services, and dairy farming became lucrative sources of income. Another innovation was the development of poultry farming, which had long been neglected. Many farmers took to raising birds imported from foreign countries. In all these side-lines to agriculture Sikh farmers took the lead. Within a few years eastern Punjab changed from a deficit to a surplus region. The impact of the Sikh peasant was felt beyond the Punjab. Because of the paucity of land many were settled in the malarial jungles of the Terai in Uttar Pradesh and in the weed-infested regions of Madhya Pradesh and Rajasthan. Sikh refugee farmers showed the mettle of their colonising forefathers in clearing the jungles and bringing barren lands under the plough. The Sikh trading classes showed the same grit as the peasants in rehabilitating themselves in their professions. Many had been reduced to abject poverty. Prosperous merchants had to start anew hawking their wares in the streets. Girls took to plying tongas; their younger brothers became shoe-shine boys. But seldom, if ever, was a Sikh man, woman, or child seen begging in the streets. And once again the Sikhs earned the respect of their compatriots as men of courage and fortitude.

The change in the political complexion of the Sikh community was significant. The exodus scattered the following of the Sikh leaders of western Punjab and weakened their position. Master Tara Singh retained his hold over the masses by becoming the spokesman of the aggrieved refugees; but others such as Gyani Kartar Singh and even more the urbanite non-Jats such as Ujjal Singh and Hukam Singh[25] were compelled to secure their future by co-operating with the party in power. By contrast, politicians from East Punjab districts gained in strength and stature. Post independence years saw the rise of men such as Pratap Singh Kairon,[26] Swaran Singh,[27] and Gyan Singh Rarewala.[28]

[25] Hukam Singh (b.1895), an Arora lawyer from Montgomery, rose to prominence in Akali politics after partition. He, along with Gyani Kartar Singh and Tara Singh, first put forward the demand for a Punjabi Suba. He was elected to the Lok Sabha twice and was made deputy speaker. He withdrew from active support of the "Suba" in 1961; in 1962 he was elected speaker of the Lok Sabha by Congress support.

[26] Pratap Singh Kairon (1901-1965), a Dhillon Jat of village Kairon took a degree in political science from the University of Michigan. He joined the Congress party in 1929, was sentenced to 5 years' imprisonment in 1932. He was elected to the Punjab Legislative Assembly in

The most significant effect of the migration was to create Sikh concentrations in certain districts of East Punjab. Although the Sikh migrants spread all over India and many thousands went abroad, more than three-fourths of their population remained in what had been the cradle of Sikhism—Malwa. This along with other factors (dealt with in the following chapter) revived the demand for a Sikh state.[29]

The East Punjab Government was organised with a temporary capital at Simla. Sir Chandu Lal Trivedi was appointed governor. Gopi Chand Bhargava was elected chief minister by the legislators who came over to the Indian side.

1936 and again in 1946. He was a member of the Constituent Assembly. He was a minister in the Bhargava Cabinet 1947-49 and the Sachar Cabinet in 1952-56. He became chief minister of the Punjab in 1956. Kairon opposed the "Suba" demand and was chiefly responsible for crushing the two movements launched in its support. He was a man of unusual drive and unconventional methods of administration. In June 1964 he was compelled to resign following a judicial pronouncement of corruption against him and his family. He was assassinated on February 6, 1965.

[27] Swaran Singh (b.1907), a Purewal Jat lawyer from village Shankar (district Jullundur), was elected to the Punjab Legislative Assembly in 1946 and made development minister. He continued in the government after partition; in 1952 he joined Nehru's cabinet as minister for works, housing, and supply; in 1957 he became minister for steel, mines, and fuel; in 1962 minister of railways; in 1963 minister for food and agriculture, and in 1964 minister of external affairs in the cabinet of Lal Bahadur Shastri.

[28] Gyan Singh Rarewala (b.1901), a Cheema Jat of village Rara in Patiala state, was chief minister of PEPSU; minister in the Kairon ministry till 1962 and thereafter the chief opponent of Kairon.

[29] Some Sikh members of the East Punjab Assembly presented a list of thirteen demands to the Constituent Assembly. They demanded 50% representation in the East Punjab Legislature; the posts of governor and chief minister of East Punjab to be alternatively Sikh and Hindu; 40% Sikh representation in the provincial service; 5% Sikh representation in the Central Legislature; and at least one Sikh minister and one Sikh deputy minister in the Central Cabinet. If these demands were not conceded then, said the signatories, they would press for a separate Sikh province. *Statesman*, November 9, 1948.

In 1948, Sikh states of the Punjab along with Maler-kotla and Nalagarh were merged to form the Patiala and the East Punjab States Union (PEPSU) with Maharajah Yadavendra Singh (who had taken the lead in persuading the princes to join the Indian Union) as *rājpramukh* (governor) and Gyan Singh Rarewala as chief minister. In PEPSU, the Sikhs formed a majority of the population.

PEPSU had a short and unstable career, with the Akalis and the Congress evenly matched in strength. Gyan Singh Rarewala was replaced by the Congressite Raghbir Singh, and, on Raghbir Singh's death, by Brish Bhan. The concentration of Sikh population and its Akali proclivities induced the government to abolish PEPSU in 1956 and merge it into East Punjab.

The first general elections in 1952 gave the Congress party an over-all majority in the Punjab. Bhim Sen Sachar became chief minister. During this ministry's tenure, the new capital of the Punjab was built at Chandigarh near the foothills of the Himalayas.[30] Sachar was displaced by Pratap Singh Kairon in 1956. The Congress party again won the elections in 1957 and 1962, and Kairon remained firmly in the saddle till he was removed from office in June 1964.

[30] Chandigarh was designed by a team of foreign experts: Le Corbusier, Jeanneret, Maxwell Fry, and his wife, Jane Drew.

CHAPTER 18

THE SIKH HOMELAND

◈◈◈◈ THE ideal of a sovereign Sikh state has never
◈◈◈◈ been very far from the Sikh mind. Ever since
◈◈◈◈ the days of Guru Gobind Singh, Sikh congregations have chanted the litany *rāj karey gā Khālsā*—the
Khalsa shall rule—as a part of their daily prayer; innumerable Sikhs gave their lives to achieve this ambition. The
establishment of the kingdom of Maharajah Ranjit Singh
confirmed the belief of the Sikhs that it was their destiny
to rule the Punjab. The fall of the kingdom was regarded
as a temporary setback. And despite their early loyalty
towards the British, when home rule for India was first
proposed, Sikh leaders began to say: "If the British have
to go, it is only right that the Punjab should be restored
to the Sikhs from whom it was wrongfully seized."

The Sikhs had to contend, however, with changing concepts of government as well as with the views of Hindus
and Muslims. The British introduced the notion of the
rule of the majority, i.e. that neither property nor prowess
mattered as much as numbers. And in the matter of numbers the Sikhs were a bare 12-13 percent of the population
of the Punjab and a little over 1 percent of the population
of India. If the right to govern was to be determined by
the simple counting of heads, then most of India would be
ruled by the Hindus and the Muslim majority areas, including the Punjab, by the Muslims. Sikh energies were
therefore directed towards frustrating the Muslim design
of ruling the Punjab.

The Sikh leaders' first move was to turn the democratic
argument against the Muslims. They aligned themselves
with the Hindus in demanding joint electorates and abolition of privileges for minority communities because they
felt that these measures would dilute Muslim communal-
ism. When the Muslims succeeded in securing separate

electorates and privileges, the Sikhs pressed for the same for themselves and began to ask for weightage so that their strength combined with that of the Hindus would outweigh that of the Muslims. They pursued these tactics for almost twenty years till they realised that no government could reduce a Muslim majority to a minority. Then a third line of resistance was evolved, viz. to ask for the redrawing of the boundaries of the Punjab so that the predominantly Muslim areas of the west might be separated from the predominantly non-Muslim areas of the east. Scant notice was taken of this proposal.[1] The Government of India Act of 1935 confirmed the worst fears of the Sikhs. The Punjab, like other provinces of India, attained autonomy. The Muslim-dominated Unionist party resumed control and with enhanced powers continued its policy of reducing Sikh representation to its numerical deserts.

The concept of the Sikh state which had never been abandoned was resuscitated. It gathered strength as the Muslim demand for Pakistan grew. In the critical years preceding the relinquishment of power by Britain, Sikh leaders allowed themselves to be guided by the leaders of the National Congress and, instead of boldly demanding a sovereign Sikh state (which the Sikh masses wanted), put the notion forward only as an argument against Pakistan. All manner of considerations—historic, economic, hydrographic, and geographic—were advanced to inflate the size of the non-Muslim part of the Punjab so that what remained would make Pakistan a mockery. Sikh leaders did not press the case for a Sikh state with sincerity. No one took their line of approach seriously.[2]

[1] This was done at the Second Round Table Conference in 1931. See Minorities Committee, III, Appendix XVII, pp. 1435-37.

[2] At the end of the war, a "Sikh homeland" plan was evolved by the Communists. This was on the eve of the 1945-46 elections and was designed to appease the Sikh masses, who had been angered by the party's enthusiastic support of Pakistan. The "Sikh homeland" scheme was pro-

In the lawlessness that prevailed during the days of partition, some Sikhs were tempted to establish a government of their own in eastern Punjab. Another version of the *sau sākhī* was unearthed; it predicted the crown for Yadavendra Singh of Patiala in *sambat* 1890 (1947); in Moti Bagh palace the popular after-dinner topic was of "Greater Patiala." The more down-to-earth Harindra Singh of Faridkot propagated the idea of a Sikh state minus the maharajah of Patiala. Sikhs of the I.N.A. vaunted their ability to effect a military coup; their visions, like those of the princes, were but vaporous creations of minds that dreamt much but dared very little.

The partition created a new situation. Sikh agricultural migration from West Pakistan was halted about the Ghaggar river with the result that in some tehsils of East Punjab and in the princely states the Sikhs came to be a majority of the population.[3] For the first time the democratic argument—the will of the majority—could, in certain areas, be put forward in support of a Sikh state. Post-partition conditions made many Sikhs doubt the wisdom of having thrown their lot with the Hindus. The scramble for land and urban property left by Muslim evacuees created ill-will between them and Hindu refugees as well as the Hindus of Hariana who had taken possession of lands left by Muslims.

Sikh cultivators were also piqued by administrative delays in the granting of rehabilitation loans. Sikh trading classes of western Punjab were more severely hit. Their

pounded by G. Adhikari, who had only two years earlier dismissed it as "not the demand of progressive Sikh nationalism."

In a letter to Prof. I. N. Madan dated January 25, 1943, Adhikari wrote: " 'Azad Punjab' is not the demand of progressive Sikh nationalism. It is a demand which is a counterblast to the demand for self-determination by the Muslims in the Punjab. It is in the interest of the Sikh people that they accept the demand of the Muslims of the Punjab and get them to accept their own rights of self-determination."

[3] Table showing the proportions of Hindus and Sikhs in 1951 on next page.*

capital was lost. There were no Muslim traders in East Punjab whose place they could take, and the government was not in a position to give them enough money to restart their business. Too proud to beg, their pride did not prevent them from being extremely bitter with a government which could never do enough for them; and bitter with the Hindus, whose sufferings they minimised. They asked themselves: "The Muslims got Pakistan, the Hindus got Hindustan; but what did we Sikhs get out of it?" In that frame of mind, it was not difficult to fan the smouldering fire of resentment against fate and create visions of a Sikh utopia.

The government showed little imagination in dealing with the Sikhs. Transport of goods by road, over which the Sikhs had virtually a monopoly, was nationalised. In Uttar Pradesh, Madhya Pradesh, and Rajasthan, Sikh settlers were regarded with the suspicion natural towards more virile strangers. In Calcutta their control over the

North-western Districts	Hindus %	Sikhs %	Northern & South-eastern Districts	Hindus %	Sikhs %	
(a) *Punjab*			(a) *Punjab*			
Hoshiarpur	73.2	26.2	Hissar	91.3	7.7	
Jullundur	42.6	56.5	Rohtak	98.5	0.7	
Ludhiana	37.4	61.7	Gurgaon	82.1	0.7	
Ferozepore	38.7	59.6	Karnal	90.3	8.9	
Amritsar	27.7	70.7	Ambala	72.2	24.6	
Gurdaspur	45.5	46.6				
(b) *Pepsu*			(b) *Pepsu*			
Patiala	52.1	47.1	Sangrur	65.4	33.4	
Barnala	21.0	71.0	Mohindergarh	99.0	0.6	
Bhatinda	21.6	78.1	Kohistan	89.0	9.0	
Kapurthala	35.5	63.6				
Fatehgarh Sahib	33.6	65.2				
				Hindus	*Sikhs*	*Others*
	(1) Punjab			63.5	33.4	3.1
	(2) Pepsu			48.8	49.3	1.9
	(3) Punjab and Pepsu			62.3	35.0	2.7

* India (Republic), Census Commissioner, *Census of India 1951*, Vol. VIII, Part II-A, pp. 298-300. In 1956, the states of Punjab and Pepsu were merged, and some of their districts combined.

taxi and bus services had to be ended to provide employment for Hindu refugees coming from East Pakistan. The
abolition of separate electorates and communal privileges
and insistence on competitive paper-examinations for entrance into services (including the official cadres of the
armed forces) adversely affected the Sikhs. It also increased
the incidence of apostasy in the army and the civilian services. Many Sikh civil servants and soldiers found that, in
a secular state, they did not have to be *kesādhārīs* to hold
their jobs; nor did the fact of being clean-shaven prejudice
their chances of promotion. Orthodox Sikhs readily
ascribed this to the machinations of a wily Hindu government.

The chief cause of Sikh uneasiness in free India was
the resurgence of Hinduism which threatened to engulf
the minorities. Renascent Hinduism manifested itself in
a phenomenal increase in Hindu religious organisations,
the revival of Sanskrit, and the ardent championing of
Hindi. The Punjabi Hindu was more aggressive than the
Hindu of other provinces.[4] Organisations, notably those
connected with the Arya Samaj and its political counter-
part, the Jan Sangh, started a campaign to persuade Punjabi-speaking Hindus to disown their mother tongue and
adopt Hindi.[5]

The resurgence of Hinduism along with the increase
in apostasy (which in effect meant lapsing into Hinduism)

[4] "The sudden emergence of this (Hindu) strong, politically conscious
minority suffering from an acute persecution complex into an absolute
statutory majority in the East Punjab transformed all their past frus-
trations into an intensely aggressive communal consciousness." Letter
from Hukam Singh in the *Tribune*, September 29, 1950. Hukam Singh
was particularly vituperative against Prime Minister Nehru's pretensions
of secularism. He wrote, "Pandit Nehru is, to say the least, the spearhead
of militant Hindu chauvinism who glibly talks about nationalism, a
tyrant who eulogises democracy and a goblian liar—in short a political
cheat, deceiver and double-dealer in the service of Indian reaction."
Spokesman, Vol. II, No. 3, January 16, 1952.

[5] In the census of 1951 there was an organised campaign by Hindu
bodies to persuade Punjabi-speaking Hindus to declare that their mother
tongue was Hindi. Hindu-Sikh riots occurred during the census operations.

of large numbers of Sikhs posed a new challenge to Sikh leadership. How could the Sikhs retain their distinct and separate identity in a state nominally pledged to secularism but in actual practice increasingly Hindu? Economic or political sanctions could no longer be invoked; the only hope lay in having a province or a state where they could insist on the teaching of the Punjabi language, Sikh scriptures and history and thus mould the minds of the younger generation to cherish the Khalsa tradition.

In 1948 the government took two steps which, in different ways, nurtured the concept of a Sikh state. The Punjab's princely states were merged into one unit—the Patiala and East Punjab States Union. PEPSU had the handsome Sikh maharajah, Yadavendra Singh, as its *rājpramukh*; a Sikh aristocrat, Gyan Singh Rarewala, as chief minister; and the majority of its population was Sikh. All that was required was to attach the Sikh majority districts of East Punjab to PEPSU to make the Sikh state a reality.

The second step gave the Sikhs the excuse they had been waiting for. The Punjab was declared a bilingual state with both Punjabi and Hindi as its languages. The Sikhs (in these matters, the Akalis spoke for the community) were quick to fasten their resentment on the language issue.[6] They argued that the spoken language of the Pun-

[6] The Indian National Congress had committed itself over and over again to the principle of linguistic provinces. But after independence, its attitude to the subject changed—inasmuch as it concerned the Punjab and the Sikhs. The Constituent Assembly appointed a commission under Justice Dar to report on the feasibility of redrawing state boundaries but excluded the Punjab from its terms of reference. The commission pronounced against any change and despite the limitation prescribed opined as follows: "The formation of linguistic provinces is sure to give rise to a demand for the separation of linguistic groups elsewhere. Claims have already been made by the Sikhs, Jats and others and these demands will in course of time be intensified and become live issues if once the formation of linguistic provinces is decided upon." *Dar Commission Report*, para 120.

The Dar Commission's recommendations were reinforced by another committee set up by the Constituent Assembly. The J.V.P. (Jawaharlal, Vallabhai Patel, and Pattabhi Sitaramaya) reviewed the Dar Commission's

jab, barring that of Hariana, was Punjabi and that most of the literature of the Punjab (except the works of the Sufis) was in Gurmukhi script. Therefore, Hariana, which had been tagged on to the Punjab at the end of the Mutiny of 1857 and was a sandy, unproductive area, should be separated and attached to its Hindi-speaking eastern neighbours, and Punjabi in Gurmukhi script should be the only language and script of the province. It was no secret that in the Punjabi Suba, as it came to be known, the Sikhs would form a majority of the population and that the basis of Punjabi language and literature was the sacred writings of the Sikhs. The demand for the Suba was in fact one for a Sikh state; language was only the sugar coating.[7] The creation of Andhra Pradesh following dis-

---

findings and reported: "We are clearly of the opinion that no kind of rectification of boundaries in the provinces of northern India should be raised at the present moment whatever the merits of such a proposal might be. . . . This does not necessarily mean that the demands for the readjustment of provincial boundaries are unjustified or without merit. We believe there is some force in them or some adjustment may ultimately become necessary."

[7] For some time both the Akalis and the government kept up the pretence and treated the issue as one of language. The Government of Punjab made both Punjabi in Gurmukhi script and Hindi in Devnagri script compulsory in primary schools. The Sachar Formula (so named after the chief minister, Bhim Sen Sachar) scotched the accusation that Punjabi was being treated as a second-class language. The Akalis came out more openly for a Sikh majority state without wholly abandoning the linguistic argument—they wanted the Punjab to be a unilingual state.

Under the Sachar Formula the Punjab was demarcated into three areas, the Punjabi-speaking, the Hindi-speaking, and bilingual. The first consisted of six districts (Amritsar, Jullundur, Gurdaspur, Ferozepur, Ludhiana, Hoshiarpur) and two tehsils of Ambala (Rupar and Kharar excluding Chandigarh). The Hindi-speaking area consisted of five districts (Rohtak, Gurgaon, Karnal, Kangra, and Hissar except Sirsa tehsil) and two tehsils of Ambala (Jagadhri and Naraingarh). The remaining areas, Simla, Ambala, Chandigarh, and Sirsa, were declared bilingual.

It was provided that in their respective areas, the language of the area would be the medium of instruction in all schools up to the matriculation standard, while the other languages would be taught as a compulsory language from the last class of the primary stage up to the matriculation standard and in the case of girls in the middle classes only. Provision was made for children whose mother tongue was other than the regional

turbances created by Telugu-speaking people and the demand for a Marathi-speaking state encouraged Sikh agitation for the Punjabi Suba.[8]

In the winter of 1953, the Government of India appointed a commission to go into the problem of redrawing state boundaries. Although at the time the most disputed issue was that of the Punjab, no Sikh was nominated to this commission.[9] The case for a Punjabi Suba was presented by the Akalis. Several Hindu bodies opposed the demand by asking for the amalgamation of Himachal Pradesh (which was overwhelmingly Hindu) and the Punjab into a *mahā* (greater) Punjab. The commission made its report two years later, rejecting the case for a Punjabi-speaking state on the ground that a "minimum measure

---

language, provided there were 40 students in the school or ten in each class requiring instruction in the other language.

PEPSU was also linguistically divided for educational purposes. The Hindi speaking region consisted of the districts of Mahendragarh and Kohistan (including Chhachrauli tehsil minus Dera Bassi) and the tehsils of Jind and Narwana. The rest of the state was declared to be the Punjabi zone. In one zone Hindi in Devnagri script, in the other Punjabi in Gurmukhi script were made the media of instruction and in both the other language was made compulsory from the fourth primary class upwards. There was no provision for choice of the medium of instruction in the Punjab.

[8] The Shiromani Akali Dal issued a manifesto stating as follows: "The true test of democracy, in the opinion of the Shiromani Akali Dal, is that the minorities should feel that they are really free and equal partners in the destiny of their country; (a) to bring home this sense of freedom to the Sikhs, it is vital that there should be a Punjabi speaking language and culture. This will not only be in fulfilment of the pre-partition Congress programme and pledges, but also in entire conformity with the universally recognised principles governing formation of provinces. (b) The Shiromani Akali Dal is in favour of formation of provinces on a linguistic and cultural basis throughout India, but it holds it is a question of life and death for the Sikhs for a new Punjab to be created immediately. (c) The Shiromani Akali Dal has reason to believe that a Punjabi speaking province may give Sikhs the needful security. It believes in a Punjabi speaking province as an autonomous unit of India." *The Spokesman*, August 29, 1951.

[9] Its members were S. Fazl Ali, H. N. Kunzru, and K. M. Panikkar.

of agreement necessary for making a change" in the existing set-up did not exist.[10]

Master Tara Singh denounced the report as a "decree of Sikh annihilation."[11] He said with some justification that if there had been no Sikhs, Punjabi would have been given a state of its own like the other major languages recognised by the Indian constitution; the refusal to concede a Punjabi state was therefore tantamount to discrimination against the Sikhs. He threatened to start a passive resistance movement. Hindus led by the Arya Samajist-Jan Sangh groups launched a counter-campaign to "save Hindi." Communal tension led to rioting between Hindus and Sikhs in many towns.[12]

The government awoke to the unpleasant reality that the notion of a Sikh state had been re-activated in the minds of the Sikhs and that PEPSU had in fact become the nucleus of a Sikhistan. It decided to merge PEPSU into the Punjab and so to create a state in which the Hindus would form a permanent majority of 65 percent against the Sikhs 35 percent. Akali leaders were hoodwinked into believing that the merger was a step towards the establishment of a Punjabi Suba.[13] They joined the Congress party en masse.

[10] *States Reorganisation Commission Report.*

[11] *The Spokesman*, October 19, 1955.

[12] The Punjab Government issued an order banning the shouting of slogans. The Akalis defied the ban as a contravention of civil liberties. More than 12,000 were arrested.

Of the many slogans for and against the Suba, two summed up the opposite points of view. The Hindu agitators—"*Hindī, Hindū, Hindustān*" versus the Sikhs—"*Dhotī, topī, Jumnā pār*" (men who wear *dhotīs* and *topīs*, i.e. Hindus, will be sent across the Jumna).

Among the leaders arrested in this agitation were Master Tara Singh, Gyani Kartar Singh, and Hukam Singh.

[13] The mirage was created through a "Regional Formula" whereby members of the Punjab Legislature were divided into two groups: one comprising those elected from the Punjabi-speaking region and the other from the Hindi-speaking region. It was provided that any measure affecting a particular region would first be considered by members of that

The truth dawned on them after a few months. Having acquiesced in the liquidation of PEPSU, they were even further away from achieving their Suba.

At this crucial juncture, Sikh leaders exhibited lamentable absence of unity. The chief supporters of Master Tara Singh in his demand for the Punjabi Suba were Gyani Kartar Singh and Hukam Singh, both from western Punjab, and hence somewhat uncertain of their political future. Both became quiescent and joined the Congress party; one to become a minister in the Punjab Government; the other, somewhat later, became speaker of the Lok Sabha. The Congress was also fortunate in finding in Pratap Singh Kairon, the chief minister of the Punjab, a man of dynamic energy who was at the same time passionately opposed to the Akalis.

Master Tara Singh was left virtually alone to lead the struggle for the Punjabi Suba. The Sikh electorate gave him its support. In the general elections of 1957, although the Congress won a majority of seats, the Akalis were able to hold the predominantly Sikh constituencies.[14] Three years later Master Tara Singh overcame the combined strength of the Congress, Communists, and other anti-Suba elements in the S.G.P.C. elections by capturing 136 out of 140 seats. Thereafter there could be little doubt that the vast majority of the Sikhs supported the Punjabi Suba.

Master Tara Singh followed up his triumph by carrying

---

region before coming up for plenary consideration. The Akalis were naïve enough to proclaim that the abolition of PEPSU and the "Regional Formula" was the first victory in the battle for the Punjabi Suba. The Sachar-language formula was to continue, and in addition it was agreed that the official language of each region at the district level and below would be the language of the region. The Punjab, in effect, was declared a bilingual state recognising both Punjabi (in Gurmukhi script) and Hindi (in Devnagri script) as the official languages of the state. Departments of Punjabi and Hindi were set up; provision was made for the establishment of a Punjabi University (opened in 1962 at Patiala).

[14] The Akalis won 19 seats in the Punjab Assembly; they carried most of the Sikh majority constituencies. Brish Bhan, who had been chief minister of PEPSU and a supporter of the merger, was defeated by an Akali.

a "Now or Never" resolution (April 30, 1960). Before the party could mature its plans, however, chief minister Kairon ordered the arrest of the leaders of the Akali Dal, including Master Tara Singh. The Master appointed Sant Fateh Singh, a *granthi*-cum-social worker, to act as "dictator" and to continue the agitation for the Punjabi Suba. Fateh Singh organised passive resistance on a massive scale. According to the Akali Dal, over 57,000 (according to the government, only 23,000) men were gaoled in the movement. Matters came to a head when Fateh Singh went on a fast unto death. The passive resistance and the fast were called off (January 9, 1961) on an assurance from the government that Sikh grievances would be looked into.[15]

The negotiations with the government did not bear any fruit. Nehru refused to accept the contention that denial of a Punjabi-speaking province amounted to discrimination against the Sikhs. In sheer exasperation Master Tara Singh undertook to fast unto death unless the Suba was conceded. He began his fast on August 15, 1961, in the sanctuary of the Golden Temple.[16] The government re-

[15] With his usual candour, Master Tara Singh admitted that the primary motive for asking for the Suba was "to protect Sikh religion and improve the position of the Sikhs"; the language issue was secondary. "You might declare it [Punjabi] language of the whole of India, would that help the Sikhs?" he asked. Tara Singh elaborated the demand, stating that a Sikh majority would improve their status in the state; it would preclude governmental interference in gurdwara affairs, give better status to Punjabi, and make Gurmukhi the sole script. With this statement began the rift between Tara Singh and Fateh Singh. "The Sant [Fateh Singh] is a religious man," said Tara Singh, explaining the other's insistence that the demand was purely linguistic, "he is not a politician and might have been misled." *The Spokesman*, January 16, 1961.

[16] Tara Singh made a statement during the fast explaining his position:

"If we face the problem open-mindedly then the situation can be summed up in three sentences:

(1) A national principle has been accepted that to make the people feel the flow of freedom states should be created on the contiguity of language affording full scope for development of one national language in one state.

fused to yield. After 43 days without food, the old warrior's spirit was broken, and he gave up the self-imposed ordeal.

Master Tara Singh saved his life but killed his political career and dealt a grievous blow to the cause of the Sikh state. He was arraigned at the Akal Takht[17] and found guilty of proving false to his oath and to the hallowed tradition of martyrdom. He was sentenced to clean the shoes of the congregation for five days. Although he carried out his penance, he was not forgiven by his community. A few months later, both the S.G.P.C. and the Akali Dal voted him out of power. Sant Fateh Singh took over as the leader of the Sikhs.

The government pressed home its triumph over the supporters of the Sikh state.[18] A three-man commission[19] under the chairmanship of S. R. Das was appointed to hear the "grievances of the Sikhs of the Punjab." The Akalis expressed lack of confidence in the personnel of the commission and its terms of reference; they asked the Sikhs to boycott the commission's proceedings. The community

---

(2) This principle has been implemented in other parts of India and even in Punjab an area has been demarcated which the government experts feel is a Punjabi-speaking area.

(3) This Punjabi-speaking area, with any adjustments that the expert opinion may deem necessary, is not being afforded the status of a state, simply because the Hindus do not agree to it."

[17] Tara Singh pleaded: "If I have committed a mistake, correct me. If I have done the right thing, march with me. If I have acted treacherously, punish me." *The Spokesman*, November 6, 1961.

[18] In the Punjab Assembly, chief minister Kairon compelled all the sitters-on-the-fence to make unequivocal declarations disavowing the Sikh state. At the centre, Hukam Singh, who had been one of the fathers of the Suba plan, confessed to his past errors: "If really there is a villain for this activity, I am here. And if he is to hang, let me be hanged." *The Spokesman*, September 4, 1961.

[19] Members of the commission were S. R. Das (chairman and ex-chief justice of the Supreme Court), C. P. Ramaswami Aiyer, and M. C. Chagla (former chief justice of Bombay, Indian ambassador in the U.S., Indian high commissioner in London, and later, minister of education).

displayed remarkable unanimity in disassociating itself from the proceedings of the Das Commission.[20]

The general elections of 1962 did little to clear the atmosphere.[21] The Congress party won in most mixed constituencies; Akali supporters of the Punjabi Suba carried the majority of Sikh voters. Before the Akalis could mature their plans to make another bid for the Suba, however, the Chinese invaded Indian frontiers.[22] The Sikhs suspended their agitation and eagerly joined in the defence of their country.

The Sikh state has been put aside for the period of the emergency but has by no means been abandoned. It will be clear from what has been said that, despite the government's ability in finding some Sikhs to oppose the movement and despite the betrayal of Communal interests by many leaders, the idea has a near-unanimous support of the Sikhs. It is also supported by many important political parties: Swatantra, the Communists, and the Socialists. It is opposed by a majority of Punjabi Hindus, the Congress, and the Hindu communal bodies such as the Mahasabha, the Bharatiya Jan Sangh, and the R.S.S.S. This opposition

---

[20] Only one nondescript group appeared to give evidence. Gopal Singh Dardi, editor of the defunct *Liberator*, had been an enthusiastic supporter of the Sikh state. Before the Das Commission, the same Dardi listed the "privileges" which the Sikhs enjoyed from the Nehru government. A few months later, the president nominated him to the Rajya Sabha.

[21] In the Punjab, the Akalis won 19 seats; in the Lok Sabha, 3. Chief minister Kairon himself had the narrowest of escapes, retaining his seat only by a dubious majority of 34 votes.

Among the notable returns was Kapur Singh for the Lok Sabha. Kapur Singh had been a member of the Indian Civil Service till his suspension in 1948. He was responsible for much of the Suba literature. Gurnam Singh, retired judge of the Punjab High Court, was returned to the Punjab Assembly and became leader of the opposition.

[22] The Punjabis' contribution in men and material equalled that of the rest of the states of India put together. The only non-Punjabi district to exceed the Punjab districts' contribution in gold was Ganganagar in Rajasthan. Ganganagar is largely settled by Sikh refugees.

is, however, qualified by a movement of Hariana Hindus to break away from the Punjab and align the region with Delhi or Uttar Pradesh.

The Suba as conceived by the Sikhs will be an integral part of the Indian Union and will comprise the Punjabi-speaking districts of East Punjab and Ganganagar tehsil of Rajasthan.[23] It will be over 35,000 square miles and hence larger than Kerala or Nagaland. It will have a population of over twelve million and therefore be more populous than Assam, Nagaland, or Kashmir. It will be economically viable with an annual revenue of over Rs. 16 crores. It will produce a surplus of food grains and have industries of its own. Sikhs will form a little more than half the population of this Sikh homeland.[24]

Postscript

A student of Sikh affairs may indulge in speculation on the future course of the two movements to which attention has been drawn in the preceding pages, viz. Sikh resistance to being absorbed by Hinduism and the movement for a Sikh state. The two are more intimately related to each other than is generally realised or admitted.

The relapse into Hinduism forms a recognisable pattern and is more evident among the rich and educated classes of

[23] "The Shiromani Akali Das has defined it as follows:

(1) *Punjab*: Districts of Gurdaspur, Amritsar, Ferozepur, Ludhiana, Jullundur, Hoshiarpur, Ambala, Karnal (except Panipat tehsil), and Hissar (only Sirsa and Fatehabad tehsils and Tohana sub-tehsil);

(2) *Pepsu*: Districts of Patiala, Barnala, Bhatinda, Kapurthala, Fatehgarh Sahib, and Sangrur (except Jind and Narwana tehsils);

(3) *Rajasthan*: District of Ganganagar.

In August 1965 Master Tara Singh's group of Akalis formally adopted a resolution that "there is no alternative for the Sikhs in the interest of self-preservation but to frame their political demand for securing a self-determined political status within the Republic of Union of India." *Tribune*, July 5, 1965.

[24] According to the census of 1961, the number of Sikhs was a little over 8 million, of whom over 7 million were in East Punjab.

Sikhs. In this class the younger generation has begun to give up the practice of wearing their hair and beards unshorn. They try to retain a sense of identity with the community by sporting other symbols—notably the *kaṛā*—and are often more punctilious in religious observance. This does not prevent their being rejected by the orthodox Khalsa as *patits* (renegades). Being too few to form a social group of their own, they soon find themselves in the accommodating embrace of Hinduism. It proves that the sense of belonging to the Sikh community requires both the belief in the teachings of the *Ādi Granth* and the observance of the Khalsa tradition initiated by Guru Gobind Singh; and that there is no such thing as a clean-shaven Sikh—he is simply a Hindu believing in Sikhism.

The absorption of the *sahajdhārī* Sikhs into the Hindu fold adds weight to the argument that there is no such thing as a clean-shaven Sikh. At one time *sahajdhārī* Sikhism was—as the meaning of the word signified, "those-who-take-time"—the halfway house to the hirsute form of Khalsa Sikhism. Now the process is reversed, and it has become a halfway house to Hinduism. The case of the *sahajdhārī* Hindus of Sindh is illustrative. Till independence, when they were living in their home province, they were distinctly more Sikh than Hindu. Today, dispersed over the Indian subcontinent, most of them have gone back to Hinduism. Even where they form compact communities as in Bombay, the altars of their temples display Hindu gods alongside the *Granth,* and Hindu ritual is fast displacing the Sikh. There are strong indications that with the passing of the present generation Sikhism will also pass out of the people of Sindh.

No statistics have been compiled to prove that the practice of taking *pahul* and wearing the hair and beard unshorn is on the decline; but that it is so is now admitted by most Sikh leaders and will be apparent to any shrewd observer. A closer study of the incidence of apostasy yields the following conclusions.

Firstly, wherever Sikhs are scattered among other people, the attachment to tradition declines and the rate of apostasy rises. This is most evident in the Sikh communities in foreign lands. In the United States, Canada, and England the number of *kesādhārī* Sikhs is extremely small and ever-diminishing. On the other hand, in countries such as Malaya or in East Africa, where Sikhs live in compact groups, incidence of apostasy is lower. The same phenomenon can be observed in India. In the Sikh districts of East Punjab, the Khalsa traditions flourish; among smaller Sikh communities in other parts of India, they are on the decline.

Secondly, the abolition of communal considerations by the Indian Government, e.g. separate electorates, weightage in services, and above all the non-enforcement of rules regarding *pahul* in the armed forces, have taken a heavy toll of the Khalsa. This was amply proven by the attitude of the untouchable castes of Sikhs. By the Scheduled Castes Order 1950-1951, while all Hindu untouchable castes were given special privileges, only four sub-castes of untouchable Sikhs were included in the list. The sub-castes excluded from the schedule showed little reluctance in abandoning the Khalsa tradition and declaring themselves Hindus in order to claim the benefits. It proved more than ever that religious sentiment is a poor argument against economic benefit.

Thirdly, there is close connection between the Punjabi language and Sikhism. In families where Punjabi has been replaced by other languages—English among the rich and the anglicised, Hindi amongst those desirous of getting the best in a Hindu-dominated India—the study of the *Granth*, the observance of Sikh ritual and Khalsa traditions have had a short lease of life.

Fourthly, with the resurgence of Hinduism, the official commitment to secularism is being reduced to a meaningless clause in the constitution. The emphasis on Sanskrit and Hindi, study of the Aryan classics, insertion of cow-protection as a directive clause of the constitution, the increase in the number of cow-protection societies, the growth of Hindu political groups such as the Bharatiya Jan Sangh and the militant R.S.S.S., and the suspicion with which other minorities have come to be regarded are but some indications of the way the wind is blowing. Hindus, who form 80 percent of the population, will in due course make Hinduism the state religion of India.

The four conclusions listed above lead to the fifth: the only chance of survival of the Sikhs as a separate community is to create a state in which they form a compact group, where the teaching of Gurmukhi and the Sikh religion is compulsory, and where there is an atmosphere of respect for the traditions of their Khalsa forefathers.

OPUS EXEGII

PART VI

APPENDICES

APPENDIX 1

CULTURAL HERITAGE OF THE SIKHS

Punjabi Language, Literature, and Painting

Language. Punjabi, like other languages of northern India, is derived from Sanskrit, the language of the Aryans. Sanskrit retained its purity by refusing to admit words of local languages and was soon restricted to a small group of purists. The common people began to develop local accents, coin words of their own or borrow them from indigenous non-Aryan languages. In the Punjab, the Sanskrit of the Aryans mingled with the languages of the Jat tribes who had moved northwards from Rajasthan into the Punjab. The mélange produced a variety of regional dialects[1] from which was evolved, some time about the 11th century, the Punjabi language.

The Punjabi of the 11th century was then subjected to many other linguistic influences. Muslim invaders brought Arabic, Persian and Turkish. The British introduced English. The languages of the conquerors enriched the vocabulary of Punjabi without altering its basic structure. Since the Muslim invaders settled in the Punjab, words of Arabic, Persian, and Turkish, found their way into the diction of the peasants. This did not apply to the same extent to English, which was restricted to matters of administration and technology and was used only by the educated classes.

Gurmukhi Script. Scholars still dispute the origin of Gurmukhi script. The popular belief is that it was invented by the second guru, Angad.[2] This is, however, disproved by the fact that Guru Nanak used the thirty-five letters in composing his acrostic. From this some scholars have concluded that Nanak was the creator of Gurmukhi letters. Recently, documents written before the time of Nanak have been found which conclusively prove that the thirty-five letters of the alphabet (known also as the *Paiṅtī*—35) now called Gur-

[1] Hindko, Multani, Pothohari, Majhi, Malwai, Puadhi, Doabi, Dogri, and Pahari.
[2] Vir Singh, *Sri Aṣt Guru Camatkār*, p. 140.

mukhi[3] were current a long time before the gurus. Pritam Singh, whose authority is now generally accepted, is of the opinion that Gurmukhi, like many other scripts in use in northern India, was derived from Brahmi letters which were in use at the time of Emperor Asoka (3rd century B.C.),[4] but no precise dates can be fixed about its evolution.

Literature. Punjabi scholars (like the scholars of other languages) vie with each other in pushing back the antiquity of their literature. But there is little real evidence of Punjabi writing before the settlement of the Muslims in the Punjab and the incorporation of their language in the local dialects. The earliest examples of the use of what may be described as Punjabi poetry were heroic ballads *(vārs)* which were composed during the Muslim invasions. These heroic ballads were sung to specific tunes, many of which find mention in the compositions of the fifth guru, Arjun, in the *Ādi Granth,* e.g. *Rāi Kamāl dī vār, Tuṇḍey asrāje kī vār,* etc.

The Sufis

The first great name in Punjabi literature is that of Farid Shakarganj (12th century). He made his home in Pak Pattan, where his successors (who also took on the name Farid) continued to reside, write religious verse, and propagate Sufi doctrines. It is not possible to say with certainty which of the many Farids was the author of a particular line of the verse: 112 slokas ascribed to Farid are incorporated in the *Granth* (see Vol. I, Appendix V, pp. 319-21).

Farid's chief preoccupation was with death.[5] He described himself "lying on the bed of care on the mattress of sorrow under the quilt of loneliness"; a strain of melancholy is consequently present in much of his writing. In the tradition of

---

[3] The name "Gurmukhi" appears to have been used in the time of Guru Amar Das (1479-1574). Prior to that the 35-letter alphabet was referred to by a variety of names. When this alphabet came to be used by the gurus, the other names gave way to "Gurmukhi"—from the mouth of the guru. *Panjāb,* pp. 407-10.

[4] *Ibid.,* p. 391.

[5] A sloka of Farid sung at obsequial ceremonies runs as follows:

> A heron sporting by the river bank
> Happy and free of care,
> Down swoops the falcon of death
> And takes the heron unaware.

the Sufis and the Bhaktas, Farid wrote of a man's search for God in the same terms as a woman's physical longing for her lover. This tradition was continued by the Sikh gurus and up to recent times by poets treating religious themes; it is the dominant motif of Punjabi poetry and can be discerned even in what might at first sight appear simple love stories such as the three great epics of Punjabi literature—*Heer Rānjhā, Sassī-Punnoo,* and *Sohnī Mahiwāl.* In all of them, after a lifetime of separation and longing, lovers meet in death.

The Sufis lived in villages and their vocabulary was refreshingly rustic. The day-to-day activities of peasants, artisans, and their women folk, the complicated emotional relationships between the various members of joint families—a sister's love for her brother, the tension between co-wives, the tyranny of a mother-in-law, etc.—gave them all the similes and metaphors they needed. The Sikh gurus, particularly Nanak, made much use of these familiar pastimes and situations to convey their message.

Another notable contribution of the Sufis was the popularisation of certain forms of verse which became distinctive of Punjabi literature, e.g. the *kāfī, bārā-māh,* and the *siharfī.* *Kāfī* (a verse of four lines in which the first, second, and the fourth are in rhyme) was well known to Persian poets and is popular today in Urdu verse. The *bārā-māh,* or the twelve months, gave poets full liberty to describe the beauty of the seasons and with that convey their message. Some of the richest descriptions of nature in Punjabi poetry owe their origin to the practice of composing *bārā-māh.* Warris Shah has a memorable one in his *Heer Rānjhā,* and that of Guru Nanak in the *Ādi Granth* is probably the most beautiful of all in the language.[6] The *siharfī,* or the acrostic, takes a letter of his alphabet as its cue. This acrostic was used by the Sikh gurus but was abandoned soon after them and never revived.

The Sikh Gurus

Most of the Sikh gurus were given to versification. The three whose works are most widely read as literature are Nanak, Arjun, and Gobind Singh.

6 See Vol. I, Appendix 5, pp. 351-57.

Guru Nanak preached through his poetry, and his works have a didacticism explaining his philosophy of life and exhorting others to a particular way of living. Most didactic poetry suffers from a cramping narrowness imposed by the purpose for which it is written, but Guru Nanak's poetry displays a remarkable freedom of expression. The beauty of pastoral Punjab aroused him to religious and poetic frenzy. The commonplace was for him pregnant with symbolism of moral significance.[7]

Guru Arjun expresses the same deep sentiments in his poetry as Guru Nanak. His verse abounds with jewelled phrases and has a haunting melody produced by the use of alliteration and repetition of words. Guru Arjun is undoubtedly the most sung of all poets of the language.[8]

Guru Gobind Singh was perhaps the most erudite of all the Sikh gurus and was familiar with both Hindu mythology and Islamic theology. He wrote in Sanskrit, Persian, and Punjabi. Unlike his predecessors, he did not restrict himself to expressing the glory of God; his writings have a moral as well as political significance. The martial spirit which he infused among his followers is expressed in the vigorous poetry of his famous *zafarnāmā*—Epistle of Victory—addressed to Emperor Aurangzeb. His *Jāp Sāhib* is to this day a source of inspiration to his followers.

No literature of any merit was produced by the Sikhs during their struggle for power nor during the brief period of Sikh rule when more store was set on Persian than on Punjabi. But while the Sikhs were busy conquering and consolidating their kingdom, two Muslims, Bulhey Shah (1680-1758) and Warris Shah (1735-1798), wrote verse which is the finest example of romantic and mystic Punjabi poetry. Bulhey Shah's *kāfīs* and Warris Shah's *Heer Rānjhā* are most popular and are recited and sung in every village in the province. They have also influenced subsequent generations of Punjabi writers.

Contemporary Punjabi Writing

For nearly half a century following the commencement of British occupation little literature was produced in India.

[7] For examples, see Vol. I, Chapter 2 and Appendix 5.
[8] For examples, see Vol. I, Appendix 5, pp. 361-76.

It took many years to recover from the effects of the political change and to size up western values. Early English rulers were convinced that all oriental culture was worthless and that the best thing the Indians could do was to adopt the Europeans. One generation of Indians agreed with this opinion and anglicised themselves to the extent that they lost all contact with Indian tradition and learning. The next generation discovered the folly and proceeded to blow away the dust of the archives housing the achievements of ancient India. This process took place all over the country. Since the Punjab was the last to be subjected to these western complexes, it was the last to shake off their effect. The renaissance in Punjabi writing was consequently somewhat later than in the rest of the country.

Post-annexation Punjabi writing corresponded roughly to the social and political changes produced by the Singh Sabha movement followed by the Akalis and the Communists. In each case, the literary output bore the impress of the problems which faced the protagonists of these movements. There were, however, some writers who remained oblivious to social and political problems and wrote, as it were, for the sake of writing.

The literary output of the Singh Sabha movement is the most important part of its contribution to Sikhism. The person to whom it owes most is Bhai Vir Singh, who re-created interest in Punjabi and established a landmark in the history of the language. Vir Singh (1872-1956) wrote fiction, poetry, and commentaries on the sacred texts.

Vir Singh's early writing has to be viewed with reference to the social and political conditions at the end of the 19th century. His novels, which made him known in millions of homes, were written at a time when the Punjabis were beginning to doubt the achievements of their ancestors. English historians harped on the crude and corrupt Sikh rule, which they had replaced by an "enlightened" one. Sanskrit scholars belittled the religion of the Sikhs as a poor imitation of the Vedic and ridiculed its forms and symbols as barbarous. Vir Singh's novels, *Sundarī, Vijay Singh, Satwant Kaur,* and *Bābā Naudh Singh,* had as their central theme the heroism and chivalry of the Sikhs and the ethical excellence of their religion. This was set in contrast to the servility of the Hindu masses and the oppression of the Pathan and Mughal rulers. The Sikhs devoured Vir Singh's novels with enthusiasm and gratitude. But with the passing of that peculiar mental state, the novels lost their appeal. To the present-day reader, they appear somewhat insipid. Their place is not in literature but in history.

Vir Singh himself gave up writing fiction and turned to translating and explaining the scriptures in a series of pamphlets and in his weekly paper, the _Khālsā Samācār_. Along with these appeared his poems, which gave him the most honoured place among Punjabi poets.

Vir Singh first experimented in blank verse. A long poem, _Rānā Sūrat Singh_, was published in 1905. The theme, as usual, was religion. His technique and mastery over the language was impressive. No one had successfully written blank verse in Punjabi before; Vir Singh turned out a work of sustained excellence, where alliteration and onomatopoeia, rhythm, and repetition produced a lilting melody with all the langourous sensuousness of a summer afternoon. Thereafter Vir Singh wrote the biographies of two Sikh gurus, the founder, Nanak, and the last, Guru Gobind Singh. _Kalgīdhar Camatkār_, the life of Guru Gobind, appeared first and was followed three years later by _Guru Nānak Camatkār_.

In between these biographies, Vir Singh published several collections of verse employing a short metre not used by Punjabi poets. The most popular of these were in the form of _rubāis_ (familiar to the readers of Omar Khayyam). In these he expressed his philosophy and mysticism, where the love of God and human beings, the spiritual and the sensual, moral and divine, moved in a colourful kaleidoscope, beautiful and baffling. There was always an underlying sense of humility, at times almost masochistic. Bhai Vir Singh had not given up experimenting even in his later years. In _The Vigil_, published posthumously, he recaptured his ability to describe nature and invest physical longing with divine attributes:

> Shades of twilight fell,
> A gentle gloom had spread.
> I mused: maybe today
> You would come when it was dark.

I blew out the street lamp,
Put out the light in the niche,
Smothered the taper in the house.

I sat in the dark and was lost in waiting.
Maybe tonight You might wish to come
With soft, unsounding tread,
In absolute stillness, in absolute dark.

* * *

Hark! What was that noise?
Was He coming?
I went and looked out of my window,
There was lightning and thunder.

My heart stopped.
Maybe tonight You might come
With fireworks
And with flaming torches!

I rose in a hurry,
Put on the light in the house,
Touched with flame the taper in the niche,
Relit the lamp in the street
With eager, impatient haste.
I mused: Maybe You would come seeing the
                                light,
          Maybe You would turn back if the house
                              were in darkness
          And I be left waiting for ever and ever.

* * *

Clouds gathered, black and lowering,
Torn by flashes of lightning,
Then came rain in torrents,
Lanes and streets became muddy swamps.

The lightning is over,
Gone in a flicker of an eye-lid
As if it knew my heart's desire.

Even the dark clouds are gone
Baring a sky clean-washed and shining,
Carrying the moon in its lap like a babe
With the stars scattered around.
Still I sit and wait.

The moon also awaits.
Look, how the moonbeams have spread
Their shimmering silver over the mud,
Spread a carpet of velvet-white on Your path!

*　　　*　　　*

The first ray of dawn has lit the sky,
The sparrow twitters,
The morning breeze,
Soft, sweet, fluting,
Enfolds me in its embrace.
Great Giver! Light of the Morning!
Everything, everywhere wakes to life,
Expectant are dawn and daylight.

The longing burgeons with the morning.
The sun is risen
As yesterday it rose and every day.
People have woken from their slumbers
And go about the streets and by-lanes.
Only I sit and wait.
Lord, what else can I do!
Lord, what more can I do![9]

Two contemporaries of Bhai Vir Singh, Puran Singh (1881-1931) and Dhani Ram "Chatrik," deserve mention. Puran Singh wrote both in Punjabi and English. He was influenced by the writing of Walt Whitman and himself produced some vigorous blank verse in both languages.[10] His sojourn abroad also made him a passionate admirer of the land of his birth:

Here are vast expanses free,
Here is a joyous impulse flooding the hearts of men,

[9] Vir Singh won the Sahitya Akademi award for literature in the year 1955.
[10] Puran Singh's better known works in English are *Sisters of the Spinning Wheel* and *Spirit Born People*.

Here the mountains melt in love,
Here is a celestial disembodied song
Echoing in the field and the meadow.

Dhani Ram "Chatrik" (1876-1954) published several collections of verse. His lyrics were surfeit with Punjabi colloquialisms—charming in the original but extremely hard to translate.

Poetry remains the most popular form of literary expression to this day. Newspapers and magazines devote a large part of their space to poems, and a symposium (*kavī darbār*) will still draw a larger crowd than a political or a religious meeting.

Most of this new poetry is, however, of indifferent quality. Two exceptions are Mohan Singh and Amrita Pritam.

Mohan Singh (b.1905) made a promising start with his *Sāve Patr* (Green Leaves) and soon came to be recognised as the best of the younger poets. His later work, published after partition, showed a strong left-wing bias, where political emotion was given precedence over poetical form—a malaise which has afflicted a large number of younger writers who label themselves "progressive." In the case of Mohan Singh, the first flush of Marxism soon settled down to simple championing of the underdog and an exhortation to work. He was once more able to recapture the spontaneous beauty of his earlier writing:

The pitch-black within the pitcher has burst
Spilling the milk-white of the moonlight.
It is time we talked of a new dawn
And gave up the gossiping of the night.

I grant that autumn's touch
Hath robbed some leaves of their sap.
Sorrow not for what is lost and gone,
With hope anew fill thy lap.

How long on the ancient vault of heaven
Idle fantasies draw and hold them dear?
Come let us caress the earth's tresses,
Come let us talk of something near.[11]

[11] Mohan Singh was the recipient of the Sahitya Akademi award for literature in 1959.

Amrita Pritam (b.1919) published her first collection of poems when she was only seventeen. Her earliest efforts were heavy with criticism of evil social customs. Although she has given up preaching, the hard lot of Indian women remains the dominant theme in most of her poetry and prose. Her writing has improved steadily as the songstress in her gained dominance over the suffragette, but the feminist protest has never been totally silenced. She was influenced by her pseudo-Marxist contemporaries, became "progressive" and at times propagandist. The great famine of Bengal of 1943 moved her to declaim that "the talk of love and beauty is talk of idle times and idle people." But once again the mother in her triumphed over the Marxist and her writing took the form of a soulful dirge rather than an angry denunciation. She became in her own words, "the chronicler of India's misfortunes." The internecine massacres of 1947, which took such heavy toll of human life, stirred her to write one of her most memorable poems. She addressed it to Warris Shah and exhorted him to rise from his grave and see the havoc wrought in his own land.

> O, comforter of the sorrowing, rise and behold
> thy Punjab
> Its fields are strewn with corpses, blood runs
> in the Chenab

In recent years, Amrita Pritam's poetry has been veering towards the sentimental and the romantic, with delicate allusions to natural phenomena:

> SPRING is here again,
> Flowers are silken clad
> For the festival of colours,
> But thou art not here.

> THE days have lengthened,
> The grape is touched with pink,
> The scythe hath kissed the corn,
> But thou art not here.

> CLOUDS are spread across the sky,
> The earth hath opened her palms
> And drunk the draught of kindness,
> But thou art not here.

THE trees are touched with magic,
Lips of the winds that kiss the woodlands
Are full of honey,
But thou art not here.

BEWITCHING seasons have come and gone,
Many moons have woven plaits
On the black tresses of night,
But thou art not here.

TODAY again the stars did stay
In life's mansion, even now
The lamps of beauty are still aflame,
But thou art not here.

RAYS of the sun did also whisper,
In the deep slumbers of the night
The moon is ever awake,
But thou art not here.

Amrita Pritam has not achieved the same distinction in her fiction as she has in her poetry. Her characterisation is often weak and her plots so contrived as to appear manifestly unreal. The Indian film industry has exercised on her, as it has on many Indian writers of her generation, a most baneful influence; the narratives of their novels are interspersed with song, and people find themselves in situations which seldom obtain in real life in India. These shortcomings are manifest in her most popular novel, *Dr. Dev.* Amrita is at her best in *Pinjar*—The Skeleton. *The Skeleton* is the story of a Hindu girl, Pooro, who is abducted and forcibly married to a Muslim and whose hatred for her ravisher gradually turns to love. Together they help Hindu and Sikh refugees to escape from Pakistan to India. Through Pooro, the chief character of the story, Amrita expresses her resentment against social conventions, male lustfulness, and sorrowful resignation to fate which, according to her, is the lot of Indian womanhood.[12]

Two other poets deserve mention as examples of trends in contemporary writing. Tara Singh, a carpenter by profession, is also representative of the reaction to obscurity which had

[12] Amrita Pritam was the recipient of the Sahitya Akademi's award for literature in 1956. *The Skeleton* is the only novel of the Punjabi language to have been translated and published in English.

at one time come into vogue. He is a favourite of the *kavī darbārs*, where rapport between the bard and his audience is essential. *The Lovers' Plight* is a sample of his technique:

> In the months of May and June,
> In the summer's heat, on a hot afternoon,
> Like a fluff of thistledown floating in the air
> Casting its shadow on a piece of straw
> For a fleeting moment; so hath
> Thy love been to me.

> Beloved mine! Thy face is like the moon
> New risen in the hours of early dawn.
> I have treasured the memory of Thy love.
> As traveller numb and cold
> Seeks shelter in a wayside hut, and
> When rain and sleet beat upon its thatched roof
> He lights a fire, guards the glowing embers
> In his embrace and lets the dirty water
> Leaking through the roof drip upon his back,
> So have I cherished thy love.

Prabhjot Kaur (b.1927), like most of her contemporaries, has tried her hand at poems, short stories, and translations. But she, like Amrita Pritam, is best in her poetry. She is less inhibited in her expression—her poems are more candidly amorous than Amrita's.

> Neither you
> Nor I
> Nor anyone else knoweth
> What your eye hath said
> To mine.

> As a flash of lightning
> Rents the veils of heaven;
> So longing burst the bonds of discretion,
> Freed itself of its fetters
> And I fled into your arms.

> You sounded the depth of my heart
> Undid the knot of passion;
> You saw the tears on my eyelashes
> And pressed your lips on mine.

In your hands you held my hands,
In the hush of the dark night.
You heard the clamour of desire
And with soothing fingers silenced it.[13]

Belles Lettres, Fiction, and Drama

The outstanding figures in Punjabi prose are Gurbaksh Singh (b.1895), editor of the monthly magazine, *Prīt Laṛī*, and Dr. Balbir Singh, younger brother of the poet, Vir Singh. Gurbaksh Singh is closely associated with the Communist party and has been the main influence on many of the Punjab's younger writers. His manifestly propagandist writing is, however, redeemed by a felicity of style and diction. Gurbaksh Singh has written novels, plays, short stories, and essays. Dr. Balbir Singh is deeply religious; he is also the most erudite of contempory Sikh writers. His essays display a knowledge of both European and Sanskrit literature and are written in the most chaste and simple Punjabi. He has only published two books *Kalam dī Karāmāt* (The Miracle of the Pen) and *Lamī Nadar* (Grace Abounding)—both of which have been acclaimed by critics.

The novel as a form of writing came somewhat late to the Punjab. The best known contemporary novelist, Nanak Singh (b.1898), has written over two dozen novels and is the most widely read Punjabi writer. His language is of the less educated class of Indians and is interspersed with English words; his plots are untrue to Indian life.[14]

Punjabi literature's most notable achievement is in its short stories.[15] By introducing modern techniques, the Punjabi writer has been able to develop the tradition of the fable. Sant Singh Sekhon (b.1908) abandoned the straightforward narrative and made dexterous use of illusion, understatement, and auto-suggestion. Kartar Singh Duggal (b.1919) is the leading writer of short stories and introduced the dialect of Rawalpindi dis-

[13] Prabhjot Kaur renewed the Sahitya Akademi's award for literature in 1965 for her collection of poems *Pabbi* (plateau).

[14] Nanak Singh was the recipient of the Sahitya Akademi's award for literature in 1961 for his novel *Ik miān do talvārāṇ* (One Scabbard, Two Swords) based on the life of Kartar Singh Sarabha of the Ghadr party.

[15] See *Land of the Five Rivers*, by Jaya Thadani and Khushwant Singh. Jaico, 1965.

trict into Punjabi writing. His collections *Sver Sār* (Early Morning) and *Navān Ghar* (The New Home) are noteworthy. In the same way Kulwant Singh Virk injected the dialect of the Jats of Majha into his short stories. Virk's later work has become somewhat sophisticated and he has begun to write of the lower middle-class life in small towns.

The most neglected aspect of Punjab writing is the drama. Only recently did the Punjab build its first proper theatre at Chandigarh; it still has no professional actors or producers. The Punjabi dramatists' exposition has been confined to writing plays for broadcasting or suffering them to be performed by amateurs at drama festivals. Nevertheless Balwant Gargi (b.1918) has written a book on the Indian stage[16] and has had some of his plays translated and enacted in the Soviet Union.

Future Prospects of Punjabi

Most Sikh politicians have tried at one time or the other to write or versify, e.g. Master Tara Singh, Gurmukh Singh Musafir, Sohan Singh Josh, Hira Singh "Dard," Teja Singh Swatantra. They have novels, short stories, or collections of poems to their credit. This emphasis on literary prowess was undoubtedly one of the factors behind the united demand for official recognition of Punjabi, the setting up of a Punjabi-speaking zone and a Punjabi Akademi. Official recognition has thus compensated for the loss sustained by the recognition of Urdu in Pakistan and the patronage of Hindi in India.

Punjabi literature continues to depend largely on Sikh writers using the Gurmukhi script. The dialects are disappearing; with use of a more standardised diction, Punjabi is beginning to lose some of its rustic vigour. These shortcomings are being partly offset by the production of translations of classics of other languages and the infusion of alien concepts and literary forms. Punjabi writers have to compete with Hindi and Urdu as well as English and French writings translated into Punjabi. Impatience with the poor standard of contemporary writing has also produced a school of critics who have broken the tradition of restricting appraisal to praise

[16] *Rang Manc* was the recipient of the Sahitya Akademi's award for 1962.

and have begun to demand better work from the novelists and the poets. The yeast has begun to ferment; Punjabi is on the eve of its long awaited renaissance.

Sikh Writers of Other Languages

Not many writers have written in other languages than Punjabi. Of these few, one, Rajinder Singh Bedi (b.1908), has achieved notable success as a Urdu novelist. His novel *Ik cādar mailī sī* (The Soiled Sheet) has been acclaimed by critics as the best novel written on Punjabi village life. It tells of a young Jat boy forced into marriage with his elder brother's elderly widow. The plot is not contrived; the story is stark and powerfully honest.

Dr. M. S. Randhawa (b.1912) is one of the most prolific Sikh writers of the day. His chief interests are folk songs of the Punjab and painting. Under his patronage, folk songs of all the districts of the Punjab have been compiled and published. He himself has collected paintings from the Punjab hill states. Several volumes of these have been published.

A Sikh writer of popular science has achieved international distinction in his field. Jagjit Singh (b.1912), an official in the railways, has published *Mathematical Ideas—Their Nature and Daily Use* and *Great Ideas and Theories of Modern Cosmology*, both of which were acclaimed by critics. In 1963, Jagjit Singh was awarded the Kalinga Prize for the popularisation of science.

Sikh Painting

A Sikh school of painting came into existence as the Sikhs rose to power. In the early stages, it consisted largely of calligraphists who produced *gutkās*—books of daily prayer (*nit nem*). The pages of these prayer books were garnished with floral designs and paintings of the gurus at appropriate pages. Most of these painters followed the techniques and patterns of the schools of painting which had evolved under the patronage of the Rajput chieftains around the hills of Kulu, Kangra, and Basohli. When the Sikhs became rulers of the Punjab, painters flocked to their courts. In addition to the paintings of religious themes, they made portraits of their patrons and other pictures—often erotic—for their patrons' delectation. Many Sikh chiefs commissioned artists to paint frescoes in their palaces.

Maharajah Ranjit Singh, despite his philistine upbringing, was a generous patron of the arts. After he reduced Raja Sansar Chand of Kangra in 1809, there was a virtual exodus of painters from the hills to the plains of the Punjab. Hari Singh Nalwa, the Bedis of Una, the Attariwalas, and the raja of Kapurthala shared Ranjit Singh's interest in painting and commissioned illustrated books, portraits, and frescoes. Ranjit Singh employed these artists to do the frescoes and other decorations in the Golden Temple at Amritsar; the most distinguished of the craftsmen employed was one Kehar Singh. Much of the *pietra dura* designs and frescoes in the Golden Temple are the work of this man. The painters of the temple were in all probability also responsible for the frescoes in Ranjit Singh's mausoleum in Lahore.

Kehar Singh created a school of *naqāśes*—craftsmen—who continued to work in the many appurtenances of the Golden Temple. He was also a gifted caricaturist and displayed his skill in portraits of nihangs and other Punjabi rustic types. Gyan Singh (1883-1953) and his sons after him continued the tradition of Kehar Singh and spent their lives working in the Golden Temple.

The most outstanding Indian painter of recent times was the Sikh, Amrita Shergil (1911-1941). Amrita was the daughter of Umrao Singh Shergil (elder brother of Sunder Singh Majithia) and his Hungarian wife. She was trained in Paris, and her early work shows the influence of French masters, chiefly Gaugin. When she returned to India, she jettisoned the European technique and became an ardent traditionalist. Her best work is reminiscent of the Rajasthani and Kangra schools but is executed on large canvas and in brighter oranges and whites. Amrita Shergil died at the age of thirty. Whatever she did in those short years has become the most coveted national treasure of India. Her canvases hang in the National Gallery in New Delhi.

Contemporary Sikh artists have not distinguished themselves. The best known are Sobha Singh and S. G. Thakur Singh. Sobha Singh has painted pictures of the Sikh gurus and illustrated themes from Punjabi folklore. S. G. Thakur

Singh is the head of an Academy of Arts in Amritsar. He paints both portraits and landscapes. His forte is photographic likenesses of the subject. Following in his tradition is a young artist, Kirpal Singh, who has illustrated macabre incidents in Sikh history. Kirpal Singh's paintings are exhibited in the picture gallery attached to the Golden Temple.

A large number of young Sikh painters and sculptors are at work today. The most promising of them are Serbjeet Singh and Jaswant Singh. Serbjeet Singh (b.1923) is also cartographer and a film producer. His best works are the mountain landscapes of the Ladakh region. He is bold in his outline and choice of colours. There is nothing imitative or abstract in Serbjeet Singh's work.

Jaswant Singh (b.1922) is a natural-born painter. He received no training of any kind and has evolved a distinct style of his own. He veers strongly towards the abstract. Among his best works are his stylistic renderings of the *rāgās* of Indian music.

APPENDIX 2

TREATY BETWEEN THE BRITISH GOVERNMENT AND THE STATE OF LAHORE, MARCH 9, 1846

WHEREAS the treaty of amity and concord, which was concluded between the British Government and the late Maharajah Runjeet Sing, the Ruler of Lahore, in 1809, was broken by the unprovoked aggression, on the British Provinces, of the Sikh Army, in December last; and Whereas, on that occasion, by the Proclamation, dated 13th December, the territories then in the occupation of the Maharajah of Lahore, on the left or British bank of the River Sutlej, were confiscated and annexed to the British Provinces; and since that time hostile operations have been prosecuted by the two Governments, the one against the other, which have resulted in the occupation of Lahore by the British troops; and Whereas it has been determined that, upon certain conditions, peace shall be re-established between the two Governments, the following treaty of peace between the Honorable English East India Company and Maharajah Dhuleep Sing Bahadoor, and his children, heirs and successors, has been concluded on the part of the Honorable Company by Frederick Currie, Esquire, and Brevet-Major Henry Montgomery Lawrence, by virtue of full powers to that effect vested in them by the Right Hon'ble Sir Henry Hardinge, G.C.B., one of Her Britannic Majesty's Most Honorable Privy Council, Governor-General, appointed by the Honorable Company to direct and control all their affairs in the East Indies, and on the part of His Highness Maharajah Dhuleep Sing by Bhaee Ram Sing, Rajah Lal Sing, Sirdar Tej Sing, Sirdar Chuttur Sing Attareewalla, Sirdar Runjore Sing Majeethia, Dewan Deena Nath and Fakeer Noorooddeen, vested with full powers and authority on the part of His Highness.

Article 1

There shall be perpetual peace and friendship between the British Government on the one part, and Maharajah Dhuleep Sing, his heirs and successors on the other.

Article 2

The Maharajah of Lahore renounces for himself, his heirs and successors, all claim to, or connection with, the territories lying to the south of the River Sutlej, and engages never to have any concern with those territories or inhabitants thereof.

Article 3

The Maharajah cedes to the Honorable Company, in perpetual sovereignty, all his forts, territories and rights in the Doab or country, hill and plain, situated between the Rivers Beas and Sutlej.

Article 4

The British Government having demanded from the Lahore State, as indemnification for the expenses of the war, in addition to the cession of territory described in Article 3, payment of one and half crore of rupees, and the Lahore Government, being unable to pay the whole of this sum at this time, or to give security satisfactory to the British Government for its eventual payment, the Maharajah cedes to the Honorable Company, in perpetual sovereignty, as equivalent for one crore of rupees, all his forts, territories, rights and interests in the hill countries, which are situated between the Rivers Beas and Indus, including the Provinces of Cashmere and Hazarah.

Article 5

The Maharajah will pay to the British Government the sum of 50 lakhs of rupees on or before the ratification of this Treaty.

Article 6

The Maharajah engages to disband the mutinous troops of the Lahore Army, taking from them their arms—and His Highness agrees to re-organise the Regular or Aeen Regiments of Infantry, upon the system, and according to the Regulations as to pay and allowances, observed in the time of the late Maharajah Runjeet Sing. The Maharajah further engages to pay up all arrears to the soldiers that are discharged, under the provisions of this Article.

Article 7

The Regular Army of the Lahore State shall henceforth be limited to 25 Battalions of Infantry, consisting of 800 bayonets each—with twelve thousand cavalry—this number at no time to be exceeded without the concurrence of the British Government. Should it be necessary at any time—for any special cause—that this force should be increased, the cause shall be fully explained to the British Government, and when the special necessity shall have passed, the regular troops shall be again reduced to the standard specified in the former clause of this Article.

Article 8

The Maharajah will surrender to the British Government all the guns—thirty-six in number—which have been pointed against the British Troops—and which, having been placed on the right bank of the River Sutlej, were not captured at the Battle of Subraon.

Article 9

The control of the Rivers Beas and Sutlej, with the continuations of the latter river, commonly called the Gurrah and the Punjnud, to the confluence of the Indus at Mithunkote—and the control of the Indus from Mithunkote to the borders of Beloochistan, shall, in respect to tolls and ferries, rest with the British Government. The provisions of this Article shall not interfere with the passage of boats belonging to the Lahore Government on the said rivers, for the purposes of traffic or the conveyance of passengers up and down their course. Regarding the ferries between the two countries respectively, at the several ghats of the said rivers, it is agreed that the British Government, after defraying all the expenses of management and establishments, shall account to the Lahore Government for one-half of the net profits of the ferry collections. The provisions of this Article have no reference to the ferries on that part of the River Sutlej which forms the boundary of Bhawulpore and Lahore respectively.

Article 10

If the British Government should, at any time, desire to pass troops through the territories of His Highness the Maharajah, for the protection of the British Territories, or those of their Allies, the British Troops shall, on such special occasion, due notice being given, be allowed to pass through the Lahore Territories. In such case the Officers of the Lahore State will afford facilities in providing supplies and boats for the passage of rivers, and the British Government will pay the full price of all such provisions and boats, and will make fair compensation for all private property that may be endamaged. The British Government will, moreover, observe all due consideration to the religious feelings of the inhabitants of those tracts through which the army may pass.

Article 11

The Maharajah engages never to take or to retain in his service any British subject—nor the subject of any European or American State—without the consent of the British Government.

Article 12

In consideration of the services rendered by Rajah Golab Sing, of Jummoo, to the Lahore State, towards procuring the restoration of the relations of amity between the Lahore and British Governments the Maharajah hereby agrees to recognise the Independent Sovereignty of Rajah Golab Sing, in such territories and districts in the hills as may be made over to the said Rajah Golab Sing, by separate Agreement between himself and the British Government, with the dependencies thereof, which may have been in the Rajah's possession since the time of the late Maharajah Khurruck Sing, and the British Government, in consideration of the good conduct of Rajah Golab Sing, also agrees to recognise his independence in such territories, and to admit him to the privileges of a separate Treaty with the British Government.

Article 13

In the event of any dispute or difference arising between the Lahore State and Rajah Golab Sing, the same shall be referred to the arbitration of the British Government, and by its decision the Maharajah engages to abide.

Article 14

The limits of the Lahore Territories shall not be, at any time, changed without the concurrence of the British Government.

Article 15

The British Government will not exercise any interference in the internal administration of the Lahore State—but in all cases or questions which may be referred to the British Government, the Governor-General will give the aid of his advice and good offices for the furtherance of the interests of the Lahore Government.

Article 16

The subjects of either State shall, on visiting the territories of the other, be on the footing of the subjects of the most favoured nation.

This Treaty, consisting of sixteen articles, has been this day settled by Frederick Currie, Esquire, and Brevet-Major Henry Montgomery Lawrence acting under the directions of the Right Hon'ble Sir Henry Hardinge, G.C.B., Governor-General, on the part of the British Government, and by Bhaee Ram Sing, Rajah Lal Sing, Sirdar Tej Sing, Sirdar Chuttur Sing Attareewalla, Sirdar Runjore Sing Majeethia, Dewan Deena Nath, and Fuqueer Noorooddeen, on the part of the Maharajah Dhuleep Sing, and the said Treaty has been this day ratified by the seal of the Right Hon'ble Sir Henry Hardinge, G.C.B., Governor-General, and by that of His Highness Maharajah Dhuleep Sing.

Done at Lahore, this ninth day of March, in the year of Our Lord one thousand eight hundred and forty-six, corresponding with the 10th day of Rubbee-ool-awul, 1262 Hijree, and ratified on the same date.

(Sd.) H. Hardinge

(Sd.)   Maharajah Dhuleep Sing
       Bhaee Ram Sing
       Rajah Lal Sing
       Sirdar Tej Sing
       Sirdar Chuttur Sing Attareewalla
       Sirdar Runjore Sing Majeethia
       Dewan Deena Nath
       Fuqueer Noorooddeen

APPENDIX 3

ARTICLES OF AGREEMENT CONCLUDED BETWEEN THE BRITISH GOVERNMENT AND THE LAHORE DURBAR ON MARCH 11, 1846

WHEREAS the Lahore Government has solicited the Governor-General to leave a British force at Lahore, for the protection of the Maharajah's person and of the Capital, till the re-organisation of the Lahore army, according to the provisions of Article 6 of the Treaty of Lahore, dated the 9th instant, and Whereas the Governor-General has, on certain conditions, consented to the measure; and Whereas it is expedient that certain matters concerning the territories ceded by Articles 3 and 4 of the aforesaid Treaty should be specifically determined, the following eight Articles of Agreement have this day been concluded between the aforementioned contracting parties.

Article 1

The British Government shall leave at Lahore, till the close of the current year, A.D. 1846, such force as shall seem to the Governor-General adequate for the purpose of protecting the person of the Maharajah and the inhabitants of the City of Lahore, during the reorganisation of the Sikh army, in accordance with the provisions of Article 6 of the Treaty of Lahore. That force to be withdrawn at any convenient time before the expiration of the year, if the object to be fulfilled shall, in the opinion of the Durbar, have been attained—but the force shall not be detained at Lahore beyond the expiration of the current year.

Article 2

The Lahore Government agrees that the force left at Lahore for the purpose specified in the foregoing Article, shall be placed in full possession of the Fort and the City of Lahore, and that the Lahore troops shall be removed from within the city. The Lahore Government engages to furnish convenient quarters for the Officers and men of the said force and to pay to the British Government all the extra expenses in regard to the said force; which may be incurred by the British Government, in consequence of the troops being employed away from their own cantonments and in Foreign Territory.

Article 3

The Lahore Government engages to apply itself immediately and earnestly to the reorganisation of its army according to the prescribed conditions, and to communicate fully with the British Authorities left at Lahore, as to the progress of such reorganisation, and as to the location of the troops.

Article 4

If the Lahore Government fails in the performance of the conditions of the foregoing Article, the British Government shall be at liberty to withdraw the force from Lahore at any time before the expiration of the period specified in Article 1.

Article 5

The British Government agrees to respect the bona fide rights of those jaghiredars, within the territories ceded by Articles 3 and 4 of the Treaty of Lahore, dated 9th instant, who were attached to the families of the late Maharajahs Runjeet Sing, Kurruk Sing and Shere Sing; and the British Government will maintain those jaghiredars in their bona fide possessions during their lives.

Article 6

The Lahore Government shall receive the assistance of the British Local Authorities in recovering the arrears of revenue justly due to the Lahore Government from the kardars and managers in the territories ceded by the provisions of Articles 3 and 4 of the Treaty of Lahore, to the close of the khureef harvest of the current year, viz. 1902 of the Sumbut bikramajeet.

Article 7

The Lahore Government shall be at liberty to remove, from the forts, in the territories specified in the foregoing Article, all treasure and State property, with the exception of guns. Should, however, the British Government desire to retain any part of the said property, they shall be at liberty to do so, paying for the same at a fair valuation, and the British Officers shall give their assistance to the Lahore Government in disposing on the spot of such part of the aforesaid property as the Lahore Government may not wish to remove, and the British Officers may not desire to retain.

Article 8

Commissioners shall be immediately appointed by the two Governments to settle and lay down the boundary between the two States, as defined by Article 4 of the Treaty of Lahore, dated March 9th, 1846.

(Sd.) H. Hardinge

(Sd.)   Maharajah Dhuleep Sing
Bhaee Ram Sing
Rajah Lal Sing
Sirdar Tej Sing
Sirdar Chuttur Sing Attareewalla
Sirdar Runjore Sing Majeethia
Dewan Deena Nath
Fuqueer Noorooddeen

APPENDIX 4

ARTICLES OF AGREEMENT CONCLUDED BETWEEN THE BRITISH GOVERNMENT AND THE LAHORE DURBAR ON DECEMBER 16, 1846

WHEREAS the Lahore Durbar and the principal Chiefs and Sirdars of the State have in express terms communicated to the British Government their anxious desire that the Governor-General should give his aid and assistance to maintain the administration of the Lahore State during the minority of Maharajah Dulleep Sing, and have declared this measure to be indispensable for the maintenance of the Government; and Whereas the Governor-General has, under certain conditions, consented to give the aid and assistance solicited, the following Articles of Agreement, in modification of the Articles of Agreement executed at Lahore on the 11th March last, have been concluded on the part of the British Government by Frederick Currie, Esquire, Secretary to Government of India, and Lieutenant-Colonel Henry Montgomery Lawrence, C.B., Agent to the Governor-General, North West Frontier, by virtue of full powers to that effect vested in them by the Right Hon'ble Viscount Hardinge, G.C.B., Governor-General, and on the part of His Highness Maharajah Dulleep Sing, by Sirdar Tej Sing, Sirdar Shere Sing, Dewan Dena Nath, Fukeer Nooroodeen, Rai Kishen Chund, Sirdar Runjore Sing Majethea, Sirdar Utter Sing Kaleewalla, Bhaee Nidhan Sing, Sirdar Khan Sing Majethea, Sirdar Shumshere Sing, Sirdar Lal Sing Morarea, Sirdar Kher Sing Sindhanwalla, Sirdar Urjun Sing Rungrungalea; acting with the unanimous consent and concurrence of the Chiefs and Sirdars of the State assembled at Lahore.

Article 1

All and every part of the Treaty of peace between the British Government and the State of Lahore, bearing date the 9th day of March 1846, except in so far as it may be temporarily modified in respect to clause 15 of the said Treaty by this engagement, shall remain binding upon the two Governments.

Article 2

A British Officer, with an efficient establishment of assistants, shall be appointed by the Governor-General to remain at Lahore, which officer shall have full authority to direct and control all matters in every Department of the State.

Article 3

Every attention shall be paid in conducting the administration to the feelings of the people, to preserving the national institutions and customs, and to maintaining the just rights of all classes.

Article 4

Changes in the mode and details of administration shall not be made except when found necessary for effecting the objects set forth in the foregoing Clause, and for securing the just dues of the Lahore Government. These details shall be conducted by Native officers as at present, who shall be appointed and superintended by a Council of Regency composed of leading Chiefs and Sirdars acting under the control and guidance of the British Resident.

Article 5

The following persons shall in the first instance constitute the Council of Regency, viz., Sirdar Tej Sing, Sirdar Shere Sing Attareewalla, Dewan Dena Nath, Fukeer Nooroodeen, Sirdar Runjore Sing Majethea, Bhaee Nidhan Sing, Sirdar Utter Sing Kaleewalla, Sirdar Shumshere Sing Sindhanwalla, and no change shall be made in the persons thus nominated, without the consent of the British Resident, acting under the orders of the Governor-General.

Article 6

The administration of the country shall be conducted by this Council of Regency in such manner as may be determined on by themselves in consultation with the British Resident, who shall have full authority to direct and control the duties of every department.

Article 7

A British Force of such strength and numbers, and in such positions as the Governor-General may think fit, shall remain at Lahore for the protection of the Maharajah and the preservation of the peace of the country.

Article 8

The Governor-General shall be at liberty to occupy with British soldiers any fort or military post in the Lahore Territories, the occupation of which may be deemed necessary by the British Government, for the security of the capital or for maintaining the peace of the country.

Article 9

The Lahore State shall pay to the British Government twenty-two lakhs of new Nanuck Shahee Rupees of full tale and weight per annum for the maintenance of this force, and to meet the expenses incurred by the British Government. Such sum to be paid by two instalments, or 13,20,000 in May or June, and 8,80,000 in November or December of each year.

Article 10

Inasmuch as it is fitting that Her Highness the Maharanee, the mother of Maharajah Dulleep Sing, should have a proper provision made for the maintenance of herself and dependents, the sum of one lakh and fifty thousand rupees shall be set apart annually for that purpose, and shall be at Her Highness' disposal.

Article 11

The provisions of this Engagement shall have effect during the minority of His Highness Maharajah Dulleep Sing, and shall cease and terminate on His Highness attaining the full age of sixteen years, or on the 4th September of the year 1854, but it shall be competent to the Governor-General to cause the arrangement to cease at any period prior to the coming of age of His Highness, at which the Governor-General and the Lahore Durbar may be satisfied that the interposition of the British Government is no longer necessary for maintaining the Government of His Highness the Maharajah.

This Agreement, consisting of eleven Articles, was settled and executed at Lahore by the Officers and Chiefs and Sirdars above named, on the 16th day of December 1846.

(Sd.) F. Currie

H. M. Lawrence

(Sd.) Sirdar Tej Sing
Sirdar Shere Sing
Dewan Dena Nath
Fukeer Nooroodeen
Rai Kishen Chund
Sirdar Runjore Sing Majethea
Sirdar Utter Sing Kaleewalla
Bhaee Nidhan Sing
Sirdar Khan Sing Majethea
Sirdar Shumshere Sing
Sirdar Lal Sing Morarea
Sirdar Kher Sing Sindhanwalla
Sirdar Urjun Sing Rungrungalea

(Sd.) Hardinge

Dulleep Sing

Ratified by the Right Honorable the Governor-General, at Bhyrowal Ghat on the left bank of the Beas, the twenty-sixth day of December One Thousand Eight Hundred and Forty-six.

(Sd.) F. Currie,

Secretary to the

Government of India

APPENDIX 5

MR. SUHRAWARDY'S STATEMENT ON THE
RIOTS, SEPTEMBER 30, 1946

"I AM deeply disturbed to find that the suspicion and distrust amongst Muslims against Sikhs still continues. I still hear rumours circulated from time to time and in various localities that the Sikhs are congregating in certain places for the purpose of attacking Muslims. Each one of these reports has been investigated and has been found to be false. Places supposed to be full of Sikhs armed for the purpose have been searched and the report has been found to be absolutely without substance.

"I have personally looked into many of these cases and can definitely state that these reports are absolutely false and are merely the outcome of panic. Sikhs went about in their taxis and their buses during those dangerous five days for the purpose of rescuing their women and children and removing their belongings. Immediately rumours got abroad that they were moving about for the purpose of attacking Muslim mohallas. Not one Muslim mohalla has been attacked by the Sikhs thus far, and yet the rumours still go on.

"There are stories of one or two Sikhs here and there in those days of carnage having taken part in the riots. Some of these may be true and others may not. But that does not mean that the Sikh community is up against the Muslims.

"I have been in constant touch with the Sikh leaders and I am absolutely convinced regarding their bona-fides and the attempts that they are making to keep themselves neutral and not to be involved in any kind of dispute. More than that during the riots they have saved as many as 5,000 Muslims from dangerous areas and carried these Muslims to safe places. Surely they deserve something better from the Muslims than this suspicion and distrust and hostility against them.

"Small incidents take place here and there and misunderstanding grows. Let us give some examples which may help to clear the situation. A report is received that Muslims are being assaulted in a Hindu area; a bus comes along which is driven by a Sikh driver, and this bus contains both Hindus and Muslims; the Muslims stop the bus and request the Muslims to get out and not to go into the dangerous area; the Hindus in the bus think that the Muslims are being taken out for the purpose of assaulting the Hindus, and they urge upon the Sikh driver to drive fast; the Sikh driver drives fast and the Muslims outside think that he is running away with some Muslim so that he may be killed in the Hindu area, and they start throwing stones. This is how misunderstanding arises.

"We know of one case where a Sikh driver did not stop at a particular place as he got into a panic seeing a Muslim crowd standing by; the Muslim in the bus who wanted the Sikh driver to stop thought that the Sikh driver was running away with him, he jumped out of the bus and injured himself. Immediately rumours got about that bodies had been thrown out of the bus, that Sikhs had killed Muslims, that Sikhs had attacked Muslims with knives and so on.

"All this must cease. My Muslim brethren must believe me when I say that this propaganda against the Sikhs is false and must stop at once, and the Sikh drivers whether of buses or of taxis must not be stoned or molested in any way. In fact I should very much like that attempts should be made by the Muslim localities to contact Sikh leaders who are their neighbours so that mutual confidence may be restored.

"I hope that Muslims will respond to this appeal wholeheartedly and stop molesting the Sikhs; and also stop this anti-Sikh propaganda which has no basis in fact and which must be put an end to at once for the sake of peace and general restoration of confidence."

The Statesman, October 1, 1946.

BIBLIOGRAPHY

GURMUKHI

Manuscript Source

Ram Singh, Maharajah Raṇjit Singh—Diary, Khalsa College MSS, Amritsar.

Published Sources

Arjun, Guru, *Ādi Grañth*, 1604 (see Vol. 1, Appendices 2 and 5).

Bhagat Singh, *Srī Nankānā dā Purātan Hāl.*

Chakravarty, I. S., *Kūkiāṇ Bāre*, Puran Singh Ravendrapal Singh, Patiala 1956.

Daljit Singh, *Singh Sabhā dey Modhī, Jīwan Britānt Bhāī Dit Singh*, Shiromani Khalsa Biradari, 1951.

Durlabh Singh, *Nirbhai Yodhā*, Hero Publications, Lahore 1942.

Ganda Singh, *Kūkiāṇ dī Vithiā*, Khalsa College, Amritsar 1944.

———, *Sardār Shām Singh Attārīvālā*, K. S. Gangawala, Amritsar 1949.

———, *Sikh itihās bāre*, Khalsa College, Amritsar 1942.

———, *Sikh itihās wal*, Khalsa College, Amritsar 1945.

Gobind Singh, Guru, *Dasam Grañth* or *Dasveṇ Pādśāh kā Grañth* (see Vol. 1, Appendix 4).

Gurbachan Singh, *Babbar Akālī*, Hoshiarpur 1950.

Gurbaksh Singh, *Śahīdī Jīvan*, Gurdwara Committee, Nankana Sahib 1938.

Gurcharan Singh Sainsra, *Ghadr Pārtī dā Itihās*, Desh Bhagat Yadgar Committee, Jullundur 1961.

Gurdit Singh, *Zulmī Kathā*, Akal Press, Amritsar.

Gurdit Singh Gyani, *Amar Gāthā*, Desh Bhagat Prakashan, Ludhiana.

Gurmukh Singh "Gurmukh," *Tawārīkh Nābhā*, Pratap Singh Sunder Singh, Amritsar.

Gur Sikhāṇ dī ardās, Youngmans Nirankari Association, Amritsar 1955.

Gyan Singh, Gyani, *Tawārīkh Gurū Khālsā*, Durbar Publishing House, Amritsar.

Hira Singh Dard, Gyani, *Niraṅkārī Gurmat Modhī Srī Bābā Dayāljī*, Youngmans Nirankari Association, Amritsar 1955.

BIBLIOGRAPHY

Jagjit Singh, *Ghadr Pārtī dī Lahr*, Sundarshan Press, Amritsar 1955.

Jagjit Singh Alakh, *Ik Jīvan—ik Itihās* (Life of Seva Singh Thikrivala), Awami Printing Press, Jullundur 1959.

Kahan Singh, Bhai, *Ham Hindu Nahin*, Nabha 1897.

Karam Singh, *Shām Singh Attārīvālā*, Jawahar Singh Kripal Singh, Amritsar.

Khazan Singh Gyani, *Itihās Gurdwārā Śahīd Gaṅj, Lahore*, published by the author, Lahore 1937.

Kirpal Singh, *Sikhān dī Sevā*, Khalsa College, Amritsar.

Kohli, S. R., *Vār Shāh Mohammed*, Punjabi Sahitya Akademi, Ludhiana 1957.

Kohli, Surinder Singh, *Panjābī Sāhit dā Itihās*, Lahore Book Shop, Ludhiana 1950.

Mahinder Singh, *Sardār-i-Āzam*, Panthic Tract Society, Amritsar 1950.

Mohan Singh, Bhai, *Bhayānak Sākā Nankānā Sāhib*, Taran Taran.

Nahar Singh, Gyani, *Azādī diyān Lehrān*, Gyani Harbhajan Singh, Amritsar 1960.

Nidhan Singh Alam, *Jag Paltāū Satgūrū*, Naya Hindustan Press, Delhi 1947.

Niraṅkārī Hukumnāmā, Youngmans Nirankari Association, Amritsar 1955.

Niraṅkārī Prem Prakāś, Youngmans Nirankari Association, Amritsar 1955.

Piara Singh Padam, *Sankhep Sikh Itihās*, Sardar Sahit Bhavan, Patiala 1963.

Pratap Singh, *Gurdwārā Sudhār*, Singh Brothers, Amritsar 1951.

Prem Singh, Baba, *Jīvan Britānt Mahārājāh Sher Singh*, Lahore Book Shop, Ludhiana 1951.

——, *Jīvan Britānt Mahārājāh Nao Nihāl Singh*, Lahore Book Shop, Ludhiana.

Randhawa, M. S., *Panjāb*, Bhasha Vibhag, Patiala 1960.

Sardha Ram, *Sikhān de Rāj dī Vithiā*, Jullundur 1956.

Sardul Singh Caveeshar, *Sākā Nankānā Sāhib*, Akali Agency, Lahore 1921.

Seva Singh, Bhai, *Panjāb te Sikh*, Amritsar 1922.

BIBLIOGRAPHY

Shah Mohammad, *Kissā Larāī Rāj Singhān*, ed. Labh Singh, Amritsar 1922.
Shamsher Singh, *Sikh Rāj dā Aṅt*, Ludhiana 1951.
Shiv Dayal, *Sār Bacan*, Radha Soami Satsang, Agra.
Sundar Singh Makhsuspuri, *Babar Akālī Lahar*, Singh Brothers, Amritsar 1961.
Surinder Singh Narula, *Panjābi Sāhit dā Itihās*, Sikh Publishing House, New Delhi 1954.
Tara Singh, Master, *Merī Yād*, Sikh Religious Book Society, Amritsar 1944.
Teja Singh, *Jīwan Kathā Sant Attar Singh jī Mahārāj*, 2 vols., published by author, Patiala 1950.

PERSIAN AND URDU

Ajudhia Parshad, *Wāq-i-Jaṅg-i-Sikhāṇ, 1845-46*, Punjab University Library, Lahore.
Mohammad Naqi, *Tārīkh-i-Punjab (Sher Singh Nāmā) , 1843*, Punjab University Library, Lahore.
Parmanand, Bhai, *Tārīkh-i-Hind*, Hindustan Ghadr, San Francisco.
Punjab Government, *Achū ± Qaumen*, Information Bureau, Punjab, Lahore 1925.
Suri, Sohan Lal, "Umdāt-ut-Tāwārīkh," Daftars IV and V, MSS, India Office Library.

HINDI

Dayanand Saraswati, *Satyārth Prakās*, new edn., Vedic Sahitya Sada, Delhi 1965.
Nahar Singh, *Nāmdhārī Itihās*, Eastern Printing Press, Delhi 1956.

ENGLISH

Original Sources

PRIVATE PAPERS

Auckland Papers, British Museum.
Broughton Papers, India Office Records (Home Miscellaneous Series, Vols. 833-862) and British Museum.
Chelmsford Papers, India Office Library (closed) .
Dalhousie Papers, Scottish Record Office, Edinburgh.

BIBLIOGRAPHY

Ellenborough Papers, Public Record Office, London.
Hardinge Papers [Henry], McGill University, Canada.
Irwin Papers, India Office Library (closed).
Lawrence Papers [Henry], India Office Library, MSS Eur. F. 85.
Lawrence Papers [John], India Office Library, MSS Eur. F. 90.
Minto Papers [3rd Earl of], National Library, Edinburgh.
Morley Papers, India Office Library, MSS Eur. D. 573.
Willingdon Papers, India Office Library (closed).

Manuscripts

Home Miscellaneous Series, India Office Records, 1846—.
Miller, Allen, "An Ethnographic Report on the Sikhs (E) Indians of the Sacramento Valley," University of California, Berkeley 1950.
Pearse, G. G., "Journal Kept during the Siege of Multan, the Punjab War 1848—1849." India Office Library, MSS Eur. B. 115.
Political Consultations, Foreign Department, National Archives of India, New Delhi.
Sahni, R. R., "History of My Times," Patiala Archives, Patiala.
Secret Consultations, Foreign Department, National Archives of India, New Delhi.
"U.S.A. *vs* Bopp & Others. San Francisco, 1917-1918," India Office Library, MSS Eur. C. 138, Vols. 1-40, 61-65.

Secondary Sources

UNPUBLISHED THESES

Abdul Karim Bin Bagoo, "The Origin and Growth of the Malaya State Guides (1873-1919)," University of Singapore 1954.
Arora, G. S., "New Frontiersmen: A Study of Sikh Immigrants in Great Britain," London University 1963.
Bal, S. S., "British Policy towards the Panjab 1844-49," London University 1962.
Brown, Giles T., "The Hindu Conspiracy and Neutrality of United States 1914-17," University of California, Berkeley 1941.
Joginder Singh Jessy, "The Indian Army of Independence," University of Singapore, 1957-1958.

Letchmanan, M., "The F.M.S. Police Force 1896-1928," University of Singapore 1961.

Lowes, George H., "The Sikhs of British Columbia," University of British Columbia 1952.

Marenco, Ethne K., "Caste and Class among the Sikhs of North West India," Columbia University 1963.

Mayer, Adrian C., "A Report on the East Indian Community in Vancouver," University of British Columbia n.d.

Mehr Chand, "Sikhism in Canada," University of British Columbia 1916.

Morse, Eric W., "The Immigration Status of British East Indians in Canada," University of British Columbia n.d.

Mosbergen, R. W., "The Sepoy Rebellion (A History of the Singapur Mutiny, 1915)," University of Singapore 1954.

Mutambikwa, Jarius Grey, "A Study of the East Indian Community of British Columbia," University of British Columbia 1959.

Nayar, Baldev Raj, "Contemporary Political Leadership in the Punjab," University of Chicago 1963.

Oren, Stephen, "The Sikhs and Punjab Politics 1921-1947," University of British Columbia 1964.

Strasser, Marsland Keith, "American Neutrality: The Case of Consul-General Bopp," University of California, Berkeley 1939.

PUBLISHED SOURCES

Adhikari, G., *Sikh Homeland through Hindu-Muslim-Sikh Unity*, People's Publishing House, Bombay 1945.

———, *Pakistan and National Unity*, People's Publishing House, Bombay 1944.

Ahluwalia, M. L., *Relations of the Lahore Durbar with China; Mai Chand Kaur's Rule in the Punjab; Sher Singh and the First War of Succession; Some Facts behind the Second Anglo-Sikh War; Ladakh's Relations with India*, Proceedings of the Indian Historical Records Commission, Vols. XXX–XXXIII.

Ahluwalia, M. L. and Kirpal Singh, *The Punjab's Pioneer Freedom Fighters*, Orient Longmans, Calcutta 1964.

Ahluwalia, M. M., *Kukas, The Freedom Fighters of the Punjab*, Allied Publishers, Bombay 1965.

Aitchison, Sir Charles, *Lord Lawrence*, Clarendon Press, Oxford 1892.

Akali Dal and Shiromani Gurdwara Prabandhak Committee, C.I.D. Report compiled by V. W. Smith, Superintendent of Police, published by Superintendent of Government Printing, Simla 1922.

Alexander, H., *India Since Cripps*, Harmondsworth 1944.

Amar Nath, *The Development of Local Self-Government in the Punjab 1849-1900*, P.G.R.O., Lahore 1929.

Amar Singh, *Memorandum of the Central Akali Dal*, West End Press, Lahore 1946.

Ambedkar, B. R., *Pakistan or the Partition of India*, Thacker & Co., Bombay 1946.

Argyll, 8th Duke of, *India under Dalhousie and Canning*, Longmans Green & Co., London 1865.

Army in India and Its Evolution, Govt. Printing Press, Calcutta 1924.

Arnold, Edwin, *The Marquis of Dalhousie's Administration of British India*, 2 vols., Saunders, Otley & Co., London 1862-1865.

Arora, F. C., *Commerce by River in the Punjab*, P.G.R.O., Lahore 1930.

Ashraf, M., *Cabinet Mission and After*, Islamic Literature Publishing House, Lahore 1946.

———, *Speeches and Writings of Mr. Jinnah*, Ashraf, Lahore 1942.

Attar Singh, *Basic Facts Regarding Punjabi Language*, published by the author, Ambala 1961.

Ayer, S. A., *Unto Him a Witness*, Thacker & Co., Bombay 1951.

Azad, Maulana, *India Wins Freedom*, Orient Longmans, Calcutta 1959.

Bahadur Shah, Proceedings on the Trial of, Superintendent of Govt. Printing Press, Calcutta 1895.

Baird, edited by J. G. A., *Private Letters of the Marquess of Dalhousie*, William Blackwood & Sons, Edinburgh 1911.

Bamford, Lt. Col. P. G., *1st King George V's own Battalion*, Gale & Golden Ltd., Aldershot 1948.

Bamzai, P. N. K., *A History of Kashmir*, Metropolitan Book Co., Delhi 1962.

Barkat Ram Kalia, *A History of the Development of the Police in the Punjab 1849-1905*, P.G.R.O., Lahore 1929.

Barkley, D. G., *Directions for Revenue Officers in the Punjab*, Superintendent of Govt. Press, Lahore 1875.

Barstow, A. E., *Sikhs*, Government of India, Publications Branch, Calcutta 1928.

Bell, Evans, *Annexation of the Punjab and the Maharajah Duleep Singh*, Trubner, London 1882.

———, *Retrospects and Prospects of Indian Policy*, Trubner, London 1868.

Bengal Army, Officer of the, *Letters on Recent Transactions in India*, Smith Elder & Co., London 1842.

Benson, edited by A. C. and V. Esher, *The Letters of Queen Victoria*, Vol. II—1844-53, London, 1908.

Bertie-Marriott, C., *Le Maharajah Duleep Singh et l'Angleterre*, L. Sauvaitre, Paris 1889.

Bingley, Capt. A. H., *Handbook for the Indian Army*, Govt. Printing Press, Calcutta 1899.

———, *Handbook on the Sikhs*, Simla Govt. Central Printing Office, 1899.

Birdwood, C., *A Continent Experiments*, Skeffington & Co., London 1947.

Birdwood, Col. F. T., *The Sikh Regiment in the Second World War*, Jarrod & Sons Ltd., Norwich.

Bolitho, H., *Jinnah, Creator of Pakistan*, Murray, London 1954.

Bondurant, Joan V., *Regionalism Versus Provincialism: A Study in Problems of Indian National Unity*, University of California Press, Berkeley, 1958.

Bosworth Smith, R., *Life of Lord Lawrence*, 2 vols., Smith Elder & Co., London 1883.

Brayne, F. L., *Socrates in an Indian Village*, Oxford University Press, Bombay 1929.

———, *Remaking of village India*, Oxford University Press, Bombay 1929.

———, *Socrates Persists in India*, Oxford University Press, Bombay 1932.

Briggs, Major General, *What are we to do with the Punjab?* James Madden, London 1849.

Broadfoot, W., *Career of Major George Broadfoot*, John Murray, London 1888.

Buist, G., *Annals for the year 1848 to the end of the Sikh War in March, 1849*, Times Press, Bombay 1849.

Burton, R. G., *The First and the Second Sikh Wars*, Govt. Central Branch Press, Simla 1911.

California and the Oriental: Japanese, Chinese and Hindu, State Board of Control of California, Sacramento 1922 (report of Governor William D. Stephens of California to the Secretary of State).

Callard, Keith, *Pakistan*, Allen & Unwin, London 1957.

Calvert, H., *The Wealth and Welfare of the Punjab*, Civil & Military Gazette Press, Lahore 1927.

Campbell, Sir Colin, *Memorandum on the part taken by the Third Division of the Army of the Punjab at the Battle of Chillianwala*, James Ridgway, London 1851.

Campbell, George, *Memoirs of my Indian Career*, Macmillan, London, 1893.

Campbell-Johnson, A., *Mission with Mountbatten*, Robert Hale, London 1951.

Canada, Royal Commission (on Oriental Immigration), Report by W. L. MacKenzie King, Ottawa 1908.

Carmichael Smyth, Major G., ed., *History of the Reigning Family of Lahore*, W. Thacker & Co., London 1847.

Caulfield, General, *The Punjab and the Indian Army*, London 1846.

Cavalry Officer, *Military Services and Adventures in the Far East*, London 1847.

Cave-Browne, J., *The Punjab and Delhi in 1857*, 2 vols., William Blackwood & Sons, London 1861.

Census Reports, Punjab, 1855 onward, Govt. Printing Press, Calcutta.

Chaddha, T. R., *A Study of the Communist Movement in the Punjab*, Jyoti Prakashan, Ghaziabad 1954.

Chandrashekhar, S., "Indian Immigration in America," *Far Eastern Survey* (July 26, 1944).

Charan Singh, Maharaj, *Light on Sant Mat*, Radha Soami Satsang, Beas 1960.

Chhabra, Dr. G. S., *Advanced Study in History of the Punjab*, 2 vols., Sharanjit, Ludhiana 1960.

Colchester, Lord, *History of the Indian Administration of Lord Ellenborough*, Richard Bentley & Sons, London 1874.

Cole, J. J., *A Sketch of the Siege of Multan*, P. S. Rozario & Co., Calcutta 1849.

Coley, James, *A Journal of the Sutlej Campaign, 1845-46*, Smith Elder & Co., London 1856.

Colvin, Ian, *The Life of General Dyer*, William Blackwood & Sons, Edinburgh 1931.

Congress and the Problem of Minorities, All India Congress Committee, published by Shankar Rao Deo, Allahabad 1947.

Congress Punjab Inquiry Report 1919-1920, Karnatak Printing Press, Bombay 1920.

Cooper, Frederic, *The Crisis in the Punjab*, Smith Elder & Co., London 1858.

Corbett, D. C., *Canada's Immigration Policy—A Critique*, University of Toronto Press, Toronto 1947.

Cork, Barry Joynson, *Rider on a Grey Horse*, Cassell, London 1958.

Coupland, R., *The Constitutional Problem in India*, Oxford University Press, Bombay 1944.

Cunningham, Alexander, *Report of a Tour in the Punjab, 1878-79*, Superintendent of Govt. Printing, Calcutta 1882.

Cunningham, J. D., *History of the Sikhs*, 1st edn. 1849; 2nd edn. 1853; 1955 edn. edited by H. L. O. Garrett and published by S. Chand & Co., Delhi 1955.

Cust, R. N., *Memoirs of Past Years of a Septuagenarian*, printed for private circulation, London 1904.

———, *Linguistic and Oriental Essays*, Trubner & Co., London 1906.

Dadabhoy, Yusuf, "Circuitous Assimilation among Rural Hindustanis in California," *Social Forces*, 33 (1954), 138-141.

Dar Commission, *Report of the Linguistic Provinces Commission*, Govt. of India Press, Delhi 1948.

Darbara Singh, *The Punjab Tragedy*, Steno Press, Amritsar 1949.

Darling, M. L., *The Punjab Peasant in Prosperity and Debt*, Oxford University Press, Bombay 1925.

————, *Wisdom and Waste in the Punjab Village*, Oxford University Press, Bombay 1934.

Das, R. K., *Hindustani Workers on the Pacific Coast*, Walter De Gruyter & Co., Berlin 1923.

Das, S. R., *Commission Report on Grievances of the Sikhs*, Govt. of India Press, Delhi 1962.

Deva Singh, *Colonisation in the Rechna Doab*, P.G.R.O., Lahore 1929.

Dhami, Sadhu Singh, *The Sikhs and their Religion: A Struggle for Democracy*, K. D. Society, Vancouver 1943.

Dharam Pal, *Administration of Sir John Lawrence 1864-1869*, Minerva, Simla 1952.

Dharam Yash Dev, *Our Countrymen Abroad*, All India Congress Committee, Delhi 1940.

Diver, Maud, *Honoria Lawrence*, John Murray, London 1936.

Dodwell, H., *A Sketch of the History of India 1858-1918*, Longmans, Green & Co., London 1925.

Douie, Sir J. M., *The Punjab, North West Frontier Province and Kashmir*, Cambridge University Press, Cambridge 1916.

Druhe, D. N., *Soviet Russia and India*, Communist Bookman Associates, 1959.

Duleep Singh, Maharajah, *The Maharaja Duleep Singh and the Government*, W. S. Orr & Co., London 1884.

Dunbar, Sir George, *India and the Passing of the Empire*, Nicholson & Watson, London 1951.

Dunlop, J., *Mooltan during and after the Siege*, W. S. Orr & Co., London 1849.

Dunn, H. H., "The Stranglers," *World Wide Magazine*, Vol. 25, pp. 338-351.

Durand, H. M., *Life of Major General Sir Henry Marion Durand*, W. H. Allen & Co., London 1883.

Durlabh Singh, *The Valiant Fighter*, Hero Publications, Lahore 1942.

Edwardes, Herbert, *A Year on the Punjab Frontier in 1848-49*, 2 vols., Richard Bentley, London 1851.

Edwardes, H. B. and Merivale, H., *Life of Sir Henry Lawrence*, Smith Elder & Co., London 1873.

Edwardes, Lady Emma, *Memorials of the Life and Letters of Major General Sir Herbert B. Edwardes*, 2 vols., Kegan Paul, Trench & Co., London 1886.

Edwardes, M., *The Necessary Hell: John and Henry Lawrence and the Indian Empire*, Cassell, London 1958.

Edwards, W., *Reminiscences of a Bengal Civilian*, Smith Elder & Co., London 1866.

Elsmie, G. R., *Thirty-Five Years in the Punjab, 1858-93*, David Douglas, Edinburgh 1908.

Encyclopaedia of Religion and Ethics, edited by James Hastings, T. & T. Clark, Edinburgh 1926.

Falcon, R. W., *Handbook on the Sikhs for Regimental Officers*, Govt. Printing Press, Allahabad 1896.

Farquhar, J. N., *Modern Religious Movements in India*, Macmillan, London 1929.

Fauja Singh Bajwa, *Military System of the Sikhs*, Moti Lal Banarsi Das, Delhi 1964.

Fitchett, W. H., *The Tale of the Great Mutiny*, John Murray, London 1939.

Forbes, A., *The Afghan Wars*, Macmillan, London 1892.

———, *Sir Colin Campbell, Lord Clyde*, Macmillan, London 1916.

———, *Havelock* (Englishmen of Action), Macmillan, London 1924.

Forbes, Angus, "East Indians in Canada," *International Journal* (1947), pp. 47-50.

Forbes-Mitchell, W., *Reminiscences of the Great Mutiny*, Macmillan, London 1910.

Forsyth, Douglas, *Autobiography and Reminiscences*, Richard Bentley, London 1887.

Francis, R. A., "B. C.'s Turbaned Tribe," *Canadian Business*, 25 (February 1952), 44-45.

Furneaux, R., *Massacre at Amritsar*, Allen & Unwin, London 1963.

Ganda Singh, *History of Gurdwara Shahid-Ganj, Lahore, from its Origin to November, 1935*, published by the author, Amritsar 1935.

Ganda Singh, "Some Correspondence of Maharaja Duleep Singh," *Journal of Indian History*, Vol. xxvii, Part i, No. 79.

———, *A History of the Khalsa College*, Khalsa College, Amritsar 1949.

———, *The Punjab in 1839-40*, Sikh History Society, Amritsar 1952.

———, *Private Correspondence relating to the Anglo-Sikh Wars*, Sikh History Society, Amritsar 1955.

Gardner, Ray, "When Vancouver Turned Back the Sikhs," *Macleans Magazine* (November 8, 1958), p. 65.

Gazette of India, Govt. Printing Press, Calcutta.

Gazetteers of India, Imperial, Oxford University Press, Oxford 1908.

Ghadr, *Report of the Senate Fact-Finding Committee of Un-American Activities to the 1953 Regular California Legislature*, California State Printing Office, Sacramento 1953.

Ghosh, K. C., *The Roll of Honour*, Vidya Bharati, Calcutta 1965.

Gibbon, F. P., *The Lawrences of the Punjab*, J. M. Dent, London 1908.

Glegg, Lieutenant Colonel J. A., *Notes on the History of the Samana*, Fort Lockhart, July 1940.

Gojra, *Jangal Vichch Mangal* (the story of a canal colony in the land of the Five Rivers), compiled by E. F. E. Wigram Wesley Press, Mysore.

Goldsmid, F. J., *James Outram, A Biography*, 2 vols., Smith Elder & Co., London 1880.

Gopal, S., *Viceroyalty of Lord Ripon, 1880-84*, Oxford University Press, Oxford 1953.

———, *Viceroyalty of Lord Irwin, 1926-31*, Oxford University Press, Oxford 1957.

Gore, M., *Remarks on the Present State of the Punjab*, James Ridgway, London 1949.

Gough, C. and A. D. Innes, *The Sikhs and the Sikh Wars*, A. D. Innes & Co., London 1897.

Gough, Lord, *War in India, Dispatches*, Ackermann & Co., London 1846.

Government Allegations against the Sikhs, Hyderabad 1922.

Government of India Records, *Agricultural Indebtedness and*

Land Transfers, Vol. II, Punjab Correspondence, Govt. Central Printing Office, Simla.

Graham-Bailey, T., *Studies in North India Languages*, Lund Humphries & Co., London 1938.

Grant, I. F., "Sikh Wars" (everyday letters written during the 1st and 2nd wars), *Army Quarterly* (1921).

Grant, Rev. K. J., "Among the Hindus of British Columbia," *Missionary Messenger* (1915).

Greenwood, J., *Narrative of the late Victorious Campaigns in Afghanistan under General Pollock with Recollections of Seven Years' Service in India*, Henry Colburn, London 1844.

Grey, C., "Panchayat Rule of the Khalsa Army 1841-45," *Journal of the United Services Institution of India* (1932).

Griffin, Lepel, *Law of Inheritance to Chiefships as observed by the Sikhs Previous to the Annexation of the Punjab*, Superintendent of Govt. Printing, Lahore 1869.

———, *Rajas of the Punjab*, Trubner & Co., London 1873.

Griffiths, C. J., *A Narrative of the Siege of Delhi with an Account of the Mutiny at Ferozepore in 1857*, ed. H. J. Yonge, John Murray, London 1910.

Gubbins, M. R., *An Account of the Mutinies in Oudh and of the Siege of Lucknow Residency*, Richard Bentley, London 1858.

Gulab Singh, *Thorns & Thistles* (autobiography of a revolutionary), National Information Publications, Bombay 1948.

Gupta, H. R., *Punjab on the Eve of the First Sikh War*, University of Punjab, Hoshiarpur 1956.

Gurbachan Singh and Gyani Lal Singh, *The Idea of a Sikh State*, Lahore Book Shop, Lahore 1946.

Gurbachan Singh Talib, *Muslim League Attack on Sikhs and Hindus in the Punjab*, S.G.P.C., Amritsar 1950.

Gurdit Singh, *The Voyage of the Komagatamaru*, published by the compiler at 32, Ashutosh Mukherjee Road, Calcutta.

Gurnam Singh, *A Unilingual Punjabi State and the Sikh Unrest*, Super Press, New Delhi 1960.

Gyan Singh Naqqash, *Gian Chitravali*, G. S. Sohan Singh, Amritsar 1956.

Handa, R. L., *A History of the Development of the Judiciary in the Punjab, 1846,* P.G.R.O., Lahore 1927.

Hansard's Parliamentary Debates, Hansard Publishing Union, London.

Harbans Singh, *Sikh Political Parties,* Sikh Publishing House, Delhi.

———, *The Heritage of the Sikhs,* Asia Publishing House, Bombay 1964.

Hardinge, Charles, *Viscount Hardinge,* Clarendon Press, Oxford 1900.

———, *Despatches of Lord Hardinge,* Parliamentary Papers, London 1846.

———, *My Indian Years, 1910-16,* John Murray, London 1947.

Harnam Singh, *Punjab: The Homeland of the Sikhs,* Civil & Military Gazette Press, Lahore 1945.

Harris, Mrs., *A Lady's Diary of the Siege of Lucknow,* London 1858.

Hilton, Major General Richard, *The Indian Mutiny,* Hollis and Carter, London 1957.

History of the Campaign of the Sutlej and War in the Punjab (memoirs of many distinguished officers), Charles Edmonds, London 1846.

Hodson, W. S. R., *Hodson of Hodson's Horse or Twelve Years of a Soldier's Life in India,* J. W. Parker & Son, London 1859.

Holland, Sir Robert, "Indian Immigration into Canada: the Question of Franchise," *Asiatic Review* (April 1943), p. 167.

Hollingsworth, L. W., *The Asians of East Africa,* Macmillan, London 1960.

Holmes, T. R. E., *A History of the Indian Mutiny,* W. H. Allen & Co., London 1888.

Honigberger, J. M., *Thirty Five Years in the East,* H. Bailliere, London 1852.

Horniman, B. G., *Amritsar and Our Duty to India,* Fisher Unwin, London 1920.

Hough, W., *Political and Military Events in British India from the Years 1756 to 1849,* 2 vols., William Allen & Co., London 1853.

Hukam Singh, *The Sikh Problem & its Solution,* Shiromani Akali Dal, Amritsar 1951.

Humbley, W. W., *Journal of a Cavalry Officer including the Sikh Campaign of 1845-46*, Longmans, Green & Co. 1854.

Hunter Committee's Report, *Disorders Inquiry Committee Report, 1919-20*, Govt. Printing Press, Calcutta 1920.

Hunter, W. W., *The Marquess of Dalhousie* (Rulers of India Series), Clarendon Press, Oxford 1895.

Husain, Azim, *Fazl-i-Husain (a political biography)*, Orient Longmans, Green & Co., Calcutta 1946.

Hutchison, L., *Conspiracy in Meerut*, Allen & Unwin, London 1935.

Hutton, Martin, "The Sikhs in Malaya," *Straits Times Annual*, Singapore 1951, p. 96.

Ibbetson, D. C., *Punjab Census, 1881*, 3 vols., Central Gaol Press, Lahore, 1883.

Immigration: Report of the Commission General for Immigration, 1919-1920, U. S. Govt. Printing Office, Washington, D.C.

Indera Pal Singh, "A Sikh Village," *Journal of American Folklore*, Vol. 71 (July–September 1958).

India in 1923-24, Govt. Printing Press, Lahore, 1924.

Indian Historical Records Commission, Proceedings, 1940 onward, Manager of Publications, Delhi.

Indian History Congress, Proceedings, 1938 onward, Manager of Publications, Delhi.

Indian Reforms Scheme: Report of the Working of the Sikh Deputation to England, 1920, Mufid-i-Am Press, Lahore 1921.

Innes, J. J. M., *Sir Henry Lawrence, the Pacificator* (Rulers of India Series), Oxford University Press, Oxford 1898.

Intelligence Reports concerning the Tribal Repercussions to the Events in the Punjab, Kashmir and India, Govt. Printing Press, Lahore 1948.

Isemonger, F. C., and J. Slattery, *An Account of the Ghadr Conspiracy*, Superintendent of Printing, Punjab, Lahore 1921.

Iyer, S. Ranga, *Diary of the Late Maharaja of Nabha*, Lucknow 1924.

Jacoby, Harold S., *A Half Century Appraisal of Indians in the United States*, College of the Pacific, Stockton 1956.

Jacoby, Harold S., "More Thind against than Sinning," *Pacific Historian*, Stockton 1958.

Jagat Singh, Maharaj, *The Science of the Soul*, Radha Soami Satsang, Beas 1961.

Jaito, the Struggle for Freedom of Religious Worship in, S.G.P.C., Amritsar 1924.

James, D. H., *The Rise and Fall of the Japanese Empire*, Allen & Unwin, London 1952.

James, Hugo, *A Volunteer's Scramble through Sing, the Punjab, Hindustan and the Himalayan Mountains*, 2 vols., W. Thacker & Co., London 1854.

Johnson, Dr. Julian, *The Path of the Masters*, Radha Soami Satsang, Beas 1939.

Kapurthala State: Its Past and Present, Pioneer Press, Allahabad 1921.

Kapurthala State: The Ruler and Method of Administration, compiled by an official, published by Dhani Ram Muni Lal.

Kartar Singh Campbellpuri, *The Plight of the Sikhs*, Servants of Sikhs Society, Lahore 1944.

Kaul, P. H., *Census of India, 1911*, Punjab vols., Civil and Military Gazette Press, Lahore 1912.

Kaye, Sir Cecil, *Communism in India*, Govt. Press, Delhi 1926.

Kaye, J. W., *History of the War in Afghanistan*, 2 vols., Richard Bentley, London 1851.

Kaye, Sir J. and T. R. E. Holmes, *Lives of Indian Officers*, 3 vols., W. H. Allen & Co., London 1888-1889.

Kaye, Sir J. and G. B. Malleson, *Indian Mutiny of 1857-58*, 6 vols., Longmans, Green, London 1897.

Kennedy, R. H., *Narrative of the Campaign of the Army of the Indus in Sindh and Kabul in 1838-1839*, London 1840.

Khaliquzzaman, Choudhry, *Pathway to Pakistan*, Longmans, Lahore 1961.

Khilnani, N. B., *The Punjab under the Lawrences*, P.G.R.O., Simla 1951.

Khosla, G. D., *Stern Reckoning*, Bhawnani & Sons, New Delhi 1949.

Khushwant Singh, *Fall of the Kingdom of the Punjab*, Orient Longmans, Calcutta 1962.

Knollys, Col. H., ed., *Life of General Sir Hope Grant*, 2 vols., William Blackwood & Sons, London 1894.
Kohli, S. R., *Trial of Dewan Mulraj*, P.G.R.O., Lahore 1932.
———, *Catalogue of Khalsa Durbar Records*, 2 vols., Govt. Printing Press, Lahore 1919.
Komagata Maru Commission of Enquiry Report, 1914, Govt. Printing Press, Calcutta 1914.
Krishen, Indra, *An Historical Interpretation of the Correspondence of Sir George Russell Clerk, Political Agent at Ambala and Ludhiana, 1831-43*, published by the author, Simla 1952.
Kukas: Papers Relating to the Kuka Sect (selections from the records of the Government of the Punjab), Lahore 1872.
Kukas: Parliamentary Paper No. 356 on the Kuka Outbreak (reply to an address in the House of Commons, July 22, 1872).

Lajpat Rai, *Story of My Deportation*, Jaswantrai, Lahore 1908.
———, *Arya Samaj*, Longmans, Green, London 1915.
———, *Young India: An Interpretation and a History of the Nationalist Movement from Within*, B. W. Huebsch, New York 1917.
———, *Reflection on the Political Situation in India*, Olto Wigand, Leipzig 1917.
———, *India's Will to Freedom: Writings and Speeches on the Present Situation*, Ganesh & Co., Madras 1921.
———, *The Agony of the Punjab*, Tagore & Co., Madras 1920.
———, *Autobiographical Writings*, ed. V. C. Joshi, University Publishers, Delhi 1965.
Lake, Edward, *Sir Donald McLeod*, Religious Tract Society, London 1874.
Lakshman Singh, Bhagat, *Autobiography*, ed. Ganda Singh, Sikh Cultural Centre, Calcutta 1965.
———, *The Sikh and his New Critics*, published by the author, 1918.
Landau, Henry, *The Enemy Within*, Putnam, London 1937.
Latif, Syed M., *History of the Punjab*, Calcutta Central Press, Calcutta 1891.
———, *Lahore, Its History, Architectural Remains and Antiquities*, republished by Mohammed Minhajuddin, Lahore 1957.

Law, Sir A., *India Under Lord Ellenborough*, London 1926.
Lawrence-Archer, J. H., *Commentaries on the Punjab Campaign of 1848-1849*, W. H. Allen, London 1878.
Lawrence, George, *Reminiscences of Forty-Three Years in India*, London 1874.
Lawrence, Henry M., *Essays, Military and Political, Written in India*, Henry Colburn, London 1859.
————, *Some Passages in the Life of an Adventurer in the Punjab*, Henry Colburn, London 1846.
Lawrence, R., *Charles Napier*, John Murray, London 1952.
Lawrence, W. R., *The Valley of Kashmir*, Henry Frowde, London 1895.
Lee Warner, Wm., *The Life of Marquess of Dalhousie*, Macmillan, London 1904.
Leigh, M. S., *The Punjab and the War*, Govt. Printing Press, Lahore 1922.
Lewis, *Campaign on the Sutlej, 1845-1846*.
Lockley, F., "The Hindu Invasion—A New Immigration Problem," *Pacific Monthly*, 17 (1907), 584.
Login, E. D., *Lady Login's Recollections*, Smith Elder & Co., London 1916.
Login, Lady, *Sir John Login and Duleep Singh*, W. H. Allen & Co., London 1890.
Lumby, E. W. R., *The Transfer of Power in India*, Allen & Unwin, London 1956.
Lumsden, P. S. and G. R. Elsmie, *General Sir Harry Lumsden of the Guides*, John Murray, London 1899.

MacKinnon, Capt. D. H., *Military Services and Adventurers in the Far East*, 2 vols., London 1845.
MacLagan, E. D., *Census of India 1891*, Punjab vols., Govt. Printing Press, Calcutta 1892.
MacLagan, M., *"Clemency" Canning: Charles John, 1st Earl Canning, Governor General and Viceroy of India 1856-62*, Macmillan, London 1962.
MacMunn, Sir G., *The Indian Mutiny in Perspective*, G. Bell & Sons, London 1931.
————, *The History of the Sikh Pioneers (23rd, 32nd, 34th)*, Sampson Low & Co., London 1936.
————, *Romance of the Indian Frontier*, Jonathan Cape, London 1936.

———, *Vignettes from Indian Wars*, Sampson Low & Co., London 1932.

———, *Turmoil and Tragedy in India in 1914 and After*, Jarrolds, London 1935.

Maconachie, R., *Rowland Bateman*, London Church Missionary Society, London 1917.

Mahajan, J. M., *Circumstances leading to the Annexation of the Punjab 1846-49*, Kitabistan, Allahabad 1949.

———, *Private Correspondence of Sir Fredrick Currie 1846-48*, Saraswati Publications, New Delhi 1947.

Mahajani, Usha, *The Role of Indian Minorities in Burma and Malaya*, Vera & Co., Bombay 1960.

Mahendra Pratap, *My Life Story of Fifty-Five Years*, World Federation Centre, Dehra Dun 1947.

Majumdar, R. C., *History of the Freedom Movement in India*, 2 vols., Mukhopadhyay, Calcutta 1963.

Malleson, G. B., *Decisive Battles of India, 1746-1849*, Reeves & Turner, London 1914.

———, *Indian Mutiny of 1857*, 6 vols., 9th edn., Seeley & Co., London 1906.

Marshman, J. C., *Memoirs of Major General Sir Henry Havelock*, Longmans, Green & Co., London 1860.

Masani, M. R., *The Communist Party of India*, Derek Verschoyle, London 1954.

May, Capt. C. W., *History of the 2nd Sikhs, 12th Frontier Force Regiment 1846-1933*, Mission Press, Jubbulpore.

Maynard, Sir John, "The Sikh Problem in the Punjab, 1920-23," *Contemporary Review* (September 1923).

Mead, Henry, *The Sepoy Revolt, Its Causes and Its Consequences*, John Murray, London 1857.

Medley, J. G., *A Year's Campaign in India (March 1857–March 1858)*, Thacker & Co., London 1858.

Mehta, H. R., *A History of the Growth and Development of Western Education in the Punjab, 1846-1884*, P.G.R.O., Lahore 1929.

Menon, V. P., *The Story of the Integration of the Indian States*, Orient Longmans, Bombay 1956.

———, *Transfer of Power in India*, Orient Longmans, Bombay 1957.

Merewether, Lt. Col. J. W. B. and Sir Fredrick Smith, *The Indian Corps in France*, John Murray, London 1917.

Minto, The Countess of, *India, Minto and Morley 1905-10*, Macmillan, London 1934.

Mitra, Nripendra Nath, *Indian Annual Register*, 1919 onward, Annual Register Office, Calcutta.

Montagu-Chelmsford Report, *Indian Constitutional Reforms Report*, Govt. Printing Press, Calcutta 1918.

Moon, Penderel, *Divide and Quit*, Chatto & Windus, London 1961.

Morrison, J. L., *A Survey of Imperial Frontier Policy from Alexander Burnes to Fredrick Roberts*, Oxford University Press 1936.

————, *Lawrence of Lucknow, 1806-1837*, G. Bell, London 1934.

Morse, Eric W., "Some Aspects of the Komagatamaru Affair, 1914," *Canadian Historical Association Journal* (1936), pp. 100-108.

Mosley, Leonard, *The Last Days of the British Raj*, Weidenfeld and Nicholson, London 1961.

Mouton, Col., *Un Rapport sur les Derniers Événements du Punjab*, Paris 1846.

Mutiny of the Bengal Army, by a Retired Officer, Bosworth and Harrison, London 1857.

Nabha, *Truth about*, S.G.P.C., Amritsar 1924.

Nahar Singh, *Gooroo Ram Singh and the Kuka Sikhs, Documents 1863-1871*, Amrit Book Co., New Delhi 1965.

Naidis, M., "Propaganda of the Gadar Party," *Pacific Historical Review*, Vol. 20 (1951).

Nair, Kusum, *The Story of the I.N.A.*, Padma Publications, Bombay 1946.

Nand Singh Sehra, "Indians in Canada," *The Modern Review* (Calcutta), Vol. 14, No. 2 (1913), p. 140.

Nanda, J., *Punjab Uprooted*, Hind Kitabs Ltd., Bombay 1948.

Napier, W., *Life and Opinions of General Sir Charles James Napier*, John Murray, London 1857.

Narendra Nath, *Memorandum on the Rights Claimed by the Hindu Community of North West India*, Civil and Military Gazette Press, Lahore 1928.

Nehru-Fateh Singh Talks, Synopsis of the (on the issue of the formation of Punjabi Speaking State), published by the Secretary, Shiromani Akali Dal, Amritsar 1961.

Nehru, Moti La, *Nehru Report of the All Parties Conference*, published by the Secretary, Indian National Congress Committee, Allahabad 1928.

Norgate, Lt. Col. T. R. and Lt. Col. Phillott, *From Sepoy to Subedar*, Calcutta 1911.

O'Donnell, C. J., *The Causes of Present Discontent in India*, Fisher Unwin, London 1908.

O'Dwyer, M., *India as I Knew It, 1885-1925*, Constable, London 1925.

Old Punjabee: *The Punjaub and North-West Frontier of India*, Kegan Paul & Co., London 1878.

Onn, Chin Kee, *Malaya Upside Down*, Jitts and Co., Singapore 1946.

Overstreet, G. and M. Windmiller, *Communism in India*, University of California Press, Berkeley and Los Angeles 1959.

Panikkar, K. M., *Founding of the Kashmir State: 1792-1858*, Allen & Unwin, 1930.

Pardaman Singh, *Ethnological Epitome of the Hindustanees of the Pacific Coast*, Khalsa Diwan Society, Stockton 1922.

Parker, Mrs. A., *Sadhu Sundar Singh*, Christian Literature Society, 1962.

Parker, C. S., *Sir Robert Peel*, John Murray, London 1899, Vol. III.

Parliamentary Papers Relating to the Punjab: 1847-49, Harrison & Son, London.

Parmanand, Bhai, *The Story of My Life*.

Parry, R. E., *The Sikhs of the Punjab*, Dranes, London 1921.

Patiala and the Great War, Medici Society, London 1923.

Pearse, Hugh, ed., *The Memoirs of Alexander Gardner*, William Blackwood & Sons.

Punjab Administration Reports, 1849 onward, Punjab Govt. Press, Lahore.

Punjab Cavalry: History of Second Punjab Cavalry, 1849-1886, Kegan Paul & Co., London 1888.

Punjab Government Records, *Lahore Political Diaries*, 1846-1849, Vols. III, IV, V, VI.

———, *Mutiny Reports*, Vol. VII, Parts I & II; Vol. VIII, Parts I & II.

Punjab Legislative Council Debates (later called the Punjab Legislative Assembly), 1897 onward, Punjab Govt. Press, Lahore.

Punjab Regiment, 14th, A Short History (1939-1945), Lund Humphries, London 1945.

Qureshi, Major Mohammed Ibrahim, *The First Punjabis* (history of the First Punjab Regiment, 1759-1956), Gale and Polden, Aldershot 1958.

Radha Soami Colony, Beas and its Teachings, Radha Soami Satsang, Beas 1960.

Rahmat Ali, *Pakistan, The Fatherland of the Pak Nation*, published by the author, Cambridge 1940.

———, *The Millat and its Mission*, published by the author, 3d edition, Lahore 1946.

Rait, R. S., *The Life and Campaigns of Viscount Gough*, 2 vols., Archibald Constable and Co., London 1903.

Rajput, R. B., *The Muslim League: Yesterday and Today*, Ashraf, Lahore 1948.

Rallia Ram, K. L., *Report on the Firing into the Gurdwara Sis Ganj, Delhi*, S.G.P.C., Amritsar 1930.

Ram Chandra, *India Against Britain*, Hindustan Ghadr, San Francisco 1916.

———, *Exclusion of Hindus from America due to British Influence*, Hindustan Ghadr, San Francisco 1916.

Randhawa, M. S., *Out of the Ashes*, New Jack Printing Works, Bombay 1954.

Randhir Singh, *The Ghadr Heroes*, People's Publishing House, Bombay 1945.

Rattigan, Sir W. H., *Digest of Civil Law for the Punjab*, 1909.

Reid, Robie L., "The Inside Story of the 'Komagatamaru,'" *British Columbia Historical Quarterly*, Vol. 5 (1941).

Roberts, Field Marshal, *Forty-One Years in India*, Macmillan, London 1898.

Ross, D., *The Land of the Five Rivers*, Chapman & Hall, London 1883.

Round Table Conference Proceedings (Government of India), Calcutta 1931-1933.

Rowlatt Committee Report, *Sedition Committee Report 1918*, Bengal Secretariat Press, Calcutta 1918.

Roy, M. N., *Memoirs*, Allied Press, Bombay, 1964.

Roy, P. C., *Gurcharan Singh's Mission in Central Asia*, Indian Historical Records Commission, Vol. 34, Part II, Trivandrum 1958.

R.S.S.S. in the Punjab, Govt. Printing Press, Lahore 1948.

Sahni, Ruchi Ram, *Struggle for Reform in Sikh Shrines*, ed. Ganda Singh, Sikh Itihas, Amritsar 1965.

———, *The Gurdwara Reform Movement and the Sikh Awakening*, Desh Sewak Book Agency, Jullundur 1922.

———, *Guru Ka Bagh Congress Inquiry Committee*, Hindi Press, Lahore 1924.

Sanders, C. W., *The Inner Voice*, Radha Soami Satsang, Beas 1960.

Sandford, D. A., *Leaves from the Journal of a Subaltern during the Campaign in the Punjab, September 1848–March 1849*, William Blackwood & Sons, London 1849.

Sant Singh, *Akali Problem*, 1955.

Sapru, A. N., *The Building of the Jammu and Kashmir State*, P.G.R.O., Lahore 1931.

Sapru, T. B., *Constitutional Proposals of the Sapru Committee*, Padma, Bombay 1946.

Saragarhi Memorial, History of the, Graduate Printing Press, Ferozepur 1955.

Sarasfield, Landen, *Betrayal of the Sikhs*, Lahore Bookshop, Lahore 1946.

Sardul Singh Caveeshar, *Sikh Politics*, National Publications, Delhi 1950.

Sarkar, Sir Jadunath, "Bibliography of Sikh History," *Modern Review* (Calcutta 1907).

Saund, D. S., *Congressman from India*, Dutton & Co., New York 1960.

Seaton, Major Gen. Sir Thomas, *From Cadet to Colonel*, London 1866.

Seetaram, *From Sepoy to Soobadar*, James Thomas Norgate, Lahore 1880.

Selections from State Papers Preserved in the Military Department, ed. George W. Forrest, 4 vols., Govt. Printing Press, Calcutta 1893-1912.
Sen, N. B., History of Koh-i-Noor, New Book Society, New Delhi 1953.
Sen, S. N., Eighteen Fifty Seven, Govt. of India Publications Division, Delhi 1957.
Sethi, G. R., Sikh Struggle for Gurdwara Reform, Union Press, Amritsar 1927.
Sethi, R. R., John Lawrence as Commissioner of the Jullundur Doab 1846-1849, P.G.R.O., Lahore 1930.
——, Trial of Raja Lal Singh, P.G.R.O., Lahore 1933.
Settlement Reports of the Punjab, Civil and Military Gazette Press, Lahore.
Sewa Ram Singh, Reforms and the Sikhs, Mufid-i-Am Press, Lahore 1920.
Shadwell, Lt. Gen., Life of Colin Campbell, Lord Clyde, London 1881.
Shah Nawaz Khan, My Memories of the I.N.A. and its Netaji, Raj Kamal Publication, Bombay 1946.
Sharma, S. R., Mahatma Hans Raj, Arya Pradeshik Pratinidhi Sabha, Lahore 1941.
Sikh Invasion and British Victories on the Sutlej, Blackwood & Page, London 1847.
Sikh Memorandum to the Boundary Commission, Mercantile Press, Lahore 1947.
Sikh Plan, Note on the, Government Printing Press, Lahore 1948.
Sikh Representation, Memorandum on (presented to the Indian Statutory Commission), Superintendent of Printing, Calcutta 1930.
Sikh Settlement, Voice of India on the, Director, Information Bureau, Punjab 1925.
Sikhs in Action, Government Printing Press, Lahore 1948.
Sikhs, Regimental Records, 35th, 1887-1922, Sham Lall & Sons, Peshawar 1923.
Sikhs War Records, 47th, The Great War 1914-18, privately published.
Simon Commission Report, Indian Statutory Commission Re-

port, Government of India Central Publication Branch, Calcutta 1930.

Smillie, Emmaline E., "An Historical Survey of Indian Migration within the Empire," *Canadian Historical Review*, 4 (1923), 217-257.

Smith, Lt. Gen. Sir Harry, *Autobiography*, ed. G. C. Moor, 2 vols., John Murray, London 1902.

Smith, Marian, "Synthesis and Other Processes in Sikhism," *American Anthropologist*, 50 (July-September 1948), 457-462.

———, "The Misal: A Structural Village Group of India and Pakistan," *American Anthropologist*, 54 (January-March 1952), 41-56.

———, "Social Structure in the Punjab," *The Economic Weekly*, 5 (November 21, 1953).

———, "Sikh Settlers in Canada," *Asia and the Americas*, 44 (August 1944), 359-364.

Smith, R. B., *Agricultural Resources of the Punjab*, Stewart & Murray, London 1849.

Speary, Earl E., and Willis M. West, *German Plots and Intrigues in the United States During the Period of Our Neutrality*, Red, White & Blue Series, No. 10, Committee of Public Information.

Spellman, John W., "The International Extensions of Political Conspiracy as illustrated by the Ghadr Party," *Journal of Indian History*, 31 (1959) 23-45.

States Reorganisation Commission Report, Government of India Press, New Delhi 1955.

Steinbach, Lt. Col., *The Punjaub: Being a Brief Account of the Country of the Sikhs*, Smith, Elder & Co., London 1845.

Stephens, Ian, *Pakistan*, Ernest Benn Ltd., London 1963.

Stevens, Lt. Col. G. R., *History of the 4th Indian Division*.

Sufi, G. M. D., *Kashmir*, Vol. II, University of Punjab, Lahore 1949.

Sullivan, John, *The Koh-i-Noor or Mountain of Light: To Whom does it Belong?* Effingham Wilson, London 1850.

———, *Are We Bound by Our Treaties?* Effingham Wilson, London 1853.

Sundram, G. A., *Guru-ka-Bagh Satyagrah*, Madras 1923.

Swarup Singh, Sadhu, *The Sikhs Demand their Homeland,* Lahore Bookshop, Lahore 1946.

Tandon, P., *Punjabi Century,* Harcourt, Brace, New York 1960.

Taylor, A. C., *General Sir Alexander Taylor,* 2 vols., William & Norgate, London 1913.

Teja Singh, *Growth of Responsibility in Sikhism,* Sikh Tract Society, 2nd edn., Lahore 1921.

――――, *Gurdwara Reform Movement and the Sikh Awakening,* Desh Sewak, Jullundur 1922.

――――, *Sikhs as Liberators,* Sikhs Sammelan, Simla 1948.

Temple, R. C., *Men and Events of My Time in India,* John Murray, London 1882.

――――, *Names and Name Places,* Bombay Education Society, Bombay 1883.

――――, *The Legends of the Punjab,* 3 vols., Bombay Education Society, Bombay 1884.

――――, *Lord Lawrence,* Macmillan, London 1890.

Thackwell, E. J., *Narrative of the Second Sikh War 1848-1849,* Richard Bentley. London 1851.

Thomas, Wendell Marshall, *Hinduism Invades America,* Beacon Press, New York 1930.

Thompson, Edward, *The Other Side of the Medal,* Hogarth Press, London 1930.

Thorburn, S. S., *Mussalmans and Money Lenders in the Punjab,* William Blackwood & Sons, London 1886.

――――, *Report on Peasant Indebtedness and Land Alienations to Money-Lenders in Parts of the Rawalpindi Division,* Civil and Military Gazette Press, 1896.

――――, *The Punjab in Peace & War,* William Blackwood & Sons, London, 1904.

Tilak Raj Chadha, *A Study of the Communist Movement in the Punjab,* Jyoti Prakashan, Ghaziabad 1954.

Tinker, Hugh, *India and Pakistan,* Praeger, New York 1962.

Toye, Hugh, *The Springing Tiger,* Cassell, London 1959.

Trevaskis, H. K., *The Land of Five Rivers,* Oxford University Press, Bombay 1928.

――――, *The Punjab of Today,* 2 vols., Civil & Military Gazette Press, Lahore 1931.

Trials, Two Historic, *I.N.A. Court Martial of 1945 and the*

Trial of Emperor Bahadur Shah 1858, Moti Ram, Delhi 1946.

Trotter, L. J., *Life of Lord Lawrence*, Oxford University Press, Oxford 1880.

——, *History of India under Queen Victoria from 1836-1880*, 2 vols., W. H. Allen & Co., London 1886.

——, *Life of Marquess of Dalhousie*, Oxford University Press, Oxford 1889.

——, *A Leader of Light Horse: The Life of Hodson of Hodson's Horse*, J. M. Dent, London 1901.

——, *Life of John Nicholson*, John Murray, London 1904.

Tuker, Lt. Gen. Sir Francis, *While Memory Serves*, Cassell, London 1950.

Tupper, C. L., ed., *Punjab Customary Law*, 3 vols., Govt. Printing Press, Calcutta 1883-1908.

U.S. Congress, House Committee on Immigration and Naturalization, *Hearings* on Hindu Immigration, February 13 to April 30, 1914, U.S. Govt. Printing Office, Washington, D.C. 1914.

Wade, Lt. Col. C. M., *History of the Campaign on the Sutlej and the War in the Punjab*, G. Butler, London 1846.

——, *A Narrative of the Services Military and Political*, G. Butler, London 1847.

——, *On the State of our Relations with the Punjab and the Best Mode of their Settlement*, Ryde, Isle of Wight 1848.

——, *War in the Punjab*, G. Butler, London 1849.

Waiz, S. A., *Indians Abroad*, Imperial Indian Citizenship Association, 2d edn., Bombay 1927.

Wilkins, Charles, *The Sikhs and their College at Patna*, ed. Ganda Singh, Khalsa College, Amritsar 1940.

Williams, D. Elwyn, "Makers of the Sikh Army," *Army Quarterly*, Vols. 55-56 (1947-48).

Woodruff, P., *The Men who ruled India*, Jonathan Cape, London 1954.

Wylly, edited by H. C., *Military Memoirs of Lieutenant General Sir Joseph Thackwell*, John Murray, London 1908.

Younghusband, G. J., *Story of the Guides*, Macmillan, London 1908.

JOURNALS AND MAGAZINES

The British Columbia Historical Quarterly, Vols. 5 (1941) and 6 (1942), Vancouver.
Calcutta Review, 1844 onward, Calcutta.
Canada and India, 1915 onward, Vancouver.
Journal of the Asiatic Society of Bengal, 1839 onward, Calcutta.
Journal of Indian History, 1922 onward.
Journal of the Punjab University Historical Society, 1932 onward, Lahore.
The Khalsa, 1929-1932, Lahore.
The Outlook (August 1924), New York.
Pacific Monthly, 1900-1920.
Thought, 1940 onward, New Delhi.

NEWSPAPERS

Aryan, Victoria, Canada 1911.
Civil and Military Gazette, Lahore 1876 onward.
Dawn, Karachi, 1946-1949.
Desh Sewak, Vancouver.
Englishman, Calcutta 1839-1934.
Examiner, San Francisco.
Friend of India, Serampore Press, 1839-1877.
Ghadr, San Francisco 1913.
Harijan, Ahmedabad 1946.
Hindustanee, Vancouver.
Khalsa Herald, Vancouver 1911.
Modern Review, Calcutta 1908 onward.
Portland Telegram, Oregon, Canada 1914.
San Francisco Chronicle 1910-1919.
Sansar, Vancouver 1913.
Spokesman, New Delhi 1940 onward.
Statesman, Calcutta 1940 onward.
Times, London 1880 onward.
Tribune, Lahore 1881 onward.
Vancouver Sun 1910-1919.

INDEX